£35.00

NUCLEAR POWER
TECHNOLOGY

NUCLEAR POWER TECHNOLOGY

Available separately

T-

NUCLEAR POWER
TECHNOLOGY : Nuclear radiation

EDITED BY

A- W. MARSHALL

Volume 3
Nuclear Radiation

CLARENDON PRESS · OXFORD
1983

Oxford University Press, Walton Street, Oxford OX2 6DP

London Glasgow New York Toronto
Delhi Bombay Calcutta Madras Karachi
Kuala Lumpur Singapore Hong Kong Tokyo
Nairobi Dar es Salaam Cape Town
Melbourne Auckland

and associated companies in
Beirut Berlin Ibadan Mexico City Nicosia

Oxford is a trade mark of Oxford University Press

Published in the United States
by Oxford University Press, New York

British Library Cataloguing in Publication Data
Nuclear power technology.
Vol. 3: Nuclear radiation
1. Atomic power
I. Marshall, W
621.48   TK9145
ISBN 0–19–851959–1

Library of Congress Cataloging in Publication Data
Nuclear power technology.
Contents: v. 1. Reactor technology – v. 2. Fuel cycle –
v. 3. Nuclear radiation. 1. Atomic power.
I. Marshall, W. (Walter), 1932–
TK9145.N83 1983   621.48   83–4124
ISBN 0–19–851959–1 (v. 3)

Printed in Great Britain
by The Thetford Press,
Thetford, Norfolk

PREFACE

Some time ago the Oxford University Press asked if I would be interested in preparing a book on nuclear power oriented towards increasing public knowledge and for the public interest. The United Kingdom Atomic Energy Authority was approaching its twenty-fifth anniversary and it therefore seemed appropriate to gather a set of chapters reviewing the state of nuclear science. The obvious way of doing this was to list all the subjects involved and then persuade an expert in each subject to write a chapter. Having chosen authors of wide experience in their fields, the result is an authoritative source book on the major aspects of nuclear science and nuclear power.

To achieve some cohesion, I set up an editorial board which has reviewed all the chapters to make sure they are factually correct, and we believe that in all the papers the choice of language makes it clear what is fact and what is opinion.

The chapters do not represent an official UKAEA point of view. Each one is very much the personal opinion of the individual author, and I have not attempted to influence his perspective of the subject. The chapters are, therefore, presented in a variety of styles, but it has been our intention throughout that they should be free of unnecessary technical jargon and comprehensible to the non-specialist. While in a publication of this standard it has been necessary to treat the technical and scientific basis for some of the subjects in depth. I hope that the book will prove helpful and informative to the general reader who, conscious of the 'Nuclear Debate' taking place around him, wishes to have access to a reliable reference document.

Many of the chapters contain bibliographies so that the reader may delve further into the technical facts and figures if he so chooses. There is also a summary of each chapter and, at the end, a comprehensive glossary and index to complete the texts.

Most of the authors come from within the UKAEA. My special thanks are due to Dr S. H. U. Bowie, who was Chief Consultant Geologist to the UKAEA from 1955 to 1977, for completing the series by contributing an article.

I especially thank Dr R. H. Flowers for the part which he has played, as Deputy Editor, in bringing this work to completion and Mrs N. M. Hutchins, as secretary to the Editorial Board, for organizing and progressing the contributions.

May 1981

W. MARSHALL
Chairman,
United Kingdom Atomic Energy Authority

ACKNOWLEDGEMENTS

Acknowledgements are due to the Editorial Board set up by the Chairman of the UKAEA to review the articles during their various stages of preparation. The members of this Editorial Board were:

Dr W. Marshall, Chairman (UKAEA) and Chairman of the Editorial Board
Dr R. H. Flowers, Deputy Editor

Mr J. G. Collier
Mr J. M. Hutcheon
Dr P. M. S. Jones
Dr A. B. Lidiard

Dr R. G. Sowden
Mr J. G. Tyror
Mr P. N. Vey
Dr B. O. Wade

Acknowledgements are due also to Mr G. Gibbons who was responsible for the artwork, to Mr J. A. G. Heller, who commented extensively on the articles from the lay-reader's point of view, to Miss P. E. Barnes, who undertook the vast typing task and to Mrs N. M. Hutchins who, as secretary to the Editorial Board, organized the authors contributions and did a large amount of editorial work.

Special thanks are due to Mr S. U. Bowie, now retired from the Institute of Geological Sciences, who prepared the article on Uranium and Thorium Raw Materials.

R. H. FLOWERS
Deputy Editor

CONTENTS

CONTRIBUTORS

W. ABSON *Instrumentation and Applied Physics Division, Harwell*

J. G. CUNINGHAME *Chemistry Division, Harwell*

G. V. EVANS *Nuclear Physics Division, Harwell*

T. F. JOHNS *Radiological and Safety Division, Winfrith*

G. H. KINCHIN *Director, Safety and Reliability Directorate, Culcheth*

R. L. OTLET *Nuclear Physics Division, Harwell*

P. A. H. SAUNDERS *Environmental and Medical Sciences Division, Harwell*

A. N. B. STOTT *Environmental and Medical Sciences Division, Harwell*

B. O. WADE *Environmental and Medical Sciences, Division, Harwell*

SYMBOLS AND ABBREVIATIONS

Abbreviation or Symbol	Name of unit and quantity measured	Notes, Units, Value
A	ampere, electric current	
α	alpha particle (He^{++})	
amu	atomic mass unit	1.66×10^{-27} kg
bar	bar, pressure	10^5 Pa
barn	unit of cross-section	10^{-28} m^2
β	beta particle (electron)	
Bq	becquerel, radioactivity	s^{-1}
c	velocity of light	3×10^8 m s^{-1}
C	coulomb, electric charge	A s
°C	celsius temperature interval	degree celsius
Ci	curie, radioactivity	3.7×10^{10} Bq
d	day, time	
EFPH	effective full power hours	
eV	electronvolt, energy	1.59×10^{-19} J
g	gram, mass	
γ	gamma radiation (photon)	
Gy	gray, absorbed dose	J kg^{-1}
h	hour, time	
h	Planck's constant	$6.6255 \ 10^{-34}$ J s
Hz	hertz, frequency	s^{-1}
J	joule, energy	
k	Boltzmann constant	1.3805×10^{-23} J K^{-1}
K	kelvin, absolute temperature interval	kelvin
m	metre, length	
M	concentration	10^3 mol m^{-3}
min	minute, time	
mol	mole, amount of substance	gram-molecule
MW(e)	unit of power station output	megawatt, electrical
MW(t)	unit of power station output	megawatt, thermal
n	neutron	
N	newton, force	kg m s^{-2}
p	proton	
Pa	pascal, pressure	1 newton m^{-2}
pH	unit of acidity	$-\log_{10} M_{H^+}$
rad	absorbed dose	10^{-2} Gy
rem	absorbed dose equivalent	10^{-2} Sv
s	second, time	
s.t.p.	standard temperature and pressure	1 bar 273.16 K
SWU	separative work unit	see Chapter 2
Sv	sievert, absorbed dose equivalent	J kg^{-1}
t	metric tonne	1000 kg
T	tesla, magnetic flux density	V s m^{-2}

tce	tonne coal equivalent	
tha	tonne heavy atoms	
V	volt, potential difference	
W	watt, power	$J\,s^{-1}$
y	year, time	

Prefixes

Multiple	Prefix	Abbreviation
10^{-18}	atto	a
10^{-15}	femto	f
10^{-12}	pico	p
10^{-9}	nano	n
10^{-6}	micro	μ
10^{-3}	milli	m
10^{-2}	centi	c
10^{3}	kilo	k
10^{6}	mega	M
10^{9}	giga	G
10^{12}	tera	T

Additional less commonly used symbols and units are explained and defined as they occur in the text.

The Elements
A complete list of the elements and their symbols, is included here for reference.

Element	Symbol	Element	Symbol	Element	Symbol
Actinium	Ac	Dysprosium	Dy	Lutetium	Lu
Aluminium	Al	Einsteinium	Es	Magnesium	Mg
Americium	Am	Erbium	Er	Manganese	Mn
Antimony	Sb	Europium	Eu	Mendelevium	Md
Argon	Ar	Fermium	Fm	Mercury	Hg
Arsenic	As	Fluorine	F	Molybdenum	Mo
Astatine	At	Francium	Fr	Neodymium	Nd
Barium	Ba	Gadolinium	Gd	Neon	Ne
Berkelium	Bk	Gallium	Ga	Neptunium	Np
Beryllium	Be	Germanium	Ge	Nickel	Ni
Bismuth	Bi	Gold	Au	Niobium	Nb
Boron	B	Hafnium	Hf	Nitrogen	N
Bromine	Br	Helium	He	Nobelium	No
Cadmium	Cd	Holmium	Ho	Osmium	Os
Caesium	Cs	Hydrogen	H	Oxygen	O
Calcium	Ca	Indium	In	Palladium	Pd
Californium	Cf	Iodine	I	Phosphorus	P
Carbon	C	Iridium	Ir	Platinum	Pt
Cerium	Ce	Iron	Fe	Plutonium	Pu
Chlorine	Cl	Krypton	Kr	Polonium	Po
Chromium	Cr	Lanthanum	La	Potassium	K
Cobalt	Co	Lawrencium	Lr	Praseodymium	Pr
Copper	Cu	Lead	Pb	Promethium	Pm
Curium	Cm	Lithium	Li	Protactinium	Pa

Element	Symbol	Element	Symbol	Element	Symbol
Radium	Ra	Sodium	Na	Titanium	Ti
Radon	Rn	Strontium	Sr	Tungsten	W
Rhenium	Re	Sulphur	S	Uranium	U
Rhodium	Rh	Tantalum	Ta	Vanadium	V
Rubidium	Rb	Technetium	Tc	Xenon	Xe
Ruthenium	Ru	Tellurium	Te	Ytterbium	Yb
Samarium	Sm	Terbium	Tb	Yttrium	Y
Scandium	Sc	Thallium	Tl	Zinc	Zn
Selenium	Se	Thorium	Th	Zirconium	Zr
Silicon	Si	Thulium	Tm		
Silver	Ag	Tin	Sn		

18

Radiation and its control

P. A. H. SAUNDERS, B. O. WADE

The discovery of radiation and radioactivity at the end of the nineteenth century led immediately to a number of practical applications. The use of X-rays and radium in medicine led to major advances in diagnosis and treatment, and techniques involving the use of radiation were applied to many areas of scientific research and later in industry. But it was soon recognized that these benefits were accompanied by a risk of damage to human health. Thus in parallel with the beneficial exploitation of radiation, the science of radiological protection evolved. Progress was particularly rapid after the discovery of fission in 1938, and its exploitation for military and later for civil purposes. This chapter outlines the major steps in the evolution of radiation protection philosophy and quantifies the residual risk associated with modern practices in the context of nuclear electricity generation.

The diverse range of electromagnetic waves and particles encompassed by the term *ionizing radiation* is described, together with their general effects on organic and inorganic materials. The development of methods for measuring radiation culminated in the modern units for defining the biological effects of radiation. The somatic and genetic effects in man are expressed in terms of these units, and the evidence on which numerical estimates of risk can be made is outlined. Recommendations for practical protection methods are developed by the International Commission for Radiological Protection (ICRP). The ICRP philosophy and the secondary and derived standards are incorporated in the legislation which governs virtually all activities involving radiation hazards in the UK.

The major component of the radiation dose to the population arises from the natural background. The contributions from cosmic rays, the cosmogenic radionuclides generated in the atmosphere, and the primordial radionuclides remaining from the formation of the earth are discussed. The man-made and man-enhanced sources of radiation contribute one fifth of the total dose, mainly arising from medical practices. The practical control of radiation is described, including the wide variety of available instruments. Finally, the radiation hazards from the nuclear industry are quantified, demonstrating that employment in that industry is one of the safest occupations, and that the consequent radiation hazard experienced by the general public is trivial.

Contents

2 The properties of radiation

    2.1 Types of radiation
    2.2 Radioactivity
    2.3 The absorption of radiation
    2.4 Effect of radiation on matter
    2.5 The measurement of radiation

3 Radiological protection

    3.1 The effect of radiation on man
    3.2 Partial body exposures
    3.3 Committed doses
    3.4 Population risks
    3.5 The evolution of radiation dose limits
    3.6 Current radiological protection philosophy
    3.7 Secondary and derived exposure standards
    3.8 Legislative control

4 Natural background

    4.1 Cosmic radiation
    4.2 Naturally occurring radionuclides
    4.3 Doses to man from external sources
    4.4 Internal doses to man
    4.5 Summary of exposures from natural sources

5 Man-made and man-enhanced radiation

    5.1 Medical irradiation
    5.2 Fallout from nuclear explosions
    5.3 Other man-made and man-enhanced sources of radiation
    5.4 Occupational exposures
    5.5 Summary of radiation exposures of the UK population from all sources

6 The practical control of radiation

    6.1 Methods of detection
    6.2 Practical radiation measurement
    6.3 The control of radiation dose

7 Radiation hazards from the nuclear industry

    7.1 Occupational hazards
    7.2 Hazard to the general public

References

1 Introduction

Although public concern about ionizing radiation is today closely associated with nuclear power, our scientific understanding of this phenomenon predates the discovery of nuclear fission by several decades. It was the discovery of X-rays at the end of the last century which launched the study of radiation as a branch of scientific endeavour, and a great deal of information was accumulated on the properties and effects of radiation long before the discovery of fission by Otto Hahn in 1938. During this period it was realized that radiation was not solely man-made, but that mankind had evolved in a natural radiation field. In fact the vast majority of the radiation dose currently being accumulated by the world's population arises from such natural sources.

Our understanding of radiation and its effects has evolved slowly as hypotheses based on observations have been confirmed or disproved by subsequent attempts to test their validity. Contributions have been needed from physics, chemistry, biology, and medicine, and only with the advent of nuclear fission have some elements of this understanding and their experimental verification become possible. As a result of scientific endeavour over nearly a century we now have enough knowledge to estimate the effects of radiation and hence control its hazards with great confidence, whilst there remain areas of considerable uncertainty over the precise mechanisms of the biological effects of radiation.

1.1 **Historical development**

The key discoveries were made in an exciting period of five years at the very end of the nineteenth century.[1] During 1895, in the course of experiments on electrical discharges in gases, Röntgen in Germany discovered that his Crookes tube generated a previously unknown radiation he called X-rays, capable of penetrating solid objects. The practical possibilities were rapidly recognized, and within a few months the first medical X-ray picture was obtained, to locate shotgun pellets in a man's hand. In 1896, Becquerel in France reported the first observation of radioactivity from measurements of the ionization caused by pitchblende (an ore of uranium) and later that year Pierre and Marie Curie announced the concentration of the small fraction of radium in this ore.

Three years later, Rutherford demonstrated that the radiation from pitchblende had two components of different penetrating power which he labelled alpha and beta. The beta rays were identified by Becquerel as electrons, and Rutherford later showed that the alpha radiation comprised helium nuclei. During this period Villard identified a third component, gamma rays, shown later to be electromagnetic radiation similar to X-rays.

Thus by the beginning of the twentieth century most of the key discoveries needed to understand man's radiation environment had been made, the only important exception being the discovery of the neutron, identified by Chadwick in 1932. The stage was set for the development of applications of radiation in medicine, industry, and scientific research.

Throughout the first half of the century there was a steady progress in elucidating the properties of radiation as a result of research into the physics of the nucleus and the widespread use of X-rays. Progress in unravelling the effects of radiation was particularly rapid during and after Word War II, when the nuclear weapons programme and the prospect of electricity generation from nuclear fission justified a major scientific programme. Extensive studies on animals and on human populations exposed to radiation have resulted in a better understanding of the hazard from radiation than from many other physical or chemical agents.

2 The properties of radiation

The term radiation is used to describe a quite diverse range of electromagnetic waves and particles. Only electromagnetic radiation can normally be detected by the human senses, as light for a narrow band of wavelengths around 1/2500 mm and as heat for longer wavelengths up to around 10 cm. Otherwise, the human body is quite unconscious of any incident radiation. It is therefore of interest to outline the properties of radiation[2] as a basis for the later discussion of its effects on man and the methods of detection. The outline will be restricted to ionizing radiation, a generic term which encompasses

(1) directly ionizing radiation, such as charged particles, and
(2) indirectly ionizing particles, carrying no electric charge, such as neutrons, X-rays and gamma rays.

In passing through matter both these types of radiation can displace electrons, leaving a trail of ion pairs (electrons and charged atoms or ions). This process of ionization affects the physical and chemical properties of the material. Non-ionizing radiation, such as from radio transmitters, will not be considered, nor the rather different problems associated with lasers.[3]

2.1 Types of radiation

The X-rays discovered by Röntgen are electromagnetic radiation but of much shorter wavelength than that of light, around one millionth of a millimetre or less. An X-ray is produced[4] by the same process as light, through the excitation of one of the cloud of electrons surrounding the nucleus of an atom: when the vacancy left by the excited electron is filled by one from a lower energy position, electromagnetic radiation is emitted with an energy corresponding to the change in the electron energy. However, whereas the lightly bound outer electrons of an atom can be excited by high temperature to produce radiation in the visible region, the much more energetic X-rays are only produced when the tightly bound inner electrons are excited, by a powerful electron beam for example.

In contrast, most other radiation of interest arises from excitation of the nucleus of the atom[5] rather than the surrounding electrons. Such nuclear excitation occurs, for example, in the particle accelerators used by nuclear physicists to explore the properties of the nucleus. It also occurs in the atmosphere when nuclear particles from space (cosmic rays) interact with the nuclei of oxygen and nitrogen, and excited nuclei remaining from the nuclear reactions which formed the primordial materials of the earth are responsible for its natural radioactivity. However, this discussion will be limited to the nuclear excitation and consequent radiation associated with the nuclear industry; in this case the major cause is the impact of neutrons, produced in large numbers in a nuclear reactor. Six main types of radiation are produced as the excited nuclei formed in a nuclear reactor decay to a stable configuration:

(1) *alpha particles*, comprising the nuclei of helium atoms,
(2) *beta particles*, which are either positive or negative electrons (normally electrons have negative charge, but some excited nuclei emit positively charged electrons),
(3) *gamma radiation*, which comprises electromagnetic radiation of even shorter wavelength than X-rays,
(4) *fission fragments*, comprising the nuclei of atoms produced when the original nucleus is sufficiently unstable to rupture completely (fission) into two or more lighter nuclei,
(5) *neutrons*, which invariably accompany fission, but can also arise without fission, and
(6) *protons*, either emitted directly from a nucleus or produced by recoil when a neutron is scattered by a hydrogen atom.

Several types of radiation may be produced in the decay of a single excited nucleus. Thus gamma radiation invariably accompanies the emission of an alpha or beta particle, and fission yields gamma radiation and neutrons as well as fission fragments. In addition, the decay of an unstable nucleus through the emission of radiation may result in another unstable nucleus; thus there may be a series of decays before a stable nucleus is reached.

2.2 Radioactivity

All excited nuclei have a finite lifetime which delays the appearance of the reaction products. For some the delay is very short, so that for all practical purposes the nuclear reaction can be regarded as instantaneous; an example of this is the neutron-induced fission reaction in uranium. But for many excited nuclei the decay products appear an appreciable time after the initial excitation; for example, this is invariably the case with alpha and beta decay. Such nuclei are described as *radioactive* and are referred to as radioisotopes or radionuclei.

Each radioisotope can be characterized by a *half-life*, the time taken for half the radioactivity to decay. In two half-lives the radioactivity is reduced to a quarter of its original level, and in ten half-lives to about one thousandth. Over a thousand radioisotopes are known,[6] and their half-lives vary from fractions of a second to millions of years.

In the nuclear industry, radioisotopes are produced by neutron capture, and the fission fragments are themselves radioactive nuclei. Table 18.1 lists the half-lives and radiation generated in the decay of a few of the more important radioisotopes produced in nuclear reactors. Naturally occurring radioisotopes, including some with very long half-lives generated around the time of the earth's formation, are summarized later in Tables 18.11–13.

Table 18.1 Some important radioisotopes[6]

Isotope	Half-life	Mode of decay	Principal particle energies (MeV)	Principal gamma energies (MeV)
Tritium (^{3}H)‡	12.3 y	β^-	0.019	—
Cobalt-60	5.27 y	β^-	1.49, 0.67, 0.32	1.17, 1.33
Strontium-90‡	28.8 y	β^-	0.55	—
Ruthenium-106‡	366 d	β^-	0.039	—
Iodine-131‡	8.04 d	β^-	0.81, 0.61	0.08, 0.28
Caesium-137‡	30.2 y	β^-	1.17, 0.51	0.66
Plutonium-239	24 000 y	α	5.16, 5.15, 5.11	0.013, 0.03
Americium-241	432 y	α	5.48, 5.43	0.02, 0.06

‡ these isotopes are among the 100 or so species produced in fission, though some of them can also occur through activation

2.3 The absorbtion of radiation

All directly ionizing radiations (alpha and beta particles, protons, and fission fragments) rapidly lose energy by ionization of any matter through which they pass.[5,7,8] The heavier and more highly charged alpha particles are stopped by a sheet of paper, and even the lighter beta particles will not penetrate thin sheets of metal. Table 18.2 gives the stopping distances in common materials.

Indirectly ionizing radiation (gamma radiation and neutrons) lose energy through interacting with electrons or nuclei to produce secondary radiation which itself dissipates by ionization.[9] However, since in general the interactions are much more widely spaced, the penetration distances are greater than for directly ionizing radiation. The processes of energy loss are complex,[9] and cannot be characterized by a single stopping distance; at deep penetrations the absorption profile is roughly exponential. The thicknesses of shielding required vary from a few centimetres of water or lead for laboratory gamma or neutron sources to several metres of concrete for the much higher intensities emitted from a nuclear reactor.

Table 18.2 The absorption of directly ionizing radiation.[5, 7, 8]

Radiation	Energy* (MeV)	Penetration distances				
		air (cm)	water (mm)	aluminium (mm)	iron (mm)	lead (mm)
Beta particles	1	400	5	2	1	0.6
	3	1200	15	7	2.5	2
Protons	1	3	0.03	—	—	0.01
	5	40	0.4	0.2	—	0.1
Alpha particles	1	0.5	—	—	—	0.003
	5	3.5	0.07	—	—	0.02
Fission fragments	65–97	2–2.5	—	—	—	—

* the energy of radiation is invariably measured in electronvolts (eV), the energy gained by an electron in being accelerated through a pontential of one volt. See Table 18.4 for multiples

2.4 Effect of radiation on matter

The way matter is affected by the passage of radiation[10] depends on the same processes that cause the radiation to be absorbed: the production of ionization and, in the case of neutrons, the production of radioactive nuclei. The effects can be described at different levels, from the way individual atoms behave to the changes produced in the properties of bulk material.

At the atomic level, ionization affects mainly the outer electrons surrounding the nucleus. Since it is just these electrons which are involved in chemical bonding of atoms into molecules, it is not surprising that the chemical behaviour of atoms is altered by radiation. The development of nuclear reactors has been accompanied by the development of a new science, *radiation chemistry*, which deals with the new dimension added to conventional chemistry by the presence of ionized atoms. The removal of electrons either in the course of ionization or as a result of the recoil of nuclei involved in an interaction may, for example, break up a molecule, and the fragments, depending on their chemical stability, may combine in some different way with the surrounding material. Thus attempts to use organic liquids as moderator or coolant in a nuclear reactor, which is attractive for some purposes, have been frustrated largely by the degradation of the organic material which occurs in a radiation field. Similarly, radiation at sufficiently high doses may be used to kill bacteria, a technique now in common use for sterilizing some medical supplies.

Organic solids, and some inorganic solids such as the alkali halides, are similarly affected by the electronic excitation caused by radiation. This may manifest itself, for example, through changes in colour, or through the emission of light (scintillation) as the excitation decays. However, in solids such as metals and ceramic oxides the major effect of radiation arises from momentum transfers to atoms in the crystal lattice, the displaced atoms leaving vacancies in the lattice and occupying interstitial positions. These processes cause changes in the physical properties of the solid, for example changes of shape and swelling due to voids formed as vacancies migrate.

These effects are important in materials exposed to high radiation fields inside nuclear reactors, such as the fuel element cans designed to contain the fission products. At low temperatures there may be an accumulation of stored energy in the displaced atoms, an effect which was the basis of the accident to the Windscale production reactor in 1957, where an attempt to release the energy stored in the graphite moderator escalated into a fire. This cannot happen in the Magnox and AGR reactors, which operate at sufficiently high temperature to keep the graphite continuously annealed.

Reactions between radiation and the nuclei of atoms are not generally as important to the physical properties of material as those involving the surrounding electron cloud. Exceptions to this arise, however, where the neutron absorption cross-section is very large, as it is for lithium and boron, and also for fissile materials; in such cases the reaction products may be produced on a sufficient scale to cause swelling and gross changes in physical properties. The helium nuclei from neutron reactions producing alpha particles can also be important, through providing nucleation centres on which vacancies accumulate to create voids.

The effect of radiation on biological material arises through the changes induced in the chemistry of individual cells. The simplest result may be the death of the cell. For human exposures, such acute effects are only of concern at very high radiation levels, usually associated with accidents, where too large a fraction of the cells in the body are affected for life to remain sustainable. At the much lower levels with which we are concerned in radiological protection, any cells killed are readily replaced by the normal metabolic processes. The effects then of importance are the much more subtle chemical changes which lead to the development of cancer or the induction of genetic damage in future generations. These 'delayed effects' of radiation are not generally understood in terms of detailed chemistry, but in §3.1 the phenomenological evidence is reviewed.

2.5 The measurement of radiation

The quantitative description of radiation effects depends on a system for measuring radiation. The International Commission on Radiation Measurements and Units (ICRU), set up by the First International Congress of Radiology in 1925,[11] has developed internationally-agreed quantities and units of radiation and radioactivity and has established suitable procedures for their measurement together with the necessary physical data. A comprehensive treatment can be found in ICRU publications; this discussion will be limited to the primary units summarized in Table 18.3.[12]

The earliest need was to establish a unit of X-ray *exposure*. Initially this was done in terms of the ionization of air, and the Second International Congress of Radiology in 1928 adopted the röntgen (R) as the quantity of X-radiation which produced 1 electrostatic unit (esu) of charge (0.3×10^{-9} coulomb) in a cubic centimetre of air at standard temperature and pressure.

Table 18.3 Summary of radiation units

Quantity	Name	Abbreviation	Units
Radiation exposure	röntgen	R	1 esu in 0.001293 g air or 2.58×10^{-4} C/kg air
Radioactivity	curie	Ci	3.7×10^{10} disintegrations/second
	becquerel*	Bq	1.0 disintegration/second
Absorbed dose	rad	rad	100 erg/g (0.01 J/kg)
	gray*	Gy	1 J/kg ($=$ 100 rad)
Dose-equivalent	rem	rem	rad $\times Q$‡
	sievert*	Sv	Gy $\times Q$ ($=$ 100 rem)

* SI units
‡ An explanation of Q is given in the text

This was later changed to refer to mass rather than volume (0.001293 g of air), and extended to gamma rays (initially from radium) by including all the ionization from secondary particles produced in that mass of air.

The unit of *radioactivity* is the curie (Ci), originally defined as the disintegration rate of the quantity of radon gas in equilibrium with one gram of radium. To avoid slight alterations from each improved measurement of this disintegration rate, the curie was later defined as a precise disintegration rate close to the measured value of the earlier definition:

$$1 \text{ Ci} = 3.7 \times 10^{10} \text{ disintegrations per second.}$$

The relationship between radioactivity and exposure depends on basic interaction processes between radiation and air, a topic discussed in many standard text books. However, for gamma rays with energies in the range 70 keV to 2 MeV (which covers many practical situations) an approximation is:

$$\text{exposure} \approx 0.5 \frac{E}{d^2} \text{ R h}^{-1} \text{ Ci}^{-1},$$

where E is the gamma energy in MeV and d the distance from the source in metres. Thus one curie of activity emitting 1 MeV gamma rays will deliver 0.5 R/h at a distance of one metre. Because of this roughly linear dependence on energy, gamma activities are often quoted in Ci MeV, obtained by multiplying the activity in curies by the gamma energy in millions of electron-volts.

As the use and understanding of radiation developed, it was found convenient to measure radiation in terms of energy deposition. The unit of *absorbed dose* adopted was the rad, where

$$1 \text{ rad} = 100 \text{ erg/g or } 0.01 \text{ joules per kilogram (J/kg).}$$

The rad can be related to the exposure in röntgens via the energy required to produce an ion pair, one röntgen giving an absorbed dose in air of 83 erg/g, i.e. 0.83 rad. However, this value is specific to air, the same exposure giving different energy deposition rates in different materials. For example in soft human tissue, 1 R gives 93 erg/g or 0.93 rad.

For radiological protection purposes the rad proved to be a satisfactory unit for measuring X-rays, gamma rays, and electrons, because the biological damage from these radiations was found to be proportional to the energy deposited to a sufficiently good approximation. However, this proportionality was found not to hold for more heavily ionizing radiation such as alpha particles. The correction for this effect depends on the ionization energy per unit length of radiation path, a quantity which will vary for different points along the path of any individual particle. However, for practical purposes it proves sufficiently accurate to use a *quality factor (Q)* to convert the energy deposition measured by the absorbed dose into the *dose-equivalent*, proportional to the biological effectiveness of radiation in causing malignancies or genetic defects. The dose-equivalent is measured in rem:

$$1 \text{ rem } = 1 \text{ rad} \times Q,$$

where $Q = 1$ for electrons and all electromagnetic radiation,
$\quad Q = 10$ for fission neutrons and protons, and
$\quad Q = 20$ for alpha particles, heavy recoil particles, and fission fragments.
The rem measures the biological effectiveness of radiation for producing delayed effects whatever its type, and is the main unit used in the later discussion. However, the concept of a quality factor is only valid at low or moderate radiation levels; at high doses where the acute effects dominate the rad is the appropriate unit.

It should also be noted that the possibility of other modifying factors in addition to Q is allowed for in the detailed formulation by ICRU, but these are currently assigned a value of unity.

New radiation units are in the course of introduction to conform to the SI system. The gray (Gy), the becquerel (Bq), and the sievert (Sv) will eventually supersede respectively the rad, the curie, and the rem. The relationship between these units is shown in Table 18.3.

It is common practice to use standard prefixes with all units to indicate multiples and sub-multiples in factors of a thousand, as summarized in Table 18.4. Thus the inventory of a particular radioisotope in a power reactor might be given in millions of curies, or MCi, whereas a teaching laboratory source might be measured in millionths of a curie, or μCi.

3   Radiological protection

The rapid expansion of the use of radiography, mainly for medical purposes, following the discovery of X-rays in 1895 soon led to radiation injuries. Many radiographers and researchers were affected by over-exposure, particularly their fingers and hands, and there were also cases of patients with skin burns. As early as 1897 a US court awarded damages to a patient affected by over-exposure.

Table 18.4 Standard scaling factors

Prefix	Abbreviation	Scaling factor
exa	E	10^{18}
peta	P	10^{15}
tera	T	10^{12}
giga	G	10^{9}
mega	M	10^{6}
kilo	k	10^{3}
milli	m	10^{-3}
micro	μ	10^{-6}
nano	n	10^{-9}
pico	p	10^{-12}
femto	f	10^{-15}
atto	a	10^{-18}

During the next few decades a great deal of information and understanding accumulated on the need for protection. Techniques improved steadily with the use of collimators, filters, more efficient X-ray sets, better screens, and the use of lead shields. Initially the application of protection measures depended on the professional skill of the radiographer, but gradually more formal protection guidelines were developed in the leading countries involved. By the time of the Second International Congress of Radiology in 1928 there was a broad consensus that internationally agreed recommendations were desirable and the Congress launched the International Commission on Radiological Protection (called initially the International X-ray and Radium Protection Committee).[13]

The International Commission on Radiological Protection (ICRP) has no legislative role, but its recommendations have formed the basis for regulations controlling the use of radiation in many countries. Although other bodies such as the US National Committee on Radiation Protection and Measurement (NCRP) and later the UN Scientific Committee on the Effects of Atomic Radiation (UNSCEAR) have made important contributions to its deliberations, ICRP has remained independent of governments, responsible only to its peers.

3.1 The effect of radiation on man

The acute effects of radiation on man, causing death within days or weeks at sufficiently high doses, are well established.[14] From the analyses of a number of accidents the single whole-body radiation dose giving a 50 per cent chance of death (LD_{50}) is about 400 rads, whereas below 100 rads there is virtual certainty of recovery. A much higher total dose can be tolerated if it is delivered in fractions separated in time, so that the repair mechanisms in the body have time to operate between each fraction.

However, radiological protection is generally concerned with much smaller doses of radiation where the acute effects are negligible. The hazards of importance are then the delayed effects of radiation on the individual: the induction of leukaemia and cancers (the somatic effects), and the damage to genes and chromosomes transmitted to subsequent generations (the hereditary effects). Quantitative estimates of these hazards to man arise largely from a rather limited number of cases where groups have received sufficiently high doses for the effects to be measurable against the general background of other risks to which human populations are exposed.[15] The principal examples of this are given in Table 18.5. In addition, there is a vast amount of data from animal experiments which has contributed significantly to the interpretation and extrapolation of the data on human populations.

Table 18.5 Principal population groups in which radiation hazards have been measured

Occupational exposure	early radiographers
	underground metalliferous miners
	radium luminizers
Medical exposure	treatment of ankylosing spondylitis
	treatment of ringworm
	diagnostic X-rays
	radiotherapy
Military exposure	Hiroshima and Nagasaki survivors
	Marshall Islanders

There is continuing debate as to how the human data for the groups listed in Table 18.5, mainly relating to radiation levels of tens or hundreds of rem, should be extrapolated to the much lower dose levels associated with the operation of the nuclear industry. The most widely accepted assumption, recommended by ICRP, is that there is no dose threshold for the onset of somatic or genetic effects, and that the chance of these effects occurring is linearly dependent on radiation dose at low dose levels.[16] This linear no-threshold hypothesis has been criticized as too conservative by some (for example, in the 1980 report of the BEIR Committee),[17] particularly for exposure to X-rays, gamma rays and electrons, but there is no consensus on this point. On the other hand, very few experts have suggested that the hypothesis may underestimate the low-dose effects of radiation, and the arguments put forward in favour of such views have been strongly disputed.

The linear no-threshold hypothesis thus remains the accepted basis for estimating radiation effects at low doses. The most recent ICRP estimate of the somatic hazard on this basis[16] gives an average risk from radiation of 125 fatal cancers for every million rem collective whole-body dose-equivalent accumulated in a population. Thus, if a million people each received an additional rem above natural background during their lifetime, the incidence of cancer deaths would increase from the 200 000 normally expected to 200 125. Such a small increase, should it occur, would not be detectable against the normal variability of cancer frequency. From the range of other

Table 18.6 Estimates of the human effect of radiation[15] [16] [17] [18]

Somatic effects	Fatal cancers per million per rem	
ICRP (1977)	125	
Other estimates:		
BEIR I (1972)	117–621	
UNSCEAR (1977)	100	
BEIR III (1980)	67–226	

Genetic effects	Genetic disorders per million live births per lifetime rem	
	1st generation	all generations
ICRP (1977)	20	80
Other estimates:		
BEIR I (1972)	5–80	24–600
UNSCEAR (9177)	25	74
BEIR III (1980)	2–26	24–440

estimates (Table 18.6), it can be inferred that the uncertainty in this average risk estimate is about a factor of two; for safety purposes this uncertainty is of no significance.

Much higher estimates of the risk from radiation were proposed as a result of the study of mortality among radiation workers at Hanford in the US.[19] This study has been strongly criticized,[20] and a later analysis of the same data using acceptable methodology gave quite different results.[21] Moreover, the high risks proposed did not seem consistent with the absence of any detectable effect from variations in the natural background. The ICRP risk estimates therefore remain the most reliable and best substantiated.

No hereditary effects of radiation have been observed in human populations at any dose level. Even among the survivors of Hiroshima and Nagasaki, children subsequently conceived have shown no enhanced incidence of genetic damage.[22] The estimates of human genetic effects therefore rely on data from animal experiments, studies of cell cultures, and theoretical considerations. The most recent estimates of the genetic hazard in man by ICRP is 80 genetic disorders spread over all subsequent generations per million live births per rem of lifetime whole-body dose-equivalent. The range of other estimates imply an uncertainty of perhaps a factor of five, but it must also be noted that the absence of evidence of genetic damage among children born subsequently to the bomb survivors makes it unlikely that the ICRP figure is a serious underestimate.[15] It is widely agreed that the measures taken to protect individuals from somatic effects automatically ensure that hereditary effects are adequately controlled.[24]

Some variation from the average levels of hazard already quoted can be distinguished for sub-groups of the total population. The most notable is between men and women because of the significant contribution from female breast cancer. The risks are substantially higher for the very young and for the foetus, and there are some indications that the risk rises again with age. Table 18.7 shows the components of the average risks distinguished by ICRP. For most practical purposes these variations are of no great significance, largely because radiation exposure affects mainly whole populations, or radiation workers who are predominantly men. The main exception arises with female radiation workers, where steps are taken to limit radiation exposure during pregnancy.

Table 18.7 Variations in the somatic risk distinguished by ICRP[16]

	Fatal cancers per million per rem
Men and women, all ages	125
Men, all ages	100
Women: all ages	150
during reproductive years	200

3.2 Partial body exposures

The risk estimates of ICRP are given in terms of the dose-equivalent to the whole body. In many practical situations only part of the body may be irradiated, or the radiation exposure may vary appreciably between different tissues. To deal with this problem, ICRP recommends weighting factors (W_T) by which the dose equivalent to individual organs should be multiplied to give the *effective whole-body dose-equivalent*:

$$\text{effective dose-equivalent} = \Sigma W_T \times \text{dose-equivalent to organ } T,$$

where Σ denotes a summation over all the organs concerned. Table 18.8 gives the weighting factors for the six principal organs at risk, and for the next five organs or tissues receiving the highest dose-equivalent; the exposure of all remaining tissues can be neglected.

Table 18.8 ICRP weighting for partial-body exposure[16]

Tissue	W_T
Gonads	0.25
Breast	0.15
Red bone marrow	0.12
Lung	0.12
Thyroid	0.03
Bone surfaces	0.03
Other tissues‡ (each)	0.06

‡ applied to the next five organs or tissues receiving the highest doses, the stomach, small intestine, upper large intestine, and lower large intestine being treated as four separate organs

3.3 **Committed doses**

For direct external radiation, the estimate of risk from whole-or partial-body exposure is straightforward. The annual effective dose-equivalent can be measured or estimated, and this can be used to control the risk from radiation as discussed later. However, for internal exposure due to ingesting or inhaling radioactive material, the dose to tissue may continue far beyond the period of intake if the radionuclide concerned has a long half-live and is retained in the body.

To measure the risk from such continuing exposure it is then necessary to sum the annual effective dose-equivalent over time. The time period adopted by ICRP is 50 years, and the resulting integrated dose is termed the *committed dose-equivalent*.

Committed dose-equivalent = annual dose-equivalent summed over 50 years.

Where partial-body exposures are involved, the dose-equivalent is replaced by the effective dose-equivalent, so that the overall individual risk in the general case is measured in terms of the *committed effective dose-equivalent*. For convenience, this quantity will be generally abbreviated to *dose* measured in rem.

3.4 **Population risks**

Because it is accepted that the risk from radiation increases linearly with exposure to radiation, the total hazard to a population is directly proportional to the sum of all the effective dose-equivalents for the individuals in the population. For example, a dose of one rem to each of a million people represents the same hazard to the whole population as a dose of 10 rem to every tenth person within that population; as a whole, the population is receiving a million man-rem, which will cause eventually about 125 deaths and about 80 genetic defects on the basis of the ICRP risk estimates. Thus it is convenient to talk in terms of the collective dose in man-rem even where the levels of individual exposure are so low as to make the risk to the individual quite negligible:

Collective dose (man-rem) = sum of individual doses (rem).

For direct exposure to radiation, the appropriate dose which measures the risk is the *effective dose-equivalent* (§3.2), and where inhalation or ingestion is involved the *committed effective dose-equivalent* (§3.3) must be used. However, populations can also suffer exposure from radionuclides released to the environment with half-lives much longer than the 50 years over which the committed dose to the individual is integrated. For example, nuclear power plants can give rise to the release to the biosphere of carbon-14, an isotope with a half-life of over 5000 years. One such release will continue to irradiate successive generations of the world population, albeit with decreasing intensity. To measure this collective risk, the dose must be integrated over all time, and this is denoted the *dose commitment* to distinguish it from the *committed dose* relevant to the individual. Thus

effective dose-equivalent commitment = effective dose-equivalent summed to infinity.

There is much philosophical debate as to whether summing to infinity is a sensible measure of the overall risk. Where half-lives of millions of years are involved, such a procedure makes exceedingly small risks to a single generation add up to a much larger risk over all time, and it has been questioned whether this is a sensible approach. After all, once the risk to a particular generation has decayed to a negligible level, if may be judged appropriate to ignore the trivial risk to all subsequent generations. On these grounds the calculation of dose commitment is often terminated at a time well short of infinity.

3.5 The evolution of radiation dose limits[13,25]

At its first meeting in 1928, ICRP made recommendations based on proposals put forward by the British X-ray and Radium Protection Committee. These included minimum thicknesses of lead shielding for X-ray and radium sources, as well as requirements for good housekeeping and working conditions, but did not include any limitations on dose. At that time it was widely thought that there was a threshold below which radiation would cause no damage. This is well illustrated by the suggestion of Mutscheller and Sievert in 1925[38] that the annual limit should be one tenth of the dose observed to cause skin damage. The radiation dose required to produce skin burns varies with the X-ray energy, determined by the voltage at which the X-ray tube operates: practical values at the time were typically 100–200 kV, and at these levels the suggested limit corresponds to about 30–70 rem per year.

It was not until its third meeting in 1934 that ICRP recommended a permissible level of occupational exposure. This recommendation of 0.2 R/day, corresponding to around 70 rem/year, remained until 1950. The surge of interest in nuclear energy initiated during the Second World War led to a number of important developments in radiological protection during the 1950s: it was recognized that the genetic effects were less important than the somatic effects; the conservative view was adopted that radiation is harmful down to the lowest levels without any damage threshold; and the Commission was reorganized to cope effectively with the greater importance of radiological protection following the advent of atomic energy. In 1950, on the basis of the large body of information which had by then accumulated, mainly from the United States, the ICRP lowered the maximum permissible dose for radiation workers to 0.3 R/week, corresponding to about 15 rem/year and introduced a quality factor of 10 for fast neutrons. For the first time maximum permissible concentrations in the body of a number of isotopes were included in the recommendations, and this list was greatly enlarged in 1953.

A further reduction in occupational dose was recommended in 1956 to 5 rem/year with the accumulated dose up to age 30 not to exceed 50 rem; and much greater emphasis was placed on the earlier cautions to keep doses as low as possible below the recommended limits. In 1958 the limits were refined by requiring the accumulated dose to age N not to exceed the value $5(N-18)$ rem with a quarterly dose limit of 3 rem. Thus the annual adult dose could be 12 rem provided the average value from age 18 did not exceed 5 rem. This recommendation lasted until 1977, when a dose limit for radiation workers of 5 rem/year was adopted, coupled with the recommendation that doses should be optimized through balancing the risks and the benefits as discussed in the next section.

Recommendations regarding the exposure of the general public were first made by ICRP in 1953, when a limit of one-tenth of the occupational exposure was promulgated. This approach has remained ever since, although in the period 1958–77 it was supplemented by a limit of 5 rem in 30 years for whole populations to limit genetic damage. The 1977 recommendations dropped this population limit on the grounds that it was not likely to be reached under the system of dose control then enunciated.

The recommendations of national bodies have broadly followed those of ICRP. The National Committee on Radiation Protection (NCRP) in the United States adopted 0.1 R/day in 1934, rather than the 0.2 R/day of ICRP, and this remained until 1947 when NCRP adopted 0.3 R/week, the level recommended by ICRP in 1950. In 1956 NCRP adopted the same general recommendations as ICRP. In the UK, the Medical Research Council recommended 0.5 R/week in 1949. In 1956 the ICRP recommendations were adopted, but coupled with lifetime dose for radiation workers of 200 rad of which not more than 50 rad were to be achieved by age 30. More recently, the National Radiological Protection Board endorsed the 1977 recommendations of ICRP as the basis for radiological protection in the UK.[26]

The ICRP recommendations concerning occupational exposure are designed to ensure that the associated risks are comparable with the safest industries. It will be seen later that actual mortality experience in the nuclear industry is consistent with this intention. The recommendations concerning the general public have resulted in exposures well below the levels considered acceptable. The associated risk to the public from the nuclear industry will be shown to be quite negligible. As far as other living species are concerned, it is the view of ICRP that if man is adequately protected, then other life-forms are also likely to be sufficiently protected.

3.6 Current radiological protection philosophy

The regulations in the UK relating to radiological protection are largely based on the ICRP recommendations of 1959. The more recent recommendations of ICRP in 1977[16] do not change the numerical dose limits in any major practical respect, but they do advance the philosophy of the way these limits are applied. This advance is important to the practice of radiological protection, and the new thinking is being implemented even though it is not yet mandatory in this country. An outline of the latest ICRP views is therefore presented here.

In making its latest recommendations, ICRP identified the following three primary objectives:

1. All practices involving radiation exposure should be justified, with the benefits outweighing the detriment.
2. Radiation doses should be as low as reasonably achievable (ALARA), economic and social factors being taken into consideration.
3. All radiation exposures should be within the recommended dose limits.

The change in emphasis embodied in these objectives is the relegation of dose limits, summarized in Table 18.9, to the role of a protection backstop, whilst introducing the concept of optimizing the radiological design of plant, Fig. 18.1, so that where the cost (C) of reducing exposure is less than the detriment (D) arising from that exposure, then the exposure should be reduced.

Table 18.9 ICRP recommended annual dose limits[16]

Occupational exposure	
Any tissue	50 rem
Eye lens	15 rem*
Whole body‡	5 rem
Public exposure	
Any tissue	5 rem
Whole body‡	0.5 rem

* reduced from 30 rem at the 1980 meeting of ICRP, see ICRP-30, part 2.
‡ or the committed effective dose-equivalent for non-uniform exposures

Such a cost-benefit approach is not easy to apply in many cases. Implementation by the plant design engineer requires the detriment from radiation to be expressed in monetary terms, and as yet there is no consensus as to the money value of a man-rem. A value commonly floated in the US is equivalent to £500/man-rem; but it is also suggested that exposures near the dose limit should have a higher value than those well below that limit, which has led to values from less than £100/man-rem to over £2500/man-rem. In the UK, a range from £10–£4000/man-rem has been discussed.[27]

The resolution of these problems is one of the current challenges in radiological protection, and it will take some time for all the implications to be resolved. Undoubtedly for large and complex plants it will be necessary

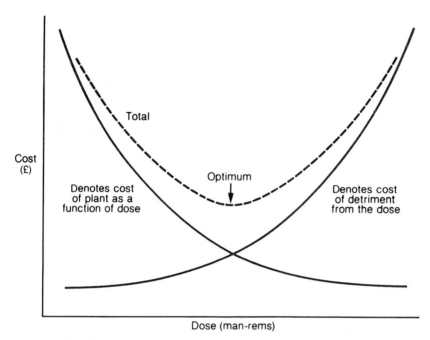

Fig. 18.1 Optimization of exposure in plant design

to undertake major optimization studies. For smaller-scale systems it seems unlikely that the cost of such sophistication can be justified by the potential advantages, so simpler guidelines may be expected to emerge based on model analyses.

3.7 Secondary and derived exposure standards

The relationship between the radiation dose to man and the concentration of radionuclides in the air he breathes or the water he drinks involves a detailed understanding of the body processes defining the fate of the inhaled or ingested fluid. To assist in the practical application of the dose limits, ICRP has developed a metabolic model of the human body, and carried through the quite complex calculations relating dose to radionuclide concentration. The results of this analysis are presented as an *annual limit of intake* (ALI) and *derived air concentration* (DAC) for each individual radionuclide, which result in a committed dose equal to the annual limit of occupational exposure.[28] These values are used in applying the basic exposure limits recommended by ICRP.

　A similar approach[29] is used to control radioactive emissions from nuclear plant, where there is dispersion in the environment causing dilution before the radioactive material reaches man. The calculation of the relationship between the quantity of a radioisotope discharged and the dose to an individual[37] is invariably specific to a particular site. It involves the geographical distribution of population, the mobility of individuals and their dietary habits, as well as the processes of radionuclide migration through the food chain. Generally the calculation of a *derived limit* (DL) requires a detailed investigation of these factors for the site concerned, although in particular cases of some practical importance (e.g. tritium or noble gas discharges) a conservative calculation is straightforward.

3.8 Legislative control

Much of the law relating to the control of radiation derives directly or indirectly from international treaties and conventions, or from the recommendation of international bodies, principally ICRP, but also including, for example, the International Atomic Energy Agency recommendations on the transport of radioactive materials. All these recommendations and agreements have legal effect only to the extent that they are incorporated into national legislation, although it is the general practice to observe their provisions. An exceptional case arises from the accession of the UK to the Treaty of Rome: under the European Communities Act 1972, which provides the legal basis for UK membership of the EEC, the ECSC, and Euratom, Regulations of the Council and the Commission of the European Communities are legally binding in this country.

The main Acts of Parliament from which statutory radiological protection measures derive[30] are the

Radioactive Substances Act 1948 and 1960,
Factories Act 1961,
Nuclear Installations Act 1965 and 1969, and
Health and Safety at Work Act 1974.

However, there is a host of other legislation which has some relevance to radiological protection; a summary of the more important examples is given in Table 18.10.

This body of legislation has effect mainly by giving Ministers the authority to promulgate regulations, the detailed procedures varying widely under the different Acts. With successive reorganization of the machinery of government, the Minister currently responsible for a particular aspect (Table 18.10) may be different from the original designee.

The last 30 years have seen the hazards from radiation brought firmly under legislative control. The relevant regulations, summarized in Table 18.10, cover the production, sale, use, storage, and disposal of radioactive substances and plant or machines generating ionizing radiation in virtually every sphere of activity. Future development of this control of radiation is likely to be through more detailed regulations under existing legislation, rather than through further Acts of Parliament. In particular, the Health and Safety at Work Act 1974 is being used to develop a more extensive framework of regulations, codes of practice, and general guidance, which in due course will supersede much of the existing provisions under earlier legislation.

4 Natural background

Mankind has evolved in a naturally radioactive environment. The earth is bombarded by cosmic rays from the sun and from outside the solar system, and all matter contains some traces of radioactive substances. Man is exposed to external radiation, consisting of the cosmic radiation and radiation from the decay of the naturally occurring radionuclides in his immediate environment and internal radiation from the decay of the naturally occurring radionuclides taken into the body.[15]

4.1 Cosmic radiation

The primary cosmic radiation incident on the top of the earth's atmosphere consists of a small solar component, with particle energies in the range 1–200 MeV, and a much larger galactic and possibly extra-galactic component, with particle energies up to at least 10^{13} MeV. The radiation consists largely of protons, with 10 per cent alpha particles and some heavier nuclei, electrons, photons, and neutrinos. At high energy ($>10^4$ MeV) the flux is uniform and isotropic, approximately equal to 10 per square centimetre per second ($10\,\mathrm{cm^{-2}\,s^{-1}}$), and constant in time. At lower energies the galactic flux is modified by the earth's magnetic field, resulting in a higher flux in polar regions, and by disturbances due to solar activity, resulting in the flux being at a minimum at the peak of the 11-year solar cycle. The solar component is associated with solar flares and is at its maximum at the peak of the solar cycle.

The primary cosmic radiation is substantially altered by its passage through the atmosphere. The proton flux is reduced from about $10\,\mathrm{cm^{-2}\,s^{-1}}$ to about $2 \times 10^{-4}\,\mathrm{cm^{-2}\,s^{-1}}$. The alpha component is almost entirely eliminated. Interactions between the primary particles and the atmosphere result in the production of electrons, photons, neutrons, and mesons. The fluxes at sea level are highly anisotropic, with a sharp maximum in the vertical direction, and vary with time as a result of atmospheric and solar changes. Both the temporal variations and the variations with latitude, however, are small and the main factor that influences dose-rate is altitude.

The approximate average values of cosmic-ray fluxes at sea level are
(1) total charged particle flux $2 \times 10^{-2}\,\mathrm{cm^{-2}\,s^{-1}}$, and
(2) neutron flux, $8 \times 10^{-3}\,\mathrm{cm^{-2}\,s^{-1}}$.
The corresponding average dose-equivalent rates are
(1) directly ionizing component,   28 mrem/y, and
(2) neutron component,   3 mrem/y.
The dose rate increases with altitude near sea level at approximately 0.5

Table 18.10 Principal legislation concerning radiological protection (March 1979)

Act of Parliament	Minister responsible	Principal powers relating to the nuclear environment	Principal regulations in force †
Import, Export and Customs Powers (Defence) Act 1939	SoS for Trade	Control of imports and exports generally	Import of Goods (Control) Order, SI 1954 No.23 Export of Goods (Control) Order, SI 1970 No.1288
Education Act 1944	SoS for Education and Science	Control of direct grant schools	Direct Grant Schools Regulations 1959, SI 1959 No.1837 amended by SI 1965 No.1
Atomic Energy Act 1946	SoS for Energy	Carrying out research into matters connected with atomic energy	
Radioactive Substances Act 1948	SoS for the Environment	Transport of radioactive substances by road (but see Health & Safety at Work Act 1974)	Radioactive Substances (Carriage by Road) (Great Britain) Regulations 1974, SI 1974 No.1735 Radioactive Substances (Road Transport Workers) (Great Britain) Regulations 1970, SI 1970, No.1827 amended by SI 1975 No.1522
	SoS for the Social Services	Licensing and regulation of therapeutic users	(not used)
	SoS for Education and Science	Regulation of imports and exports of radio-active substances	(not used)
Civil Aviation Act 1949	SoS for Trade	Conditions for the carriage of goods by air	Air Navigation Order 1976, SI 1976 No.178
Post Office Act 1953	SoS for Industry	Conditions for the carriage of goods by post	Post Office regulations
Atomic Energy Authority Act 1954 & 1959	SoS for Energy	AEA right to manufacture, use, dispose of and research into radioactive substances	
Food and Drugs Act 1955	Minister of Agriculture Fisheries and Food and SoS for the Social Services	Control of irradiation of food for human consumption	Food (Control of Irradiation) Regulations 1967, SI 1967 No.385 amended by SI 1972 No.205 Food (Control of Irradiation) (Scotland) Regs. 1967, SI 1967 No.388 amended by SI 1972 No.307
Local Government Act 1958	SoS for Education and Science	Control of Schools and Colleges of Education	Schools Regulations 1959, SI 1959 No.364 amended by SI 1965 No.3 Further Education Regulations 1969, SI 1969 No.403

(Table 18.10 *Continued*)

Act of Parliament	Minister responsible	Principal powers relating to the nuclear environment	Principal regulations in force †
Radioactive Substances Act 1960	SoS for the Environment	Accumulation and disposal of radioactive waste. Registration of users of radioactive material and mobile radioactive apparatus (see also the Continental Shelf Act 1964, Section 7)	Used only to give a large number of exemptions, including civil defences, fire detectors, electronic valves, testing instruments, exhibitions, luminous articles, storage in transit, phosphates, rare earths, lead, uranium and thorium and their components, hospital waste, schools, lightning conductors
Factories Act 1961	SoS for Employment	Radiation levels in factories and other premises	Ionizing Radiation (Unsealed Sources) Regulations 1968, SI 1968 No.780 Ionising Radiation (Sealed Sources) Regulations 1969, SI 1969 No.808
Transport Act 1963	SoS for Trade	Conditions for carriage of goods by rail (Implements the International Convention)	British Rail regulations – Dangerous Goods by Freight Train and by Passenger Train or Similar Service, List of Dangerous Goods and Conditions of Acceptance, Class 7
Merchant Shipping Act 1964	SoS for Trade	Gives effect to the International Convention for the Safety of Life at Sea, 1960	Merchant Shipping (Dangerous Goods) Rules 1978, SI 1978 No.1543
Nuclear Installations Act 1965 and 1969	SoS for Energy	Issue of site permits for isotopic enrichment and processing of irradiated matter Nuclear site licensing (but see Health & Safety at Work Act 1974) Implements the International Conventions on Third Party Liability	Nuclear Installation Regulation 1971, SI 1971 No.381 Nuclear Installations (Dangerous Occurrences) Regulations 1965, SI 1965 No.1824 (see also Regs. under the Health & Safety at Work Act 1974 Nuclear Installations (Insurance Certificate) Regs. 1965, SI 1965 No.1823, amended by Nuclear Installation (Insurance Certificate) (Amendment) Regulations 1969, SI 1964 No.64 Nuclear Installations (Excepted Matter) Regulations 1978, SI 1978 No.1779

(Table 18.10 *Continued*)

Act of Parliament	Minister responsible	Principal powers relating to the nuclear environment	Principal regulations in force †
The Atlantic Treaty Act 1967	SoS for the Environment	Prohibits waste disposal in Antarctica as agreed under the Antarctic Treaty	
The Medicines Act 1968	SoS for Health	Control of medicines	Medicines (Radioactive Substances) Order 1978, SI 1978, No.1004 Medicines (Committee on Radiation from Radioactive Medicinal Products) Order 1978, SI 1978 No.1005 Medicines (Administration of Radioactive Substances) Regulations 1978, SI 1978, SI 1978 No.1006
Radiological Protection Act 1970	SoS for the Social Services	Appointment and direction of the National Radiological Protection Board	
European Communities Act 1972		Makes Directives of the Council of the European Commission effective in the UK	Council Directive 76/579/Euratom of 1st June 1976 laying down the revised basic safety standard for health protection Nuclear Installations Act 1965 (Repeats and Modifications) Regs. 1974, SI 1974 No.2056
Health & Safety at Work Act 1974	SoS for Employment	Replacement of certain provisions of the Radioactive Substances Act 1960 and the Nuclear Installations Act 1965 by a system of regulations and codes of practice approved by the Health and Safety Commission Transferred responsibility for Nuclear Site Licence to the Health and Safety Commission	Radioactive Substances Act 1948 (Modification) Regulations 1974, SI 1974 No.1821
Control of Pollution Act 1974	SoS for the Environment	Control of pollution in addition to provisions of Radioactive Substances Act 1960	Control of Pollution (Radioactive Waste) Regulations 1976, SI 1976 No.959

† many other regulations have been made under these and other Acts of Parliament which may affect the legal position in some respects

mrem/y for every 100 m. Above a few hundred metres the dose-rate increases more rapidly with increasing altitude: in many parts of the world substantial populations live at altitudes of a few thousand metres where dose-rates are three of four times those at sea level.

4.2 Naturally-occurring radionuclides

About 70 radionuclides have been found in nature. They can be divided into two classes:
   (1) radionuclides produced by cosmic rays—cosmogenic radio-nuclides—and
   (2) radionuclides with half-lives of the same order of magnitude as the earth, assumed to be the remnants of the primordal inventory of radionuclides, and members of their decay series.

1. *Cosmogenic radionuclides.* The principal cosmogenic radionuclides of radiological interest are ^{3}H, ^{7}Be, ^{14}C, and ^{22}Na. They are produced by the interaction of cosmic-ray protons and neutrons with nitrogen, oxygen, and argon in the atmosphere. Production rates and inventories are given in Table 18.11.

   Some other radionuclides are also produced but they contribute negligible radiation dose to man at ground level.

2. *Primordial radionuclides.* These are of two types:
   (1) singly occurring radionuclides with long half-lives,
   (2) members of the families of radioactive heavy elements, originating in ^{238}U, ^{235}U, and ^{232}Th.
Both types are distributed throughout the earth's crust. They are the source of geothermal energy, generating a heat flux of about 65 mW/m^2.

   Seventeen singly occurring radionuclides have been detected, the majority being rare earths with long half-lives and very low concentrations, having negligible radiological significance. The two nuclides that contribute significant doses to man are ^{40}K and ^{87}Rb. They are found in all rocks, soils and water, and in man. Typical concentrations are given in Table 18.12.

   The two families of radioactive elements originating with ^{238}U and ^{232}Th account for much of the natural radioactivity to which man is exposed. A third family, originating with ^{235}U, is also present but does not contribute significant radiation dose.

   Typical concentrations of the principal members of the two families are given in Fig. 18.2. Uranium, thorium, and radium are dissolved from rocks and soils and suspended in the air as dust particles, and ingestion and inhalation results in a typical adult man containing approximately 100 μg of uranium and some 40 pCi of radium (thorium, being relatively insoluble, is not found in man in significant quantities). Inhabitants of areas of high

Table 18.11 Principal cosmogenic radionuclides

Nuclide	^{3}H	^{7}Be	^{14}C	^{22}Na
Half-life	12.3 y	53.6 d	5730 y	2.62 y
Number of atoms produced per unit time per unit area of earth's surface (cm^{-2} s^{-1})	0.25	8×10^{-2}	2.5	9×10^{-5}
Global inventory (MCi)	34	1	300	0.01
Distribution as % of inventory:				
stratosphere and troposphere	8	72	2	27
land surface and biosphere	27	8	4	21
oceans	65	20	94	52

Table 18.12 Singly occurring primordial radionuclides

Nuclide	^{40}K	^{87}Rb
Half-life	1.26×10^9 y	4.8×10^{10} y
Typical activity:		
concentration in rock and soil (pCi/g)	2–30	3
activity concentration in man (pCi/kg)	1600	230

natural radioactivity have much higher body burdens of these elements. Radon, being a gas, emanates from solids, and concentrations depend on such factors as soil condition, and, for buildings, construction methods and ventilation rates. The relatively long-lived nuclides ^{210}Pb and ^{210}Po are concentrated in some plants (10–100 pCi/kg) and significant doses can result from ingestion and inhalation. An average adult man contains approximately 500 pCi of ^{210}Pb and ^{210}Po.

4.3 Doses to man from external sources

The doses received from external sources of radiation originate from cosmic rays and from gamma-emitting radionuclides in man's immediate environment. Both contribute essentially whole-body doses.

4.3.1 *Doses from cosmic radiation*

The average flux of ionizing cosmic radiation at sea level results in an average ion-pair production rate of 2.1 cm^{-3} s^{-1}. Assuming each ion pair requires 33.7 eV to be produced, the corresponding absorbed dose-rate in air is 3.2 μ rad/h. The relationship between absorbed dose-rate in air and absorbed dose in human tissue depends on the stopping powers of the radiation in air and tissue, and on geometrical factors. The average annual dose depends on the amount of time spent outdoors; buildings can provide considerable shielding from some cosmic radiations. If this structural shielding

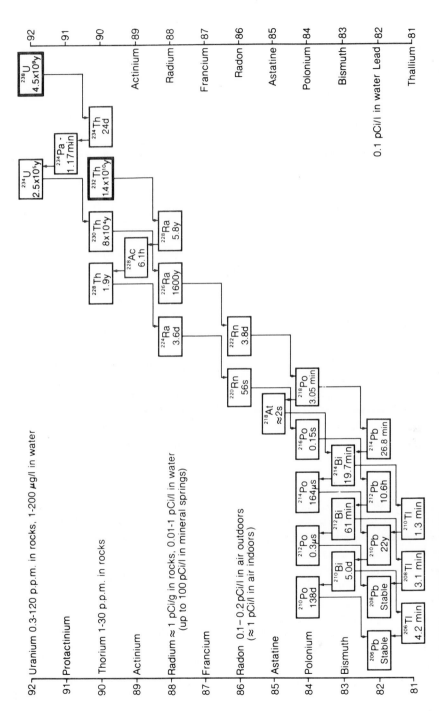

Fig. 18.2 ^{238}U and ^{232}Th decay series

Table 18.13 External doses from radionuclides in the ground

Radionuclide	Absorbed dose-rate in air 1 m above ground μ rad h^{-1} pCi^{-1} g^{-1}
^{40}K	0.16
^{238}U	1.58
^{232}Th	2.45

effect is not taken into account, the average annual absorbed dose in human tissue for the ionizing component of cosmic radiation at sea level is the figure of 28 mrem given above.

A similar calculation for the neutron component gives an annual absorbed dose in human tissue of 3 mrem.

Because cosmic-ray intensities increase rapidly at high altitudes, passengers and crew in aircraft are exposed to additional cosmic radiation. The average dose-rate at the cruising height of a jet aircraft is 0.4 mrem/h.

4.3.2 *External doses from naturally occurring radionuclides*

The decay of the naturally occurring radionuclides produces alpha, beta, and gamma radiations. Practically all the alpha and beta radiation is absorbed in surface tissues, and doses to the more critical organs result from the gamma contribution. The principal sources of gamma radiation outdoors are ^{40}K, and ^{238}U and ^{232}Th and their decay products. The absorbed dose-rates in air corresponding to unit activity concentrations of these nuclides in a representative soil are given in Table 18.13. It is assumed that the decay products of ^{238}U and ^{232}Th are in equilibrium with their precursors.

In practice, the dose-rates in air depend on the characteristics of the soil or rock, moisture content, snow cover, and atmospheric conditions. The average value of the absorbed dose-rate in air, at 1 m above the ground, is estimated by UNSCEAR[15] to be 4.5 μ rad/h. The contributions from the cosmogenic radionuclides to external radiation dose is insignificant in comparison. The majority of the world's population lives in areas where the outdoor absorbed dose-rate in air varies between 3 and 7 μ rad/h, but in some areas, with populations of several thousands, levels of 100–200 μ rad/h have been found, and in some more localized areas levels are even higher. The highest quoted figure is 10 000 μ rad/h.[15]

Indoors, exposure depends on the extent of shielding from the outdoor exposure and on the construction materials used in the building. In wooden and prefabricated houses with thin walls, there is only a small attenuation of the outdoor radiation, but in more substantial houses, outdoor radition is almost completely shielded, and the exposure results largely from the radio-activity in the building materials. The average indoor absorbed dose-rate in air is approximately 5 μ rad/h, with the majority of the world's population living in buildings where the range of values lies between 2 and 9 μ rad/h.

The corresponding average annual absorbed dose in tissue, assuming 80 per cent of time spent indoors, is 32 mrem (world figure, see ref. 15; for UK average see Table 18.14), with the majority of the world's population receiving 21 to 43 mrem. Some groups in areas of high background radiation receive annual doses of several hundred mrem and a few receive 1–3 rem.

4.4 Internal doses to man

Calculation of the doses from internal exposure following ingestion and inhalation of naturally occurring radionuclides requires knowledge of the way the body absorbs and metabolizes these materials. Estimates are largely based on measurements of the nuclide content of the various organs of the body and models of the mechanisms by which the materials reach these organs. Unlike external sources, which contribute uniform whole-body doses, the absorbed doses from internal sources vary considerably from organ to organ.

4.4.1 *Internal doses from cosmogenic radionuclides*
The cosmogenic radionuclides only contribute a small fraction of the total natural background dose. The most important of these is ^{14}C, which contributes 1.3 mrem per year of whole-body dose; ^{3}H, ^{7}Be and ^{22}Na together contribute a total of some 30 μ rem/year.

4.4.2 *Internal doses from primordial radionuclides*
Only ^{40}K and ^{87}Rb, of the singly occurring radionuclides, contribute significant internal doses and of these two ^{40}K is the more important. An average adult man contains approximately 16 mg, from which he receives an annual whole-body absorbed dose of some 17 mrem. Approximately 0.4 mrem is contributed by ^{87}Rb, with an average body content of about 200 mg.

For the uranium and thorium series, the most highly exposed organ is the lung, which is exposed to alpha radiation from radon and its short-lived decay products. The dose is not distributed uniformly throughout the lung. The deposition and fate of the inhaled material depends on the physical characteristics of the material (such as particle size), the way of breathing (nose or mouth breathing, depth of respiration), and clearance methods within the lung. Many measurements of radon exposure have been reported in terms of a working-level month (WLM), a unit used in controlling occupational exposure to radon and radon daughters in mines. A working level (WL) is defined as any combination of short-lived radon daughters per litre of air that will result in the emission of 1.3×10^5 MeV of alpha-particle energy; a WLM is an exposure for one working month (170 hours) to a concentration of 1 WL. The use of this unit avoided the difficulty of inter-preting the non-uniform dose distribution within the lung in terms of the effective dose equivalent. However, there is now consensus that 1 WLM is equivalent to 1 rem in the mining environment but to not more than 0.5 rem in the general environment.[49] The average annual dose from naturally occurring radon and short-lived daughters is 0.16 WLM equivalent to 80 mrem whole body dose.[50] The other nuclides of the two series irradiate mostly the bone-lining cells and the red bone marrow, and somewhat smaller doses are delivered to the gonads; total annual doses to these organs are approximately 120, 25, and 14 mrem, respectively.

4.3 Summary of exposures from natural sources

The estimated average effective whole-body dose-equivalents from natural sources are summarized for the UK in Table 18.14. Much higher doses are received by people living at high altitudes and in a few regions of high natural radioactivity, such as those listed in Table 18.15, which also gives UK and USA figures for comparison.[23]

Table 18.14 Summary of exposures from natural sources—UK[31]

Source of irradiation	Average annual effective whole-body dose-equivalent (mrem)
External irradiation	
Cosmic rays	31
Primordial radionuclides	38
Internal irradiation	
cosmogenic radionuclides:	
^{3}H, ^{7}Be, ^{22}Na	0.01
^{14}C	1.3
primordial radionuclides:	
^{40}K	17
^{87}Rb	0.4
U and Th series	98*
Total (to 2 significant figures)	190*

* including 80 mrem from radon and its daughters

Table 18.15 World variations in annual dose-equivalent from natural background radiation excluding the contribution from radon and its daughters

	mrem/y
UK average:	110
London	90
Aberdeen	90–170 (av. 130)
USA average:	100
minimum (east coast)	90
maximum (Colorado)	250
Sri Lanka, granite areas	3000–7000
Kerala, India	800–8000
Minas Gerais, Brazil	1700–12 000
Rio de Janeiro beaches, Brazil	550–1250
At cruising altitude of subsonic jet	3500*
At cruising altitude of supersonic jet	17 500*

* resulting in typical dose for transatlantic flight $\approx$ 4 mrem

5 Man-made and man-enhanced radiation

The natural background contributes approximately four-fifths of the total annual average radiation dose in the UK. Man's technological activities contribute the balance.[15,31] Some of this balance is directly man-made—radiation from X-ray sets and t.v. tubes, or from radioactive elements created in accelerators; the rest results from man's manipulation of naturally occurring radioactive materials—their extraction from the earth and their use in medicine, consumer goods, nuclear weapons, and the nuclear power industry. By far the largest part of this balance comes from the use of X-rays and radioactive materials in medical diagnosis and therapy.

5.1 Medical irradiation

Medical irradiation contributes the highest man-made dose to which the average human being is exposed. It differs from most other types of exposure in that it is generally delivered at high instantaneous dose-rates and usually only involves limited regions of the body. It is also unique in the sense that it is used with the express purpose of directly benefiting the exposed individual.

Because from the point of view of the individual the benefit of medical irradiation normally exceeds the risk, the factor that is normally considered in assessing possible detrimental impact is the risk of hereditary damage to future generations, expressed in terms of the genetically significant dose (GSD).

Radiation is used in medicine in three ways:
    (1) diagnostic radiology,
    (2) diagnostic use of radiopharmaceuticals, and
    (3) radiotherapy

The use of diagnostic radiology in many technically developed countries is growing at a rate of 5–15 per cent p.a.; the growth-rate in the developing countries is generally higher. There is a great range in annual number of X-ray examinations from country to country; for example, 1530 diagnostic examinations are carried out per 1000 of population each year in the Federal Republic of Germany, while the figure for India is 35 per 1000.[15]

Diagnostic use of radiopharmaceuticals is growing very rapidly, many countries reporting a doubling of the number of tests every 3–5 years.

Radiotherapy is used for the treatment of malignant and non-malignant disease. The number of radiation treatments for non-malignant diseases has fallen rapidly in recent decades because of the availability of alternative and safer forms of treatment. Radiotherapy remains an important treatment for malignant disease, and the need for such treatment is likely to increase as causes of death other than cancer, such as malnutrition and tuberculosis, are gradually eliminated with improvement in the world's living standards. The high doses (up to several thousands of rads) that are needed to destroy tumours inevitably affect surrounding healthy tissue, with some associated risk of late effects of the radiation. This risk is normally acceptable because of the seriousness of the primary disease.

Because of the large variations of medical practice from country to country, figures relating to the UK will be used. The most complete study of radiological exposure in the UK remains the Adrian survey of 1957.[32] This survey reported a total Genetically Significant Dose (GSD) of 19.3 mrem per person per year from all medical practices, made up of 14.1 mrem from diagnostic radiology, 0.2 mrem from radiopharmaceuticals and 5 mrem from radiotheraphy. A survey is being carried out by NRPB to bring these figures up to date. Their study of diagnostic radiology, just completed,[33,34,35] shows that, while the number of investigations has been increasing at 2 per cent per annum since 1957, technical improvements have resulted in a lower GSD per investigation. As a result, the current average annual dose from this source has decreased by about 15 per cent since 1957 to 11.8 mrem.

Investigations using radiopharmaceuticals are carried out less frequently than those using X-rays; typical numbers range from a few thousand to a few tens of thousands of investigations per annum in the UK. Doses vary considerably according to the techniques used and the part of the body being investigated. NRPB estimate an average GSD of less than 0.3 mrem per person per year.[31]

Because of the decreasing use of radiotherapy for non-malignant disease the annual GSD from this source in the UK is likely to have decreased since the Adrain survey. NRPB's estimate for therapy for both malignant and non-malignant disease is an average of 1 mrem per person per year.[31]

5.2   Fallout from nuclear explosions

The natural background and medical irradiation contribute 98 per cent of the radiation dose received by the general public. Of the remaining sources, the most important is the fallout of radioactive material produced in nuclear explosions. The three bombs exploded during the war, at Alamogordo, Hiroshima, and Nagasaki, and subsequent tests of fission bombs prior to the first thermonuclear explosions in 1952, all had exposive powers equivalent to kilotons of TNT. The radioactive debris, apart from the larger particles that were deposited within a few hundred kilometres of the explosion, was injected into the lower regions of the atmosphere (the troposphere), carried by winds around the earth and deposited hundreds or thousands of kilometres from the explosion within two months. The thermonuclear bombs tested mainly during the periods 1955–8 and 1961–2 had yields of up to 50 million tons of TNT. The debris from these explosions reached the upper atmosphere (the stratosphere) and gave rise to worldwide fallout, the major part of which was in the hemisphere of injection. The residence time of a radionuclide in the stratosphere, before transfer to the troposphere and subsequent deposition on the surface, depends on particle size and on the latitude, altitude, and time of year of the explosion. The mean residence time varies from a few months to a few years. Essentially all the debris has therefore by now entered the biosphere, and the contribution that it makes to man's radiation dose depends on the same factors of distribution, intake, and metabolism as the naturally occurring radionuclides.

The main nuclides from the point of view of radiation dose are ^{14}C, ^{90}Sr and ^{137}Cs; all these were produced in MCi quantities. The debris also contained 5 tonnes of plutonium. The radiological impact of fallout has now passed its peak; the current average annual dose in the UK from this source is now approximately 1 mrem compared with about 8 mrem in 1963.

5.3 Other man-made and man-enhanced sources of radiation

The natural background, medical irradiation, and fall-out contribute over 99 per cent of the radiation to which the average member of the UK public is exposed. The remainder comes from consumer goods, principally luminous watches, contributing 0.8 mrem per annum and from the nuclear industry, contributing 0.3 mrem per annum. The maximum authorized discharge levels from nuclear installations are set in such a way as to ensure that no member of the public shall receive more than 0.5 rem in any one year, and that the whole population shall not receive an average of more than 1 rem per person in thirty years. In practice, exposures are very considerably below these levels for the vast majority of the public. Nuclear reactors and nuclear fuel fabrication contribute negligible doses to average members of the public. The only significant nuclear source is the low-level radioactive effluent discharged into the sea from the Windscale fuel reprocessing works. The main component of the effluent from the point of view of radiation dose is ^{137}Cs, with some ^{134}Cs. These radionuclides are distributed throughout the Irish Sea, north-east Atlantic and the North Sea by ocean currents and can reach the population as a result of consumption of fish caught in these waters. Levels were negligible before about 1970 but rose in the mid-1970s because of corrosion of the cladding of some Magnox fuel elements and subsequent leaching of caesium from the uranium fuel rods by storage pond water. The annual average dose to members of the UK population from this source increased from less than 1 μ rem from the early 1970s to 0.25 mrem in 1976 and 1977, and is expected to fall again as new water treatment plant is commissioned.

Some members of the public receive significantly higher doses than the average, either because they live particularly close to some nuclear installations or as a result of certain specific pathways by which radioactive material can reach them.[37] The annual excess doses range from a few milirems up to a few tenths of a rem for small groups of consumers of fish caught in the vicinity of the Windscale discharge to sea. Table 18.16 lists UK nuclear installations and shows the maximum dose to the critical group or individual as a percentage of the ICRP limit.[36]

Table 18.16 Exposures resulting from the UK nuclear industry on a percentage of ICRP dose limits (1977)[36]

Source	Critical pathway	Indiv. dose (max.) as % of ICRP limit
UKAEA		
Winfrith	shellfish	< 0.2
Harwell	drinking water	< 1
Dounreay	external dose	< 1
BNFL		
Windscale	fish/shellfish	30
Springfields	external dose	< 1
Chapelcross	external dose/shellfish	◁ 1
CEGB		
Berkeley/Oldbury	external dose/fish	< 0.1
Bradwell	fish	< 0.3
Dungeness	external dose/fish	< 0.1
Hinkley point	external dose/fish	< 0.2
Sizewell	external dose/fish	◁ 0.2
Trawsfynydd	lake fish	3
Wylfa	external dose/fish	< 0.1
Defence establishments		
Chatham	external dose	< 0.1
Devonport	external dose	◁ 0.1
Faslane	external dose	◁ 0.1
Holy Loch	external dose	< 0.1
Rosyth	external dose	< 0.1

5.4 Occupational exposures

It has been shown that by far the largest contribution to radiation dose for general members of the public comes from the natural background and from medical irradiation. This is not the case for certain groups who are exposed to radiation in the course of their work. The most highly exposed group is industrial radiographers, with those employed on sites other than factories receiving an annual average of 2.7 rem. The excess average exposure to radiation workers in the nuclear industry ranges from less than 0.1 rem to workers in fuel enrichment plant to 1 rem to workers in fuel reprocessing plant. Medical workers involved with diagnostic and therapeutic uses of radiation are exposed to an average of 0.2 rem. Typical values of occupational exposure, together with the number of workers exposed, are given in Table 18.17.[31]

5.5 Summary of radiation exposure of the UK population from all sources

Table 18.18 shows the average annual per caput radiation exposure for the UK population from both the natural background and man-made sources.[31] The most significant departures from the average are inhabitants of areas of high terrestrial radiation, such as Aberdeen, and those exposed to radiation in the course of their work. The nuclear industry contributes the smallest component of the total.

Table 18.17 Occupational exposures in the UK[31,50]

Type of work	No. of workers	Annual average dose (rem)
Industry		
Industrial radiographers		
(factory)	5 000	0.9
(site)	2 000	2.7
Manufacture of radiochemicals	900	0.78
Aircrew	20 000	0.12
Others	11 300	0.43
	39 200	0.46
Nuclear industry		
Fuel fabrication	2 200	0.25
Fuel enrichment	600	0.07
Reactors	7 300	0.34
Fuel reprocessing	4 400	1.1
	14 500	0.55
Research		
Nuclear (UKAEA/CEGB/SRC)	9 600	0.4
Universities/Polytechnics etc	10 000	0.25
	19 600	0.32
Medical		
General medical	33 000	0.21
Dental	20 000	0.16
Veterinary	4 000	0.06
	57 000	0.18
Metalliferous mining	2 600	2.7
All occupational exposure (collective dose 49 500 man-rem)	132 800	0.42

6 The practical control of radiation

The detection of radiation depends invariably on the ionization associated with all types of radiation. Since ionization can be detected with great sensitivity, it is generally possible to measure radiation exposure to levels far below those of interest in radiological protection. It is this sensitivity which has led to the use of radioisotopes as tracers in medicine and coastal surveys, and which makes possible carbon-14 dating of archaeological specimens.

The highest sensitivity is achieved in laboratory measurements, where the full range of detection techniques can be combined with spectrometry and chemical extraction. However, quite adequate sensitivity can usually be achieved with the compact hand-held instruments needed for practical measurements in the field, and it is on this area that attention will be focused here. The exceptions arise where very low energy radiation or radionuclides taken into the body must be monitored: an important practical example is the measurement of plutonium in the lung, where the 17 keV X-ray from plutonium-239 is shielded by the body tissues, making sophisticated equipment necessary for measurements.

Table 18.18 Radiation dose per caput in the United Kingdom[31,50]

	Whole-body dose-equivalent (mrem/y)		Genetically significant dose* (mrem/y)	
Natural background				
Cosmic radiation	31		31	
Terrestrial sources	38		38	
The human body	37		30	
Atmospheric radon	80		—	
Total, natural background		186		99
*Geographic variations in natural background***				
London—total (min)	160		180	
Aberdeen—total (max)	250		170	
General public exposure, man-made				
Medical:				
diagnostic X-rays	~ 45		11.8	
radiopharmaceuticals	~ 1		~ 0.3	
radiotherapy	~ 4		~ 1	
		50		13
Fallout from weapon tests		1		0.7
Miscellaneous sources:				
luminous watches	0.2		0.1	
air travel	0.6		0.3	
television sets	0.0002		0.0002	
		0.8		0.4
Nuclear power generation:				
fuel production	0.0004		< 0.0004	
nuclear power stations	0.03		0.03	
reprocessing	0.25		0.21	
research establishments	0.003		0.003	
		0.28		0.24
Occupational exposures, man-made				
Metalliferous miners	0.13		0.002	
Non-nuclear industry	0.32		0.22	
Medical, dental and veterinary	0.19		0.08	
Nuclear power industry	0.14		0.06	
Research	0.11		0.06	
		0.9		0.4
Total, man-made sources		53		15
Total, natural and man-made		239		114

  * the GSD measures the dose to the reproductive organs. It may differ from the whole-body dose because of factors such as the age distribution of the exposed group, the spatial variation in the exposure of the body and, in the case of internal radiation, self-shielding.
 ** excluding the variation in the radon dose which is known to exceed 100 mrem between individual dwellings but is not yet sufficiently well documented to define regional variations.

6.1 Methods of detection

Detailed discussion of the different techniques for detecting radiation can be found in many standard textbooks.[39] This discussion will be limited to a summary of the principal features of techniques used in radiological protection.

6.1.1 *Photographic emulsions*

Radioactivity was discovered by Becquerel through the ability of charged particles and gamma rays to blacken photographic emulsions. The technique has become highly developed, with the inclusion of radiation filters over different portions of the film, enabling information on the energy and type of radiation to be deduced. The energy response is effectively linear from 20 keV to 3 MeV, and the dynamic range is from 5 mrem to 1000 rem, conveniently covering exposures of practical interest. However, there is no means of continuous read-out, the results being obtained only after development and measurement of the film.

6.1.2 *Ion chambers*

Ionization can be measured directly by applying a voltage between two electrodes; the resulting electric field causes the positive and negative ions to drift towards the electrodes, giving a current proportional to the ionization produced by charged particles or gamma rays. It is also possible to operate ion chambers in a pulse mode, collecting the ionization from each particle track as a current pulse. The dynamic range of an ion chamber can readily cover six decades, and with appropriate chamber dimensions it is possible to measure from a fraction of a μ R/h to over 1000 R/h.

An alternative way of using an ion chamber is as an integrating device. The two electrodes can be regarded as the plates of a capacitor. When charged up to a suitable voltage, ionization between the plates causes the capacitor to discharge, the change in voltage being proportional to the integrated ionization between the plates. A common configuration is to combine an integrating ion chamber with a quartz-fibre electroscope (q.f.e.) and a simple optical viewing system. In this way an instantaneous reading can be obtained, usually on a scale up to 5 R.

6.1.3 *Proportional counters*

By using higher electric field gradients than in an ionization chamber, the free electrons from the primary ionization can be accelerated to sufficient energy to cause secondary ionization, so that successive electrons multiply to form a cascade which is collected at the anode as a current pulse proportional to the initial ionization. This is then amplified electronically and fed to a ratemeter. The high field gradient is achieved by making the anode in the form of a fine wire. In practice such proportional counters may operate with multiplications up to several hundred, making it easier to distinguish the signal from the electronic noise.

6.1.4 *Geiger counters*
If the electric field is increased beyond the level used in a proportional counter, then the atoms excited in producing the local electron cascade emit sufficiently energetic radiation in decaying to the ground state to cause further ionization, and an avalanche of electron cascades is propagated along the whole length of the counter. Special measures must be incorporated to quench the process, either by reducing the applied voltage after the initial pulse or by including gases (alcohol, halogens) which absorb energy by photodissociation rather than ionization. Because of the need for quenching, there is a dead time of about a millisecond after each pulse, limiting the maximum counting rate, but very little pulse amplification is needed so that instruments can be particularly robust as well as portable.

6.1.5 *Scintillation counter*
An early method of detecting charged particles, used by Rutherford, was to observe the light flashes they produce on a zinc sulphide screen. Many organic and inorganic crystals as well as solutions of organic materials are now known to exhibit this property, and with the advent of the modern photomultiplier, the scintillation counter has become one of the commonest of radiation detection instruments. The light flashes are due to excited or ionized atoms returning to their ground state, releasing energy in the visible range. The pulse length varies from a few microseconds in inorganic crystals to a few tens of nanoseconds in certain organic scintillators.

The scintillation counter combines a number of advantages: it has a much higher density than a gas counter, giving greater efficiency in detecting gamma rays; it can operate up to very high count-rates; it can be provided with a very thin window so that alpha particles can be detected; and it can be constructed with a very large sensitive volume. However, the photomultiplier requires high voltages, and perhaps lacks the robustness of a Geiger counter.

6.1.6 *Solid-state detectors*
In general it is not possible to measure the ionization produced in solids. Charge collection is difficult from insulators, and in conductors the free electrons swamp the effect from ionizing radiation at the levels of interest for radiological protection. However, an exception arises with semiconductors. A sandwich of p-type and n-type semiconductors behaves like a diode: when a reversed voltage is applied, virtually no current flows because of the presence of a depletion layer at the junction of the two types of material, which is free of electrons or holes. However, any ionization produced by radiation in the depletion layer will be collected, constituting a small current pulse against an electronically quiet background.

Pure single crystals of silicon give good energy resolution for alpha and beta particles. For gamma-ray measurements a higher atomic number material is necessary if there is to be a reasonable probability of the whole gamma energy being absorbed in a single photoelectric event, as is necessary for good energy resolution; germanium is commonly used in the laboratory, where cooling to liquid-nitrogen temperatures can be used to reduce the background from thermally excited electrons.

An alternative type of solid-state device is the thermoluminescent detector (t.l.d.) in which electrons (or holes) caused by exposure to ionization become trapped in the crystal lattice at normal temperatures. When the detector is heated, the trapped electrons return to the ground state, accompanied by the emission of light. Several inorganic materials exhibit this property, for example lithium fluoride (LiF). The light output of LiF is proportional to dose over the range of 10 mrem to 500 rems. It can be conveniently impregnated in p.t.f.e. discs, and if necessary the ^{6}Li isotope can be depleted to reduce the sensitivity to neutrons. This type of detector is only suitable as an integrating dosimeter, and is similar to the photographic emulsion in this respect.

6.1.7 *Neutron detectors*
Because neutrons are not directly ionizing, they are not generally detected by the methods already described. However, all these devices can be made sensitive to neutrons if a material is included which has a good chance of capturing a neutron and promptly emits a charged particle. The materials commonly used for this purpose are boron, in which the boron-10 isotope has a very large neutron cross-section for generating alpha particles, and uranium-235, in which thermal neutrons generate heavily ionizing fission fragments.

Thus an ionization chamber coated internally with boron or uranium-235, or a counter incorporating boron trifluoride gas, can be used to detect thermal neutrons. Fast neutrons can be measured by incorporating a moderator (e.g. polythene) in the detector to slow them down to thermal energies for measurement with a thermal-neutron detector; by careful design, the response of a neutron counter to neutrons of different energies can be made to match the variation with energy of the biological effectiveness of neutrons in tissue. Fast neutrons can also be detected from the ionization produced by proton recoils, caused when neutrons collide with the nuclei of hydrogen atoms. The application of this technique is mainly limited to the laboratory.

6.2 **Practical radiation measurement**

For most radiation measurements a wide choice of options is available. The selection of a particular method of detection will often depend on factors such as weight or robustness, as well as sensitivity or energy resolution. However, there are areas where the choice is restricted: alpha radiation is best measured by scintillation or solid-state detectors, with the latter type preferred where good energy resolution is helpful in reducing interference from other types of radiation.

Table 18.19 lists some typical examples of instruments used in radiological

Table 18.19 Typical examples of radiological-protection instruments

General application	Instrument Purpose	Type	Radiation sampled	Detector	Dose range	Display
Personal monitoring	integrated dose	—	beta/gamma	photographic film	0.005–800 rem	none
	integrated dose	1760 A	X-ray/gamma	integrating ion chamber	0–0.2R	q.f.e. (optical)
	external dose-rate	0023	gamma	geiger	0–1 R/h	audible
	internal dose	0434–1	alpha (on dust)	filter paper	—	separate measurement
	integrated dose	3271–1	neutron	proportional counter	1 mrem–10 rem	preset audible and readout
Portable	general	0537–1	gamma	geiger	1 mR/h–2 R/h	3 decade log
	field	R02	beta/gamma	ion chamber	0–5 R/h	4 range linear
	survey	0950–1	neutron	proportional counter	0.1 mrem/h–1 rem/h	4 decade log
	hotspot	3248–1	beta/gamma	geiger	5 R/h–5000 R/h	3 decade log
Contamination	portable	0339/AP3	alpha	ZnS scintillator	0.1–1000 DL	4 decade log
	survey	0339/1828A	beta	geiger	0.1–1000 DL	log
Installed area monitors	external radiation	0467	gamma	geiger	0.1–100 mR/h	log+visual+audible
	hands, feet, and body contamination	NE–1 PM–6	alpha/beta	gas flow proportional counter	typically down to 1 DL	meter and alarm (visual and audible)
	Pu-in-air tritium-in-air	3200	alpha	filter paper	0.2–4000 DL	log+visual+audible

protection. Much more extensive lists can be found in manufacturers' catalogues, and evaluations of some instruments are published by the National Radiological Protection Board.

In addition to the instruments for measuring radiation in the working environment, a number of techniques are available for making measurements on radionuclides taken into the body. A whole-body counter[40] can be used to make direct measurements—the subject is scanned by a number of large scintillation counters in a shielded room. The count-rates are invariably low, necessitating counting times of around an hour, and corrections are required for the natural radioactivity of the body. The method is being used increasingly for periodic measurements of plutonium workers to cross-check the estimates of inhaled plutonium based on personal or installed plutonium monitors. In addition, urine and faecal measurements can be used to estimate the intake of radionuclides, although the interpretation of the results depends on the extent of knowledge about the way particular radionuclides are metabolized.

One further method of biological dose measurement is the analysis of chromosome damage in blood cells.[41] Although these cells do not normally divide, a blood sample can be cultured to cause cell division, and the individual chromosomes can then be examined for damage under the microscope. By examining perhaps a 1000 cells in this way, a whole-body dose can be determined with a sensitivity of about 10 rems providing no confounding factor (e.g. exposure to chemicals) is present. The method is useful for verifying suspected cases of overexposure, particularly where other estimates are not available (as, for example, when exposure results from a stolen industrial radiography source).

6.3 The control of radiation dose

The control of radiation, to meet the statutory standards of protection deriving from the ICRP recommendations, is a major factor both in the design of nuclear plant and in its operation. The following are the four primary elements in the control process.

1. *Shielding*. This attenuates the radiation[9], commonly using concrete, steel, and lead. The most heavily shielded plant is the nuclear reactor, where several metres of reinforced concrete may be used, whilst laboratory experiments may only require a few centimetres of lead. Water is also a very convenient shielding material in some applications; for example, irradiated fuel elements are commonly stored and handled in deep ponds both at nuclear reactors and at reprocessing plants.

2. *Containment*. This controls radioactive gases or airborne dust. In a reactor, the fuel element cans prevent the release of gaseous fission products from the fuel to the coolant circuit, and a further layer of containment is provided by the coolant pressure circuit. In the laboratory, sealed gloveboxes are commonly used to prevent radioactivity escaping to the atmosphere, operating at sub-atmospheric pressure to ensure any leaks are inward and with filters in the extract system. Radioactive-isotope sources are frequently sealed to very high standards to prevent any significant airborne hazard.

3. *Distance*. This takes advantage of the inverse square attenuation of radiation and can be a useful control measure in many practical situations. Thus radioactive sources are frequently handled using long tongs, and the boundary fence of a nuclear site may be set at a sufficient distance to reduce the maximum levels acceptable for radiation workers to the lower levels set for exposure of the general public.

4. *Time limitation*. This prevents the unnecessary accumulation of radiation dose. In this way the dose to radiation workers can be reduced even further below the acceptable levels, conforming to the ALARA principle (as low as reasonably achievable).

By applying these measures appropriately, all nuclear plant can be designed and operated in a manner which conforms to the regulations controlling radiation exposure.

7   Radiation hazards from the nuclear industry

The hazard from radiation is one of the most closely controlled risks in our society. The effects of radiation on man are well understood, and the legislative framework ensures that the high standards of protection recommended by ICRP are applied to all operations involving radiation exposure. In contrast, there are many other hazards in our domestic and working lives which are much less well understood or controlled. However, since it is accepted that there is no threshold to radiation effects, the residual exposure to radiation carries with it some small degree of risk. The component of this risk which arises from the nuclear industry can be calculated by combining the ICRP assessment with the results of the extensive monitoring of public and occupational radiation exposure, and by examining the health record of the nuclear industry.

7.1   Occupational hazards

The groups most at risk are those who work with radiation. On average each radiation worker receives an annual dose of about 0.5 rem, and combining this with the ICRP risk estimate (for men) of 10^{-4} deaths/rem, the annual risk of death from occupational radiation exposure is 1 in 20 000. If this value is compared with the average annual risk of death from all causes of about 1 in 80 and the average annual risk of death from accidents of 1 in 3000, it is clear that radiation is a minor hazard.

An alternative way of viewing this risk is to represent it as the extent to which the average life is shortened.[42] This is a more satisfactory basis to the extent that it distinguishes between early deaths, as may occur with ordinary industrial accidents, and deaths which are delayed, as with pneumoconiosis and cancer. The average life-shortening corresponding to the hazards of manufacturing industry generally is 20 days (Table 18.20), which may be compared with 7 days from the radiation hazard to the average radiation worker.

These comparisons may overstate the effects of radiation to the extent that the ICRP risk estimates are conservative. It is therefore of interest to examine actual mortality experience.[43] Table 18.21 shows the standardized mortality ratio (SMR) for each of the standard industrial classifications, a quantity which measures the frequency of death after correction for differences in age distribution. Compared with the average SMR over all occupations of 100, the values range from 144 for miners and quarrymen to 73 for professional and administrative occupations. On the same basis, the SMR for employees of the UKAEA and BNFL is found to be 75. The deaths among radiation workers have included a few cases where the balance of probability was held to be that death was due to radiation exposure, but the proportion of such cases is very small in comparison with occupational mortality in industry generally.

It is thus clear that employment in the nuclear industry is one of the safest occupations, and that occupational radiation risks are both small in absolute terms and substantially lower than most other occupational risks.

7.2 Hazard to the general public

The average per caput exposure of the general public from the activities of the nuclear industry is 0.3 mrem/y. On the basis of the ICRP estimates, the corresponding annual risk of death is 1 in 30 million. That level of risk corresponds to the risk of being killed in travelling one mile by car or in 1–2 hours typical factory work; or the risk that a man aged 60 will die from natural causes in one minute.

The very small scale of the risk is confirmed by comparing the annual public radiation dose with the natural background. The 0.3 mrem/y from the nuclear industry is over 100 times less than the variation in dose between London and Aberdeen, a variation which itself appears to be of no significance to health. The hazard is thus quite negligible.

This close control of the routine radiation hazards associated with the operation of nuclear plant could be vitiated if accidents made a major contribution to the overall radiological risk. The most serious accident risk arises with nuclear reactors, rather than with other types of nuclear plant, because of the high energy density and complex engineering features of a reactor.   ·

It is not physically possible for a reactor to explode like a bomb—the fuel is too dilute for the very short neutron lifetime required for detonation to be achieved—but a reactor could accidentally overheat and it might then leak some radioactive materials. Many precautions are taken to prevent such occurrences and to mitigate their consequences:

(1) very high standards are adopted in the design, construction and operation of nuclear reactors;

(2) multiple safety provisions are incorporated in a reactor to prevent or mitigate the effect of failures; and

(3) independent checking by the Nuclear Installation Inspectorate is imposed throughout the whole life of a reactor, from the initial design stage through to final decommissioning.

In this way an exceptionally high standard of safety is achieved; but, of course, there must be a residual risk.

Table 18.20 Life-shortening due to occupational hazards[42]

Whole-life occupation	Life-shortening
	(days)
Deep-sea fishing	1400
Coal mining	150
Railway employment	95
Construction	93
All manufacturing	20
Paper printing and publishing	12
Radiation worker (0.5 rem/y)	7

Table 18.21 The relative frequencies of deaths among different occupations[43]

Occupation	Standardized mortality ratio*
All occupations	100
Armed forces	147
Miners and quarrymen	144
Labourers	141
Furnace, forge, foundry etc. workers	122
Service, sport and recreation workers	116
Leather workers	114
Construction workers	111
Painters and decorators	111
Transport and communication	111
Textile workers	110
Food, drink, and tobacco workers	110
Glass and ceramic workers	109
Warehousemen, storekeepers, etc.	108
Gas, coke, and chemical workers	107
Electrical workers	104
Engineering and allied trades	104
Drivers of cranes, etc.	103
Clothing workers	103
Clerical workers	99
Woodworkers	96
Farmers, foresters, fishermen	91
Paper and printing workers	91
Sales workers	90
Makers of other products	84
Professional, technical workers, artists	75
Administrators, managers	73
UKAEA and BNFL employees‡	75

* the SMR measures the frequency of death relative to the average of the whole population, corrected for differences in age distribution in the occupational groups. The data is for men aged 15–64

‡ 1962/74 data for men aged 15–64. The SMR for UKAEA and BNFL employees of 65 and over is 74

The most comprehensive estimate of this residual level of risk is provided by a major US study[44] led by Professor Rasmussen of MIT. Figure 18.3 shows the annual probability of an accident as a function of the number of deaths, including delayed deaths, which the study estimated for a programme of 100 reactors. This calculation indicates that an accident causing a few deaths, mainly from cancer, can be expected less than once in 100 years, with larger accidents decreasing in frequency. By comparison, many other hazards of life are much more probable, as shown by the other curves on Fig. 18.3.

The Rasmussen analysis was reviewed by a committee[45] chaired by Professor Lewis of the University of California, which criticized the executive summary of the report and judged that the errors in the calculation had been under-estimated, but which endorsed the method of calculation. A further review of the work by the Electric Power Research Institute[46] evaluated the numerical effect of a number of detailed criticisms, showing that, although the bounds of uncertainty were increased, the upper limit of uncertainty was virtually the same as that estimated by Rasmussen whilst the median was lowered. It was also concluded that the excellent safety experience accumulated in operating reactors over a quarter of a century showed that the upper limit of accident frequency could not have been underestimated. Further support for the Rasmussen analysis (Fig. 18.3) has been provided recently by an independent German study,[47] which yielded virtually identical numerical results.

Although the analyses discussed above relate to accidents to light water reactors, the standards of safety applied to other types of reactor are equally stringent. In particular, the numerical estimates of accident frequency for the UK Magnox stations[48] are consistent with the Rasmussen analysis. Whilst nuclear plant other than reactors also involve a finite risk, the potential for accidents in these plants is much lower than for reactors, and because the same safety philosophy is applied their contribution is considered negligible.

These studies show that the average hazard to the whole population from reactor accidents is small compared with that due to radiation exposure from the routine operation of nuclear plants, itself a very minor risk. It is clear that reactors are not particularly susceptible to large accidents, and that an accident is much more likely to be due to some non-nuclear cause than to a reactor for a given number of fatalities.

The high standard of reactor safety can be illustrated in a number of ways. For example, the chance of a reactor accident causing 100 deaths (including delayed deaths) is less than the chance of 100 people being killed simultan-eously by an aircraft crashing on them. Accidents of this size from any cause are fortunately very rare indeed—only a handful of cases have occurred in the UK within living memory—and reactor accidents would contribute less than 1 in 100 of such cases, even after completing a major programme of nuclear stations. The same argument applies irrespective of the size of accident considered.

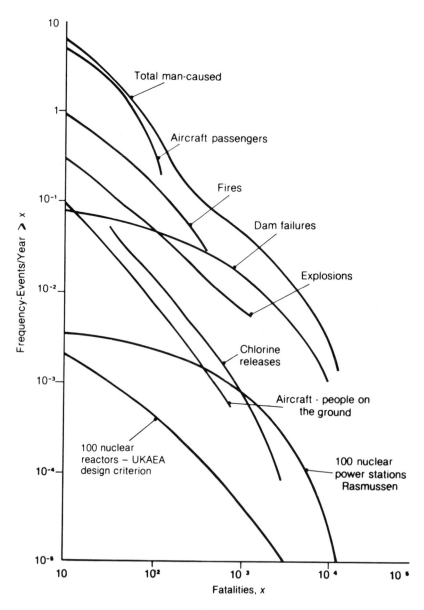

Fig. 18.3 Frequency of man-made events involving fatalities

References

1. HENRY, H. F. *Fundamentals of radiation protection.* Wiley-Interscience, Chichester (1969).
2. HINE, G. J. AND BROWNELL, G. L. *Radiation dosimetry.* Academic Press, London (1956).
3. BRITISH STANDARDS INSTITUTION. *Protection of personnel against hazards from laser radiation. BS* 4803 (1972).
4. COMPTON, A. H. AND ALLISON, S. K. *X-rays in theory and experiment.* Van Nostrand, London (1935).
5. EVANS, R. D. *The atomic nucleus.* McGraw Hill, Maidenhead (1955).
6. LEDERER, C. M. AND SHIRLEY, V. S. (eds.) *Table of isotopes* (7th edn). Wiley-Interscience, Chichester (1978).
7. INTERNATIONAL COMMISSION FOR RADIOLOGICAL PROTECTION. *Data for protection against ionizing radiation from external sources.* ICRP Publication 21, Pergamon Press, Oxford (1973).
8. US NATIONAL ACADEMY OF SCIENCE. *Studies in Penetration of Charged Particles in Matter.* USNAS Washington, Publication 1133 (1964).
9. SCHAEFER, N. M. *Reactor shielding for nuclear engineers. TID* 25951. United States Atomic Energy Commission, Washington (1973).
10. HUGHES, A. E. AND POOLEY, D. *Real solids and radiation.* Wykeham Publications (London) Ltd. (1975).
11. TAYLOR, L. S. History of the International Commission on Radiological Units and Measurement (ICRU), *Health Phys.,* **1**, 306, (1958).
12. INTERNATIONAL COMMISSION ON RADIATION UNITS AND MEASUREMENTS. *Radiation quantities and units.* ICRU-33 (1980).
13. TAYLOR, L. S. History of the International Commission on Radiological Protection (ICRP). *Health Phys.* **1**, 97, (1958).
14. HEMPELMANN, L. H., LISCO, H. AND HOFFMAN, J. G. The acute radiation syndrome. *Annals of Internal Med.,* **36**(2), 279 (1952).
15. UNITED NATIONS SCIENTIFIC COMMITTEE ON THE EFFECTS OF ATOMIC RADIATION. *Sources and effects of ionising radiation.* UNSCEAR, New York (1977).
16. ICRP. *Recommendations of the International Commission on Radiological Protection,* ICRP Publication 26, *Ann. ICRP,* **1**, no. 3.
17. US NATIONAL ACADEMY OF SCIENCE. *The effects on populations of exposure to low levels of ionising radiation.* Report of the Biological Effects of Ionizing Radiation (BEIR) Committee. USNAS, Washington (1980).
18. —.*The effects on populations of exposure to low levels of ionizing radiation.* Report of the BEIR Committee. US National Academy of Science, Washington (1972).
19. MANCUSO, T., STEWART, A., AND KNEALE, G., Radiation exposures of Hanford workers dying from cancer and other causes, *Health Phys.* **33**, 369, (1977).
20. REISSLAND, J. A. *An assessment of the Mancuso study. NRPB-R79.* National Radiological Protection Board, Harwell (1978).
21. (a) GILBERT, E. S. AND MARKS, S. An analysis of the Mortality of workers in a nuclear facility. *Radiat. Res.* **79**, 122 (1979).
    (b) DARBY, S. C. AND REISSLAND, J. A., Low Levels of Ionizing Radiation and Cancer—are we underestimating the risk? *J. R. Statist. Soc.* **144**, part 3 (1981).
22. KATO, H., A review of 30 years' study of Hiroshima and Nagasaki bomb survivors: early genetic surveys and mortality study. *J. Radiat. Res.,* **16**, (suppl.), 67 (1975).
23. EICHHOLZ, G. G. *Environmental aspects of nuclear power.* Ann Arbor Science, Michigan (1976).

24. *Nuclear power and the environment, sixth report of the Royal Commission on Environmental Pollution. Cmnd.* 6618. HMSO, London (1976).
25. TAYLOR, L. S. *Organization for Radiation Protection, the operations of the ICRP and NCRP 1928–1974.* DoE/TIC-10124. US Dept. of Energy (1979).
26. NRPB. Recommendations of the International Commission on Radiological Protection (ICRP Publication 26): *Statement by the NRPB on their Acceptability for Application in the UK, NRPB–ASP 1.* (1978).
27. NATIONAL RADIOLOGICAL PROTECTION BOARD. The application of cost-benefit analysis to the radiological protection of the Public: a consultative document. NRPB, Harwell (1980).
28. ICRP. *Limits for intakes of radionuclides by workers.* ICRP Publication 30. Pergamon Press, Oxford (1979).
29. PRESTON, A. *The United Kingdom approach to the application of ICRP Standards to the controlled disposal of radioactive waste resulting from nuclear power programmes. IAEA-SM-*146/9. International Atomic Energy Agency, Vienna (1978).
30. SIM, D. F. *Law of atomic energy and radioactive substances. In* HALSBURY, H. S. G. (ed.) Halsbury's Laws of England vol 16, part 2, para 224-500. 4th edition. London, Butterworth (1976).
31. TAYLOR, F. E., AND WEBB, G. A. M. *Radiation exposure of the UK population. NRPB–R77* (1978). See also NRPB–R118 and R119
32. COMMITTEE ON RADIOLOGICAL HAZARDS TO PATIENTS. *Final report to the Minister of Health and the Secretary of State for Scotland.* HMSO, London (1966).
33. KENDALL, G. M., DARBY, S. C., HARRIES, S. V., AND RAE, S. *A frequency survey of radiological examinations carried out in National Health Service hospitals in Great Britain in 1977 for diagnostic purposes. NRPB–R*104 (1980).
34. WALL, B. F., FISHER, E. S., SHRIMPTON, P. C., AND RAE, S. *Current levels of gonadal irradiation from a selection of routine diagnostic X-ray examinations in Great Britain, NRPB–R*105 (1980).
35. DARBY S. C., KENDALL, G. M., RAE, S. Y. and WALL, B. F. *The Genetically significant dose from diagnostic radiology in Great Britain in 1977. NRPB-R*106 (1980).
36. DEPARTMENT OF THE ENVIRONMENT, SCOTTISH OFFICE, AND WELSH OFFICE. *Annual survey of radioactive discharges in Great Britain 1978.* HMSO, London (1979).
37. JOHNS, T. F. *Environmental pathways of radioactivity to man.* Atomic Energy Establishment, Winfrith Report *AEEW–R*1288. HMSO, London (1979).
38. SIEVERT, R. *Acta Radiologica* **4**, 61 (1925).
39. TAIT, W. H. *Radiation detection*, London, Butterworth (1980). (See also Chapter 20.)
40. RAMSDEN, D. Whole body monitoring. *Electronics and power*, **25**(1), 36 (Jan. 1979).
41. LLOYD, D. C., PURROTT, R. J., PROSSER, J. S., AND WHITE, A. D. *Doses in radiation accidents investigated by chromosome aberration analysis, X, a review of cases investigated 1979. NRPB–R*96 (1980).
42. REISSLAND, J., AND HARVIES, V. A scale for measuring risks. *New Scient.* **83**, 809 (1979).
43. WADE, B. O. The safety of nuclear power. *R. Soc. Health J.*, **99**, 239 (1979).
44. US NUCLEAR REGULATORY COMMISSION. *Reactor safety study–an assessment of accident risks in US commercial nuclear power plants. WASH*–1400 (*NUREG* 75/014). USNRC, Washington (1975).
45. LEWIS, H. W., BUNDITZ, R. J., KOUTS, H. J. C., AND LOWENSTEIN, W. B. *Risk Assessment Review Group Report to the US Nuclear Regulatory Commission. NUREG/CR*0400 (1978).
46. ELECTRIC POWER RESEARCH INSTITUTE. *Comparison of the EPRI and Lewis Committee Review of the Reactor Safety Study. EPRI–NP*–1130 (1979).

47. THE FEDERAL MINISTER OF RESEARCH AND TECHNOLOGY. *The German risk study.* (1979). Bundesministerium für Forschung und Technologie, Bonn (1979).
48. FARMER, F. R., AND BEATTIE, J. R. Nuclear power reactors and the evaluation of population hazards. *Adv. Nucl. Sci. Technol.* **9**, 1 (1976).
49. EVANS, R. D., HARLEY, J. H., JACOBI, W., MCLEAN, A. S., MILLS, W. A., AND STEWART, C. G. Estimate of risk from environmental exposure to Radon-222 and its decay products. *Nature, 290* **98**, 12 March 1981.
50. *Living with radiation*, 2nd edn, NRPB, 1981.

19

The biological background to the recommendations of the ICRP

A. N. B. STOTT

An account is given of the historical origins of the International Commission on Radiological Protection. The Commission's most recent recommendations issued in 1977 are based on a philosophy of avoiding unncessary radiation exposure and justifying such exposures as do occur. In addition, annual individual levels of exposure are set which the Commission recommend should not be exceeded.

These levels are derived from information on the effects of radiation obtained from fundamental radiobiological studies but mainly from epidemiological data on human subjects irradiated accidentally or for medical reasons. These data are reviewed in the article. The Commission use these to make numerical estimations of the risk incurred in receiving doses of radiation.

In setting the levels the Commission have attempted to establish degrees of risk for workers and the public at large which will compare favourably with risks generally regarded as acceptable. Although there are still considerable uncertainties about radiation effects, particularly at very low doses, it is unlikely that the Commission's estimates of risk from radiation are misleadingly optmistic.

Contents

1 Introduction

The intense excitement in the scientific world occasioned by the researches of William Konrad Röentgen has been well described.[1] His discovery of 'a new kind of ray' which penetrated not only glass and celluloid but also opaque substances and human bodies took place on 8 November 1895. By January 1896 not only had there been a preliminary publication of his observations in the Proceedings of the Physical Medical Society of Wurzburg, but he had already sent reprints and radiographs to colleagues in England, France, Germany, and Austria. They immediately started reconstructing his experiments and proved for themselves the existence of the ray which he had termed 'X', since its nature was unknown.

Although Röentgen himself was little interested in the biological effects of X-rays others foresaw many uses in this area. The widespread use, for example, of ionizing radiation for medical sterilization was hinted at in 1896 by Minck,[2] who investigated the killing effects of X-rays on bacteria. An even more prophetic utterance was made in the same year by Joseph (later Lord) Lister, the initiator of antiseptic surgical techniques and the foremost physician of his era. In his presidential address to the annual meeting of the British Association for the Advancement of Science he referred to the exciting prospects for medical radiography using the new rays. He then cautioned 'If the skin is long exposed to their action it becomes very much more irritated, affected with a sort of aggravating sunburning. This suggests that their transmission through the human body may not be altogether a matter of indifference to internal organs!' This 'aggravating sunburning' was clearly evident to Rutherford when he visited the Curies in Paris in 1903. 'We could not help but observe' (he states) 'that the hands of Professor Curie were in a very inflamed and painful state due to exposure to radium rays.'

Many similar observations and the subsequent development of cancers in the early workers with X-rays and radium led to the creation in Britain in

1921 of an X-ray and Radium Protection Committee to try to establish safer conditions for such work which was then largely confined to the medical field. In 1925 there took place the first International Congress of Radiology (ICR), during which the need for standardized radiation units was met by the formation of the International Commission on Radiologial Units (ICRU). That same year two scientists, A. Mutscheller and R.M. Sievert, separately recommended a maximum possible dose from X-rays and radium of 0.1 of an erythema dose per year.[3] (This empirical biological quantity was a tenth of the dose necessary to produce the erythema or skin inflammation referred to by Lister.) At the second meeting of the ICR in 1928 there was established, on the pattern of the British model, the International X-ray and Radium Protection Committee, which published the first set of international recommendations for protection from ionizing radiation, using the röentgen as the unit of exposure. This Committee continued to give guidance on radiation protection, but from 1945 its recommendations became of greater significance because of the rapid post-war developments in the nuclear energy field. In 1950 it asssumed its present organization and title of the International Commission on Radiological Protection (ICRP). In this form it is widely regarded as the appropriate body to provide guidance on standards in the field of radiological protection. Its policy is to formulate the fundamental principles upon which regulatory measures might be based and to review and revise these in the light of changing knowledge.

Its recommendations will also be influenced by the uses of ionizing radiation within society. Over the years there have been substantial reductions in the dose limits recommended for workers with ionizing radiation (Table 19.1). In 1966 the Commission emphasized that these reductions did not arise because of evidence that the previous levels set in 1949 had been found to be harmful, but because of the much greater usage of sources of radiation of all kinds with a greater potential for human exposure. The most recent set of recommendations, issued by the ICRP in 1977 as *Publication 26*, goes much farther along this path of societal considerations in addition to taking into account the considerable corpus of new information on dose–effect relationships and hence on radiological risk estimates. The need to be quantitative about such estimates even in the absence of rigorous certainty of information has been well argued by Pochin.[4] Unless numerical values are attributed to the possible consequences of varying radiation exposures it would be impossible to prescribe realistic control measures and difficult to compare the risks

Table 19.1 Recommended limits for worker exposure

year	Exposure or dose limit
1925	70 rem/year (0.1 erythema dose)
1934	0.1 rem/day, 0.5 rem/week, 25 rem/year
1949	0.3 rem/week or 15 rem/year
1966	3 rem/13 weeks or 5 rem/year

(1 rem = 0.01 sievert)

from radiation with those experienced in other human activities. The back-ground to the knowledge on which the ICRP based their recommendations with some indications of the areas of uncertainty will form the basis of this chapter.

2 Fundamental radiobiology

Although the ability of ionizing radiation to produce malignant change in tissues was soon recognized, for many years it was thought that such change occurred only in organs already visibly heavily damaged by radiation. Such a phenomenon was familiar to physicians who saw similar developments following the chronic inflammations of commonplace infections such as tuberculosis or syphilis. There is now good evidence that cancers in man can arise from apparently normal tissues[5] following radiation doses well below the levels at which observable immediate effects occur. Since this suggests that the events which initiate malignant change (carcinogenesis) take place at the level of one or only a few cells, the knowledge derived from cellular radiobiology is worth considering.

Two other factors reinforce this consideration. Whereas in the 1930s and 1940s the observable harmful effects of radiation on experimental animals were attributed to complex radiobiochemical changes, it is now considered that most of these effects can be attributed to the loss of proliferative ability (*cell death*) in a high enough number of cells in an irradiated tissue.[6] Furthermore, although the initial mechanisms of carcinogenesis are still far from unravelled there is increasing evidence that one prerequisite is an effect on the hereditary macromolecule, DNA. In the field of chemical carcinogenesis such effects, demonstrating mutational changes in cells treated with the suspected carcinogen, have been shown to be strongly predictive of cancer production in the whole animal.[7]

If cells in culture are exposed to ionizing radiation then for most effects produced it can be shown that such effects are modified by a number of factors. Of these, clearly the most important is the *amount* of radiation energy absorbed by the cells. (This absorbed energy per unit mass is measured in grays (Gy) and the term *dose* henceforth used in this chapter implies the more correct term *absorbed dose*.)

Another important variable lies in the *quality* of the radiation. Since biological effects arise from the ionization and excitation of the irradiated medium, it follows that the greater effects will be produced in the areas of most frequent ionization. A densely ionizing radiation will give rise to greater effects than sparsely ionizing radiation. Since the amount of ion-ization is dependent on the energy released, then the quality of different types of radiation can be compared on the basis of the average energy released per unit length along the track they follow through the irradiated medium. This quantity is termed the *linear energy transfer* or LET of the radiation.

The LET of any type of ionizing radiation depends in a complicated way upon the mass, energy, and charge it possesses. Electromagnetic radiations such as X-or γ-rays will have a low probability of interaction with the atoms of irradiated material and will release their energy over a relatively long path. Heavy particulate radiations such as alpha particles or neutrons will release their energy over a short track. The former (X and γ) are therefore termed low-LET radiations, whereas the latter (α, neutrons) are high-LET radiations (see Fig. 19.1).

When LET values are high, then within the given target area there will be many ionization events with a high probability of harmful biological effect even at relatively low dose. Conversely, with low-LET radiation these events will be isolated so that effects are low and molecular repair possible, although this spacing will become less significant at higher radiation doses.

When the effects of high- and low-LET radiation are contrasted experimentally on cell cultures, then for most end-points a clear difference emerges as illustrated in Fig. 19.2. Curve A shows that the incidence of effect with high-LET radiation is uniformly proportional to the dose down to the lowest dose measurable. Curve B shows that at lower doses the effect per unit dose of low-LET radiation is less than at higher doses.

Other important factors relative to both radiation protection and radiotherapy can be demonstrated with cell studies. Effects of radiation can be shown to be markedly less for a given radiation dose if that same total dose is given as a series of smaller doses (fractionation) or over a longer period of time (protraction). This is found only in the case of low-LET radiation, and in both instances is attributed to repair processes in the cell. Certain chemicals have been shown to have the facility to make the cell more or less sensitive to radiation. The most dramatic example of this chemical interaction is the presence or absence of oxygen. Oxygen-deficient cells are much less affected by low-LET radiation. Once again, this is not observed with high-LET radiation and there is consequent interest in the benefits to be gained therapeutically by using high-LET radiation for the destruction of those human cancers which are deficient in oxygen supply.

Cellular radiobiology has also been useful in confirming the increased radiosensitivity of cells in the process of division. It is possible to select progressively a population of cells synchronous in their life cycle and expose them to ionizing radiation. It is clear that greater damage is inflicted on cells when they are dividing, and it is the length of this mitotic phase rather than the frequency of division which determines sensitivity.

There seems to be general agreement for the theoretical radiobiological model proposed by Kellerer and Rossi[8] involving a 'dual radiation action'. This postulates that the lesions produced by ionizing radiation are proportional to the absorbed dose (D) and that it will require two such lesions close enough in space and time to interact to cause a biological effect. In the case of sparsely ionizing (or low-LET radiation) such lesions will be produced by independent charged particles and their number will be proportional to the

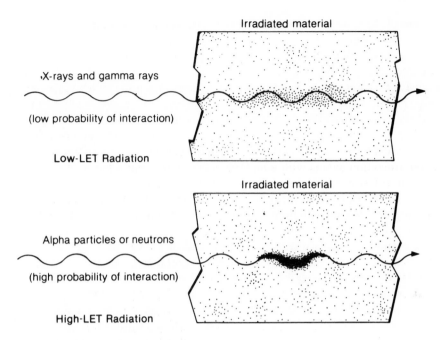

Fig. 19.1 High and low LET radiation

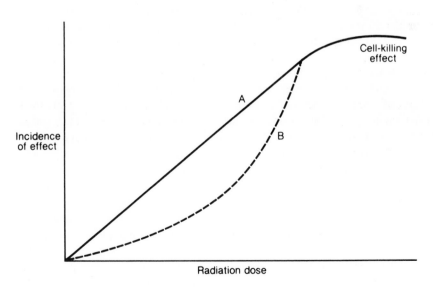

Fig. 19.2 Dose-effect relationships

square of the dose. However, because of the stochastic nature of the inter-action of radiation with matter (i.e. the non-uniform deposition of energy), the yield of biological lesions will be proportional to both dose and dose squared, that is, equal to $aD + bD^2$ where a and b are constants. For high-LET radiation the yield will always be proportional to dose, i.e. aD (Fig. 19.2).

If the effect looked for (e.g. cell transformation or mutation) depends on the survival of the cell, then as doses increase to an extent where substantial cell killing takes place, the effect will be less evident. Because of the greater biological efficiency of high-LET radiation, this response will be more pronounced, but it can also occur with low-LET radiation (Fig. 19.2). For this reason, there may be apparent anomalous effects per unit dose at high doses, particularly with carcinogenesis, and errors in extrapolation to lower doses.

The value of studies at the cellular level rests in the comparative ease with which variables, such as the type of radiation, total dose, dose-rate, stage in cell cycle, and so on, can be altered. In general it can be said that the effectiveness per unit dose of low-LET radiation is reduced at low doses and low dose-rates, whereas that of high-LET radiation is relatively less dose and dose-rate dependent. The variations with dose, dose-rate and LET differ, however, from one type of effect to another, and the conclusions cannot be applied with confidence at the exposure levels associated with occupational or background irradiation. Furthermore, effects produced in cells in artificial conditions and isolated from other body controls, cannot be regarded as representative of effects produced in tissues in the whole animal. There are hormonal and immunological mechanisms which regulate normal and abnormal cell behaviour which will be absent in cell culture sitautions. Damage to a cell will not inevitably lead to expression of mutation and cancer. Watson *et al* have described gross chromosomal damage in the skin cells of eight patients who had received radiotherapy years previously, without subsequent cancer development, illustrating that carcinogenic transformation is a rare event.[9] It is commonplace in chemical carcinogenesis to talk of one substance (A) as an *initiator* of the cancer process, which will only become manifest if one or several *promoters* (B, C, D, ...) are simul-taneously present. It may be that the primary radiation lesions in a cell can also be regarded in this light.

3 Animal experience

In addition to experimentally induced cancers, chromosome aberrations and mutations have been studied following irradiation of animals. All three effects show that, as with cells, the dose–effect curve for low-LET radiation increases in slope with increasing dose and dose-rate through the low to intermediate dose range. Similarly the curves for high-LET radiation rise more steeply with dose, are more nearly linear, and are much less affected by dose-rate. Indeed for the production of mammary cancers in one species of rat, the efficiency of tumour induction per unit dose seems greater at low neutron doses than at higher levels.[10]

With both high- and low-LET radiation at very high dose, effects per unit dose are reduced for the reasons of cell-killing already mentioned.

It is also easier to study in animals the influence that biological variables have in modifying the radiation response. From such studies it is clear that the age, the sex, and species characteristics can all influence this response.

4 Human effects

The final evaluation of radiation risks to man, while utilizing all the information derived from cellular and animal sources, must ultimately be derived from human experience. As stated earlier, much of this experience was derived from fortuitous exposures in the first half of the century, and many of the more immediately apparent effects of radiation were well known. The late effects of heavy radiotherapy doses were also well documented (as graphically described by Solzhenitsyn in *Cancer Ward*). The more insidious effects of lower doses were only recognized within the last 25 years.

It is now customary to describe the effects of radiation as being *somatic* if they occur in the individual who is irradiated or *hereditary* if they occur in his or her progeny. Effects produced by irradiation of the foetus after conception are somatic effects, whether they result in malformations (teratogenesis) or in subsequent malignancies in post-natal life. In considering somatic effects these must be treated as being produced in a *non-stochastic* or a *stochastic* fashion.

4.1 Non-stochastic effects

Non-stochastic effects which are produced by relatively high doses of radiation will occur in all or most irradiated subjects according to the level of dose. They are strongly dose-dependent, and for a given effect there will be a threshold of dose below which this effect will not appear. For example, above 0.5 Gy delivered at a high dose-rate to the testis there will be depression of the spermatozoa population. Above 1 Gy of high dose-rate irradiation of most of the body there will be a depopulation of the circulating blood cells, more marked at higher doses. Other non-stochastic effects include loss of hair, inflammation and ulceration of the skin, loss of the lining of the gastro-intestinal tract, and so on. Death will follow high dose-rate whole-body irradiation of around 6 Gy if medical intervention is not possible and will certainly occur at doses of 10 Gy even with treatment.

These effects are attributable in the main to cell death or loss of proliferative ability in sensitive tissues. Although most evident at high dose-rates, there may be non-stochastic effects produced by smaller but repeated radiation doses which ultimately will also affect the function of an organ. Fibrosis and chronic ulceration are longer-term effects well recognized as following high doses to, say, lung or skin. Such effects, then can be generally regarded as totally avoidable if such doses are not sustained.

4.2 Stochastic effects

It has become clearly evident that in any irradiated individual there is a chance that he may develop certain effects attributable to the radiation which will only appear at long time intervals after the irradiation event. This evidence has been derived from the study over many years of large groups of persons who were known to have received significant doses of radiation.[11] Since such effects are probabilistic and cannot be predicted for any one individual, they have been termed *stochastic*. The most notable of these effects are carcinogenesis and mutagenesis, and the possibility of their development in an individual exposed at low doses of radiation is now regarded as the most important consideration in radiation protection. It is this consideration which forms the basis of the ICRP risk estimates and their consequent recommendations. It is appropriate, therefore, to review the most important human experience in this respect. The prerequisites for the validity of such information have been well set out in the UNSCEAR report of 1977.[11] They are,

(1) a sufficiently long period of study (several decades) of the irradiated populations to ensure development of all the effects which may occur;
(2) reliability of diagnosis and detection of such effects;
(3) a sufficient number of effects to give statistical confidence when compared to those of a control population;
(4) a valid control population;
(5) knowledge of the absorbed dose, dose-rate, or dose fractionation, and variations of these for different individuals;
(6) a sufficiently uniform dose distribution in the whole body or tissue of interest;
(7) a method of comparing the effect of radiation of different quality at different dose levels.

When these criteria have been fulfilled, another problem remains. Although there are many groups of persons in whom the late effects of radiation are undisputed, only a few studies can be regarded as quantitatively reliable. Even in these the dose–effect response is usually estimable only for doses in the higher ranges. To gauge the effects of the doses of the few tenths of Gy encountered in the radiation protection situation, certain assumptions have to be made. The first is that the incidence of the effect (e.g. the frequency of induction of cancer) is proportional to the dose received; the second, that every dose above zero has a probability of causing such an effect, regardless of the rate at which it is received. This concept of a linear, non-threshold dose–effect relationship is now central to the recommendations of the ICRP, but is still conjectural. The bulk of the evidence from cell and animal experimental data suggests that this concept will tend to overestimate the risks from low doses of radiation when derived from frequency of effect at high doses, especially in the case of low-LET radiation. The extent of such over-estimation, however, may not be so great as is frequently claimed,[12] and may be an under-estimation when used for high-LET radiation.[13] This will be discussed again after a review of some human studies from which risk estimates can be tentatively derived.

4.3 Risk estimates

For a linear relationship the risk coefficient for cancer induction R may be defined by the equation $(O-E)/N = R \times D$, where O is the observed number of cancers, E the expected number in the population N, and D the average dose to the tissue in which cancer arises. As mentioned above, only a few studies have permitted a reasonably confident derivation of R for a limited number of tissues and these can now be described.

4.4 Leukaemia

The three sets of data on leukaemia mortality from which risk coefficients can be estimated are given in Table 19.2.

The Japanese figures are derived from the well-known study of the survivors from the atomic bomb explosions at Hiroshima and Nagasaki, which covers the period 1950–74.[14] The population studied were 7482 persons irradiated at Nagasaki who received exposure doses above 0.1 Gy. From this the average bone marrow dose can be calculated.[11] The control population was a group of 11 406 persons whose exposure dose was less than 0.1 Gy. (Even with the most meticulous refining of these doses there must inevitably be substantial uncertainties because of inadequate recollection of an individual's position at the time of the explosion, the effect of partial shielding

Table 19.2 The risk coefficients for leukaemia from the currently available data

Radiation exposure group	No. of persons	$O-E$	Average dose to bone marrow (Gy)	Risk coefficient $10^{-4}\,\mathrm{Gy}^{-1}$ *
LSSS Nagasaki	7843	13.6	0.57	32
Ankylosing spondylitis	6656	23.5	3.2	11
Metropathia haemorrhagica	2068	4.7	1.3	17

* a rounded representative value is taken as $20 \times 10^{-4}\,\mathrm{Gy}^{-1}$

by buildings etc.) Considerable uncertainties still exist on the magnitude of the neutron component of the radiation from the Hiroshima weapon. Since the exact value of this factor is not known, the Hiroshima data cannot be used to estimate the risk coefficient for low-LET radiation. In both cities there is a clear difference in induction rate with age at exposure, with greater sensitivity to leukaemia induction in the age groups below 10 years and above 50 years at the time of the bomb.

Two sets of radiotherapy patients also appear in Table 19.2. In these situations the dose can be estimated with more certainty because of reasonably standard therapeutic techniques and the availability of individual records. Court, Brown and Doll[15] published cancer mortality data on 14 554 patients, predominantly young males in their third and fourth decades, who were given X-ray treatment to spine and pelvis for ankylosing spondylites. (This is a disabling condition of the joints of the spine and pelvis more prevalent in young men, which can be relieved by irradiation.) Further data were recently published[16] on a subgroup of 6656 patients who received a single course of treatment. The average follow-up time in this subgroup was 16.2 years and about 30 leukaemias were observed with only 6.5 expected. Calculations, allowing for the non-uniformity of bone-marrow dose and the fact that about 60 per cent of the marrow was outside the radiation field, estimated an average dose over all the marrow of 3.2 Gy[11]. The other radiotherapy group were 2068 women, mainly in the age-group 40–50 years, treated for metropathia hamorrhagica, a condition of excessive menstrual blood loss cured by inducing an artificial menopause by irradiation.[17] The follow-up averaged 19 years per patient and 7 leukaemias were observed against 2.3 expected. Again the dose to bone marrow was non-uniform but averaged over all red bone marrow was estimated to be 1.3 Gy. A representative value for leukaemia induction from these three groups is given as 20 per 10^4 Gy when averaged over all age groups.

Leukaemia occurs in several forms depending on the type of parent white blood cell which is undergoing uncontrolled proliferation. In none of the above studies has chronic lymphatic leukaemia been observed. At Hiroshima the induction rates for chronic granulocytic leukaemia (and a few other acute forms) were four or five times greater than at Nagasaki. Chronic granulocytic leukaemia formed only a small minority of the total leukaemia incidence in the ankylosing spondylitics. This seems to indicate a neutron-dependent response varying between different cell types.[14]

4.5 Thyroid cancer

A summary of the four major surveys of thyroid cancer associated with irradiation is given in Table 19.3. Data on the thyroid cancers among Japanese survivors is obtained from the health survey conducted during the period 1958 to 1971.[18] The participants in this study have been clinically examined every second year since 1958 and thyroid cancers diagnosed

Table 19.3 Estimates of the risk of thyroid cancer in groups of exposed persons

Irradiated group	No. in survey	Excess cancers $O-E$	Average dose to thyroid (Gy)	Risk coeff. 10^{-4} Gy^{-1}
Japanese A-bomb survivors	10 000	23	1.2	20
Thymic enlargement	2 872	24	1.2	70
Tinea capitis treatment	10 902	10	0.1	92
Marshall Is.				
<10 years	87	2	3.5	65
>10 years	156	5	1.4	230

during the clinical investigation. In 10 000 persons receiving an average dose of 1.2 Gy to the thyroid there developed 31 cancers. Only 8 were found in an almost equal number of unexposed persons. It should be noted that only one *death* attributable to thyroid cancer has occurred in the total of 39 cases in both groups.

In the 1930s in the USA several illnesses of infancy were attributed to enlargement of the thymus gland in the upper part of the chest. Shrinkage of this gland was induced by X-irradiation, but the exposure field also included the thyroid gland. Follow-up studies of 2872 such persons have now gone on for about 40 years, and Hempelmann and his colleagues published in 1975 the up-dated results.[19] An excess of 24 thyroid cancers has been demonstrated, with an average thyroid dose of 1.2 Gy. Females have a risk per Gy 2.3 times that of males. Only one death attributable to thyroid cancer occurred out of the 24 diagnosed. Hempelmann also identified a sub-group who were all treated by one radiologist. Most of his patients belonged to a closely-related religious sect and they appear to be at greater risk than a heterogeneous population, with the females having a very high relative risk.

During the first 12 years of mass immigration to Israel (1948-60) nearly 17 000 children were treated by irradiation of the scalp for tinea capitis, a fungal infection of the skin of the head. The irradiation was done at three medical centres using 75–100 kV superficial X-ray machines. The details of irradiation technique such as focal skin distance and filtration are well known and doses to the scalp are reliably estimated as being from 3.5–4.0 Gy. The thyroid gland is estimated as receiving doses in the range 0.05–0.17 Gy.[20] Altogether, 10 902 children have been followed for periods between 12 and 23 years and data on cancer incidence obtained from two matched control groups; 12 thyroid cancers were observed in the irradiated group and two were expected.[21] The risk coefficient is about the same as that for the infants studied by Hempelmann.

Following the explosion of the first US hydrogen bomb at Bikini atoll in the Pacific Ocean in 1954, three of the islands in the Marshall Group were accidentally showered with radioactive fallout. The people of the islands were exposed to external radiation from this fallout. Additionally, many radioisotopes of iodine are produced in a nuclear explosion and some of these were inhaled directly. Some of the longer-lived isotopes entered the body from contaminated water or locally grown vegetables. Iodine is concentrated in the thyroid gland which was consequently irradiated from this source as well as from external radiation. The thyroid dose varied with age, younger people receiving higher doses from a given iodine intake than older people because of the lower mass of the thyroid in the younger age group. In Table 19.3 the exposed persons have been divided into two age groups. Two excess cancers occurred in the lower age group and five in the upper group.[22] The statistical significance is not high, but it does not appear that the younger thyroids were more radiosensitive.

From these four surveys of thyroid cancer a rounded value of 100 per 10^4 per Gy could be taken as representative. It should be noted that mortality from thyroid cancer is considerably less than incidence owing to the effective treatment now available.

4.6 Bone cancer

In general it appears that bone has a low sensitivity to cancer induction by radiation. Although cases have been described following radiotherapy,[11] the numbers are small and useless for the estimation of risk coefficients. There are no excess bone cancers in the Japanese bomb survivors. The risk of inducing bone cancer by low-LET radiation seems to be small. Most of our present knowledge of radiation-induced cancers in bone comes from two studies of individuals occupationally or medically exposed to radium-226 in the USA during the first half of this century,[23] and from patients treated with radium-224 for ankylosing spondylitis and tuberculosis in Germany about 30 years ago.[24] These are both α-emitting isotopes of radium which follow the metabolic pathways of calcium in the body and become deposited in the bone. Radium-226 has a half-life of 1620 years and radium-224 only 3.6 days. The spatial and temporal distributions of dose in the bone will therefore be quite different, the radium-226 being much more uniformly distributed through the bone. In the ^{226}Ra subjects both osteosarcomas and carcinomas were produced, the latter arising from the radon diffusing into the air spaces of the sinuses of the skull. Dolphin[25] summarized the latest data from the Argonne National Laboratory[26] on the status of the radium cases they have been studying (Table 19.4). He allocated the 1933 cases to arbitrary dose groups according to the calculated average skeletal dose. No osteosarcomas or cancers have occurred at doses less than 9 Gy and 6 Gy, respectively. The risk coefficients have been calculated for each dose range and for both types of malignancy, with a footnote showing the risk coefficients for each for doses up to 30 Gy. Above this level the risk seems to decrease possibly because of the influence of cell-killing at very high doses. It should be noted that these results are biased by the fact that malignant cases are much more likely to find their way into this study. The risk assessments are therefore probably over-estimates.

Table 19.4 Sarcomas and carcinomas in the 1933 cases included in the Argonne radium study[27]

Dose range (Gy)	0	3	3–10	10–30	30–100	100 +
Number of cases	466	1167	88	89	89	43
Total dose (man-Gy $\times$ 10³)	0	0.41	0.50	1.5	5	7.8
Number of sarcomas	—	—	1	14	26	15
Number of cancers	—	—	1	6	16	6
Risk coefficient (per 10⁴ per Gy)						
sarcomas	—	—	20	93	52	19
cancers	—	—	20	39	31	7

Risk coefficients: sarcoma = 60×10^{-4}
cancer = 30×10^{-4}

The osteosarcomas occurring among the adults treated with ^{224}Ra in Germany were analysed by Mays and Spiess[27] for a protracted regime of injections. Taking the dose to cells lining the bone spaces, the risk coefficients (high-LET radiation) turn out at 25 per 10⁴ per Gy for children and 20 per 10⁴ per Gy for adults.

4.7 Lung cancer

With a malignant condition so universally prevalent as lung cancer there are serious difficulties in establishing a pure causal relationship with irradiation even when there are apparent excess cases in populations under study.

The major complicating factor is the difference in smoking habits between study and control groups and between individuals in these groups. A further complexity is the rapid increase in lung cancer incidence over the past 30 years, particularly among women.

In the Japanese A-bomb survivors, lung cancers in excess have only occurred in victims irradiated when older than 35 years,[14] with the induction rate accelerating for those over 50 years. The mortality data up to 1974 shows no excess in the Nagasaki victims, making it impossible to establish a risk coefficient for low-LET radiation. There is, however, an excess of 23 lung cancers at Hiroshima in dose groups receiving more than 0.05 Gy absorbed dose to lung. A crude risk coefficient can be obtained (without quantifying the increased effectiveness of neutron irradiation) at about 40 per 10⁴ per Gy.

Excess lung cancer has been extensively studied in hard rock miners, particularly uranium miners, who in the past were exposed to radon gas and its radioactive daughters which permeate the mine atmosphere. The greater part of the dose to lung comes from the α -emitting daughter products, polonium-218 and polonium-214 which are deposited mainly in the respiratory passages where they irradiate the surface cells. It is difficult to establish a relationship between measured radon atmospheric contents in the mines and dose delivered to these cells from its daughters. Jacobi[28] has derived a relationship suggesting a value of 200 lung cancers per 10⁶ per *working level month* (WLM). (Working level is defined as any combination of radon daughter products in one litre of air resulting in the emission of a prescribed amount of potential alpha energy. A working level month is the exposure to one working level over 170 hours.) He postulates a relationship of 1 WLM equivalent to 5 m Gy dose to the bronchial epithelium. This gives a crude risk coefficient of 100 per 10^4 per Gy for α-irridation, much higher than the neutron value suggested for Hiroshima.

In ankylosing spondylitis patients treated by X-radiation, central positions of both lungs were included in the X-ray field during irradiation of the spine. In 6656 patients who only received one course of treatment over 30 excess lung cancers developed.[17] The mean lung dose has still not been calculated with certainty so that risk coefficients are uncertain. Since 24 excess leukaemias also occurred, it might suggest that red bone marrow and lung have about the same sensitivity, about 60 per 10^4 per Gy. A related study[29] showed that excess lung cancer does not occur in irradiated subjects with ankylosing spondylitis.

4.8 Female breast cancer

Five surveys provide the main evidence of radiation carcinogenesis in the female breast.

From the Japanese survivors an excess of breast cancer of 33.9 cases was shown in the dose group greater than 0.1 Gy, compared to those of the under 0.1 Gy group.[30] No cancers occurred in those who were under 10 years at the time of the bombs. Absorbed doses to breast were calculated using factors of 0.8 and 0.55 for gamma rays and neutrons respectively to convert exposure values to absorbed dose. The neutrons were estimated to have the same biological effectiveness as the gamma rays and the absorbed doses were added without modification. The risk coefficient (Table 19.5) calculated applies to cancers induced in a time interval 5–24 years after irradiation. A longer follow-up period would probably give a higher value.

Two groups of patients receiving fluoroscopy in Nova Scotia[31] and Massachusetts[32] were being treated by artificial pneumothorax for pulmonary tuberculosis. This technique involves deflating the lungs by admitting air into the chest and requires frequent radiological surveillance. Since cancer is known to occasionally follow tuberculosis, control groups had to be carefully selected to eliminate bias in finding E, the expected number of cancers. Each fluroscopic examination gave only very low dose and the total estimated dose was therefore accumulated over a long period of time. The risk co-efficient applies to women irradiated between the ages of 5 and 55 years and covers a risk of 30 years following exposure (Table 19.5). Boice's study suggests that the rate of induction may be higher in the adolescent breast and also that the risk coefficient is greater for doses *less* than 1 Gy although this observation is not statistically significant.[11]

Mastitis is an inflammatory condition of the breast occasionally occurring after a mother has given birth. A total of 606 women with this condition were treated by X-irradiation of the breast (or occasionally both breasts) with a calculated mean breast exposure over the series of 2.5 Gy. Three control groups were used in estimating a possible excess of cancers in the irradiated patients: siblings of the treated groups, non-related women treated for mastitis by methods other than radiation, and siblings of the latter group. This eliminates the possibility that mastitis itself leads to cancer development, but not the possibility that inflamed tissues subjected to irradiation may be unduly susceptible to cancer induction. The risk coefficients (Table 19.5) deduced apply to women treated in the age range 15–20 years and for cancers developing between 10 and 34 years after treatment.[33]

The Swedish survey (Table 19.5) included among the 1115 women studied, a large number treated for fibroadenomatosis of the breast, a condition which may predispose to subsequent cancer development. Hence the high risk coefficient may be an over-estimate.

It should be noted that, as with thyroid cancer, incidence does not equate with mortality. Where good treatment facilities exist, the 20-year survival rate in breast cancer is nearly 50 per cent.[34]

Table 19.5 The risk coefficient for breast cancer following irradiation calculated from data given in 5 published surveys

Group	No. in survey	Excess breast cancers attributed	Average dose* (Gy)	Risk coefficient $10^{-4}\,Gy^{-1}$
Japanese LSS	11 968‡	33.9	0.64§	44
Fluoroscopy (Massachusetts)	1 047	18	1.5	115
Fluoroscopy (Nova Scotia)	326	27.7	12.1	70
Mastitis (Rochester)	606	20	2.47	134
Benign diseases (Sweden)	1 115	93.3	4.2	198**

* average dose to both breasts
‡ women over 10 years at time of bomb with known doses of over 0.1 Gy
§ 0.58 Gy absorbed dose from gamma radiation plus 0.06 Gy absorbed dose from neutrons
** rounded value for Swedish data

4.9 Other cancers

Excess cancer induction has been reported in several other organs (or tissue systems), but in most cases the small number of cancers involved lead to low level of confidence in risk coefficient estimates (Table 19.6).[4]

4.10 Relative radiosensitivity of organs to cancer induction

Some organs and tissues appear to be of greater consequence than others when assessing the total risk of cancer induction by irradiation. This may be

Table 19.6 Summary of risk coefficients (per 10^4 per Gy) derived in this chapter

Organ	Risk coeff. in this paper		
	X-or𝛾-rays	neutrons	alphas
Female breast	100	44*	
Red bone marrow	20		
Thyroid	100‡		
Bone (osteosarcoma)	low		60/100
Lung	20§	40*	100
All cancers	80–100**		

* derived from the LSS data from Hiroshima with the uncertainties of the magnitude of neutron component
‡ this estimate is for cancer incidence and mortality may only be 5% of this value
§ by comparison with red bone marrow
** excluding breast cancer

so because they are indeed more radiosensitive for this particular end-point. Their prominence in epidemiological surveys may arise, however, by the comparative highlighting of a tumour which is ordinarily rare and thus easily detected. One way of checking on whether all expected malignancies have become manifest is to determine the ratio of total malignancies to the total of leukaemia alone. In the surveys already described the excess incidence of leukaemia seems to decline around 15 years after exposure and to have almost ceased after about 25 years. Data from a study of a contemporary group of US radiologists who developed excess cancer incidence can be used to evaluate such a ratio since this group (1920-9) have now nearly all died and all malignancies will have revealed themselves.[35] Table 19.7 shows the ratios for three irradiated groups. The Japanese data extend to 1976, and although most leukaemias have occurred, the so-called *solid* cancers continue to appear at the same rate; hence this ratio will probably increase with time. The average follow-up time for the particular sub-group of ankylosing spondylitics[17] is about 16 years, and this ratio will also increase with time as all the leukamias seem to have occurred.

If the risk coefficient for leukaemia is taken to be 20 per 10^4 per Gy low-LET radiation, then by using the ratio for the US radiologists the risk coefficient for all cancers lies between 80 and 100 per 10^4 per Gy. This range will exclude female breast cancer since the radiologists of this cohort were predominantly male.

Table 19.7 The ratio of excess deaths from all cancers to those from leukaemia

Irradiated group	Number	Excess cancers	Excess leukaemias	Ratio
Japanese LSS Nagasaki	7860	29	13.6	2.1
US Radiologists	1117	36	8.4	4.3*
Ankylosing spondylitics	6656	91.5‡	23.5	3.9

* 1920–9 cohort of radiologists relative to a similar cohort from the American College of Physicians
‡ excess cancers in the heavily irradiated sites in those patients receiving a single course of treatment

5 Discussion of epidemiological data

It has already been mentioned that risk estimations based on a linear dose–effect relationship are thought probably to over-estimate risk at low doses and low dose-rates when based on cancer incidence occurring only at considerably higher single doses. Most of the data from the studies described tend to support this. One or two, however, are not concordant with such a view. The estimated risks per unit dose, for instance, in the tinea capitis patients who received mean thyroid doses of only 0.1 Gy of low-LET radiation are no smaller than in those who received therapeutic doses to the thymus 10 times higher. It may be that other factors such as an effect on pituitary function in the tinea cases may distort this, but the findings seem more consistent with a linear than a curvilinear dose–effect relationship. A similar conclusion must be reached on consideration of the breast cancer data. The doses given at fluoroscopy examinations are relatively small and separated in time. There is no evidence however of a reduced risk per unit dose despite this protraction. One study not mentioned so far is that of childhood malignancies following antenatal X-ray irradiation of the foetus. Both those of Stewart and MacMahon suggest that such cancers follow absorbed doses of only a few tenths of a Gy.[35]

There are other interesting aspects of the epidemiological data. Hempelmann's study of thymus-irradiated subjects seemed to disclose a sub-group of peculiarly susceptible persons. It may be that other such groups exist so that protection standards require to take account of this.

Whereas neutrons can be assigned a relative effectiveness 20 times that of gamma irradiation for leukaemia induction, they seem to be no more effective than gamma irradiation in inducing breast cancer. Mole[13] has postulated that the diverse types of leukaemia in fact represent different diseases with different dose–response relationships.

It is also clear that age and sex differences are important apart from the obvious case of breast cancer. Incidence of lung cancer following irradiation seems to be greater in the older age groups; thyroid cancer seems to show the reverse and in addition is more prevalent in the female. Leukaemia cancer induction rates are greater in the young and the elderly. Since none of the studies have followed the irradiated group through to death of all the irradiated individuals, there may yet be significant expression of cancers with long latent periods of development. Conversely, cancers induced in middle-age with very long latent periods may never appear. All of these unresolved discrepancies have to be considered when prescribing a set of recommendations which will be universally applicable.

6 Hereditary risks

In addition to the stochastic somatic risks, attention has to be paid to the genetic effects of radiation first demonstrated 50 years ago by Muller[36] in the fruit fly, *Drosophilia melanogaster*. Twenty-six years ago when the British Medical Research Council produced its major work on *The hazards to man from nuclear and allied radiation*, the genetic risk from radiation was thought to be the most important factor in protection against its effects. The studies described above and the lessening apprehension about genetic effects have altered this view, so that cancer induction is now given greater emphasis. The mutations however which lead to cancer expression in the somatic cells of the body may similarly lead to transmissible changes in the reproductive cells of male and female. Such changes may be point mutations affecting single genes, chromosome number anomaly, or chromosome rearrangements. Information about their frequency of occurrence in the offspring of irradiated animals has been gained mainly from large-scale experiments with irradiated male and female mice. Such experiments have shown that the natural rates of at least five separate types of genetic abnormality in the mouse are doubled by roughly similar radiation doses and it is currently accepted that the so-called *doubling dose* is around 1 Gy of low-LET irradiation at low dose-rate.

Naturally occurring hereditary effects in humans have been reviewed recently by the Medical Research Council.[37] The birth frequency of the four major causes of hereditary effects are shown in Table 19.8 taken from UNSCEAR 1977.[11]

Table 19.8 Birth frequency of hereditary effects and estimated hereditary effects of 1 Gy per generation of low-dose low-LET irradiation on a population of 10^4 individuals (doubling dose assumed to be 1 Gy)*

Abnormality	Natural incidence per 1000 live births	Per 10^4 live-born per Gy/generation	
		1st gen.	equil.
Dominant and X-ranked	10	20	100
Recessive	1	—	—
Chromosomal	4	38	40
Polygenic,	90‡	5	45
multifactorial		63	185

* data from this table is taken from UNSCEAR 1977[11]
‡ only 5% of these effects are assumed to be affected by single mutations

The dominant and sex-linked mutations appear in the first generation and reach an equilibrium level within a few generations. Radiation-induced recessive mutations make little contribution to subsequent effects. The chromosome alterations which might be induced by radiation will turn up mainly in the first generation.

Effects which arise from several genetic alterations are the most common at birth, but it is recognized that the frequency of these is little altered by single mutations within the system such as those induced by radiation.

Therefore, this type of abnormality does not contribute much to radiation-induced effects in future generations.

Although studies have been made of populations living in areas of the world with high natural radiation exposure levels, no confirmed evidence of increased hereditary abnormality has been found. The only large group of irradiated adults and offspring studied in a systematic way is in the Japanese A-bomb survivors. During the period 1948–53, 70 000 children born in Hiroshima and Nagasaki were examined for hereditary defects during the first year of life. From this initial stage it was concluded that there were no differences in the inherited effects in the 30 000 children born to irradiated parents compared with the 40 000 control children of unirradiated parents. This study has continued with nothing of significance emerging. Kato[38] concluded that these data show that the doubling dose must be greater than 0.7 Gy when a factor of five is applied to take into account the presumed greater effectiveness of fission neutrons in producing hereditary effects. This estimate is reassuring since it adds support to the use of the doubling dose of 1 Gy derived from the experiments with mice.

Estimates are given in Table 19.8 for the frequency of effects per 10^4 live-born per Gy per generation, for the first generation and in equilibrium. The doubling dose is taken to be 1 Gy for all types of abnormality. The hereditary effects in the first generation amount to 63 and at equilibrium to 185 per 10^4 per Gy. It should be remembered that germ cell mutation cannot be of consequence in the age group where procreation is no longer possible, so that in any heterogeneous population irradiation will only be genetically significant in a section of the population.

7 The recommendations of the ICRP[39]

It is from the type of information reviewed above that the ICRP is able to formulate its recommendations (Fig. 19.3). It must assess the risk from exposure to ionizing radiation, and in the absence of evidence to the contrary it starts with the premise that any dose of radiation, however small, carries some finite risk to those sustaining it. This philosophy has been implicit for at least a decade in the Commission's recommendations. In 1959 they stated 'All doses should be kept as low as practicable and all unnecessary exposure avoided.' In 1965 this was altered to 'As any exposure may involve some degree of risk, the Commission recommends that any unnecessary exposures be avoided and that all doses be kept as low as is readily achievable, economic and social considerations being taken into account.'

The latest recommendations of 1977 and 1980 finalize this philosophy by specifying three limits of radiation protection.
1. No practice shall be adopted unless its introduction produces net benefit (JUSTIFICATION).
2. All exposures shall be kept as low as-reasonably achievable, economic and social factors being taken into account (OPTIMIZATION).

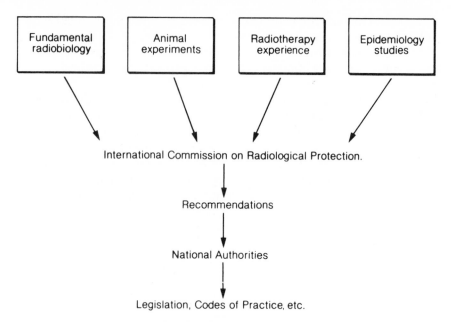

Fig. 19.3 The development of ICRP recommendations

3. The dose equivalent to individuals shall not exceed the limits recommended for the appropriate circumstances by the Commission (DOSE LIMITATION).

With regard to the third of these principles the Commission has gone further than ever before into societal considerations. Since every dose of radiation (additional to that already received from natural sources) apparently carries some risk, there must be a decision on the level of risk which people find acceptable. The difficulties in deciding (on behalf of others) what that level might be is discussed in an earlier Commission document,[40] but clearly can be partly resolved by distinguishing between persons who choose to work in situations where the possibility of receiving radiation doses exists and the public at large who do not (although in many instances receiving some benefit from the existence of such sources).

In the former case, i.e. that of workers, the ICRP have set levels of exposure which correspond with the mortality rates for industries which are generally regarded as 'safe'. In such industries the average annual risk of death is of the order of 10^{-4}, that is, with less than 100 deaths per million employed per year. Even within such industries the risk to any individual will vary with his task, and the distribution of individual risks will turn about the mean with a few values being considerably higher. The Commission have therefore taken account of the risk estimates derived from all the validated information available and set limits of exposures to workers which will achieve a level of mortality risk comparable to industries having a high standard of safety.

Before such comparisons can be made it is necessary to take account of the difference in effect of radiation of differing quality and under differing conditions of exposure. A simple estimate of absorbed dose by itself is insufficient to predict either the severity of non-stochastic effects or the probability of induction of cancer, as was seen in the difference in incidence and type of leukaemia between the Nagasaki and Hiroshima victims. It is therefore necessary for radiation protection purposes to produce a further quantity.

This quantity, called the *dose-equivalent*, *H*, is arrived at by modifying the absorbed dose by certain factors. The most important of these depends on the LET of the radiation being considered. For a spectrum of radiation an effective value of the quantity $\bar{Q}$, can be calculated and the ICRP recommend values of this as shown in Table 19.9. At present the other factors have been assigned a value of 1 so that the dose-equivalent expressed in units of sieverts (Sv) is derived by multiplying the absorbed dose, *D*, by $\bar{Q}$, i.e.

$$H(\text{Sv}) = D(\text{Gy}) \times \bar{Q}$$

Table 19.9 ICRP recommended values of the radiation quality factor, Q

X-rays, gamma rays and electrons	1
Neutrons, protons, and singly-charged particles of rest mass greater than one atomic mass unit of unknown energy	10
Alpha particles and multiply charged particles (and particles of unknown charge) of unknown energy	20
Thermal neutrons	2.3

The ICRP wishes to limit the development of non-stochastic effects and stochastic malignant and hereditary effects. To ensure protection against non-stochastic effects the ICRP recommend for workers an annual effective dose-equivalent limit for irradiation of any tissue of 0.5 Sv. The exception to this is the lens of the eye in which opacities may be produced by irradiation. For this particular tissue the limit is 0.15 Sv. If these limits are observed then it is unlikely that, over a working lifetime, the threshold for non-stochastic effects will be reached.

For stochastic effects, which by definition have no threshold, the ICRP has derived its estimation of risks in terms of dose-equivalent. These, for induction of fatal cancers in certain organs, and for hereditary risks are shown in Table 19.10. It is recognized from the epidemiological evidence available that some of these risks are dependent on the factors of age, sex, and so on already described, so that the risk will vary for any individual. It will be higher, for example, for breast cancer in females than in males, and hereditary risks will only be significant before the end of fertile life. The ICRP feel that sufficient accuracy in estimation is achieved, however, by using a single average risk level for each organ or tissue.

Using these estimations of risk there can then be derived a dose-equivalent of uniform whole-body irradiation which if not exceeded will place workers in the same category of average mortality risk, i.e. 10^{-4}, as workers in other safe industries. The ICRP has recommended that this be limited annually to

Table 19.10 Risk factors for radiation protection purposes (ICRP)

Organ or tissue	Risk factor (Sv^{-1})	Effect
Red bone marrow	2×10^{-3}	Leukaemia mortality
Bone	5×10^{-4}	Bone cancer mortality
Lung	2×10^{-3}	Lung cancer mortality
Thyroid	5×10^{-4}	Thyroid cancer mortality
Breast	2.5×10^{-3}	Breast cancer mortality
All other tissue	5×10^{-3}	Cancer mortality
Any other single tissue	1×10^{-3}	Cancer mortality
Uniform whole-body irradiation	10^{-2}	Cancer mortality
Uniform whole-body irradiation	4×10^{-3}	Hereditary effects within first 2 generations

50 mSv (Table 19.11). In so doing it has taken account of the fact that this dose-equivalent limit has been in effect for over 20 years. Experience has shown that internationally in occupational situations the resultant annual average dose-equivalent is no greater than one-tenth of the limit, with very few worker exposures approaching this limit. The dose limitation system is also based on the principle that the risk should be equal whether the whole body is irradiated uniformly or non-uniformly. If the latter, then a weighting factor can be used to adjust the risk of irradiation of only certain tissues. This takes account of the radiosenstivity of various tissues and the proportional risks of irradiation. The annual dose-equivalent in any tissue can be multiplied by its weighting factor, but the sum of such separate dose-equivalents should never be greater than the limit for uniform whole-body irradiation of 50 mSv. For such tissues the limit for non-stochastic effects must also, of course, apply. For the thyroid gland, for example, the stochastic dose-equivalent limit obtained by multiplying the limit of 50 mSv by its weighting factor 0.03 would give an implied dose-equivalent of 1.7 Sv. This however exceeds the non-stochastic limit of 0.5 Sv which must be the overriding constraint (Table 19.12).

7.1 Limits for the intake of radioactive materials

The harmful effects of the internal irradiation of organs or tissues by radioactive substances deposited or incorporated in their structure was well illustrated in the case of the Marshallese Islanders and the radium-treated patients earlier described. The ICRP has to take account of such situations and has set limits for such intakes. (It should be stressed that these limits are set for workers and should not be used without modification for any other situation.) Before such an ALI (Annual Limit of Intake) can be specified for any radionuclide, information has to be available on its chemical form, its metabolic fate with regard to excretion, retention, and distribution in the body, its own radiation characteristics and those of its daughter products.[41] In addition such a situation is postulated to take place within a *reference man*

Table 19.11 Recommended annual dose-equivalent limits

Recommended limit	Application	Tissue or organ
0.5 Sv	Workers	All tissue except lens of eye
0.15 Sv	Workers	Lens of eye
50 mSv	Workers	Uniform irradiation of whole body
5 mSv	Individual members of the public	Whole body
50 mSv		Any one organ or tissue including skin and lens of eye

Table 19.12 Tissue weighting factors

Tissue	Weighting factor (W_T)
Gonads	0.25
Breast	0.15
Red bone marrow	0.12
Lung	0.12
Thyroid	0.03
Bone surfaces	0.03
Remainder	0.30

whose anatomical and physiological characteristics are standardized. Some radionuclides will persist for many years, and hence it is recommended that their dose-equivalent be integrated over a working lifetime of 50 years and be termed the *committed dose-equivalent*. In any year of practice this value in all organs of the body must be limited, so that the resulting total risk of cancer and hereditary disorder is no greater than that from uniform whole-body irradiation of 50 mSv. As with external irradiation the non-stochastic limit of 0.5 Sv may also have to be invoked.

7.2 Pregnant women

Having regard to the possible special hazards of the unborn child, the ICRP conclude that it is unlikely that an embryo would receive more than 5 mSv during the first two months of pregnancy if women of reproductive capacity are occupationally exposed under the recommended limits and at regular rates. Such a procedure will provide appropriate protection during the period of formation of organs. The Commission also think it unlikely that a pregnancy of more than two months' duration will go unrecognized. When pregnancy has been diagnosed, arrangements should be made so that the woman can continue to work only where it is most unlikely that the annual exposure will exceed three-tenths of the annual whole-body dose-equivalent limit (15 mSv).

7.3 Dose-equivalent limits for the public

In setting these limits the Commission has once again made its own estimate of acceptable risk. On the basis of comparison with activities involving the public in risk, such as usage of public transport, the ICRP concludes that a level of acceptability of fatal risks to the public is much lower than for occupational risks and of the order of 1 in a million per year.

The assumption of a total fatal risk of the order of 10^{-2} Sv^{-1} (Table 19.9) would imply the restriction of the lifetime dose-equivalent to the individual member of the public to a value that would correspond to 1 mSv per year of lifelong whole-body exposure. The ICRP concludes that an annual dose-equivalent limit of 5 mSv to individual members of the public is likely to result in average dose-equivalent limits of less than 0.5 mSv, and hence recommends this figure (Table 19.11). Such a figure will also, taken into account with the principles of justification, prevent excessive population exposures.

8   Validity of risk estimates for low doses

The point has already been made that the ICRP base risk estimates on the premise that even the lowest dose of radiation has a probable harmful effect. The human evidence for this assumption is scanty, and except for foetal exposure we have little direct information about the effects of doses from zero to a few hundredths of a Gy. It is in this range however that lie the doses sustained by radiation workers. The risk estimates are founded largely on extrapolation from the much higher exposures of the irradiated groups described. If one seeks to find similar information for low dose levels one is immediately confronted with statistical limitations. A smaller radiation dose corresponds to a smaller excess risk, and as the excess risk decreases a progressively larger sample is required to detect it. For example, if the excess risk is proportional to dose, and if a sample of 1000 persons is necessary to detect the effect of a 1 Gy exposure, a sample of 100 000 may be needed for an exposure of 0.1 Gy and about 10 million for 0.01 Gy.

These numbers might not be so formidable if two considerations were true. If radiation caused some unique or unusual effect comparable to the rare liver cancer attributed to vinyl chloride, detection would be simpler. There is, however, no evidence of this and radiation-induced cancers are lost against the background of 'natural' cancer which causes the death of roughly one in four of the population. The other consideration would apply if the present linear hypothesis grossly under-estimates the health effects of low doses of radiation. One or two studies have recently purported to show that this may indeed be possible. The best known of these is a study by Mancuso and others[42] of the effects of occupational radiation exposure to workers at the Hanford Laboratory in Washington State in the USA.

The study was based on the causes of death over many years of 3500 males from a workforce of 25 000. It looked for correlations between these causes as shown on death certificates and radiation exposures as recorded by film badge dosimeters, and concluded that those who died of cancer had slightly higher radiation doses than those who died of other causes, and that those who received more radiation more frequently had cancer as their cause of death. There are many anomalies in the results of this study and its statistical methods have been severely criticised. One of these anomalies has been an apparent small excess in the radiation workers of cancer of the pancreas and of myeloma, a special type of blood cancer, but no excess of commonly induced radiation cancers such as leukaemia. The ICRP considered this work in 1978[43] and concluded that it provided no justification for changes in its risk estimates. The US National Academy of Sciences in its 1980 report on the effects of low-level radiation (BEIR)[44] concluded that the Hanford study was distinctly lacking in statistical power and could not influence the conclusions avilable from more consistent and statistically stable epidemiological evidence.

Considerable doubt exists whether any epidemiological study at these low dose levels will ever be able to fully satisfy stringent statistical requirements.[45] Nevertheless, several projects have been launched in the United Kingdom and elsewhere to test the hypothesis that current risk estimates are not wildly optimistic. The United Kingdom Atomic Energy Authority has commissioned the Medical Research Council to conduct such a study of approximately 40 000 ex- and serving-employees. The attributed radiation doses will be known for those employees who were radiation workers and mortality data will be obtained from central government sources. Such data will also be available for employees who were not exposed to radiation and they will serve as the most appropriate control group.

9 Conclusion

The recommendations of the ICRP are founded on two bases. The first is that there is a linear non-threshold relationship between exposure to radiation and those consequences, such as cancer induction and hereditary effects, which are regarded as the most serious possible consequences of radiation at occupational levels of exposure. It is likely that this concept neither minimizes nor too greatly exaggerates the risks of radiation.

The Commission have thus derived a quantitative risk estimate and, on the premise that an acceptable occupational risk is of the order of 10^{-4} per year and a population risk of the order of 10^{-6} per year, have set their recommended dose limits for exposure. Although there are areas of uncertainty about both these concepts it is true to say that the quantification of the risks from ionizing radiation is more secure than for any other environmental hazard and should at least be matched for reliability should any alternative risks be considered.

References

1. POSNER, E., *Brit. Med. J.*, **4**, 357 (1970).
2. MINCK, F. *Münch. Med. Wschr.*, **5**, 101 (1896).
3. STONE, R. S., *Radiology*, **58**, 638 (1952).
4. POCHIN, E. E. Why be quantitative about radiation risk estimates? Lauriston S., Taylor Lecture series in radiation protection and measurements. Lecture no. 2. National Council on Radiation Protection and Measurements, Washington (1978).
5. MOLE, R. H. *Brit. Med. Bull.*, **29**, 78–83 (1973).
6. ALPER, T. *Cellular radiobiology*. Cambridge University Press, London (1979).
7. PURCHASS, I. F. H., LONGSTAFF, E., ASHBY, J., STYLES, J. A., ANDERSON, D., LEFEVRE, P. A., AND WESTWOOD, F. R. *Nature, Lond.* **264**, 624–627 (1976).
8. KELLERER, A. M., AND ROSSI, H. H. *Curr. Top. Radiat. Res. Q.*, **8**, 85–158 (1972).
9. WATSON, G., *Proc. Assoc. of Rad. Research Meeting, Glasgow*. (1974).
10. SHELLABERGER, C. J. BROWN, R. D., RAO, A. R., AND SHANLEY, J. P., Rat mammary carcinogenesis following neutron or X-radiation. In *Proc. of a symposium on biological effects of neutron irradiation*, Neuherberg, 1973. International Atomic Energy Agency, Vienna (1974) pp. 391–401.
11. UNITED NATIONS SCIENTIFIC COMMITTEE ON THE EFFECTS OF ATOMIC RADIATION. Sources and effects of ionizing radiation: 1977 report to the General Assembly. United Nations, New York (1977).
12. BROWN, J. M., *Rad. Res.* **71**, 34–50 (1977).
13. MOLE, R. H., *Brit. J. Radiol.* **48**, 157–169 (1975).
14. BEEBE, G. W., KATO, H., AND LAND, C. E. Mortality experiences of atomic bomb survivors. Radiation Effects Research Foundation tech. report, *RERF–TR*1–77. Hiroshima (1977).
15. COURT BROWN, W. M., AND DOLL, R. *Brit. Med. J.* **2**, 1327 (1965).
16. SMITH, P., AND DOLL, R. *Late biological effects of ionizing radiation. IAEA–SM–224/711.* IAEA, Vienna (1978).
17. SMITH, P., AND DOLL, R. *Brit. J. Ridol.* **49**, 224 (1976).
18. PARKER, L. N., BELSKY, J. L., YAMAMOTO, T, AND KAMAMATO, S. Thyroid carcinoma diagnosed between 13 and 26 years after exposure to atomic radiation. Japan Tech. Rep. No. 5–73. Atomic Bomb Casuality Commission, Hiroshima (1974).
19. HEMPELMANN, L. H., HALL, W. J., AND PHILLIPS, M. *J. Nat. Cancer Inst.* , **55**, 519 (1975).
20. WERNER, A., MODAN, B., AND DAVIDOFF, M. *Phys. Med. Biol.* **13**, 247 (1968).
21. MODAN, B., BAIDATZ, D., AND MART, H., Lancet, **1**, 277 (1974).
22. CONARD, R. A. Summary of thyroid findings in Marshallese 22 years after exposure to radioactive fallout. *In* Groot, L. J., (ed.) Radiation associated thyroid carcinoma. Grune and Stratton, New York (1977).
23. POLEDNAK, A. P., J. Epidem. **107**, 3, (1978).
24. MÜLLER, W. A., AND EBERT, H. G. (eds.) *Biological effects of Ra-224*. Martinus Nijholi Med. Div., The Hague (1978).
25. DOLPHIN, G. Personal communication.
26. ROWLAND, R. E., AND STEHNEY, A. F. *Ann. Rep. for Centre for Human Radiobiology*. ANL-77-65, Pt. 2. Argonne Nat. Lab. (1977).
27. MAYS, C. W., AND SPIESS, H. Bone sarcoma risks to man from ^{224}Ra, ^{226}Ra and ^{239}Pu. *In* Müller, W. A. and Ebert, H. G. Biological effects of Ra-224. Martinus Nijhoff Med. Div., The Hague (1978) pp. 168–181.
28. JACOBI, W. Interpretation of measurements in uranium mines. *In* Nuclear Energy Agency. Personal dosimetry and area monitoring for Radon and daughter

products. Proceedings of a specialist meeting, Elliott Lake, 4–8 October 1976. Organisation for Economic Co-operation and Development, Paris (1977) pp. 33–48.

29. RADFORD, E. P., SMITH, P., AND DOLL, R. *New England J. of Med.* **297**, 572 (1977).
30. MCGREGOR, D. H., LAND, C. E., AND CHOI, K. J. *Natl. Canc. Inst.* **59**, 799-811 (1977).
31. MYRDEN, J. A., AND QUINLAN, S. S. *Ann. R. Coll. Physicians Can.* **7**, 45 (1974).
32. BOICE, J. D., AND MASON, R. R. *J. Natl. Canc. Inst.* **59**, 3 (1977).
33. SHORE, R. E. *Arch. Environ. Health* **31**, 21–29 (1976).
34. DUNCAN, W., AND KERR, G. R. *Brit. Med. J.* **2**, 781 (1976).
35. MATANOSKI, G. M., SELTSER, R., AND SARTWELL, P. E. *Amer. J. Epidem.* **101**, 3, 199 (1975).
36. MULLER, H. J. *Genetics* **13**, 279 (1928).
37. ASHE, P., VENNART, J., CARTER, C. Lancet, **1**, 849 (1977).
38. KATO, H., *J. Radiat. Res.* **16** suppl., p. 67 (1975).
39. INTERNATIONAL COMMISSION ON RADIOLOGICAL PROTECTION. *Recommendations of the International Commission on Radiological Protection.* ICRP Publication 26. Pergamon Press, Oxford (1977).
40. ICRP. *Problems of developing of index of harm.* ICRP Publication 27. Pergamon Press, Oxford (1977).
41. ICRP. *Limits of intakes of radionuclides by workers.* ICRP Publication 30 (part 1). Pergamon Press, Oxford (1980).
42. MANCUSO, T. F., STEWART, A., AND KNEALE, G. *Health Phys.* **33**, 369 (1977).
43. ICRP. Limit of intakes of radionuclides by workers. ICRP Publications 30 (part 2). Pergamon Press, Oxford (1980).
44. NATIONAL ACADEMY OF SCIENCE. *The effects on population of exposure to low levels of radiation.* Nat. Acad. Sci. Washington (1980).
45. LAND, C. E. *Science,* **209**, 1197 (1980).

20

Detection of nuclear radiation

W. ABSON

Radiation detection devices fall into three main categories, gas-ionization detectors, semiconductor detectors, and scintillation detectors. Each of these main headings covers a wide variety of different devices, and the development of various types of detector has witnessed some major advances, notably the advent of controlled gas multiplication techniques in large and small detectors, and of large-size, highly uniform single-crystal forms of semiconductor and scintillator materials.

This article examines the principles and techniques of all the major detector types and their principal applications. There are a number of specific forms of gas ionization detector, and the first part of the chapter looks at these, giving particular attention to methods of pulse amplification and pulse shaping.

Solid-state detectors include both semiconductor devices used as solid-state ionization chambers and also scintillation detectors. These are examined in the latter part of the chapter, which looks at the value of these devices in certain specific applications, in particular the high resolution in radiation energy measurements achievable with semiconductor detectors.

Radiation detectors of all types are subject to measurement errors imposed by detailed aspects of their design, which may be adjusted to suit particular applications, and these limitations are discussed. In addition there are fundamental limitations due to statistical fluctuations in the primary signals produced, and also the effects of electrical noise both in the detectors and in the associated pulse amplifiers. These limitations on accuracy of radiation energy measurement are also examined in the chapter, and an outline mathematical treatment of the subject is given in the Appendix.

Contents

1 Introduction

1.1 **Detection methods**

The development of nuclear radiation detection techniques and their application has been a continuing process throughout the history of studies in nuclear physics and the world-wide development of a nuclear power industry. The three main categories of detector are gas detectors (measuring radiation-induced ionization), semiconductor detectors (measuring ionization in high purity single-crystal semiconductors), and scintillation detectors (measuring luminescence in high-purity single-crystal scintillators). All three categories are described briefly in this introduction. Sections 2 and 3 deal in detail with the techniques and applications of gas detectors. Semiconductor detectors are described in more detail in §§4 and 5, and scintillation detectors in §6.

The main particle-type nuclear radiations are energetic, electrically charged particles, i.e.

(1) heavy charged particles such as fission fragments and alpha particles.

(2) energetic electrons (beta radiation) of much smaller mass and with longer ranges than the heavy particles, and

(3) neutrons which have the same mass as hydrogen nuclei but which have no electric charge.

The charged particles produce ionization and excitation of the atoms of the material through which they are passing; the ionization charge can be collected on the electrodes of a suitably designed detector and can then be amplified as necessary and recorded. The light which is emitted on de-excitation of excited states of atoms or molecules can be detected in suitable media using a sensitive photomultiplier tube; this arrangement is called a scintillation detector.

Neutrons can react with the nuclei of the material through which they are passing to produce energetic charged particles, which can then be detected by the methods already outlined.

A further very important category of nuclear radiation is gamma radiation. This does not exhibit either mass or charge but is a form of electromagnetic radiation with a very high photon energy. The absorption of gamma radiation in matter is best described in terms of the reactions of these photons on the electrons in the electronic shell structure of the atoms of the medium. The reactions lead to the production of energetic electrons, which can be detected and measured by ionization and scintillation detection methods.

The radiation energy initially absorbed to produce ionization and excitation is eventually dissipated in the form of heat, after recombination and de-excitation, so that calorimetric methods can be used for nuclear radiation measurement. These are applied particularly for precision measurement of total radiation energy absorption in the specific materials and media used in nuclear reactors. The calorimetric method is only suitable for use at high levels of radiation intensity. At radiation levels where it is quite safe for human beings to be exposed throughout their lifetime, the average rate of energy absorption is only a small fraction of 1 microwatt throughout the whole body. The human body is not sensitive to this low level of power absorption, nor are calorimetric methods suitable for these detection purposes. Ionization or scintillation detection techniques can be used to measure the *radiological protection* levels quite quickly. In many applications these methods are used for the measurement of radiation at intensities which are several orders of magnitude less than those of interest in radiological protection.

Becquerel's first discovery of the penetrating radiations from 'natural' radioactive ores stemmed from his observations of the 'exposure' of photographic plates stored nearby. Photograhic emulsions are still used in sophisticated nuclear physics experiments, for X-ray radiography, and also very widely for routine measurement of radiation dose to workers who may be exposed to one or more of the various types of nuclear radiation.

The ionization of gases (i.e. production of positive ions and electrons by separation of electrons from outer shells of neutral atoms) was used by the early workers on radioactivity to further their understanding of the nature and properties of nuclear radiations. Electroscopes and electrometers, discharged by conduction through the surrounding ionized gas, were used by Marie Curie and by Rutherford. Rutherford and Geiger extended the scope of gas ionization detectors by applying high enough electric fields in their ionization chambers to accelerate the primary ions to an energy where they could produce further ionization. By using this gas multiplication technique, they were able to collect a sufficiently large electric charge to detect single nuclear events producing ionization, and this type of radiation detector was developed later by Geiger and Müller into the present day *Geiger–Müller* counter. Gas ionization detectors used with or without gas multiplication now have wide application in nuclear physics and 'space' physics (e.g. cloud chambers, multiple-wire proportional counters, and spark counters); both single-event (charge) and mean-current ionization detectors play an important role in intrumentation for nuclear plant process control and for radiological protection.

Ionization in gases was also used from an early stage to observe visually the tracks of ionizing radiation. The Wilson cloud chamber uses air nearly saturated with water vapour; a separate detector system is used to determine when an ionizing event occurs and triggers off a mechanism producing a sudden expansion of the chamber gas. Preferential condensation of water vapour occurs along the ionized track, and the track is illuminated and photographed through transparent windows in the chamber. This instrument played a major part in experimental work in fundamental studies of nuclear physics. More recent types of track-indicating detector, which are still of major importance in nuclear physics, are gas-filled multi-wire spark chambers, and also *bubble* chambers where the ionization tracks in a liquid gas produce lines of bubbles along the length of particle tracks.

Rutherford also made extensive use of a scintillation screen and a low power microscrope to view the flashes of light produced by alpha particles in his studies of the scattering of alpha particles, which led to the early theories of the nature of the nuclei of atoms. This method of detection depends on excitation of molecules or molecular centres, and the subsequent emission of light when the excited state returns to its normal ground state. Curran and Craggs were the first to publish an account of the use of a light-sensitive photomultiplier tube to enable much lower intensity light flashes in luminescent materials to be detected and registered electronically. Zinc-sulphide screens are still used with photomultiplier tubes for alpha-counting; large sodium-iodide crystals are used for high-efficiency counting of high-energy gamma rays, and liquid and plastic scintillators for fast response and high-speed counting of many types of radiation. The applications of these *scintillation* counters again cover experimental sciences, nuclear plant control, and radiological protection instruments. Other luminescence phenomena used for radiation detection and measurement are photoluminescence and thermoluminescence; these phenomena are particularly suitable for integrating the total exposure to radiation over a given period of time. The amount of exposure or dose of radiation can be measured by heating the material (thermoluminescence) or exposing it to ultraviolet radiation (photoluminescence), when the material emits a visible (optical) radiation for a short period of time; the total amount of light emitted may be measured with a photomultiplier tube and is proportional to the total nuclear radiation dose to which the sample has been previously exposed. This technique is used in conjunction with, or as an alternative to, photographic film for *personal dosimeters* worn on the surface of the body.

The most recent development in radiation detectors measures ionization charge in solids. This has only become practicable on a large scale with the development of very pure single crystals of semiconductor materials in which the electrons and also the complementary *electron-holes* are mobile and can be collected under the influence of an applied electric field before recombination occurs. The two most commonly used materials for fabrication of these solid-state ionization detectors are silicon, which can be used at normal ambient temperatures, and germanium, which requires to be cooled to liquid nitrogen temperatures, to keep thermally generated conduction currents at a sufficiently low level. These developments in semiconductor detectors have resulted in a major improvement in the accuracy with which X-ray and gamma-ray energies can be measured, and also, more importantly, an ability to resolve and measure separately radiations with only small differences in energy. Large germanium crystals can now be used to analyse mixtures of radioactive materials (in terms of their characteristic gamma-ray emissions) without recourse to complicated chemical separation processes. Similarly, analysis of mixtures of non-radioactive elements and materials can be carried out by irradiating the samples under analysis with X- or gamma radiation, or with energetic electrons, to excite the characteristic

X-ray emission of the atoms of the material being analysed. Small silicon detectors with very low noise pulse-amplifier systems can be used to give resolutions comparable with those previously only attainable by the use of X-ray crystal diffractometers to measure the small wavelength (and hence energy) differences between the X-ray emissions. These high resolutions are achieved with a major increase in overall detection efficiency.

Table 20.1 lists these various types of detector and indicates the principle of operation and the detection medium used. The detector types are divided into two main categories, *signal* and *track* type detectors. In signal detectors, the radiation event or events are simply registered or counted, and the magnitude of the signal may or may not be used to measure the radiation energy; in track detectors the path of the particle is registered and displayed in some suitable form.

The track-type counters are mainly used in nuclear physics research and are of great importance in fundamental studies. It will not be possible in this chapter to deal with these developments in any detail, and emphasis will be placed on the techniques and applications of signal-type detectors, which have a much wider range of use in many different scientific disciplines and industrial procedures.

1.2 Types of radiation

The various forms of nuclear radiation and their properties are described in many books and articles on nuclear physics and applications of atomic energy. The following summary outlines the properties of the radiations, e.g. mass and charge (if any), range, and ionizing power, which may affect the design of radiation detectors for measurement of specific forms of radiation.

There are four broad categories of nuclear radiation that need to be considered.
1. *Heavy charged particles*. These include, for example, fission fragments, alpha particles (^{4}He nuclei), protons (^{1}H nuclei), and other miscellaneous 'recoil' nuclei.
2. *Beta radiations*. These are electrons emitted from the nuclei of some radioactive materials, and also high-energy electrons produced by bombardment of atoms by gamma or other high-energy radiation. These are lightweight charged particles.
3. *Neutrons*. These uncharged particles are produced notably in the fission process, but also in many nuclear bombardment processes.
4. *Gamma rays*. These are emitted from nuclei during radioactive decay and may have photon energies ranging from a few keV to several MeV. The X-rays characteristic of specific elements are not nuclear in origin, but arise from disturbance of electrons in the electron shells surrounding atomic nuclei; the photon energies range from about 100 eV for light elements to about 100 keV for heavy elements.

Table 20.1 Nuclear radiation detectors

Name	Type	Primary interaction	Medium	Mode of use
Ionization chamber	Signal	Ionization	Gas	Primary ionization measured as individual current pulses or as a mean current
Proportional counter Geiger counter	Signal	Ionization	Gas	Primary ionization increased by gas multiplication and individual current pulses amplified electronically as necessary
Scintillation counter	Signal	Excitation of electronic levels and emission of photons on return to ground states	Gas, liquid, and Solid	Light pulses measured with photomultiplier tube
Photoluminescence or thermo-luminescence	Signal	Excitation of electronic levels. Recovery to ground state by u.v. irradiation or by heating, to produce photon emission	Solid	Photo emission measured as total integrated light output using photomultiplier
Semi-conductor counter	Signal	Production of electron–hole pairs	Solid	Current pulses amplified electronically
Cerenkov counter	Signal	Production of photons by Cerenkov effect	Gas, liquid, or solid (transparent)	Light pulse measured with photomultiplier tube
Photographic emulsion	Track (single or multiple)	Ionization	Solid	After development process single tracks observed and measured optically, or mean density measured
Cloud chamber	Track	Ionization	Gas	Tracks photographed
Bubble chamber	Track	Ionization	Liquid	Tracks photographed
Spark chamber	Track	Ionization	Gas	Tracks observed by photograph, by acoustic or electronic means
Dielectric detector	Track	Ionization	Solid	Tracks developed by etching

1.2.1 *Charged particle absorption*

The first two categories, viz., heavy and light charged particles, lose energy by Coulomb interaction, i.e. by virtue of the electric field forces between the moving energetic charged particle and electrons bound to the nuclei of the absorbing medium through which it is passing. Ionization or excitation of the atoms of the medium occurs, depending on whether the electron is completely stripped away from the parent atom or displaced to another shell.

Fission fragments, alpha particles, and protons have a large mass compared with electrons and give up only a small fraction of their energy at each interaction. The paths through matter are characterized by being nearly straight lines and the tracks of ionized atoms are similarly thin tubular straight-line tracks.

Fast electrons or beta particles have the same mass as the electrons of the medium and hence a large fractional energy transfer may occur at one interaction; their tracks are no longer straight lines but a succession of bifurcations with large angles between the direction of the primary and secondary and tertiary electrons. All of these electrons subsequently lose their energy mainly by ionization or excitation. Whilst electrons of a given energy do not have a characteristic straight path-length like the heavy particles, they still have a finite penetration distance in the given medium. Both heavy particles and electrons produce approximately the same total ionization in the medium for a given energy absorbed, and in gases this is about one ion pair per 30 electronvolts (eV) of particle energy absorbed. The figure is related to the ionization potential of the gas. In solids, a smaller amount of energy is required since the electrons are more loosely bound and, in silicon for example, the average energy required to produce one electron–hole pair is 3.6 eV. Whilst ionization and excitation of atoms is the main process of energy loss for all but the higher-energy charged particles, there are two other processes which should be noted. The first is an inter-action between the moving charged particle and the electric field of the charged nuclei in the atoms of the absorbing medium. This slowing-down interaction produces electromagnetic radiation (like gamma or X-ray photons) called *bremsstrahlung* (literally 'braking radiation'). For electrons this radiative loss is proportional to $E_0 Z^2$, where E_0 is the electron energy and Z is the atomic number of the medium. For 2 MeV electrons, the specific energy loss (i.e. loss per unit path length) via the bremsstrahlung process is 3.5 per cent of the total energy transfer in silicon and 8 per cent in germanium. Bombardment of high mass number targets, such as tungsten, by electrons accelerated to high energies (e.g. 150 keV and greater) provides the con-tinuum of photon energies emitted by 'X-ray' generators used in radiography and radiotherapy.

Another source of loss of energy of fast-moving particles, which is however small compared with the other processes discussed, is by the production of electromagnetic radiation in the optical region; this was first observed by Cerenkov. Cerenkov radiation occurs when a charged particle travels through a medium of high refractive index at a speed faster than that of light in that medium. The phenomenon is analogous to an acoustic shock wave, and the disturbance of electrons along the path of the particle gives rise to radiation (optical region) which reinforces to give a conical coherent wavefront at an angle $\theta = \cos^{-1} 1/\mu \beta$ to the particle path, where μ is the refractive index of the medium and β is the particle velocity relative to that of light in a vacuum. In a dispersive medium, light of different wavelengths will be emitted at various values of θ. In water, electrons with a $\beta \rightarrow 1$ will produce some 20 photons (optical region) per mm of path length. This phenomenon has been used for particle detection and also for measurement and/or selection of particle velocities in nuclear physics experiments.

Further quantitative data on the ranges of various particles in semiconductors and scintillation phosphors as a function of particle energy are given in Figs 20.24 and 20.25.

1.2.2 *Gamma and X-ray absorption*

Gamma and X-rays can be detected by ionization or excitation effects of the fast electrons which they can produce by interaction with the atoms of the absorbing medium. There are three basic processes of interaction or absorption of gamma and X-ray photons; (1) photoelectric interaction, (2) Compton scattering, and (3) pair production.

1. In photoelectric absorption, the whole energy $(E = h\nu)$ of the photon, where ν is the frequency of the radiation, is transferred to an electron (usually in the inner or K shell closest to the nucleus). This electron is thus released with an energy $E_e = h\nu - E_b$, where E_b is the binding energy of the electron. This electron orbit is immediately filled with subsequent emission of a characteristic X-ray of energy E_b, and this low-energy photon is usually absorbed within the detector, so that the total energy transferred to ionization and excitation is proportional to E the primary gamma-ray energy.

2. In Compton scattering or absorption, a part of the primary photon energy is transferred to an electron, leaving a photon of reduced energy which may or may not be subsequently absorbed within the detection medium; the reaction can be analysed quantitatively as a classical scattering or collision process. If the scattered photon is absorbed within the detector, we again have an energy transfer to ionization and excitation which is proportional to the primary gamma-ray energy E.

3. In pair production, the energy of the primary photon is transformed into the kinetic and potential energies of an electron and a positron (same mass as an electron with an equal but opposite sign of electric charge). The process occurs near an atomic nucleus, and the primary photon must have an energy greater than 1.022 MeV, i.e. equal to the rest mass of the two particles $(= 2mc^2)$; the two particles have equal kinetic energies, the total energy being equal to the primary photon energy less 1.022 MeV. Each particle then loses most of its energy by ionization and excitation processes, and the positron then annihilates with a nearby electron and a pair of gamma rays each of energy mc^2 (0.511 MeV) are emitted in opposite directions. If these are absorbed within the detector, it is again possible for the total ionization and excitation energy transfer to be equal to E, the primary photon energy.

The probability of these reactions occurring may be expressed in terms of an effective cross-sectional area for each atom of the medium:
(1) the photoelectric absorption cross-section, $\tau \propto Z^5/E^{3.5}$;
(2) the Compton absorption cross-section, $\sigma \propto Z/E$;
(3) the pair production absorption cross-section $k \propto Z^2(E - 1.02)$.

Gamma and X-rays do not have a finite range but are attenuated continuously with distance d. For a well-collimated beam of mono-energetic gamma radiation, the intensity (I) is reduced exponentially with distance d, by the relation:

$$I = I_0 \exp(-\mu N d),$$

where,

$\mu = \tau + \sigma + \kappa$, i.e. the total absorption cross-section per atom
N = number of atoms per unit volume,
I_0 = incident intensity (photons/unit area), and
I = intensity at distance d.

A graphical representation of the partial and total absorption coefficients (μN) over a range of gamma-ray energies, for semiconductors and scintillation phosphors is given in Fig. 20.29 and Fig. 20.32. It is evident that high gamma-detection efficiencies are most readily achieved for lower energies, and that the detection medium should have as high atomic number (Z) as possible.

If a detector is required to give a measurement of the gamma photon energy, the dimensions of the detection medium must also be large enough to ensure absorption of the secondary radiations resulting from the primary gamma-ray interaction. This is a criterion which is especially important in gas detectors and limits their use for energy measurements to X- and gamma rays below 100 keV.

1.2.3 *Neutron absorption*

The interaction of uncharged neutrons with matter is quite different from that of charged particles or gamma rays. Only those interactions which are important for the detection and/or energy measurement of neutrons will be dealt with here. The simplest interaction is an elastic collision with the atoms of the medium. The maximum energy transfer occurs by collision with hydrogen nuclei (protons) which have nearly the same mass as neutrons, and the energy of the proton recoil is given by $E_p = E_n \cos^2 \theta$, where θ is the angle between the paths of the neutron and the recoil proton. E_p has a uniform (or rectangular) distribution of number versus energy, for E_p ranging from zero to a maximum of E_n (head-on collision with θ = zero). The cross-section for this reaction with hydrogen nuclei is 9.6 barns (10^{-24} cm^2) for E_n = 0.2 MeV, falling to 4.5 barns and 1.6 barns at E_n = 1.0 MeV and 5.0 MeV, respectively. The reaction is used with hydrogenous gases for pulse-type (single-event) detectors and for mean-current detectors. It is also used with liquid and plastic scintillator detectors, and with semiconductor detectors in conjunction with a hydrogenous *radiator*. This reaction is not generally suitable for neutron detection at energies less than about 0.1 MeV because the small amount of energy transferred becomes difficult to distinguish from other interactions (mainly with gamma rays) which are often associated with the neutrons to be measured.

Energetic or fast neutrons which undergo successive elastic collisions eventually reach an energy in equilibrium with the surrounding atoms of the medium; this equilibrium energy $= kT$, where T is the temperature of the surrounding atoms and k is Boltzmann's constant. (For T = 300 K, $kT = 0.025$ eV). The neutrons are then described as being completely *thermalized*. At or near this thermal energy, the probability of a neutron being captured or compounded with other nuclei becomes much greater than at high neutron energies. In a small number of cases, the compound nucleus formed is unstable and immediately disintegrates in an exothermal nuclear process with charged-particle reaction products of high energy. Examples of these processes with high cross-sections for absorption of thermal neutrons, which are used in neutron detectors are:

^{10}B $+$ n $\longrightarrow$ ^{7}Li $+$ ^{4}He (α-particle) $+$ Q (2.8 MeV)

(cross-section $\sigma_{th} = 3770$ barns)

^{3}He $+$ n $\longrightarrow$ ^{3}H $+$ ^{1}H (proton) $+$ Q (0.77 MeV)

(cross-section $\sigma_{th} = 5330$ barns)

^{6}Li $+$ n $\longrightarrow$ ^{3}H $+$ ^{4}He (α-particle) $+$ Q (4.8 MeV)

(cross-section $\sigma_{th} = 900$ barns)

^{235}U $+$ n $\longrightarrow$ fission fragments $+$ Q (160 MeV)

(cross-section $\sigma_{th} = 545$ barns).

The reaction energy Q is distributed between the reaction products. The first two reactions are commonly used with pulse-type gas multiplication or proportional counters filled with boron-trifluoride (BF_3) gas and with ^{3}He gas with suitable other gas admixtures. Boron and also ^{6}Li may be used as thin layers coated on the metal electrodes of a gas counter or on the surface of a solid-state detector. *Fission counters* usually have thin coatings of fissile material in an oxide form, on the electrodes of gas counters, and, for special studies, on or near the surface of silicon semiconductor detectors.

1.3 Radioactivity and radiation units

The different forms of nuclear radiation which have been described may be emitted spontaneously from radioactive isotopes. The disintegration of these radioactive nuclei is a completely random process, and the rate of disintegration in a particular sample is proportional to the number of radio-active atoms present (N). Thus,

$$-\frac{dN}{dt} = \lambda N.$$

which on integration gives

$$N_t = N_0 \exp(-\lambda t).$$

The decay constant λ is related to the half-life $t_{1/2}$ (time for the number of atoms in a sample to decrease by a factor two or for the disintegration rate to decrease by two):

$$t_{1/2} = \frac{\ln 2}{\lambda} = \frac{0.693}{\lambda}$$

A well-known unit of total activity (disintegration rate) in a sample is the curie, which derives from Madame Curie's work on the emanation from radium compounds found in uranium ores. This disintegration rate, i.e. 1 curie $= 3.70 \times 10^{10}$ disintegrations per second, represents a very large quantity of radioactivity; in practical applications use is made of smaller sub-units, e.g. the millicurie (mCi) and microcurie (μ Ci).

An SI unit of radioactivity is now being introduced. This new unit is the becquerel (Bq) $= 1.0$ disintegration per second.

1.3.1 *Radiation dose and dose-rate*

Dose and dose-rate are used in studies of biological effect. For a particular form of radiation, the biological effect produced (at levels where such effects can be observed) is proportional to the amount of radiation energy absorbed per unit mass of tissue or other biological material. A unit used for *energy absorbed per gram* or absorbed dose, is the rad, equal to 100 erg/g. It was established at an early stage (L.H. Gray) that the total energy absorbed is proportional to the ionization energy transfer, and from the very early days of radiation measurement, dose has been measured in terms of the ionization produced in a tissue-equivalent gas ionization chamber. The ionization is collected by applying a voltage between the chamber electrodes in order to collect and measure the rate of charge production as a mean current ($\propto$ dose-rate) or as the accumulated charge during a preset time ($\propto$ dose).

An SI unit of absorbed dose has recently been introduced. This is the gray (Gy) $= 1J/Kg = 100$ rad.

A given energy deposition can produce a greater biological effect as the specific ionization (in ion pairs per unit track length) increases. In radiological protection measurements the term *quality factor* (*QF*) is used to take account of this effect, and specific values of *QF* have been adopted on an international basis for the main types of radiation encountered in radiological protection work. Absorbed dose $\times$ *QF* is referred to as dose-equivalent for radiological protection measurements; its unit is the rem. An SI unit of dose equivalent has recently been introduced. This unit, the Sievert (Sv) $= 1$ coulomb/kg $= 100$ rem. A more detailed discussion of radiation dose and dose-equivalent, and methods of measurement for exposure of human beings to different types of radiation hazard, is given in Chapter 18.

The internationally recommended maximum permissible dose equivalent for radiation workers likely to be exposed throughout their lives is 5 rem/y (whole body). On the basis of working week of 40 hours and 50 working weeks per year, this corresponds to an average dose-rate of 2.5 mrad/h for gamma radiation. It is of interest to calculate this dose-rate in terms of power absorption:

$$2.5 \text{ mrad/h} = 7 \times 10^{-12} \text{ W/g}.$$

For whole-body radiation and assuming a body mass of 70 kg, the total power absorption is 0.5 μW. It will be shown that the dose-rates associated with these very low levels of total power absorption can be readily measured. The relative ease of measurement of radiation hazards compared with the other varied hazards arising in industrial processes and from modern methods of living has perhaps contributed to an over-emphasis in the public mind on the relative importance of the hazards arising from the nuclear industries and from atomic power generators.

2 Radiation detection techniques using ionization in gases

Gas-filled detectors may be used to measure the mean rate of ionization as a direct current, positive ions moving towards the cathode (negative electrode) and electrons towards the anode under the influence of the electric field. If a sufficiency high voltage is applied to provide an electric field which can separate all the positive ions and electrons formed in the primary tracks and also prevent any subsequent recombination of the moving charges, the current flowing in an external current-measuring device will be equal to the mean rate of ionization. Direct-current devices of this type have been in use throughout the history of nuclear radiation measurement and are still widely used, especially in high-intensity radiation fields where it may be difficult to separate individual events (e.g. in neutron-sensitive reactor control devices) and also in radiological protection instruments. The latter class give a mean ionization rate response which is directly related to the rate of energy absorption in the gas and walls of the ionization chamber. If the walls and gas are *tissue-equivalent* in terms of their absorption properties to the radiation being measured, the response is proportional to energy absorption rate or dose-rate in tissue.

Another and more widely used class of gas-filled detector measures or counts the individual current pulses due to collection of the ionization charge produced by each separate ionizing event. This class of detector may be further sub-divided into three types: (1) the pulse-type ionization chamber; (2) the proportional counter; and (3) the Geiger–Müller counter. The most commonly used electrode geometry is two coaxial cylinders with the gas between them, the outer cylinder forming the cathode. The inner cylinder, usually in the form of a fine wire, forms the anode and is held at a positive potential, V, relative to the cathode which is often at earth potential. The gas multiplication, M, is then defined as the ratio of the final electronic charge collected on the anode to the charge of either sign in the primary ionization track. Fig. 20.1 shows the relation between V and M for a gas filling of argon–CO_2 at a pressure of about 0.2 bar, in a detector of dimensions shown in the figure.

When V is very small, only a small fraction of the primary electrons are collected on the anode, and the remainder recombine with positive ions. As V is increased the electrons and positive ions become fully separated, and all electrons in the primary track are collected at the anode. Section (a) of the curve in Fig. 20.1 shows the range of voltage when the collected charge is virtually constant and is referred to as the saturated-ionizaton-chamber region. In this region $M = 1$.

A further increase in V, into the hundreds-of-volts region, produces an increase in the final charge collected, Q, owing to a gas multiplication process. As electrons reach the region of high electric field near the anode wire, they may acquire sufficient energy between collisions with gas molecules or atoms to produce ionization by collision. Each such collision produces two electrons in place of one, and a succession of such collisions produces an avalanche process. The final size of the avalanche goes on increasing as V is increased, and this is represented by section (b) in Fig. 20.1. This region is called the proportional-counter region because at any particular point in the curve the collected charge Q is proportional to the initial primary charge. The multiplication factor M is constant for a wide range in Q, for values of M up to about 100. This region may be used for measurements of particle energies. At higher voltages M continues to increase, but is no longer independent of the magnitude of the primary ionization. As the primary ionization is increased, at a given voltage, the multiplication factor M becomes smaller, because space charge reduces the electric field near the anode. This is the region of limited proportionality and is represented by section (c) of the curve in Fig. 20.1.

The avalanche size increases rapidly as V is increased but eventually, in a gas mixture containing a quenching agent (see 2.2 and 2.3), the rate of rise is reduced and the number of electrons collected at the anode becomes nearly constant and independent of the primary ionization. This is the Geiger-counter region and is represented by section (d) in Fig. 20.1. In this region the avalanche process ceases to be limited to the part of the counter anode where the primary electrons arrive. Ultraviolet photons are produced when electrons and positive ions recombine. These photons are absorbed very close to their point of origin and additional electrons are produced which may initiate new avalanches adjacent to the initial one. This process can spread in both directions along the anode wire until it reaches the end terminations of the anode. Over a range of voltage the value of Q per unit length of the counter is nearly constant, determined by space charge reducing the electric field near the wire to low values where the multiplication process ceases. When M becomes very large (e.g. 10^9 in Fig. 20.1) other secondary processes result in electrons being released into the counter gas from the cathode surface and the discharge becomes continuous.

Operation in the Geiger-counter region provides a very large signal, but

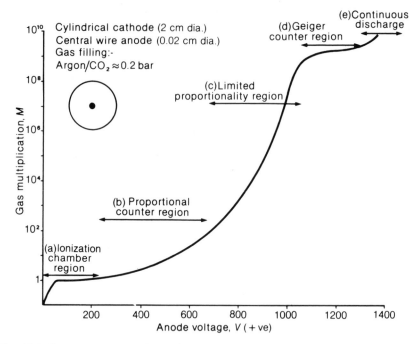

Fig. 20.1 Gas counter operating regions

there are limitations on counting speed. However, the Geiger counter continues to have many applications.

The following paragraphs give further details of pulse response, pulse amplification, and processing in systems using ion chambers, proportional counters, and Geiger counters.

2.1 Pulse response in gas ionization chambers

In the simple gas ionization chamber the pulse-signal time response will depend on the rate of collection of the primary ionization. In gases at about atmospheric pressure the positive ions have low drift velocities (0.01 m/s in an electric field of 100 V/m); free electrons have drift velocities (v) about 1000 times faster. There are, nowadays, few applications in which the slow pulse responses due to positive ions are observed as individual events, since the current pulse lengths are of the order of milliseconds in duration. Provided that the gas fillings are free from traces of electronegative gases (e.g. O_2, halogens) the electrons remain free and fast moving and can be collected in times ranging from a few microseconds in chambers with electrode spacings of a few centimetres, to a few tens of nanoseconds with 1000 V applied between electrodes spaced 1–2 mm apart. For a given primary ionization $q = Ne$, (N is the number of ions and e the charge on an electron), the current pulse on collection is $N\,eV$ and this has a duration d_a/v, for parallel-plate electrodes, where d_a is the distance between the position of the primary ionization and the anode on which the electron is finally collected and v is the electron velocity. The associated induced charge on the anode is $Ne \times d_a/d$, where d is the spacing between the parallel-plate electrodes. Thus, although a fast pulse can be obtained, the induced charge on the anode depends on the position of the ionized track as well as on the total magnitude of the charge.

2.2 Pulse response in gas proportional counters

A limitation of the pulse-type of gas ionization chamber is that radiation depositing only a small amount of energy in the detector (beta particles and cosmic radiations, and gamma and X-rays) produce signals which are not much greater than spurious electrical noise signals. This limitation may be overcome by increasing the applied voltage to a value where the primary electrons can gain enough energy in their mean free paths between elastic collisions with atoms of the gas to produce ionization of these atoms. One such ionizing collision for a primary electron produces an extra electron, which in turn can produce two electrons and a cascade multiplication process or avalanche may occur, as has already been mentioned. A cylindrical geometry with an outer electrode as cathode and a coaxial wire as a central anode favours stable proportional amplification and carefully purified gas mixtures (inert gases with a polyatomic gas as quenching agent) are also necessary. The early developments and a detailed theory of operation are well reviewed by D. H. Wilkinson and also by P. Rice Evans. (See *Suggestions for further reading.*).

When a voltage V is applied between the centre wire, radius r_1, and cathode, radius r_2 (wire potential positive with respect to the cathode), the electric field at a position radius r is given by:

$$X_r = \frac{V}{r} \ln \frac{r_2}{r_1}.$$

As the primary electrons are collected, the voltage induced on the anode is proportional to the potential ($\int X \, \mathrm{d}r$) through which the electrons have fallen. This collection of primary electrons contributes an insignificant proportion of the final signal. The field X increases rapidly near the wire and secondary ion pairs are created very close to the wire (within two or three wire diameters). There is now a charge Mq of electrons and positive ions near the centre wire with the concentration of charge increasing near the anode wire. The outward movement of the positive ions away from the anode in the high field region produces a larger induced charge on the anode than the collection of the electrons on the anode.

An approximate expression for the induced-charge signal/time response is:

$$q(t) = \frac{Mq}{2 \ln (r_2/r_1)} \ln \left[1 + \frac{2\mu + Vt}{\ln (r_2/r_1)} \right]$$

This equation represents a signal with an initial fast rise, gradually slowing down until $q(t) = Mq$ at a time when all positive ions have reached the cathode, which may take several milliseconds. However, the initial rise is so rapid that $q(t)$ may reach $Mq/2$ within a microsecond or so (depending on counter dimensions and gas filling), so that about 50 per cent of the maximum available signal may be further amplified in a fast amplifier, i.e. one with pulse-shaping circuits having short time constants. (See §2.4.)

A typical value for the mean free path between collisions is 10^{-2} mm, and a multiplication M of 128 ($= 2^7$) requires seven such paths. Thus gas multiplication need only start at a radius r_c which is quite close to the wire (r_1) e.g. within a few wire diameters. Figure 20.2(a) illustrates the drift of the electrons in the primary ionization (q/e electrons) to a position at radius r_c; Fig. 20.2(b) illustrates the start of the gas multiplication process by secondary ionization within the radius r_c for each electron of the charge q. Figure 20.2(c) shows the movement of the charge $+ Mq$ away from the wire, which produces the main signal response. Figure 20.3 shows the dependence of the multiplication factor M, in the range 2–500 times, on applied voltage and gas pressure for a cylindrical counter with an argon–CO_2 filling, a cathode diameter of 40 mm, and a wire radius of 0.12 mm. The data for $M > 100$ only applies for beta rays or electrons from X- or gamma rays.

2.3 Pulse response in Geiger-Müller counters

The effect of increasing the voltage on the anode wire above the proportional counter region in a counter containing a mixture of noble gas with a quenching agent (often a polyatomic vapour) has already been discussed briefly. The charge collected on the anode continues to increase with anode voltage increase and at a more rapid rate, although the multiplication factor M becomes dependent on the magnitude of the primary ionization q because space charge near the anode in the region where the electrons are collected, reduces the electric field.

As the final charge collected becomes larger, the avalanche process is modified by a further effect which starts at the end of the region of limited proportionality (Fig. 20.1). Ultraviolet photons are emitted as noble gas atoms, which were excited to higher energy states in the collision process, return to their ground states. These photons are heavily absorbed by the quenching agent close to their point of origin, resulting in the production of additional electrons near to the anode wires. These electrons in turn will initiate avalanches. At a slightly higher applied voltage difference between anode and cathode this effect, in which additional avalanches are produced at the edges of an initial densely ionized region, causes the discharge to propagate itself in both directions along the wire from that region. Experimental measurements indicate a velocity of spread of about 10^{-5} ms^{-1} in an argon / alcohol gas mixture. The total charge collected is limited eventually by space-charge effects from the positive-ion sheath near the anode causing

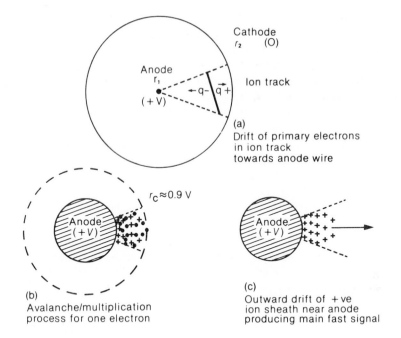

Fig. 20.2 Proportional counter action

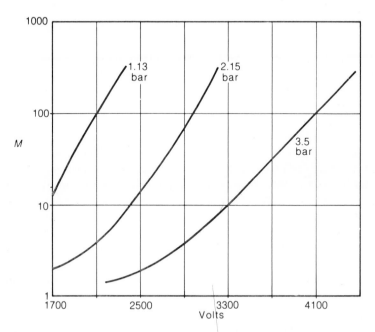

Fig. 20.3 Gas multiplication factor M vs voltage in a proportional counter: Anode wire dia. 0.21 mm; Cathode dia. 40 mm; Gas filling, argon/10% CO_2 at various pressures

a marked reduction in the electric field near the wire. This maximum or limiting charge is equivalent to about 10^7 ions per millimetre length. The total charge collected is thus proportional to the total counter length.

The avalanche process and spread down the length of the anode wire is completed within a few microseconds, but the final collection of the positive ions on the cathode takes a much longer time (1 ms).

In the absence of a quenching agent u.v. photons will reach the cathode, producing additional electrons by photoemission at locations remote from the initial avalanche. A second process generating 'spurious' electrons will occur as positively charged noble gas ions drifting outwards from the avalanche region reach the cathode and are neutralized there. The work function of the cathode surface is normally much less than the gas ionization potential and electrons will be released into the gas. Thus a further discharge, becoming continuous, will occur. This effect can be prevented by the use of external electronic quenching circuits which reduce the applied voltage, within a few microseconds after initiation of a pulse, so that further multiplication processes cannot occur until some defined time long after collection of the positive charge (fraction of a millisecond). Both these effects can also be prevented by the quenching agent. Positive ions of the main gas (e.g. argon) transfer their charge to the alcohol molecules (since the ionization potential of an alcohol molecule is less than that of argon). The positive ion sheath reaching the cathode thus consists mainly of alcohol ions and these have the property on neutralization of losing excess energy by dissociation rather than by photoemission of electrons from the cathode and eventual ionization of the counter gas. Since the dissociated alcohol molecules do not recombine, this acts as a life-limiting feature, the lifetime being determined by the initial alcohol content and by the number of Geiger discharges. A 25 mm × 50 mm Geiger counter with alcohol quenching would have a typical lifetime in the range 10^8–10^9 counts.

Thus the counter produces a large pulse (fast movement of about 10^8 ions away from the immediate region of the anode wire) lasting for a few microseconds, after which space charge effects near the anode result in a dead-time of 10–100 microseconds when it is insensitive to further ionizing events. This is followed by a recovery time (approaching 1 ms) during which any further event would produce a smaller but gradually increasing pulse size as these space charge effects due to the outward-moving positive ion sheath are progressively reduced. An electronic circuit is often employed to define the total dead-time and recovery time precisely. This circuit prevents the registration of a pulse until a fixed time after a previous pulse, and is set at a value greater than the longest likely dead-time effect due to positive ion collection.

With a Geiger counter very little additional pulse amplification is necessary before the pulse-discriminator stage.

2.4 Pulse amplification and pulse-shaping

The magnitude of the current pulses from ion chambers and proportional counters can be measured using a high-input-impedance amplifier to measure the change in voltage Q_e/C_D induced in the total detector capacitance C_D. This capacitance will include any connector-lead capacitance which will be in parallel with the detector. This dependence of output signal on input capacitance can be avoided by the use of an input circuit arrangement with a *virtual earth* input, with negative capacitative feedback between output and input; this gives an output proportional to the time-integral of current flow into the input terminals. This current integrator is often referred to as a *charge-sensitive* amplifier and the schematic circuit is shown in Fig. 20.4. The output pulse is largely independent of C_D, provided $C_f \times G$ (= capacitative input impedance of amplifier) is very much larger than C_D.

The first few stages have a gain G of about 1000 times and the output, which is in opposite phase to the input, is fed back to the input via a feed-back capacitor C_f. The input terminal of the amplifier remains virtually at the same (usually earth) potential and the pulse current flow $[I(t)]$ from the detector can be regarded as flowing directly into C_f. An exact analysis for the voltage signal at B is:

$$V_B(t) = \frac{G}{C_D + (1+G)C_f} \int I(t)\, dt.$$

and if $G \gg 1$ and $G\,C_f \gg C_D$ this simplifies to

$$V_B(t) = \frac{1}{C_f} \int I(t)\, dt.$$

This is a *step-function* pulse rising to a final value $V_B = Q_e/C_e$, where Q_e is the total effective charge flowing from the electrode to the other. Thus the signal at B is independent of the detector capacitance. This signal is still a step function which can be modified by *pulse-shaping* networks to produce a unipolar pulse. The most common pulse-shaping networks are the simple *differentiating* and *integrating* circuits shown in Fig. 20.4. If the pulse-shaping time constant $(T_s = C_s R_s)$ is long compared with the rise-time of the step function signal at B (and this rise-time is equal to the collection-time of the ionization charge in the detector), the final output signal shown diagrammatically in Fig. 20.4 is given by: [1,2]

$$V_c(t) = A_0 V_B(t) \cdot \frac{t}{T_s} \exp\left(-\frac{t}{T_s}\right)$$

The peak amplitude of the output signal V_{max}, for T_s several times greater than the charge collection time, is:

$$V_{max} = \frac{A_0 Q_e}{C_f} \cdot \frac{1}{e}$$

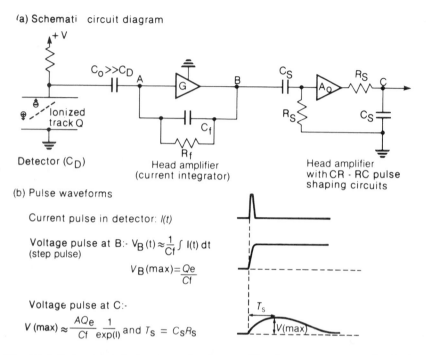

(a) Schematic circuit diagram

(b) Pulse waveforms

Current pulse in detector: $I(t)$

Voltage pulse at B:- $V_B(t) \approx \frac{1}{Cf} \int I(t)\, dt$
(step pulse)

$$V_B(max) = \frac{Qe}{Cf}$$

Voltage pulse at C:-

$$V(max) \approx \frac{AQe}{Cf}\, \frac{1}{exp(l)} \text{ and } T_S = C_S R_S$$

Fig. 20.4 Current-integrator type of pulse amplifier for measurement of radiation detector current pulses

and this peak amplitude is reached after a time $t_m = T_s$, sometimes referred to as the *peaking-time*. In a simple gas ionization chamber with parallel plate electrodes, the effective charge Q_e moving from one electrode to the other is $q \times d_a/d$, where q is the primary ionization produced and d_a is the mean distance through which this charge moves before the charge is collected on the anode. The signal amplitude is thus not proportional to the primary ionization or energy absorbed. In the proportional counter, where the signal is due to the multiplied positive charge (Mq) moving away from the anode to the cathode, the signal is proportional to the primary ionization and hence to the radiation energy deposited in the counter. The discriminator unit is a circuit which is only operated or triggered by a pulse greater than a preset level. This level is set so that only the required radiation pulses are subsequently counted. The detector/amplifier system must be designed so that the required signals are larger than spurious signals from electrical noise in the amplifier or from signals due to unwanted radiation. For example, alpha particles will in general produce larger signals than beta particles, so that a single discriminator unit can be used to count alpha particles in the presence of beta radiation. More sophisticated systems are required, e.g. multiple discriminator units or pulse-amplitude analysers, in order to register pulses within a particular amplitude range in the presence of other pulses which are outside (above or below the range). A whole spectrum of pulse amplitudes can of course be analysed and registered by the use of a multichannel pulse-amplitude analyser.

2.5 Sources of error in radiation energy measurement with gas proportional-counter systems

Inhomogeneities in detector response affecting the relation between primary ionization and final shaped output pulse from the amplifier will cause a spread in the distribution of output pulse sizes. Thus variation in anode wire diameter introduces a variation in pulse output size, but this can usually be kept to within a few per cent of the average. Distortion of the electric field at the ends of the counter where the anode wire is supported may produce larger effects, but these can be eliminated if the radiation to be measured is prevented from reaching these regions of the counter, e.g. by shielding or collimation of incident radiation. In the case of energy measurement of X- or gamma rays, errors will arise if the secondary electrons produced in the counter gas strike the cathode wall before dissipating all their energy within the gas. This effect can be reduced by using a larger diameter counter and/or a higher gas pressure. This cathode wall effect limits the use of gas proportional counters for X- and gamma ray measurement to a maximum energy of about 100 keV.

In addition to these geometrical factors there are two other sources of spread in output pulse distribution. These are (1) random fluctuations in the number of positive ions and electrons produced by the absorption of a given amount of particle energy, and (2) electrical noise in the amplifier system.

2.5.1 *Fluctuation in number of ions produced*

For a given medium the average particle energy dissipated per ion pair produced has a near constant value (W) over a wide range of particle energy, so that the number of ion pairs N produced by absorption of E eV is given by $N = E/W$. The process of ion formation is partially random, and there is a fluctuation in N which has a Gaussian distribution. The root mean square deviation in N is found experimentally to be given by:

$$(\overline{\Delta N^2})^{1/2} = (FN)^{1/2}.$$

and the full width at half maximum amplitude of the Gaussian distribution is $2.4 \times (\overline{\Delta N^2})^{1/2}$.

For counter gases the factor F varies in the range 0.1 to 0.5, and W is about 30 eV per ion pair. There is also a fluctuation in the gas multiplication factor M in gas proportional counters, and this fluctuation has the effect of adding a further variance factor $b(\approx 0.5)$ to the factor F.

Fluctuation in ion pairs produced and fluctuation in M are the dominant causes of spread in pulse-amplitude distribution in gas proportional counter systems, and the full width at half maximum (f.w.h.m.) of this distribution is a measure of the energy resolution of the system.

$$\Delta E \text{ (f.w.h.m.)} = 2.4 \, (\overline{\Delta N^2})^{\frac{1}{2}} W$$
$$= 2.4 \, (F + b)^{\frac{1}{2}} \, (WE)^{\frac{1}{2}}.$$

Thus for 10 keV X-rays the energy resolution (f.w.h.m.) possible with a gas proportional counter, $F + b = 0.6$, is:

$$\Delta E \text{ (f.w.h.m.)} = 2.4 \times (0.6 \times 30 \times 10^4)^{\frac{1}{2}}$$
$$= 1018 \text{ eV},$$

or the percentage resolution

$$\frac{\Delta E \text{ (f.w.h.m.)}}{E} \times 100 = 10\%$$

at $E = 10$ keV X-ray energy. The lower limit of detection of photons of X-ray energy in a proportional counter is set by electrical noise in the amplifier system. All sources of electrical noise are discussed in the appendix. For gas proportional counters, electrical noise generated in the first stage of the pulse amplifier (usually called amplifier *shot noise*) is the dominant noise effect. Noise generated by resistors or by currents in the amplifier input circuit, including the detector itself, can be made negligible by comparison.

The r.m.s. value of amplifier shot noise, can be expressed in terms of an equivalent noise charge in the counter:

$$Q_{n_s} = \frac{A \cdot C_D}{(T_s)^{1/2}} \text{ ion pairs.}$$

The appendix gives an expression for the constant A in terms of known parameters, for a low-noise amplifier, and also numerical data in the form of a nomograph. Thus,

$$Q_{n_s} = 4 \times \frac{C_D}{(T_s)^{1/2}} \text{ ion pairs.}$$

for C_D in picofarads and T_s in microseconds.

If spurious counts from this electrical noise are to be avoided, a pulse-amplitude discriminator following the pulse amplifier must be set at a level equivalent to an input signal of at least $5 \times Q_{n_s}$.
(Noise count will then be much less than one per second.)

Thus, the limiting radiation energy detectable in a gas proportional counter (E_L) is given by:

$$E_L \times \frac{M}{W} = 5 \times 4 \times \frac{C_D}{T^{1/2}}.$$

Thus, for $W = 30$ eV per ion pair, gas multipliation $M = 300$, and $C_D = 10$ pf,

$$E_L = 20 \text{ eV}.$$

3 Gas ionization detector designs and uses

3.1 Mean-current gas ionization chambers

Mean-current gas ionization chambers find many applications, particularly in the measurement of gamma or neutron radiation, if the mean rate of ionization within the detector is sufficient to produce a mean direct current large enough to be measured directly using a suitable d.c. amplifier. It is important in these applications that the response of the detector to the radiation to be measured is very large compared with the response to any other type of radiation which may be present. An important example is the measurement of gamma-radiation flux, and also of dose-rate.

If the ionization chamber has reasonably thick walls most particle-radiation (e.g. alpha and beta particles) will be absorbed and will produce no response. Figure 20.5 shows a cutaway drawing of a mean-current ion chamber with concentric cylindrical electrodes with hemispherical ends. The electrodes are made from a conducting plastic material with a mean atomic number very near to that of animal tissue, and the chamber is filled with dry air and the outer aluminium case sealed off with the air at a suitable pressure (e.g. 1–5 bar). The chamber is thus tissue-equivalent as regards gamma radiation and the mean current measured can be intepreted in terms of gamma dose-rate in, say, mrad/h. (For an air filling 1 mrad/h $\equiv 10^{-13}$ A/litre at n.t.p.) A positive potential (few hundred volts) is applied to the outer *polarizing* electrode, which is mounted on an insulating end plate. The collector electrode is not mounted directly to the same insulating plate, but is mounted on to a *guard* electrode via a high-quality insulator, and the guard electrode is electrically connected to the outer screening case, which is at earth potential. This arrangement has the following important advantages.

1. There is no leakage current path between the polarizing electrode and the collector electrode; the collector electrode is connected to the input of a d.c. amplifier which has a potential equal to or very close to *earth* potential, so that there is little or no voltage difference across the insulator on which the collector electrode is mounted, and hence minimal spurious or leakage current in the input circuit.

2. The use of the guard electrode defines the sensitive volume of the chamber precisely and ensures that there is an adequate electric field at all points within the sensitive volume.

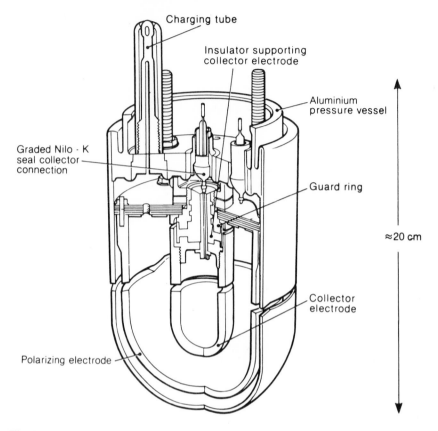

Charging tube

Insulator supporting
collector electrode

Aluminium
pressure vessel

Graded Nilo - K
seal collector
connection

Guard ring

≈20 cm

Collector
electrode

Polarizing electrode

Fig. 20.5 Mean current ion chamber, for gamma dose-rate measurement in the range
1 mrad/h to 1 rad/h

The first stage or even the whole of the d.c. amplifier may be mounted directly on the end bulk-head of the aluminium case, thus avoiding the use of cable to conduct very small currents to the d.c. amplifier.

The same design concepts may be used for d.c. ionization chambers for the measurement of neutron flux, for use in nuclear reactor control. In these designs the chambers are made entirely of metal with ceramic insulators and lead-through seals to ensure resistance to radiation damage and to enable them to be operated at elevated temperatures; they are coated with a thin layer (1 mg/cm²) of boron (enriched in ^{10}B). Chambers with a boron-coated area of 560 cm² have a sensitivity of about 5×10^{-15} A n^{-1} cm² s (for thermal neutrons). They are mounted outside the reactor core and used for reactor control with neutron fluxes ranging from about 10^3 to 10^{10} n cm^{-2} s^{-1}. These chambers have a gamma sensitivity of about 5×10^{-12} A rad^{-1} h, i.e. equivalent to a neutron flux of 1000 n cm^{-2} s^{-1}, but it is usually possible to ensure that the neutron flux to gamma dose-rate ratio is such that the gamma response is insignificant compared with the neutron response.

3.2 **Pulse-type gas ionization chambers**

Pulse-type gas ionization chambers which do not make use of gas multiplication are nowadays almost exclusively limited to use as neutron detectors. They are made sensitive to neutrons by coating the cathode electrode with fissile material, usually ^{235}U in the form of the oxide U_3O_8. Neutrons absorbed by ^{235}U produce short-range high-energy fission fragments, which produce a large ionization charge in the gas. Although this appears to be a limited application, it is an extremely important one for measurement of neutrons in very high gamma backgrounds, as in reactor physics measurements. The detectors are constructed from metal (usually stainless steel) for the electrodes and outer case, and use high-purity alumina ceramics as insulator materials. Designs range in size from 6 mm diameter (for flux scanning in materials-testing reactors) to 75 mm for high-sensitivity detectors (1 count per second per unit neutron flux) for measurement in reactor control.[45] Examples of designs capable of being used up to temperature of 500 °C are shown in Figs 20.6 and 20.7.

Another important feature of use of this fission counter type of neutron detector is that the signal due to individual neutrons is very large compared with that caused by a gamma event (from a secondary electron). The pulse amplitude ratios are of the order 10^4 and the pulse duration can be very small (50–100 ns). This means that a very large number (e.g. greater than 10^3) of gamma events can occur during a single pulse-duration event (100 ns) and the 'pile-up' effect of the multiple gamma pulses is still less than a single fission pulse instigated by neutron absorption. As a practical example, large, high-sensitivity fission-type neutron detectors, such as those shown in Fig. 20.7, can be used to measure low neutron flux levels in the presence of very high gamma-radiation levels (e.g. up to 10^6 rad/h) using pulse-amplitude discrimination to distinguish and discriminate neutron pulses from the gamma pile-up pulses, which in the example quoted would appear as very high-level *current noise*.

The nature of the gas filling is important in pulse-type gas counters. The construction of detectors must ensure that no electronegative gases are present as impurities in the counter gas, and that no such gases are released subsequently from the internal walls. The free electrons, whose transit gives rise to the short-duration current pulses and associated fast-rising induced-voltage signals, are readily captured on electronegative atoms or molecules, which then become slow-moving ions that are not observed or registered in the associated fast pulse-amplifier. Another important feature of the gas filling, which is also important in gas proportional counters using gas multiplication, is the electron velocity under the influence of an applied field. Electrons do not exhibit a constant mobility in gases, i.e. a *drift velocity* directly proportional to the applied field. The drift velocity increases initially with applied field divided by gas pressure (X/P), and this increase may be considerably enhanced in inert gases (e.g. argon) by adding a few per cent by volume of a polyatomic gas such as CO_2, CH_4, or N_2. Argon–N_2 mixtures are

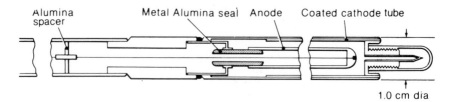

Fig. 20.6 Low-sensitivity high-temperature fission counter, for reactor control application up to 500°C operation[5] ^{235}U-coated cathode area ≈ 8 cm^2; thermal neutron
sensitivity $\approx 8 \times 10^{-3}$ counts/s per neutron cm^{-2} s^{-1}

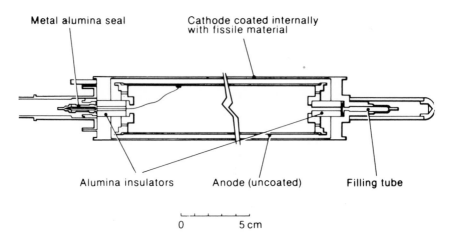

Fig. 20.7 High sensitivity high-temperature fission counter for reactor control application up to 500°C[5]. ^{235}U-coated cathode area 500 cm^2 (25 cm long cathode);
thermal neutron sensitivity 0.5 counts/s per neutron cm^{-2} s^{-1}

used in fission-counter applications where CO_2 or CH_4 may dissociate slowly
with time in high-gamma-radiation fields or at high temperatures. Figure
20.8 shows the drift velocity for electrons versus X/P for Argon with methane
(CH_4) added at various levels up to 30 per cent. Although much higher drift
velocities may be obtained with the addition of CO_2 or CH_4, it will be seen
that the drift velocity begins to decrease again at still higher levels of X/P. A
feature of argon-nitrogen mixtures is that for nitrogen at levels up to 5 per
cent, the drift velocity increases to the region of 3 cm/μs for $X/P = 1.1 \times
10^3$ V cm^{-1} bar^{-1} and remains reasonably constant for X/P up to three times
this value.

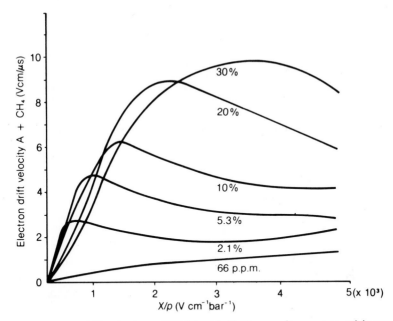

Fig. 20.8 Electron drift velocity vs X/P (electric field per unit gas pressure) in argon methane mixtures; per cent fractions refer to amount of methane in mixture; 1 bar = 10^5pa

3.3 Gas proportional counters for X-ray detection and spectrometry

The basic requirements for high-efficiency and high-resolution X-ray proportional counters are a very thin window entry for the X-rays (to minimize X-ray absorption in the window before reaching the gas) and a gas with a high atomic number Z, so that a large proportion of the incident X-ray quanta are completely absorbed by the photoelectric process and transfer the whole of their energy to secondary ionizing electrons. For spectrometry a further requirement is that the path lengths of secondary electrons within the gas are small compared with the counter dimensions, so that the electron energy produces ionization in the gas and the output signal is consequently proportional to the incident X-ray energy. Thus in a pulse-amplitude spectrum, a given X-ray energy produces pulses which are uniformly distributed about a mean value. If the counter dimensions are too small, a proportion of the secondary electrons strike the counter walls, and only a fraction of the available energy produces ionization in the gas. The resultant pulse could have any value lying between zero and the *peak* amplitude. There is thus a continuum of the pulses at energies below those in the peak pulse distribution, and these may interfere with the measurement and resolution of lower-energy X-rays when measurements are made on a range of X-ray emissions. Gas proportional counters with 50 mm diameter cathodes and with xenon gas fillings at 2 bar pressure can be used for X-ray spectro-metry up to energies of about 30 keV without serious problems arising from this effect of a continuum in the observed spectra.

Figure 20.9 illustrates a series of X-ray proportional counters, developed at Harwell, which exploit developments in brazing technology between beryllium and stainless steel.[6] Beryllium has the lowest atomic number of the durable metal elements and therefore has a low X-ray absorption co-efficient. Beryllium tube, 0.25 mm and 0.12 mm thick, is used in the cylindrical counters with *thin-window* access over 360 °. A second basic geometry, a thin end-window detector is also shown.

Figure 20.10 gives details of the detection efficiency and resolution of a 25 mm diameter cylindrical counter filled with xenon to a pressure of 2 bar, for X-ray energies ranging from 1 keV to 100 keV.

These X-ray gas proportional counters can thus deal with measurements of the characteristic X-rays of nearly all elements from the heavy actinide elements ($Z > 92$) with X-rays in the 15–20 keV range to Na ($Z = 11$) with its characteristic 1 keV X-ray. Proportional counters may also be used for detection of still lower-energy X-rays (e.g. in X-ray crystal diffractometers), but require still thinner windows, e.g. of thin plastic material; such counters

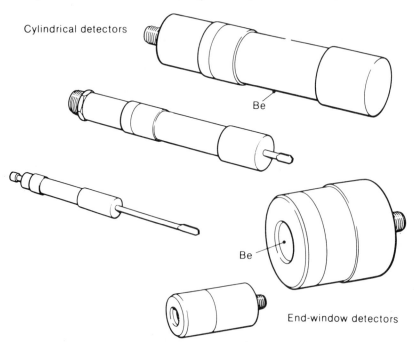

Cylindrical detectors

Be

Be

End-window detectors

Fig. 20.9 X-ray proportional counters; stainless steel construction with thin beryllium *windows*[6]
Cylindrical: 50 mm to 12 mm dia. minimum wall thickness (Be) 0.25 mm to 0.12 mm
End window: window area 750 mm², thickness 0.12 mm (Be)
              window area 125 mm², thickness 0.025 mm (Be)

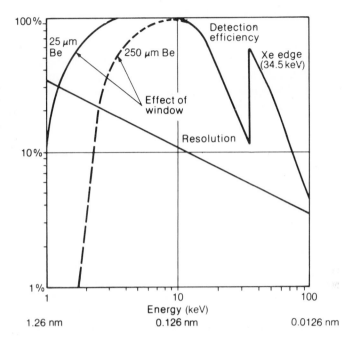

Fig. 20.10 X-ray detection efficiency and energy resolution vs X-ray energy for a 25 mm dia. proportional counter; gas filling 90% xenon + quench gas, at a pressure of 2 bar

cannot be sealed off permanently, but are used with a continuous flow of the gas mixture at a pressure greater than that existing outside the thin-window entry, to ensure purity of the counter gas. At the lower energies, e.g. 5 keV and less, the gas proportional counter is being superseded by the cooled semiconductor counter because of the better energy resolution available.

Sealed gas proprtional counters can have advantages over cooled semi-conductors counters in terms of larger windows and hence sensitivity and simplicity in use, viz. simpler amplifier systems and avoidance of liquid-nitrogen cryostat systems. These advantages often outweigh the better energy resolution available with semiconductor detectors, for both experimental and industrial use in hostile environments.

Analysis of alloys and compounds, using radioisotope X-ray sources to excite the characteristic X-rays of elements, which are then assayed using X-ray detectors and pulse-amplitude analysers, is now achieving widespread application.

3.4 Multi-wire gas proportional counters for X-ray spectrometry

Proportional counters consisting of an array of thin wires mounted in a flat plane parallel to and within flat cathode electrodes were developed initially to provide a large sensitive area. They have also been developed in the form of three (or more) layers of counters to provide means of rejecting spurious pulses from long-range particles such as cosmic rays. Figures 20.11 and 20.12 show schematically the basic principles of a single-layer multi-wire counter and a three-layer detector system incorporating anti-coincidence schemes for rejecting cosmic days. These types of counter require careful design and manufacture because the anode wires must maintain the same spacing with respect to each other and also to the cathode, within close limits; otherwise the electric field becomes distorted and changes the counter multiplication and other characteristics locally. The three-layer type of detector with anti-coincidence schemes is used as the detector section of an X-ray spectrometer system used in space satellites for study of X-ray emissions from distant galaxies.

A different variation of a multi-wire counter for X-ray spectrometry incorporating anti-coincidence detection to eliminate the effect of cosmic rays and long-range secondary electrons from high-energy gamma-ray background radiation, is shown in Fig. 20.13. This was designed to provide a large area detector for the low-level measurement of ^{239}Pu in the lungs.[7] The counter has overall dimensions of $30 \times 30 \times 10$ cm and is constructed in three main sections, which can be operated independently (to give information on any localization of ^{239}Pu in the lung area) and still share the same anti-coincidence counter system. The counter has a thin mylar window and uses a gas-flow technique to achieve gas purity, usually with an argon–10 per cent methane mixture. The effect of background radiation is reduced as far as possible by placing the whole apparatus and the subject to be monitored in a well-shielded room. This type of counter is used with a number of large-volume NaI(Tl) scintillation counters (for measurement of higher-energy gamma emitters) for *whole-body* monitoring.

^{239}Pu in the lungs is detected by virtue of the emission of uranium X-rays (energies 13.6–20.2 keV) which are emitted following 4 per cent of the disintegrations of ^{239}Pu. None of these X-rays can penetrate the bone of the rib cage or sternum, and only about 3 per cent of X-rays emitted in the lung will penetrate a chest wall of 3 cm thickness. Hence the need for reduction of spurious counter response from background radiation of all kinds. The techniques of pulse rise-time discrimination may be used to distinguish between X-rays of 13–20 keV energy, which after absorption in the argon gas produce secondary electron tracks 2–3 mm in length, and longer-range particles (secondary electrons or cosmic rays), which may deposit about the same energy in a long track. The primary ionization from the X-rays arrives at the anode within a short time interval and the pulse response time is governed by the counter design parameters (wire diameter, applied voltage, and gas filling). The primary ionization from a long track at an angle to the anode wire arrives over a longer period, and this lengthens the final effective pulse rise-time. Electronic circuits can be used to reject pulses with rise-times longer than some preset value, and this reduces pulses due to background radiation not already rejected by the anti-coincidence techniques.

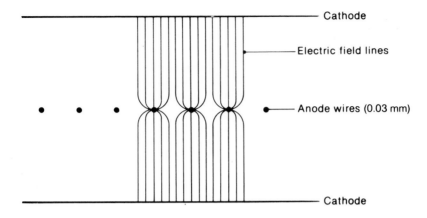

Fig. 20.11 Multi-wire proportional counter with flat plane cathodes (metal sheets, wires or wire mesh) Anode wires spaced 1–5 mm depending on counter size

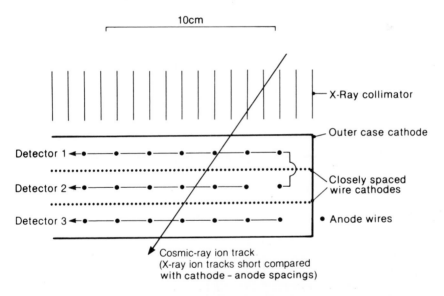

Fig. 20.12 Three layer multi-wire proportional counter system, for X-ray spectrometry with cosmic ray rejection. Counts in detectors 1 and 2 only registered as X-rays if not in time-coincidence. Cosmic-ray tracks originating in detector 2 can also be rejected since they produce time-coincident counts in detectors 2 and 3.

Figure 20.14 shows the X-ray spectrum obtained using a collimated source of ^{239}Pu. The different X-ray energies can be resolved, thus demonstrating the energy resolution capabilities of this type of counter. The energy spectrum from a subject with ^{239}Pu in the lungs, or a simulated source of the same nature, does not show this fine structure (viz. f.w.h.m. 1.5 keV at 13.6 keV). The spectrum lines are broadened by scattering of the primary X-ray

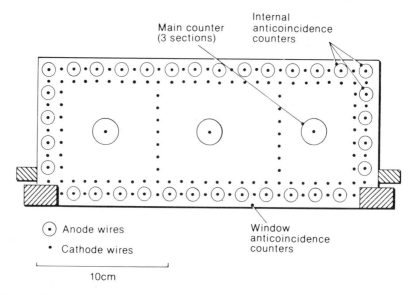

Fig. 20.13 Counter for low-level measurement of ^{239}Pu in lungs. Section of the proportional counter showing the multi-wire assembly[7]

emissions in passing through the body tissue, and energy discrimination is limited to wider bands, e.g. a 13–20 keV band.

When all precautions mentioned above are taken into account, the background count can be reduced to about 2 counts per minute. The derived minimum detectable activity for a subject of average build is 8 nCi of ^{239}Pu, for a 1-hour measurement; this is about half the maximum permissible lung burden.

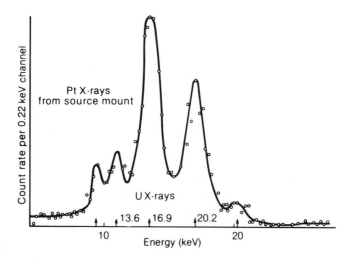

Fig. 20.14 X-ray spectrum from collimated source of ^{239}Pu, measured with counter illustrated in Fig. 20.13[7]

3.5 Neutron-sensitive gas proportional counters with $^{10}BF_3$ or ^3He gas fillings

Proportional counters for the detection of neutrons may be filled with BF_3 gas, the boron being highly enriched in the ^{10}B isotope which has a high atomic cross-section (3770×10^{-24} cm²) for capture of thermal neutrons and immediate decay to Li and He nuclei with kinetic energy of 2.4 MeV (see §1.2). Figure 20.15 shows some details of the design of a cylindrical counter for neutron counting using BF_3 gas. Special precautions in design and manufacture are necessary to achieve and maintain good counting characteristics.[8]

The count-rate versus amplifier attenuation characteristics are shown in Fig. 20.16 for a 25 mm diameter counter filled with BF_3 to a pressure of 0.5 bar. The sensitivity of this counter is about 3 counts/s for each thermal neutron cm² s^{-1}. The counter is operated with the amplifier attenuation set on the plateau region, but below the position where amplifier noise or possible gamma pile-up might produce spurious pulses. Counters of the same basic design are made in sizes ranging from 6 mm diameter and a few centimetres long up to 50 mm diameter and 1 m long, and are used in nuclear materials assay applications and for a wide variety of experiments in nuclear science and reactor physics. Sensitivities range from 0.01 counts/s per unit thermal nuetron flux, in short-length 6 mm dia. counters to 200 counts/per unit thermal neutron flux, in long 50 mm dia. counters, and are proportional to sensitive volume and BF_3 gas pressure.

An alternative gas filling for a neutron-sensitive gas proportional counter is the helium-3 isotope, used with a small percentage of CO_2 to stabilize the counting characteristics. Again, these counters are made in sizes from 6 mm diameter to 50 mm diameter. They have the advantage of providing a somewhat higher sensitivity since the cross-section per atom for the $^3He(n,p)$ reaction is 5330×10^{-24} cm² and it can be used in counters at higher gas pressures. (There are practical difficulties in filling counters with BF_3 at pressures greater than atmospheric and maintaining long-term good performance.) ^3He filled counters of a given size, though more sensitive to neutrons, have less discrimination against the effects of gamma pile-up in

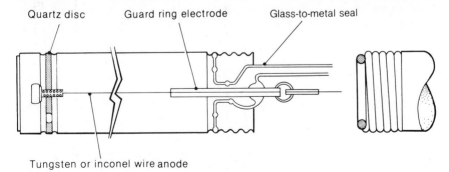

Fig. 20.15 Neutron-sensitive boron tri-fluoride (BF_3) proportional counter. Cathode dia. 25 mm, anode wire dia. 0.05 mm. Similar design uses for 6 mm, 12 mm and 50 mm dia. counters[8]. Counter body—high purity oxygen free copper

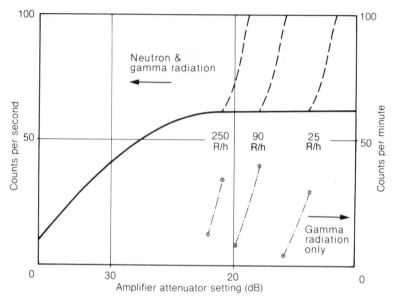

Fig. 20.16 Effect of high gamma radiation levels on neutron response of BF₃ filled proportional counter [8]. Counter 12 mm dia. × 150 mm long. BF₃ gas pressure 0.5 bar. CR–RC pulse-shaping time constant $0.16\,\mu\mathrm{sec}$.

high gamma radiation fields. This is due to the lower energy of the ^{3}He(n,p) reaction which releases particles with an energy of 0.77 MeV compared with 2.4 MeV for the ^{10}B(n, α) reaction.

3.6 Multi-wire gas proportional counters for particle position-sensing

A multi-wire proportional counter with a single plane of anode wires, between flat parallel cathodes, and with each wire connected to a separate amplifier may be used to determine the position of incidence of an incoming particle.

Figure 20.11 shows a schematic diagram of such a counter, which may have anode wire spacings as close as 1 mm for small detectors (100 × 100 mm) and 3–4 mm in very large chambers (5 × 5 m). The spatial resolution can be better than the wire spacing if account is taken of relative signals between adjacent wires. The amplifiers used in such applications are very simple systems, not requiring a very high stability or very low noise characteristics. Two-dimensional position sensing may be achieved either by having two systems similar to Fig. 20.11 placed orthogonally to each other, or by making measurements on cathode strips, again placed orthogonally to the anode wires.

The development of these types of chambers to provide high resolution in space and time was originated by Charpak, who has reviewed developments of the last decade mainly in relation to their applications in high-energy physics.[9]

The general principles of proportional counters with simple cylindrical geometry and with multi-wire arrays are described in the book by P. Rice-Evans listed in the *Suggestions for further reading*. He also deals with the applications of multi-wire gas detectors for nuclear physics studies. These include gas counters used in the spark discharge mode, for three-dimensional visualization of ionizing particle tracks.

3.7 Geiger-Müller counters

The mode of operation of Geiger counters has been described in §2. This form of counter played an important role in the early stages of nuclear studies, and has continued to find a wide range of applications. The essential attraction and advantage of this form of detector is its simplicity of construction, and provision of a very large electrical signal requiring only the simplest form of pulse amplifier in the associated electronic equipment.

The disadvantages are that it gives no direct information on particle energy and fails to distinguish between different forms of radiation, except in so far as the outer envelope may absorb the less-penetrating forms. The rate of counting is also limited because of the comparatively long dead-time ($10-200\,\mu s$) after a counting event, due to space-charge effects, before a subsequent event may be detected. Nevertheless there are still many applications for detection of gamma rays and cosmic rays and also, on a more limited scale, of beta rays. The rate-of-counting limitation can often be overcome by choice of size of counter. Most counters have cylindrical coaxial electrode structures and these can vary in size from a few mm in diameter and 10 mm long for moderately high-level radiation intensity measurement to 50 mm diameter and 2 m long, for measurements of low radiation levels. Applications of small- and large-size counters arise in radiological protection instruments. In smaller-size counters, e.g. up to 20 mm dia. × 100 mm long, the use of alcohol as a quenching agent may reduce the useful life unduly. The self-quenching action involving dissociation of the alcohol molecules eventually leads to deterioration of the counter as the alcohol is used up (e.g. 10^9 counts total). Bromine or chlorine may also be used as self-quenching gases with the advantage that after dissociation into separate atoms they can eventually recombine to form molecular bromine and chlorine (Br_2 and Cl_2). A longer counting lifetime may thus be achieved.

4 Semiconductor radiation detectors

4.1 Introduction

The most widely used forms of semiconductor detectors can be regarded as solid-state ionization chambers, in which ionizing radiation produces electrons and electron–hole pairs, which can be collected if suitable electrodes are fitted to the semiconductor material. An important difference from gas ionization chambers is that the positive electron-holes have a high mobility, comparable with that of electrons, so that the whole ionization charge (positive and negative) can be collected quickly and a short pulse signal proportional to the radiation energy absorbed can be obtained. Semiconductor detectors, like other solid-state detectors such as scintillators, can provide a much greater total absorption of incident radiation than a gas detector because of their greater density. This enables them to be used for gamma ray and X-ray measurements with a high efficiency at much greater energies.

4.2 Pulse response in semiconductor radiation detectors

Ionization in solid-state ionization detectors takes the form of creation of electron–hole pairs and, as in the case of gas ionization detectors, the aim is to collect these positive and negative charges on electrodes (cathodes and anodes) by applying a suitable voltage. It is only in very pure insulating or semiconductor materials that the electron–hole pairs can be collected before charge trapping and eventual recombination occurs at defect or impurity centres in the crystal lattice.

The only two materials currently available in single-crystal form which are suitable for making large detectors are silicon and germanium. Electron–hole carrier lifetimes in these materials can be much greater than a few milliseconds. Both positive and negative carriers have a high enough mobility for the collection time in quite large structures (100 cm^3) to be in the microsecond region. In small detectors the collection time may be a few tens of nanoseconds. Since both carriers can be collected rapidly, the output signal, even with fast amplifiers, is proportional to the total charge collection across the whole electrode distance, and the signal is thus proportional to the radiation energy deposited. A current-integrator type of pulse amplifier followed by CR–RC pulse-shaping circuits as described in §2.4 and shown in Fig. 20.4 may be used to produce a unipolar pulse output from the amplifier prior to pulse-amplitude discrimination, or analysis. More sophisticated pulse-processing systems, which can exploit more completely the potential energy resolution available with semiconductor detectors, will be described briefly later in this section.

The energy required to produce an electron–hole pair is only 3.62–3.79 eV for Si (at 300 K and 77 K respectively) and 2.94 eV for Ge (at 77 K), both much lower than the 30 eV in gases. The total number of electron–hole pairs for a given particle energy absorbed is therefore much higher than for gases, and the statistical fluctuations become a smaller fraction of the collected charge. This is a basic reason for semiconductor detectors yielding a better energy resolution than gas detectors. Silicon is used for particle and X-radiation, but its low atomic number ($Z = 14$) makes it useless for higher-energy gamma spectrometry. Germanium ($Z = 32$) used in large-volume detectors (250 cm³) provides high-resolution spectrometry and moderate efficiency for gamma rays up to about 2 MeV.

4.3 General physical principles of semiconductor detectors

The nature of the contact to the semiconductor material is vital to the construction of satisfactory detectors. If ohmic contacts were made to opposite sides of a slice of even the highest-purity silicon or germanium currently available, the thermally generated carrier densities would result in mean currents of hundreds of microamperes with 100 v/cm applied. The resulting current noise would mask the signals achieved by collection of charge produced by a single ionizing particle.

These difficulties are overcome by the use of junction contacts. To understand the reasons for this it is convenient to consider the simplified energy-band-level diagrams for electrons and holes in pure semiconductor materials, and in materials containing some impurity atoms, shown in Fig. 20.17. Figure 20.17(a) represents the pure material, with a lower band or range of energies for the valence electrons bound to the host atoms of the crystal lattice. Above this valence band there is a range or band of forbidden energies for electrons (band gap of magnitude E_g eV). In order to release electrons from their bound state and make them free to migrate in an electric field, they must be given extra energy, greater than E_g, to 'lift' them into the *allowed* range of energies constituting the conduction band. At absolute-zero temperature, all electrons are in the valence band and electrical conductivity

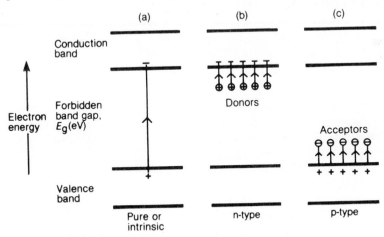

Fig. 20.17 Energy-level diagrams for electrons in semiconductors:
(a) Pure semiconductor. Conducts of thermal agitation can raise electrons from valence to conduction band levels
(b) Material with donor impurities. Conducts if thermal agitation can raise electrons from valence to acceptor band levels
(c) Material with acceptor impurities. Conducts if thermal agitation can raise electrons from valence to acceptor band levels

is zero. As the temperature is raised, increasing numbers of electrons can acquire enough energy from thermal excitation to break away from the crystal atoms and become available for conduction.The 'vacancies' left behind in the valence band (corresponding to electrons raised to the conduction band) may be filled up by an electron from a neighbouring atom and so on. In effect the vacancies behave as mobile net positive charges and are known as *positive-holes*. They have mobilities (μ_+) about half that of the free-electron mobilities (μ_-). Pure semiconductors have equal numbers of positive and negative charge carriers. At a given temperature the densities of these carriers, $n = p$, are given by:

$$n_i^2 = np = 2.3 \times 10^{31}\, T^3 \exp{(E_g/kT)}\ \text{cm}^{-3},$$

where, T is the absolute temperature in K and k is the Boltzmann constant in J K^{-1}.

Thus, for pure or intrinsic silicon $n_i = 1.6 \times 10^{10}$ charge carriers cm^{-3} corresponding to a resistivity ρ of $2.3 \times 10^5\,\Omega\,$cm ($\rho = 1/n_i e\,(\mu_+ + \mu_-)$).

Figures 20.17(b) and (c) represent the more usual practical case of a semiconductor material with impurity centres in the crystal lattice. At these centres the valence electrons of the impurity atoms can have energy values which fall within the forbidden band of the pure host material. Impurities with an extra valence electron in the outer shell compared with the host atoms, (e.g. phosphorus or arsenic etc. in silicon) can have valence electrons in narrow bands very close to the conduction band (e.g. about 0.05 eV below the lower edge—see Fig. 20.17(b)). Only a small amount of energy is required to ionize these impurity atoms and provide free electrons in the conduction band. Virtually all the impurity atoms are ionized by thermal agitation of the main crystal atoms even at reduced temperatures. Phosphorus impurity levels of 10^{15} per cm^3 in silicon (1 part in 10^9) will thus produce negative carrier (electron) densities of 10^{15} per cm^3 and a corresponding resistivity, $\rho\ (= \frac{1}{ne'\mu})$, of 5 Ω cm. Impurity centres with energy levels just below the conduction band and providing electrons as negative carriers are called *donor* centres, and material exhibiting conduction by electrons from such donors is called n-type material. The positively charged sites left behind do not provide net positive carriers, since the filling of these vacancies by valence electrons from the host material has a low probability, because the energies are in the forbidden band.

Impurity atoms with one electron fewer in the outer shell (e.g. boron or gallium in silicon) can have electron energy levels very close to and just above the upper limit of the valence energy band for silicon (see Fig. 20.17(c)). This electron deficiency at the impurity centre can be filled by a valence electron from a nearby silicon atom, thus creating a mobile positive-hole carrier in the silicon. These impurity centres (giving rise to hole conduction) are referred to as *acceptor* centres and, like the donor centres, they are not mobile after ionization but remain as fixed negative charges in the crystal lattice. Conductivity by positive carriers arising from acceptor impurities is referred to as *p-type* conduction and the material as p-type *doped*.

The relation $np = n_i^2$ also applies to the product of the electron and hole concentrations in a doped semiconductor, i.e. the product of electron and hole carrier concentrations remains constant over a wide range of doping levels and is equal to n_i^2. For n-type material with a donor concentration N_D (and $N_D \gg n_i$):

(1) the electron concentration, $n = N_D$, and

(2) the hole concentration $p = n_i^2/N_D$.

The diagrams of Fig. 20.18 indicate the carrier concentration distributions at an np *junction* between a heavily-doped n-type layer and a more lightly doped p-type material. With no applied bias a few free electrons diffuse across the junction from the n-type into the p-type region and holes diffuse from the p-type region into the n-type layer. The ionized donor and acceptor centres remain as fixed positive and negative charges, resulting in the charge and potential distributions shown. In equilibrium a self-adjusting potential barrier is created. If reverse bias voltage is applied to the junction (i.e. positive to the n-type layer) the effect is to drive free electrons away from the n-side to the p-side of the junction and free holes from the p-side to the n-side of the junction. The donor and acceptor sites remain as positive and negative fixed charge centres, with the charge distribution and resulting potential and electric field distributions as shown in Fig. 20.18. The depletion region, i.e. a region where the impurity centres are permanently ionized, exists in both the heavily doped n-type material and the lightly doped p-type side of the junction. There are equal fixed charges (of opposite sign) in these regions, and the width is therefore much greater in the p-type region, since the impurity-centre concentrations are lower here. This latter part of the depletion region is the main region of interest for nuclear radiation detection. It is equivalent to a region of perfect crystal where no carriers are generated thermally from impurity centres, but only from the valence band. (This is also the explanation of low current in a reverse-biased semiconductor junction diode: the current which does pass is due to thermal excitation from the valence band, from diffusion of carriers from the non-depleted regions contiguous with the depletion region, and also from surface leakage effects.) In practice a highly doped (p^{++}) contact is made to the p-type material on the opposite side to the n^{++}, p junction. Ionizing nuclear radiations passing through the depletion region will have sufficient energy to ionize the atoms of the main crystal lattice, i.e. produce mobile electron carriers in the conduction band and mobile positive-hole carriers in the valence band.

The width of the depletion region for the planar geometry of Fig. 20.18 can be calculated simply from Poisson's equation. If the donor concentration in the heavily doped n-type material is very much greater than the acceptor impurity concentration in the p-type material ($N_D \gg N_A$), then

$$\frac{d^2 V}{dx^2} = \frac{4\pi e}{K} \cdot N_A,$$

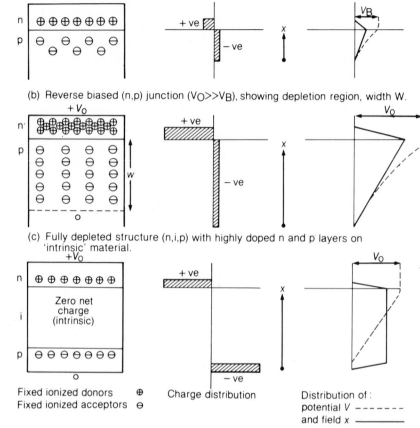

(a) (n,p) junction (n highly doped) in equilibrium with no applied voltage, V_B is junction barrier potential.

(b) Reverse biased (n,p) junction ($V_O \gg V_B$), showing depletion region, width W.

(c) Fully depleted structure (n,i,p) with highly doped n and p layers on 'intrinsic' material.

Fixed ionized donors   ⊕   Charge distribution   Distribution of :
Fixed ionized acceptors ⊖   potential V -------
                                                     and field x ————

Fig. 20.18 Semiconductor junction detectors, charge, potential and field distributions

where

V is electric potential,
X is distance,
K is the dielectric constant of the depleted semiconductor, and
e is the charge on the electron.

Integrating gives the electric field X, thus

$$X_x = \frac{dV}{dx} = \frac{4\pi e}{K} N_A x,$$

i.e. X is greatest at the junction and falls with a uniform gradient. Further integration gives the potential

$$V_x = \frac{2\pi e}{K} N_A x^2 \text{ (a parabolic distribution)}.$$

For a total applied voltage V the depletion width

$$W = \left(\frac{KV}{2\pi e N_A}\right)^{1/2}$$

The dielectric constant K is 12 for silicon and 16 for germanium. W may also be expressed in terms of the resistivity, ρ, of the higher-resistivity side of the junction, since $\rho = 1/N_A e \mu_+$, where μ_+ is the hole carrier mobility, i.e.

$$W = \left(\frac{KV}{2\pi}\right)^{1/2}(\mu_+\rho)$$

$$= 3.2 \times 10^5 (\rho V)^{1/2} \text{ cm for p-type silicon}$$

and

$$W = \left(\frac{KV}{2\pi}\right)^{1/2}(\mu_-\rho)$$

$$= 5.3 \times 10^5 (\rho V)^{1/2} \text{ cm for n-type silicon.}$$

The incremental capacitance of the detector per unit area $C = \mathrm{d}Q/\mathrm{d}V$; $\mathrm{d}Q$ ($= N_A e\, \mathrm{d}W$) is the additional charge to increase W by $\mathrm{d}W$. Thus,

$$C = \frac{\mathrm{d}Q}{\mathrm{d}W} \Big/ \frac{\mathrm{d}V}{\mathrm{d}W} = \frac{N_A eK}{4\pi N_A eW} = \frac{K}{4\pi W},$$

i.e. the same as for a parallel-plate capacitor.

Nomographs have been constructed for quick estimation of W for silicon junctions in terms of V and ρ (and impurity concentration) for p-type and n-type silicon. An example is shown in Fig. 20.19.

Fully depleted detectors with thin contacts on both sides of the semiconductor material may also be constructed. One contact is a junction (opposite type) contact as already discussed viz. n^{++} on p (high resistivity) and the back contact will be a p^{++} (highly doped and very low resistivity) layer. It is possible to operate with a voltage high enough to produce a finite field across the whole of the fully depleted structure provided that this field does not give rise to injection of carriers from the p^{++} region, leading to excessive mean current through the detector. Planar detectors of this type with fully depleted thickness ranging from a few tens of micrometers to several millimetres are used to measure the rate of energy loss $\mathrm{d}E/\mathrm{d}x$ (specific ionization) of ionizing particles in various nuclear studies.

The same principle may be used for making very thick detectors of Si or of Ge for measurement of total energy E. In these cases the base material used is intrinsic material, i.e. material with both donor and acceptor impurities present which balance or cancel each other out almost exactly. Lithium (Li) acts as a donor in silicon and germanium, and can be introduced by the lithium-ion drift process to compensate almost exactly the acceptor impurity centres in p-type material. In large volumes (up to 200 cm³ in cylindrical geometries) impurities can be compensated using the Li-ion-drift technique

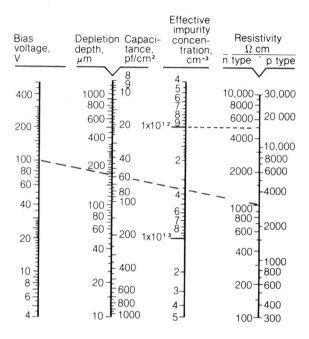

Fig. 20.19 Nomograph for the determination of the depletion layer thickness in a silicon detector

which adjusts the concentration of Li-doping to balance the p-type acceptor concentration. The process will automatically balance the level of impurity even though its concentration might vary throughout the specimen. Fully compensated material of this type is termed intrinsic-doped. Depletion layers produced in it have no net fixed charge, because there are equal numbers of ionized donor and acceptor centres, and the electric field is uniform. (See Fig. 20.18.)

4.4 Sources of error in radiation energy measurements with semiconductor detector systems

As with gas proportional counters, a variation in pulse amplitude may arise due to either inhomogeneities within the sensitive volume or distortions in the electric field leading to incomplete collection of the primary electron–hole pairs. Boundary-wall effects are not usually very significant. Statistical fluctuations in the number of primary electron-hole pairs produced provide an ultimate limitation on energy resolution, and the spread in pulse amplitude may be further increased by the effect of electrical noise in the detector–amplifier system. The magnitude of these effects is referred to in the discussion of detector designs and uses (§5). A further source of error in very high resolution systems, arising from the signal-processing system, is described in §5.6.

The appendix gives a more detailed discussion of statistical fluctuations in the pulse signals, and also of electrical noise, for all types of detector systems including semiconductors.

5 Semiconductor detector designs and uses

Figures 20.20 and 20.21 show diagrammatically the geometrical arrangement of junction and other contacts for

(1) various sizes of silicon planar detectors for alpha, beta or other particles,
(2) small-size silicon detectors for X-ray spectrometry,
(3) large planar,
(4) large coaxial geometry } Ge(Li) or high-purity Ge,
(5) large well-type coaxial.

5.1 Silicon Detectors for alpha, beta and other particle measurements

The photograph of Fig. 20.22 shows two Harwell designs for 25 mm diameter silicon detectors, mounted in stainless steel cases and used mainly for alpha detection and/or spectrometry in many systems. The junction and other contacts to the silicon follow the arrangements shown in Fig. 20.20(a), i.e.

(a) Alpha and/or beta particle detector. For mounting in steel case with wire connectors to back face. Entry face made light-tight by chromium coating

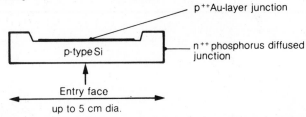

p^{++}Au-layer junction

p-type Si

n^{++} phosphorus diffused junction

Entry face
up to 5 cm dia.

(b) Small low-capacitance fully depleted detector, for use in vacuum cryostats for high resolution X-ray spectrometry

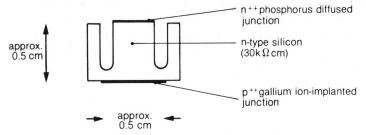

n^{++} phosphorus diffused junction

approx.
0.5 cm

n-type silicon
(30k Ω cm)

p^{++} gallium ion-implanted junction

approx.
0.5 cm

Fig. 20.20 Diagrams of construction of some silicon detectors

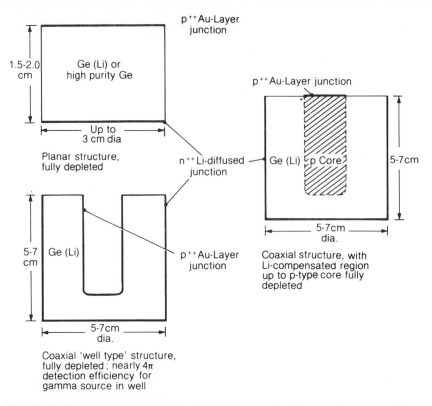

Fig. 20.21 Diagrams of large volume germanium detectors for gamma spectrometry

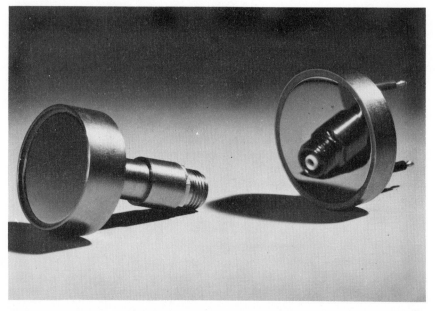

Fig. 20.22 Silicon semiconductor detectors for alpha particle measurements. 25 mm dia., mounted in stainless steel cases with silicone rubber, front surface light-proof and touch-proof. See Fig. 20.20 (a)

the silicon is p-type with a thin 'wrap-around' n^{++} junction prepared by diffusing phosphorus into the material. The contact on the opposite face is an evaporated layer of Au which makes a p^{++} or ohmic contact to the p-type silicon. Suitable thin wires are welded to the two electrodes, i.e. to the phosphorus diffused layer and to the Au layer. Robust external leads for connections to amplifier input circuits are brought out through the back of the steel casing in which the detector is mounted. The junction, on which the particles impinge, has a phosphorus diffused surface to make it 'touch' proof, and is covered with an evaporated layer of chromium to eliminate large currents from incident light photons.

Figure 20.23 shows a photograph of several Harwell-designed probe-type detectors fitted with a 12 mm diameter handle, which contains a head-amplifier unit.[10] This assembly is connected via a flexible lead to a battery-operated counting-rate meter unit. The largest detector is 50 mm diameter and is used in radiological protection applications for survey of alpha contamination on surfaces. The small cylindrical probe is for examination of the nasal passages for alpha activity and the small disc type of monitoring for alpha activity in wounds. A similar disc geometry detector is used for measuring beta activity in nuclear medicine applications, and for these

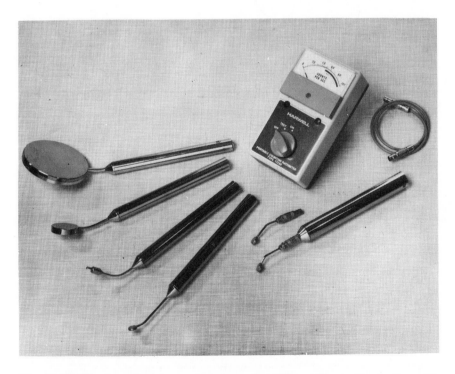

Fig. 20.23 Silicon semiconductor detector probes, 50 mm dia. to 10 mm dia., with preamplifier in prove handle and flexible connection to portable counting-rate meter. For alpha and beta surface contamination measurements including medical applications

applications a much more robust *window* (50 μ m thick stainless steel) can be used without undue absorption of beta particles. The probe is therefore robust enough for medical sterilization processes. The ranges of alpha particles, protons, and electrons in silicon and other detector materials are given in Figs 20.24 and 20.25.

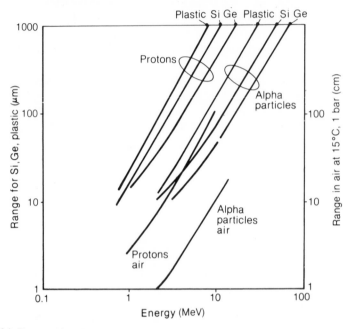

Fig. 20.24 Range of alpha particles and protons in various detector media[19]

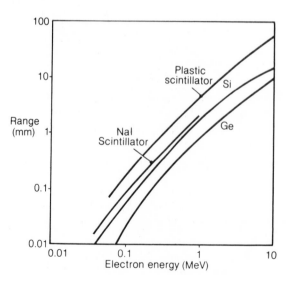

Fig. 20.25 Range of electrons in various detector media[19]

5.2 Silicon detectors for high-resolution X-ray spectrometry

Figure 20.20(b) shows a geometrical arrangement for small size *planar* detectors, using intrinsic Si(Li) material or high-purity silicon, which ensures low surface leakage currents and uniform electric field throughout the sensitive volume. Further details of fabrication using gallium ion-implantation techniques to prepare the p,n junction are described in reference (11). At low X-ray energies, particularly below about 20 keV, it is essential to reduce electrical and/or electronic noise, i.e. arising from shot noise in the field-effect transistor (FET) and current noise in the detector. Figure 20.A4 in the appendix shows the ultimate resolution achievable, i.e. governed only by statistical fluctuations in the primary signal, and the effect of electrical noise of various magnitudes, when added to this ultimate value. A small-capacitance detector is needed to minimize the effect of shot noise in the pulse amplifier and hence there is a need for small-area detectors with wide depletion depth. The detector current and the associated noise are also reduced by use of a small-volume detector. These requirements may be inconsistent with the need for larger-size detectors to improve total sensitivity, and hence some compromise on total size may have to be made to meet special applications. In general, however, the requirement is for maximum energy resolution, i.e. low-noise. FET shot noise is reduced by operation at low temperatures, and detector current and noise in *intrinsic* material are also reduced at low temperatures. Even when high-purity or intrinsic material is used, this only affects current and noise generated in the bulk of the material. In practice, surface-generated currents are the biggest problem, and special precautions and techniques are needed to 'clean' the surfaces and maintain them in an uncontaminated condition.

For X-ray spectrometry, the detector is encapsulated in an evacuated stainless steel enclosure and mounted together with the first stage of the preamplifier unit on a *cold finger*, consisting of a copper rod or tube which is in turn cooled by contact with liquid nitrogen in a Dewar-type flask. The detector is mounted with its entry face close to a thin beryllium window in the vacuum enclosure to achieve low energy absorption, and also to enable the detector to be placed as close as possible to the *source* to be measured.

Figure 20.26 illustrates a typical arrangement, and the energy spectrum of Fig. 20.27 indicates the high energy-resolution capabilities of this type of X-ray spectrometer. The electronic LED (light-emitting diode) shown in Fig. 20.26 provides charge neutralization at the input of the preamplifier on a pulse-by-pulse basis. This charge neutralization is more usually achieved on a continuous basis by the use of a high-value resistor connected across the feed-back capacitor, C_f, of the first pulse-amplifier stage (i.e. the current integrator). This resistor can contribute additional electrical noise and also give rise to other problems in maintaining resolution at high counting rates. This further aspect of the role of the complete signal-processing system in realizing the best possible energy resolution up to high counting rates is discussed more fully in §5.6, since it also applies to high-resolution gamma-ray systems.

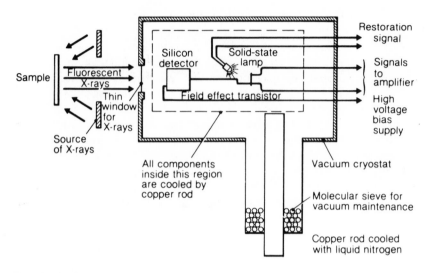

Fig. 20.26 Liquid nitrogen-cooled silicon detector system for X-ray spectrometry. Opto-electronic charge neutralization applied to detector/amplifier input

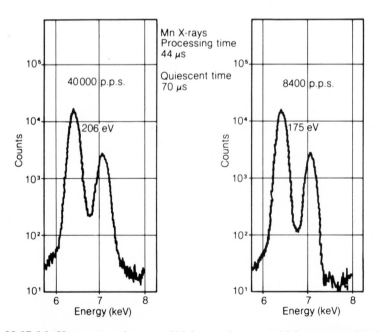

Fig. 20.27 Mn X-rays at moderate and high counting rates with long processing times in active-filter signal processing, following cooled silicon detector system of Fig. 20.26

There has been a world-wide application of high-resolution semiconductor detectors in X-ray fluorescence analysis of materials. In some applications a radioisotope source of X-rays is used to excite the characteristic X-rays of the material or materials being analysed. A more general-purpose method is the use of a beam of electrons (energy variable). Electron beam machines of this type have been marketed for many years, and used in conjunction with a crystal-type diffractometer to measure the energy of the characteristic X-rays. The semiconductor detector system has replaced or supplemented the diffractometer method. Although at low energy (few keV) the semiconductor detector method cannot yet equal the resolution performance of the diffractometer, it provides a very much higher sensitivity and an energy resolution entirely satisfactory for many analytical measurements in the laboratory and in industrial applications.

5.3 Germanium detectors for high-resolution gamma-ray spectrometry

Figure 20.21(a) shows a geometrical arrangement for a planar detector using germanium. The size of such a device may range from a few millimetres in diameter and depth to about 3 cm (vol. 20 cm³), depending on the gamma-energy range required. As mentioned earlier, as the size of the detector is increased, the proportion of pulse signals which correspond to the whole of the incident gamma-ray energy being absorbed also increases. This is because the secondary photon, produced by Compton scattering of a primary gamma photon, has a higher probability of being totally absorbed by subsequent photoelectric capture the larger the size of the detector. Coaxial structures (e.g. Fig. 20.21) 5–7 cm in diameter and 5–7 cm, or more, long (volume $\geqslant 100$ cm³) are used. The coaxial-contact electrode structure enables higher electric fields and shorter carrier collection paths, both leading to shorter pulse signals, to be achieved than does a planar structure for a given total detector volume.

Figure 20.28 shows graphically the variation of photo-peak efficiency (ratio of detected signals within the peak distribution to incident gamma photons) with gamma energy for 10 cm³ and 85 cm³ germanium detectors. The photo-peak efficiencies of 12 cm³ and 330 cm³ cylindrical NaI scintillator detectors (25mm dia. × 25mm long and 75mm dia. × 75mm long) are also shown. Much higher efficiencies are achieved with NaI scintillators over the whole energy range (0.1 MeV to about 2 MeV) shown, but superior energy resolutions are achieved with the germanium detectors, e.g. 0.2 per cent to 0.4 per cent (f.w.h.m.) at about 1 MeV, depending on whether the detector system is operating at low or very high counting rates, compared with a resolution of about 7 per cent for a good NaI scintillator system. The partial and total gamma-ray absorption coefficients, for silicon and germanium over the energy range 0.01–10 MeV, are shown in Fig. 20.29.

The valence to conduction band energy gap in germanium is 0.66 eV (cf. 1.2 eV for Si) and very large carrier densities and corresponding leakage

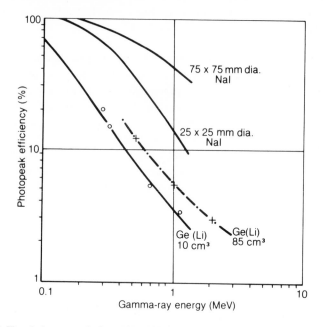

Fig. 20.28 Total photo-peak detection efficiencies vs gamma-ray energy for two sizes of Ge(Li) semiconductor and NaI scintillator detectors[20]

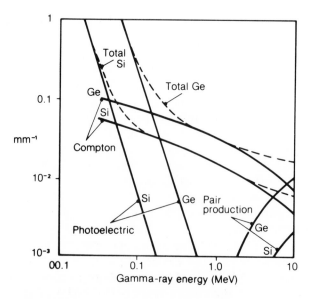

Fig. 20.29 partial and total gamma-ray absorption coefficients vs energy, for silicon and germanium[19]

currents arise in the bulk of the material at normal temperatures. Operation at liquid-nitrogen temperature is standard practice, and systems based on the use of cryostats similar to that shown in Fig. 20.26 are widely used. Many variants on shape and size have been evolved (with Dewar vessels up to 0.5 m diameter and 0.5 m high). Applications include nuclear studies, laboratory radio-chemical analysis in all disciplines affecting the nuclear power industry, medical and biological sciences, and a wide miscellany of industrial applications for field studies and plant instrumentation. The extent of application of a system requiring large liquid-nitrogen Dewar vessels has been surprising. There are still more applications which would be viable if some other method of cooling could be used. The most promising alternative to date is a system depending on Joule-Thompson cooling, by expansion of liquified or compressed gases.

An important technological development in recent years has been the production of large-size germanium crystals with a very high degree of purity (p-type impurity levels in the range 5×10^9–10^{11} per cm^3). This material can be used directly for manufacture of detectors without using the Li–ion drift process, which is only needed to compensate for the much higher p-type impurity levels in the more 'standard' quality of Ge. An important consequence is that these Ge detectors do not have to be maintained permanently at liquid-nitrogen temperatures after fabrication. In the case of Li-doped, i.e. Ge(Li) detectors, it is necessary to keep the detectors cooled to avoid migration of Li by diffusion processes, which would eventually lead to incomplete and inadequate 'compensation'. With the new high-purity Ge detectors, they may be stored (still in their vacuum-tight encapsulations) at room temperature and only need to be cooled to liquid-nitrogen temperatures when in use.

5.4 Monitoring of plutonium-contaminated waste with a Ge detector gamma spectrometer system

An example of the use of a high-resolution Ge detector (liquid-nitrogen cooled) for detecting and measuring prescribed levels of ^{239}Pu in miscellaneous waste (tissues, filters, small pieces of apparatus, etc.) is illustrated in Fig. 20.30. This waste material is collected in plastic bags and requires to be assessed for Pu-content to prescribed levels before packaging more permanently in metal containers.

The package is placed in a rotating drum and the ^{239}Pu measured by taking successive measurements on segments or slices of the package. This is achieved by automatic raising and lowering of the Ge detector in its lead collimator. The amount of ^{239}Pu in each segment is assessed from a measurement of the counts within a narrow band of energies centred on the 414 keV gamma ray emitted by ^{239}Pu. A gamma source (selenium-75), placed on the far side of the rotating drum, emits 400 keV gamma rays, and the count-rate at this energy in the detector is used to estimate the density of each segment

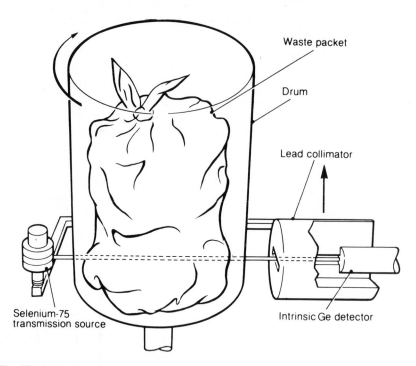

Fig. 20.30 Monitor for plutonium contaminated waste

to correct for the absorption of the 414 keV gamma rays from ^{239}Pu by the waste matrix.

5.5 Semiconductor detectors other than Si and Ge

Consideration has been given to the use of various semiconductor or insulatng compounds containing an element of high atomic number Z which might offer a higher efficiency for gamma-ray detection than Ge, and with a higher energy band gap in order to avoid cooling to liquid-nitrogen temperature. The substances examined have included Ga–As, Al–Sb, Ga–P, Cd–Te, and HgI$_2$. In all cases there are problems not only of achieving freedom from impurities, but also in achieving specimens with uniform crystalline structure, free from stoichimetric defects. None of these materials have been grown in the form of large pure crystals, and virtually all specimens exhibit a high degree of trapping of one or other of the carriers (electrons or holes). Prospects of producing large detectors with these materials are not promising.

5.6 Signal processing for high-resolution spectrometer systems, including operation at high counting rates

The following comments apply particularly to high-resolution gamma-ray spectrometry, using Ge semiconductor detectors and to high-resolution X-ray spectrometry using small silicon detectors.

The earlier discussion on the factors limiting pulse-amplitude (and hence energy) resolution dealt only with limitations due to statistical fluctuations in the number of primary charges collected and some additional limitations due to electrical noise fluctuations in the detector–amplifier input circuits. (See §§2.5 and 4.4.) These limitations are fundamental and are discussed in more detail in the appendix. They represent the best results which can be achieved with high-resolution detectors at very low counting rates if only the simple signal-processing system (cf. §2.4) is used.

Additional distortion of the pulse-amplitude spectra can arise from the pile-up of successive pulses on the decaying 'tails' of previous pulses. In the systems so far described no account has been taken of long time-constant tails arising from operation of other parts of the circuit on the signal pulses. Important sections in the input circuit which have long differentiating time consonants are R_L, C_D (load resistor and detector capacitor) and R_f, C_f. C_f is the feed-back capacitor in the first-stage current-integrator section of the amplifier, and R_f is a shunt resistor required to establish a steady-state mean voltage across C_f (otherwise the amplifier would drift into a non-linear region and either saturate or cut-off).

Suppose the longer time constant of these is T_L. The effect will be that the CR-RC shaping circuits ($CR = T_S$) will no longer give a unipolar pulse (see Fig. 20.4), but one that will have an *undershoot*, i.e. it will cross the base-line. This undershoot will be T_S/T_L times the previous positive signal. Although T_S/T_L may appear to be numerically small (e.g. 10μs/1 ms = 1/100), this small undershoot decays with a long time constant T_L. For the example chosen, with a mean pulse-rate of only 1000 counts/s, there is a high probability of a reduction of up to 1/100 (1 per cent) in the apparent height of a pulse. This can cause a significant increase in spectrum line widths obtained with high-resolution semiconductor detectors. Fortunately there are simple means of overcoming this particular problem partially by modifications to the main CR–RC shaping circuits. The circuit adjustments are referred to as *pole-zero cancellation* and are adequate for dealing with one or perhaps two long-time-constant effects in the a.c.-connected pulse amplifier. Another technique which it is usually necessary to apply is that of correction for base-line shift, which is greater of course as the mean count-rate increases. Various d.c. restoring circuits have been devised. Perhaps the most elegant is the method of *spectrum stabilization*. A secondary source with a well-defined energy emission is used, and by the use of feedback it is arranged that the peak signal due to this emission should always occupy a chosen channel in the spectrum analyser. Any variation produces an error signal which can be used to correct the d.c. bias of the system at some convenient point. Similarly, if a second reference peak is included, then any measured variation in the amplitude gap between the two peaks can be interpreted as a gain change in the system, and automatic corrective action may then be taken.

Further details of these techniques and of nuclear pulse amplifiers in general may be obtained in references (1) (2) and (19).

A big improvement in reducing undershoot effects has been the use of optoelectronic charge restoration at the input of charge-sensitive (i.e. pulse-current-integrator type) amplifiers. The use of this technique was illustrated in Fig. 20.26 dealing with a high-resolution, cooled Si detector system for X-ray spectrometry. This method virtually eliminates pulse undershoot problems and at the same time reduces electronic noise, since the equivalent noise of the feedback resistor is much greater than any noise associated with the optoelectronic device.

Optoelectronic charge neutralization at the detector was first proposed by Kandiah,[12][13] who used a light-emitting diode (LED) and a photodiode in the optoelectronic device, followed by direct-coupled amplification and a new signal processor, in which an accepted pulse was processed and measured and the whole system then restored to its initial state before accepting any further pulse into the system.

The optoelectronic system of charge neutralization has been widely adopted, and F.S. Goulding[14] proposed exposing the input FET to the light pulses from the LED, thus avoiding any additional component and increased capacitance on the input. Goulding and others have developed optoelectronic charge neutralization to the amplifier input in conjunction with high-quality a.c.-coupled amplifiers and associated systems of base-line restoration and pile-up rejection circuits (references (14) and (19)). In all the systems the optoelectronic charge restoration is carried out after several pulses have been analysed; the output from the head amplifier (a current integrator) is allowed to move up to a fixed upper limit before restoring the input (and output) back to a fixed lower limit.

Kandiah has developed further the system of optoelectronic charge restoration of the complete system after processing and measurement of each separate accepted pulse.[16][17] This system incorporates signal recognition followed by signal processing with *active* time-variant filters in place of passive filters. Timing and logic signals ensure that a recognized signal accepted into the system is processed and measured and the whole system restored to initial conditions before a further signal is accepted for measurement. The system provides a high degree of pile-up protection and there is automatic stabilization of the system zero condition and overall gain. The proportion of input pulses to output pulses is known accurately so that live-time correction can be made. It is claimed that a much wider range of input rates can be dealt with (i.e. still providing a useful output rate) than for any other system.[17] Thus, for high-resolution X-ray spectrometry with Si detectors, input rates up to 50 000 events/s can be dealt with before appreciable degradation of energy resolution occurs.

6 Scintillation detectors

6.1 **Pulse response in scintillation counters**

In scintillation detectors the light emitted on recombination of ionized atoms (or molecules), or on the return of excited atoms (or molecules) to the ground state, is observed. The scintillator medium must obviously be transparent to this light, which is in the visual or near-visual region. The various scintillation mechanisms which can be observed in gases, liquids, and solids will be described in more detail in following sections. The duration of the light pulses and their time response varies widely. Pulse durations of a few tens of nanoseconds can be obtained in certain organic solids, liquids and plastics. In inorganic crystals the pulse durations are longer, viz. in the microsecond region. Thallium-activated sodium iodide [NaI(Tl)] is widely used for gamma detection and spectrometry and it can be obtained in the form of very large crystals (e.g. 30 cm dia. × 30 cm) to provide very high-efficiency detection of high-energy gamma radiation. Liquid scintillators are widely used in biological sciences for measurement of low-energy beta emissions from ^{14}C and tritium (^3H) by adding the material to be assayed in suitable solution form to the liquid scintillator. Large plastic phosphors have wide applications in nuclear physics studies when very fast time responses are required for particle detection. The luminescence in scintillators is observed using photomultiplier (PM) tubes which consist of a photoemissive cathode followed by a series of secondary-electron multiplier electrodes or *dynodes*. The primary photoelectrons from the cathode are multiplied by a factor of 5–10 times at each secondary stage; overall gains up to 10^7 may be obtained in photomultiplier tubes with 10 secondary-emission stages.

Two scintillation counter systems are shown in Fig. 20.31. They only differ in the detailed design of the photomultiplier tube dynode systems. A commonly used size of photomultiplier tube is 4–5 cm in diameter and 10–15 cm in length. The photocathode is a thin semiconducting film deposited on the inside of the end face of the cylindrical glass envelope and the scintillator is fitted to the outside of this face in a manner which provides a good optical contact. Light flashes produced by radiation in the scintillator cause photo-electrons to be emitted from the photocathode, and these are accelerated through a potential of 100–200 volts on to the first electron-multiplier dynode. Each of these electrons causes several (5–10) secondary electrons to be emitted from the specially prepared surface. These secondary electrons are in turn accelerated through 100–200 volts on to the second electron-multiplier dynode, and this process continues throughout all the dynode stages, finally producing 10^6–10^7 electrons for each electron initially emitted from the photocathode. The final charge is collected on a *collector* electrode as shown in Fig. 20.31. Electrical connections from the photocathode, from each separate electron-multiplier dynode and from the collector electrode, are brought out through the glass envelope via connector pins as shown, so that the appropriate voltages may be applied and connection made to a pulse amplifier. The rise-time of the charge collection waveform at the collector of the photomultiplier tube (A in Fig. 20.31) is governed mainly by the luminescence time-decay characteristic of the scintillator, ranging from a few microseconds in inorganic crystals [NaI(Tl)] to a few nanoseconds in organic materials, particularly some liquid and 'plastic' scintillators.

The step-function charge collection waveform can be converted to a unipolar pulse with CR–RC pulse-shaping circuits, or with delay-line shaping to produce a very sharply rising pulse which preserves the fast response of organic phosphors. Very little additional pulse amplification is required in order to operate a pulse amplitude discriminator or analyser.

6.2 **Photomultiplier tubes**

The photocathode efficiency is an important parameter in determining the number of primary electrons produced by a scintillation pulse. The most

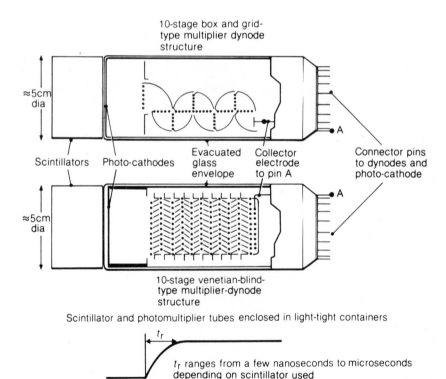

Fig. 20.31 Scintillation counter systems

efficient photoemitters are the alkali antimonides, which have a peak response in the blue region of the optical spectrum that, in general, corresponds well with the region of peak response in the most commonly used scintillators.

The photocathodes are formed as thin substrates behind the window of the photomultiplier tube, and the most generally useful cathode is the oxidized caesium–antimony (Cs_3Sb) cathode, which has a peak quantum efficiency of between 8 per cent and 15 per cent for blue light. The dark current emission is 10^4 electrons $cm^{-2}\ s^{-1}$. This response has been designated as the S11 type.

A somewhat higher efficiency (18 per cent) may be obtained with a tri-alkali cathode (Na–K–Cs–Sb), designated S20 type, which also has a lower dark current (10^3 electrons $cm^{-2}\ s^{-1}$ at 25°C).

Cs_3Sb is also used as a substrate on the dynodes to form on excellent secondary-electron emitter, and secondary-emission coefficients of 10 are obtained with 500 volts between dynodes. With 10 stages of secondary emission, multiplier gains of 10^6 to 10^7 are achieved with 2–3 kV applied across the 10 stages in series (200–300 V per stage).

In *non-focused* types of electron multiplier, e.g. the box-and-grid structure and the venetian-blind structure (Fig. 20.31), the extraction fields at the secondary-emission surfaces are usually weak, and the transit time of electrons through the system may be as long as 100 ns and the transit-time spread 10–20 ns. These types of photomultiplier tubes are, however, the most efficient for general detection and spectrometry applications. In fast-timing experiments with fast organic scintillators it is necessary to use photomultiplier tubes with specially shaped and positioned dynodes to achieve high electric fields at the secondary emitting surface. These are usually called *focused* systems and can provide transit times as low as 30 ns, transit-time spreads of 5 ns, and risetimes of 2 ns. Fast-response photo-multiplier tubes and fast scintillators are required in nuclear physics studies for measurement of particle velocities (and hence energy) by time-of-flight methods, and for experimental determination of the decay time of very short-lived nuclear states.

6.3 Sources of error in energy measurement in scintillation detector systems

Inhomogeneities in luminescence response throughout the scintillator, variations in light transmission to the photocathode of the photomultiplier tube, and variations in sensitivity over the surface of the photocathode can all cause a spread in final signal response for a given radiation energy absorbed. These effects can all be investigated separately, and inadequate scintillator specimens or photomultiplier tubes rejected. A stringent specification of these parameters is required in order to obtain the highest possible per cent resolution, e.g. with large NaI(Tl) crystals measuring relatively high gamma energies (>1 MeV).

A fundamental limitation is the statistical fluctuation in the number of photoelectrons emitted from the photocathode for a given radiation energy absorbed. At low energies and with scintillators of low luminescence efficiency, this effect can account for virtually all of the pulse amplitude spread. Electrical noise in pulse amplifiers following the photomultiplier tube is usually a negligible effect. The appendix gives a more detailed account of the effect of statistical fluctuations in signal amplitude.

6.4 Scintillation and luminescence detectors and their uses

Luminescence is a general term applied to the phenomenon of emission of light from materials caused by the return of excited states of atoms or molecules to the ground state. The initial excitation may be the result of any method of energy absorption, but in this section only the excitation from energetic charged particles will be considered. The subsequent release of the stored energy may require stimulation by further energy absorption, as for example in radiophotoluminescence (in silver-activated phosphate glass), where u.v. irradiation is required to release the stored energy in the form of visible light, or thermoluminescence (in LiF, or CaF₂ with impurity doping), where the substance must be heated to produce the luminescence. In both these processes the time integration of the luminescence produced (total light energy emitted) is proportional to the ionizing energy which was initially absorbed. This phenomenon can thus be used for measurement of the integral dose absorbed, and thermoluminescent powders (LiF) are finding application in assessing beta- and gamma-radiation doses in personal dosimeters for radiological protection. The method is adaptable to measurement of finger-tip dose (LiF incorporated into Teflon tape) and is more convenient and accurate than the use of photographic film for this particular application, though the read-out process is destructive.

The term scintillation is used to refer to the process by which de-excitation producing luminescence does not require any additional stimulus, and the luminescence is manifested by a short-period light flash immediately following the initial absorption of radiation energy.

The light associated with de-excitation and recombination of individual atoms following the absorption of radiation can be observed in gases; the light emitted is primarily in the u.v. region and occurs in about 10^{-9} s.

In certain organic solids and liquids, the energy initially dissipated by incident radiation in producing ionization and excitation can be transferred to neighbouring molecules and is eventually re-radiated as light in the visible region. The overall time delay in the emission of this luminescence is usually in the order of 10^{-8} s or less.

In some inorganic crystals a similar transference of energy can occur to neighbouring regions of the crystal lattice where there is an impurity atom defect. The impurity centres are raised to a metastable state whose lifetime determines the decay characteristic of the luminescence; the decay times are usually far greater than 10^{-8} s and may be several hours. This process is called phosphorescence and the materials are referred to as phosphors. NaI with about 1 per cent thallium incorporated at impurity centres (thallium-activated NaI) has a decay time of about 0.25 μs, and is one of the more efficient phosphors, the ratio of light energy emitted to radiation energy absorbed being about 10 per cent.

The photomultiplier tube, which converts this light flash into an electrical charge emitted from a photocathode and then multiplies this charge via a series of secondary electrodes or dynodes, provides a robust and noise-free means of amplification which can be faster than that used with any other form of detector. Fast photomultipliers used with fast-decay organic scintillators, including 'plastic' scintillators often of very large size, are used for measurement of time of arrival of particles (to about 10^{-9} s) and hence for measurement of very short time intervals in time-of-flight particle spectrometers. Inorganic phosphors are used for alpha-, beta-, and gamma-survey purposes and NaI(Tl) or CsI(Tl) for very high-sensitivity gamma detection and spectrometry (albeit with a low energy resolution in comparison with the much less sensitive Ge semiconductor detector). Single crystals of NaI(Tl) are available in sizes up to 30 cm diameter and 30 cm long.

The partial and total absorption coefficients for gamma rays in NaI and in anthracene, over the energy range 0.01–10 MeV, are shown in Fig. 20.32 and the photo-peak detection efficiencies are shown in Fig. 20.28 for two sizes of NaI. The resolution obtainable with these sizes of NaI detector, when used with a high-quality photomultiplier tube is in the region of 7 per

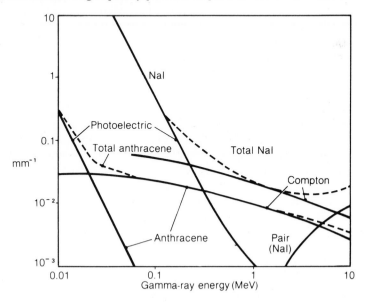

Fig. 20.32 Partial and total absorption coefficients for gamma rays vs energy for NaI and anthracene scintillators[19]

Table 20.2 Scintillators for scintillation counting

Scintillator type	Physical properties and applications

A. Inorganic phosphor types

NaI–Tl
Density 3.67. Refractive Index 1.77. Photoelectron yield per MeV: 3000 (electrons), 2400 (5 MeV alpha). Main decay time $0.25\,\mu$s.

Typical applications: gamma-ray detection and spectrometry. Single crystals (up to 30 cm dia. × 30 cm long obtainable). Since crystals of this type are damaged by moisture, they are normally sealed in a hermetically sealed container with glass or quartz windows and MgO or Al_2O_3 light reflectors.

CsI–Tl
Density 4.51. Refractive Index 1.79. Photoelectron yield per MeV: 2000 (electrons), 2900 (protons), 1650 (alpha). The light pulse rise and decay depends on dE/dx. The average scintillation pulse decay time (interpreted as exponential decay) – $0.7\,\mu$s (electrons), $0.6\,\mu$s (8 MeV proton), $0.4\,\mu$s (5 MeV alpha).

Typical applications: alpha-particle and proton detectors and spectrometers, gamma detectors and spectrometers. Single crystal, thin or thick (up to 12 cm dia. × 10 cm). Not hygroscopic. May be machined and mounted in normal atmosphere.

LiI–Eu
Density 4.06. Photoelectron yield per MeV: 1500 (electrons), 2000 (protons), 1000 (5 MeV alpha). No useful dependence reported on light decay with dE/dx. Average decay time $1.4\,\mu$s. Gamma-ray absorption very similar to NaI (Tl). Detects neutrons via a high cross-section reaction with ^{6}Li isotope.

Typical applications: Slow neutron and gamma-ray detectors. Fast neutron detectors and spectrometers (cooled to 44 K). The single crystals are very hygroscopic and are almost always mounted in sealed moisture-proof containers for attachment to photomultiplier.

ZnS–Ag
Luminescent powder, small crystals $10-100\,\mu$m. Density 4.09. Refractive index 2.36. Photoelectron yield per MeV: 4000 (alpha). Light pulse decay law $E^{-1.3}$ (alpha-particle excitation). Time for ½ total light to be emitted $3\,\mu$s. Optimum thickness for 5 MeV alpha particles 9 mg/cm². Maximum useful thickness 80 mg/cm².

Typical applications: alpha-particle detectors, soft beta-particle detectors (using delayed coincidences), neutron detectors in combination with hydrogenous or neutron-active media (see below). Available as bulk crystalline powder or mounted as thin layers on transparent backing. Alpha-particle detectors (mounted on transparent backing with light-proof alpha window on front).

ZnS–Ag-based detectors
Dispersion of ZnS in boron or mixtures of ZnS in B_2O_3 glass. Neutron detection efficiency (limited transparency of ZnS) 15-25% for thermal neutrons depending on level of gamma rejection required. Available as discs with natural boron or ^{10}B

ZnS–Ag-based fast-neutron detectors
Dispersion of ZnS in hydrogenous plastic (Hornyak buttons) with various modifications to improve light collection (Emmerich detectors). Count-rate proportional to energy transported by the fast-neutron flux. Efficiency for 1 MeV neutrons (about 1%) is reduced if higher level of gamma rejection required.

Note: The photoelectron yield per MeV absorbed applies for good optical coupling between scintillator and a photocathode with a sensitivity of 40 μA/lumen.

B. Crystalline organic scintillators

Anthracene
Organic crystals. Density 1.25. Integrated photoelectron yield per MeV: 1500 (1 MeV electrons) 450 (3 MeV protons). Light pulse decay of form $A \exp(-t/\tau)$ + low-level $t^{-1.35}$ decay. Exponential component decay time 30 ns. Fraction of integrated light in power law decay 20% (0.5 MeV electrons).

Typical applications: beta-ray spectrometry, protons and fast-neutron spectrometry using decay-time discrimination. Available as single crystals or crystalline blocks.

Table 20.2 Continued

Scintillator type	Physical properties and applications
Stilbene	Organic crystals. Density 1.16. Integrated photoelectron yield per MeV: 1200 (1 MeV electrons), 400 (3 MeV protons), 85 (5 MeV alpha). Light pulse form A exp $(-t/\tau)$ + low-level $t^{-1.35}$ decay. Exponential component of decay 6 ns.
	Typical applications: Fast coincidence counting, proton and fast neutron spectrometry using decay-time discrimination. Available as single crystals or crystalline blocks.

C. Organic mixtures

Scintillating Liquids A	Typical mixture 4 g/l PPO or p-terphenyl + 0.1 g/l POPOP in toluene. Photoelectron yield per MeV: 900 (1 MeV electrons). Fast component of decay 2–3 ns.
Scintillating Liquids B	Solutions into which water or metal organic compounds may be loaded. Typical mixtures PBD (8 g/l) + POPOP (0.05 g/l) + Naphthalene (80 g/l) + xylene to which may be added methyl borate and other metal compounds, substances dissolving in methanol or butanol. Photoelectron yield per MeV: 700–900 (1 MeV electrons) 60–80 (5 MeV alpha). Fast component of decay 2–3 ns, slow component for decay time discrimination 0.2 μs. Applications ^{14}C and ^{3}H assay.
Plastic Scintillators	Typical composition 36 g/l p-terphenyl + 1 g/l POPOP in polyvinyltoluene. 2.5% p-terphenyl + 0.08% TPB + 0.01% zinc stearate in polystyrene (for large volumes). Density 1.06. Refractive index 1.58. Photoelectron yield per MeV: 750 (1 MeV electrons), 250 (3 MeV protons), 60 (5 MeV alpha). Main decay about 3.5 ns.
	Applications: general, where relatively inexpensive and robust scintillating material is required for alpha, beta, gamma detection. Rod, blocks, discs, thick sheet, filament, granules, etc. or cut to any shape as required—weights up to 1 ton or more if required. Tube or vessel for flow counters. Thin sheets attached to transparent backing.

cent for 1 MeV gamma rays. This fractional resolution becomes larger (worse resolution) at lower energies.

Liquid scintillators have become very important as the detection system for radioactive isotopes of hydrogen and carbon in the biological sciences. Complete automated counting instruments have been developed for the measurement of tritium ^{3}H (a radioactive isotope of hydrogen, with a low-energy beta emission—22 keV max., 7 keV mean) and ^{14}C (radioactive with a low-energy beta emission of max., energy 155 keV, mean energy 50 keV).

It is possible to dissolve the materials to be counted in a suitable solvent (toluene). This may contain a primary organic scintillator such as PPO (2,5-diphenyl oxazole), which emits light in the ultraviolet region, and a secondary scintillator, e.g. POPOP (1,4-di (2-5-phenyloxazolyl)), which absorbs this light and re-emits light at a longer wavelength that more closely matches the spectral response of the photocathode, (*see Leame and Homewood, Suggestions for Further Reading*).

Automated instrument systems are available commercially which can deal with 100 or more samples in glass phials. Each glass phial is moved in turn between two photomultiplier tubes. A count is only registered if a signal pulse is received simultaneously in both detecting channels (i.e. within a short *coincidence time* of 100 ns, or even less). The primary signal may consist of only a few electrons emitted from the photocathode, and the chance of a spurious count from thermally generated electrons emitted from the photocathode is considerably reduced by the use of the *coincidence-count* system.

Scintillation counters have been one of the most successful forms of pulse detector throughout the history of nuclear physics and applied nuclear developments, and continue to have wide application. The more important properties of inorganic crystal and organic crystal or liquid scintillators are summarized with a brief reference to their main applications in Table 20.2.

7 Conclusions

Gas ionization detection techniques were the first to become established for nuclear radiation measurement in nuclear physics studies. The advent of the photomultiplier tube stimulated development of improved forms of scintillators, in particular of large single crystals of inorganic compounds (e.g. NaI, CsI), for gamma-radiation measurements, and organic crystals (e.g. anthracene, stilbene) and organic mixtures (liquids, plastics) for a variety of particle measurements. Semiconductor counters are a much more recent development, with rapid advances in techniques, design, and application over the last decade. These developments have stemmed directly from improvements in the purity and sample size of single crystals of silicon and germanium produced to meet the wider-ranging applications of other semiconductor devices.

All three detection techniques continue to find application in nuclear physics studies, in control instrumentation for nuclear reactors and nuclear materials processing plant, in measurements for radiological protection throughout the nuclear industry, and in a miscellany of instrumentation and measurement applications in laboratories and industrial processes. Future developments will include further refinements in measurement accuracy and adaptation of existing methods of measurement to new applications.

Appendix

Statistical fluctuations in pulse response and electrical noise in detector–amplifier systems

A.1 Statistical fluctuations in pulse-signal amplitude

In spectrometry systems which measure the pulse response to assess radiation energies, the accuracy of the energy measurement will depend on the statistical fluctuations in the number, N, of ions produced and collected, or on the number of photoelectrons emitted from the photocathode of the photomultiplier tube in a scintillation counter. (There are other sources of variation in pulse-signal, for a given radiation energy absorbed, notably non-uniformity in response throughout the volume of the detector, but the fundamental random fluctuations will be dealt with here.)

An important factor for gas and semi-conductor detection media is the mean particle energy required to be dissipated to produce one ion pair. This parameter is usually referred to as the W-value, and Table 20.A1 lists values for some gases and semiconductors; the gas ionization potentials and the semiconductor energy band gap (i.e. between the upper edge of the valence band and the edge of the conduction band) are also listed.

It will be seen from these W-values that a fraction from a quarter to a half of the particle energy is used in production of ionization; the rest is expended in excitation processes or kinetic energy transfer collisions. The mean number $\bar{N}$ of ions produced may be calculated from the W-values quoted, but

Table 20.A1 W-values for gases and semiconductors, with ionization potentials and energy band gaps

Gases

Medium	W for electrons (eV)	Mean ionization potential (eV)
Hydrogen	36.9	15.4
Argon	26.3	15.8
Air	34.2	—
Methane	28.1	13.1

Solids

Medium	W for electrons (eV)	Energy band gap (valence/conduction) (eV)
Silicon	3.79 (77 K) 3.62 (300 K)	1.09
Germanium	2.94 (77 K)	0.75
Cadmium Sulphide	7.3 (300 K)	2.5

Note: W-values for a given medium are fairly constant for different particle energies and particle types

there is a fluctuation in $\bar{N}$ which has a Gaussian distribution. These fluctuations were first investigated in gases by U. Fano, who found that the standard deviation, (s.d.), was $(F\,\bar{N})^{1/2}$ (or the variance was $F\,\bar{N}$), where the Fano factor F is less than 1. For counter gases F varies in the range 0.1–0.5. Recent values of F quoted for silicon and germanium have been in the region 0.1.

When gas multiplication is used, as in the gas proportional counter, there is a variance in the gas multiplication factor M. The effect of this has been found to be equivalent to adding a further numerical factor b (≈ 0.5) to F, i.e. apparent variance in N becomes $(F + b)N = 0.6N$ for an argon–CH_4-filled proportional counter.

A.2 Spread in pulse amplitude and amplitude or energy resolution

For a given radiation energy E eV absorbed, the peak pulse signal response, V_m, using a *proportional* detector and a current-integrator amplifier system with CR–RC pulse shaping, will be proportional to the mean number of ions produced ($\bar{N} = \dfrac{E}{W}$) and is given by:

$$V_m = \frac{A_0 e}{C_f\,e}\frac{E}{W},$$

where e is the electron charge (1.6×10^{-19} coulombs) and E is the radiation energy absorbed in eV.

The standard deviation of V_m will be given by

$$\text{s.d.}(V_m) = \frac{A_0 e}{C_f\,e}\left(\frac{Fe}{W}\right)^{1/2}$$

or

$$\frac{A_0 e}{C_f\,e}(F+b)^{1/2}\left(\frac{E}{W}\right)^{1/2} \quad \text{for a gas proportional counter.}$$

When a detector is used for measuring the radiation energy or distinguishing between radiations of very close energies, the energy measurement accuracy or resolution will depend on the spread of pulse heights (V_m) for radiation of the same energy. A typical pulse-height distribution is shown in Fig. 20.A1. The observed pulse-height distribution for many detector systems is Gaussian. A useful measure of the resolution obtainable is the full width at half maximum (f.w.h.m) of this curve, and for Gaussian distributions:

$$R\ (\text{f.w.h.m.}) = 2.4 \times \text{standard deviation in } V_m.$$

This resolution factor, R (f.w.h.m.), may be expressed in percentage terms:

$$R(\text{f.w.h.m.}) = \frac{\Delta V_m\ (\text{f.w.h.m.})}{\text{Pulse height at peak } (V_m)} \times 100 \text{ per cent}$$

$$= \frac{\Delta E\ (\text{f.w.h.m.})}{\text{Mean energy } E} \times 100 \text{ per cent.}$$

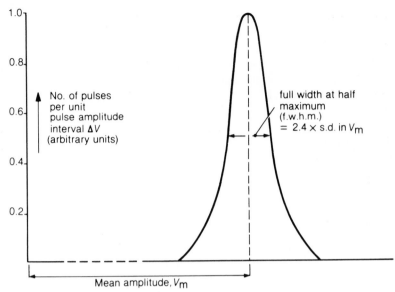

Fig. 20.A1 Pulse amplitude distribution curve for large number of pulses of a given mean amplitude

If the major source of fluctuation in signal relative to the mean level is due to the phenomena so far described,

$$R(\text{f.w.h.m.}) = 2.4 \times \left(\frac{FW}{E}\right)^{1/2} \times 100 \text{ per cent.}$$

or

$$R(\text{f.w.h.m.}) = 2.4(F+b)^{1/2} \times \left(\frac{W}{E}\right)^{1/2} \times 100 \text{ per cent for}$$
$$\text{gas proportional counters.}$$

Alternatively the resolution may be measured in terms of the spread in energy (eV) at the half maximum count point on the curve of number of counts versus energy measured.

$$\begin{aligned} R(\text{f.w.h.m.}) &= \text{Energy spread } \Delta E(\text{f.w.h.m.}) \\ &= 2.4(FW \times E)^{1/2} \text{ eV,} \\ &= 2.4(F+b)^{1/2}(WE)^{1/2} \text{ eV} \end{aligned}$$

or

for gas proportional counters.

The best achievable resolution, i.e. when statistical fluctuations in detector signal are the only source of error, are as follows:

    (1) for germanium semiconductors,
        $FW = 0.1 \times 2.94$, and hence $R = 1.30\, E^{1/2} \text{ eV}$;

    (2) for silicon semiconductors,
        $FW = 0.1 \times 3.8$, and hence $R = 1.48\, E^{1/2} \text{ eV}$;

    (3) for gas proportional counters,
        $(F+b)\cdot W = 0.6 \times 27$, and hence $R = 9.66\, E^{1/2} \text{ eV}$.

Table 20.A2 lists values of these best achievable values of resolution, R, over an energy range 1 keV to 1 MeV.

In scintillation counters the spread in mean pulse height arises partly from the fluctuation in the number of photoelectrons emitted from the photocathode of the photomultiplier tube as a result of the light pulse from the scintillator. The energy absorbed in the scintillator per photoelectron emitted

Table 20.A2 Calculated resolution at FWHM for various detectors, assuming only a variance in the number of ion pairs collected, i.e. electrical noise effects neglected

Detector type	Germanium		Silicon		Gas proportional (Argon–CH)	
	R		R		R	
Radiation energy	(eV)	(%)	(eV)	(%)	(eV)	(%)
1 keV	41	4.10	49	4.90	305	30.5
10 keV	130	1.30	150	1.50	966	9.66
100 keV	410	0.41	490	0.49	3055	3.05
1 MeV	1300	0.13	1500	0.15*	9660*	0.97*

* Silicon and gas proportional counters are not suitable for gamma-energy measurements much greater than 100 keV, but may be used for short-range particles (alpha particles) at energies of a few MeV

from the photocathode varies widely with the scintillator material and the photocathode sensitivity. The best combination for gamma radiation is a NaI (thallium-activated) scintillator with a photomultiplier tube with a Cs–Sb cathode, and the effective value of W is 300 eV per photoelectron produced. Thus for E eV radiation energy absorbed, the mean number of photoelectrons produced is $E/300$. The fluctuations in this number are random, i.e. s.d. is $57.7 \times 10^{-3} \times E^{1/2}$, and the corresponding value of f.w.h.m. is $138.5 \times E^{1/2}$ photoelectrons. Amplification of these primary photoelectrons introduces no significant increase in variance, so that on this basis one might expect a relative resolution of:

R (f.w.h.m.) $= 4.2 \times 10^{-3} E^{1/2}$ per cent,
or 4.2 per cent at $E = 10^6$ eV.

In practice the resolution for gamma radiation, with a NaI(Tl) scintillator, is not as good as the above formula suggests. The greater dispersion is due partly to inhomogeneities in scintillator response, but there is a further fundamental limitation. For gamma radiation the total energy may be absorbed by a variety of processes (e.g. 1 photoelectron, or 1 Compton + 1 photoelectron), each then producing a different variety of secondary electrons (delta rays) by further collisions. In scintillator systems including NaI(Tl) the value of W (eV electron energy absorbed per electron emitted from the photomultiplier tube photocathode) is not constant with energy but tends to increase as the electron energy decreases. This variation in W, coupled with variation in the process of energy loss, leads to a further term for the dispersion in scintillation detector response and reduces the resolution. Thus a good practical result for resolution at 1 MeV is about 7 per cent at f.w.h.m. Electrical noise in any pulse amplifier following the photomultiplier tube produces a negligible effect, because the signals at the output of the photomultiplier are usually very large compared with r.m.s. noise levels at the input of voltage or current pulse amplifiers.

A.3 Electrical noise and its effect on pulse-amplitude spread and detector system energy resolution

Another source of spread in pulse-amplitude is the presence of electrical noise in the detector or in the amplifier system. There are three main sources of noise arising from the following causes.

1. *Electrical resistance due to thermally generated random vibrations of current carriers within the conductor.* These fluctuations may be represented by a zero-impedance noise-voltage generator in series with a noiseless resistor, or by an infinite-impedance noise-current generator in parallel with a noiseless resistor.
2. *Fluctuations in any currents flowing in the detector itself or in the input circuits of the pulse amplifier.* These fluctuations may be represented by infinite-impedance noise-current generators in parallel with the input terminals.
3. *Fluctuations in the current flowing in the first component of the amplifier.* This is the anode–cathode current if the first component is a thermionic valve, or the drain–source current if the first component is a field-effect transistor (FET). This fluctuation may be represented as a zero-impedance noise-voltage generator in series with the input terminals, e.g., between the control gate of the FET and earth.

Figure 20.A2 shows these equivalent current and voltage noise generators in a simplified circuit of a nuclear radiation detector and associated pulse amplifier; the circuit is the same as that of Fig. 20.4 and is composed of a current-integrator section followed by further stages of amplification incorporating $R_s C_s$ differentiating an integrating pulse-shaping circuits.

Any resistor generates noise because of thermal random vibration of the current-carrying free electrons within the conductor (metal or semiconductor). The magnitude of this noise increases with temperature, and the spectral density of the mean-square open-circuit noise voltage developed between the ends of a resistance R is:

$$[V_n^2] = 4kTR_v \cdot \Delta f \cdot V^2 \quad \text{Hz}^{-1},$$

where T = absolute temperature, in K

k = Boltzmann's constant, in J/K (= 1.38×10^{-23}).

This noise has a uniform density throughout the spectrum and is referred to as *white noise*. It can equally well be represented as an infinite impedance current-noise generator in shunt with the resistance and this has a magnitude

$$[i_n{}^2] = \frac{4kT}{R} \Delta f \; \text{A}^2\text{Hz}^{-1}. \tag{2}$$

These noise generators associated with detector load resistor R_L and *feed-back* resistor R_f are indicated on Fig. 20.A2 with root mean square (r.m.s.) magnitudes i_{nR_L} and i_{nR_f}.

Detector current fluctuations are represented in Fig. 20.A2 by the shunt generator i_{nD} and FET gate current by $\bar{i}_{ng}$. All these noise sources generate a mean square noise current per Hz of bandwidth given by:

$$(i_n{}^2) = 2eI \cdot \Delta f, \tag{3}$$

where I is the mean current flowing, i.e. I_D from the detector and I_g from the gate. Most forms of current noise are associated with some actual direct current and are essentially due to the discontinuous nature of the current flow, i.e. flow of discrete particles (electrons) with a finite electrical charge. Such noise is often referred to as *shot* noise.

The noise-current generator representing *resistance* noise can be conveniently expressed in terms of an equivalent fictitious d.c. current I_{eq} which can be obtained from eqns (2) and (3) thus:

$$I_{eq} = \frac{2kT}{eR}. \tag{4}$$

In practical examples the resistors used in the detector and amplifier input circuits (R_L and R_f) have values of 10^9 Ω or more. The shunt current noise generator representing thermal noise in a 10^9 Ω resistor has a mean square noise current per Hertz from eqn (2):

$$i_n{}^2(\text{for } 10^9 \; \Omega) = 16 \times 10^{-30} \; \text{A}^2\text{Hz}^{-1} \text{ at } 290 \text{ K}.$$

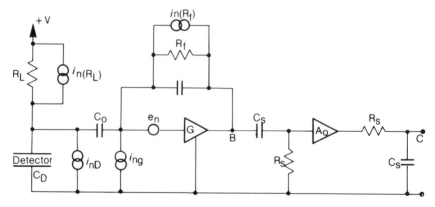

Fig. 20.A2 Detector/amplifier circuit showing equivalent electrical noise generators: equivalent noise voltage generator in series with amplifier input
equivalent noise current generator in parallel with amplifier input

The equivalent mean current giving the same mean square current noise as a $10^9 \, \Omega$ resistor can be obtained from eqn (4):

$$I_{eq} = \frac{2kT}{e \times 10^9} = 5 \times 10^{-11} \, \text{A}.$$

Gas ionization detectors will have leakage currents much smaller than 5×10^{-11} A, and FET gate currents can often be less; cooled semiconductor detectors may also have leakage currents less than 10^{-11}A, and therefore R_L and R_f in these cases should be $\gg 10^9 \, \Omega$. Large silicon detectors at room temperature may have leakage currents in the region of 10^{-6} A, and smaller values of R_L and R_f are then permissible.

The mean square noise values (or densities) are additive and all the actual currents or equivalent currents may be added together (to give I_{total}) and the mean square spectral density of the total current noise per unit bandwidth is then $2eI_{total} \, \text{A}^2\text{Hz}^{-1}$.

The fluctuation in the anode or drain current of the first amplifying valve or FET is another important source of noise, and this is conveniently expressed in terms of a noise voltage source e_n in series with the input terminal. Sometimes this is expressed in terms of r.m.s. voltage divided by the square root of frequency, particularly if the spectral density varies with frequency. If the noise is *white*, i.e. the same magnitude per unit frequency interval, the voltage noise generator e_n is more usually expressed in terms of an *equivalent noise resistance*, R_n, having the same uniform spectral density as e_n, that is

$$[\bar{e}_n^2] = 4kTR_n \, \Delta f. \tag{5}$$

The value of R_n is often quoted as $2.5/gm$ for a triode value, or $0.7/gm$ for an FET, where gm is the mutual conductance[1]. Low-input-capacitance FETs are now available with $gm = 5$ mA/V and hence $R_n = 0.7/(5 \times 10^{-3}) = 140 \, \Omega$.

The noise in semiconductor devices such as FETs is often not constant per unit bandwidth, but increases per unit bandwidth as the frequency decreases. This type of *excess* noise will not be discussed here. Further information may be obtained in Ref. (19).

These main sources of electrical noise have been indicated in Fig. 20.A2 and can be further simplified as a series noise voltage e_n in series with the input lead of amplifier G, and a single current-noise generator i_n in parallel with the amplifier input terminals.

The series and parallel noise generators have so far been quantified only as the mean square voltage or mean square current fluctuations per unit frequency interval (eqns (5) and (3)). To obtain the signal at the output of the current integrator and main amplifier, with $C_sR_s = T_s$ pulse-shaping differentiating and integrating circuits (i.e. output of circuit of Fig. 20.A2), the signals given by eqns (5) and (3) must be multiplied by the amplifier gain (a function of frequency because of the C_sR_s circuits) and integrated over all frequencies. The calculation of the total noise output for series and parallel noise generators is given in ref. (1) and ref. (18), and it is pointed out that a convenient way of expressing this noise output is in terms of an equivalent charge collected rapidly in a conduction-type detector of capacitance C_D at the amplifier system input.

For series voltage-noise generators (e.g. representing shot noise in the first amplifier component), this total equivalent noise charge (e.n.c.), Q_n, expressed in numbers of ion pairs is:

$$Q_{ns} = \left[\frac{kTR_n}{2T_s}\right]\frac{e}{e}\,C_D \text{ ion pairs.} \tag{6}$$

For parallel current-noise generators (e.g. representing noise from detector currents or leakage currents in the detector–amplifier input circuit) the equivalent noise charge is:

$$Q_{np} = \left[\frac{I_{eff}T_s}{e}\right]\frac{e}{2} \text{ ion pairs.} \tag{7}$$

It is of interest to note that $(I_{eff} \times T_s)/e$ is equal to the number of electrons comprising the total effective input leakage current which flow in one time constant T_s. The total equivalent fluctuation in this current (i.e. Q_{np}) is proportional to the square root of the number of electrons flowing in one time constant—a result to be expected from Poisson statistics.

It will be noted that Q_{ns} (representing shot noise in the first component) is directly dependent on C_D and inversely proportional to T_s, but Q_{np} (representing noise from leakage currents in the input circuits) is independent of C_D but directly proportional to T_s.

Numerical examples for Q_{ns} and Q_{np} can be obtained for a range of values of the parameters involved (R_n, T_s, I_{eff}, etc.) using the nomographs. Figs. 20.A3 and 20.A4 in this appendix.

Since Q_{ns} and Q_{np} are really r.m.s. noise/signal ratios with the same reference signal for both quantities, it follows that the resultant equivalent noise charge for both effects, Q_n, is obtained by taking the square root of the sum of the squares of each, giving

$$Q_n^2 = Q_{ns}^2 + Q_{np}^2.$$

Q_{ns}^2 is $\propto 1/T_s$ and $Q_{np}^2 \propto T_s$. The product of these terms is constant and their sum is therefore a minimum when they are equal. Minimum electrical noise is thus achieved when the shaping time constant T_s is chosen to make the two components of the e.n.c. (Q_{ns}^2 and Q_{np}^2) equal to each other. This optimum value of T_s (for minimum electrical noise) is given by:

$$T_{s_{opt}} = C_D\left(\frac{2kTR_n}{eI_{eff}}\right)^{1/2}$$

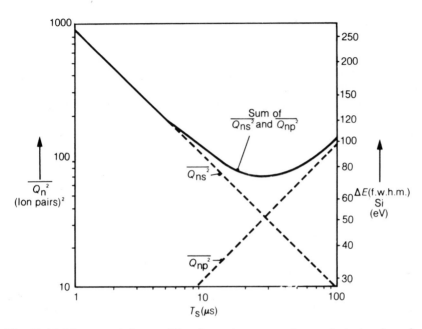

Fig. 20.A3 Nomograph for amplifier shot noise expressed as equivalent series noise voltage generator at input (V_{ns}); equivalent noise charge (e.n.c.) $Q_{ns} = V_{ns} C/e$ ion pairs[18]

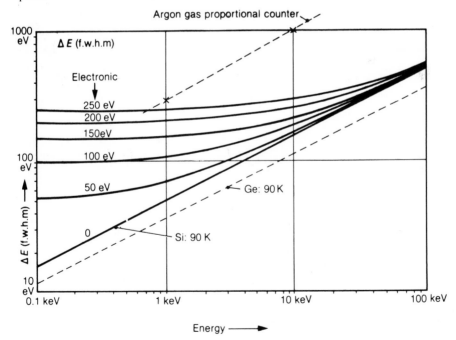

Fig. 20.A4 Nomograph for amplifier input current noise, expressed as equivalent noise charge (e.n.c.) at input (Q_{np} ion pairs)[18]

Electrical noise, due to detector leakage currents and first stage shot noise in the amplifier, is an important factor in determining the overall resolution obtainable with some forms of the semiconductor detectors and proportional counters. Electrical noise is independent of the signal amplitude in the detector (i.e. independent of particle energy) and hence may be insignificant compared with fluctuations in the number of ion pairs collected in affecting resolution when high-energy radiation is being measured. If the detector has a large capacitance, C_D, and/or a large leakage current, electrical noise may still be a significant factor. Electrical noise becomes more important in its effects on resolution when low-energy radiations are being measured, and it is important in these applications to achieve the lowest possible detector leakage current and electrical capacitance C_D.

Figure 20.A5 gives some numerical examples of electrical noise for a detector–amplifier system with a small silicon detector for a range of CR–RC pulse-shaping time constants T_s.

Separate curves are drawn for current noise due to 10^{-13} A leakage vs T_s,

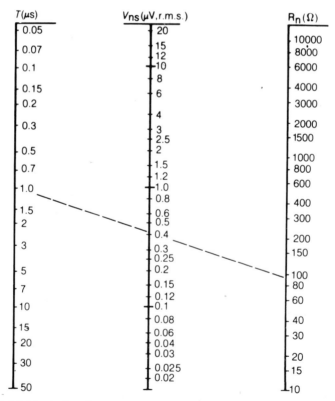

Fig. 20.A5 Equivalent input electrical noise and energy resolution as a function of pulse-shaping time constant T_s for a cooled silicon detector system. Detector temperature 77°K; amplifier input stage FET 5 mA/V at 100°K; 5 picofarad total capacitance; 10^{-13} A total input leakage[15]

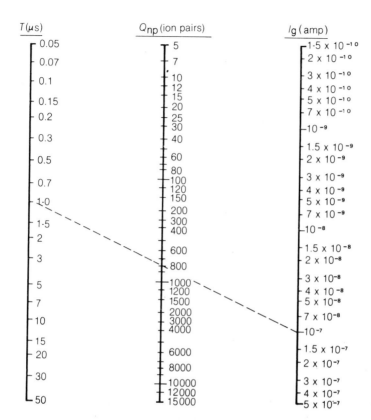

Fig. 20.A6 Energy resolution of a silicon detector system as a function of radiation energy in the range 0.1 to 100 keV. Separate curves show the overall resolution when various levels of electronic noise are present

The best achievable Ge detector resolution and best achievable resolution with an argon/CO_2 gas proportional counter are also shown, (i.e. with negligible electronic noise contribution to resolution)[15]

and for first-stage shot noise (assuming $R_n = 140\ \Omega$, e.g. for a 5 mA/V FET) vs T_s for $C_D = 5$ pF. Figure 20.A5 applies for 77 K temperature operation. Significant reductions in amplifier shot noise (by a factor of two) are obtained if the FET is operated at a low temperature. Current noise is not a function of temperature, *per se*, but semiconductor detector leakage currents are reduced by operation at low temperatures (e.g. 77 K, with liquid-nitrogen cooling). Mean square noise is expressed in terms of the square of equivalent noise charge, Q^2_n, as a mean square number of ion (electron–hole) pairs. This can be converted to equivalent particle energy $E_n = Q_n \times W$ where W, the mean particle energy in eV to produce 1 ion pair, will depend on the detector medium. The effect of E_n on pulse amplitude distribution can be expressed in terms of f.w.h.m. $= 2.4 \times E_n$ eV.

The effect of this spread in pulse amplitude and the spread due to fluctuation in the numbers of primary charges collected can be obtained by adding the two separate effects in quadrature. If R_c is the f.w.h.m. resolution due to fluctuation in charge collection (expressed in say eV) and R_n is the f.w.h.m. resolution due to electrical noise (expressed in the same units—eV), the total f.w.h.m. resolution R_T is:

$$R_T = (R_c^2 + R_n^2)^{1/2}.$$

Figure 20.A6 shows the theoretical resolution obtainable versus radiation energy with Si and Ge detectors (operated at 77 K) if no other noise source is present, i.e. the dispersion is due only to fluctuations in the number of primary ion pairs formed. The similar limiting figure for an argon–CH_4-filled proportional counter is also included. The graph shows the total resolution R_T of the silicon detector when various levels of electronic noise are also present. These levels are combinations of FET shot noise and input-circuit current noise.

Acknowledgements

The author wishes to thank colleagues at Harwell for help in the preparation of this article. Dr. J. W. Leake, Mr. J. H. Howes, and M. Awcock for assistance in choice and presentation of many of the illustrations, and Mr. R.B. Owen for permission to use the collection of data on phosphors and scintillators for scintillating counting, shown in Table 20.2.

Figures 20.24, 20.25, 20.29 and 20.32 are reprinted from *Nuclear Electronics* by P. W. Nicholson (1974) by permission of John Wiley & Sons, London. Figures 20.A5 and 20.A6 are reprinted from 'Some electronic aspects of energy measurements with solid-state detectors' by F. S. Goulding and D. A. Landis from the *IEEE transactions of nuclear science* (copyright IEEE, 1978) by permission of the IEEE.

References

1. GILLESPIE, A. B. *Low noise head amplifiers. AERE R* 6202. Atomic Research Establishment, Harwell (1969).
2. GILLESPIE, A. B. *Nuclear pulse amplifiers. AERE R* 6203 (1969).
3. HOWES, J. H. *Gamma and beta gamma survey equipments. AERE EL/R* 2336 (1957).
4. ABSON, W., PYRAH, H. S., AND SALMON, P. G. Design, performance and use of fission chambers. *Proc. IEE*, **105**(B), No. 22, 366-374 (1958).
5. ABSON, W., LOOSEMORE, W. R., AND SALMON, P. G. Developments in fission chambers for neutron flux measurements. In *Proc. 5th Inst. and Measurements Conf.* Stockholm 1960. Academic Press, New York (1961).
6. HOWES, J. H AND LEAKE, J. W. *Beryllium—a reappraisal of its use in nuclear radiation detectors. AERE M* 2193 (1969).
7. TAYLOR, B. L. A proportional counter for low-level measurement of ^{239}Pu in lungs. *Health Phys.* **17**, 50–69 (1969).
8. ABSON, W., PYRAH, S., AND SALMON, P. G. Boron trifluoride proportional counters. *Proc. IEE* **105**(B), No. 22, 357–365 (1958).
9. CHARPAK, G. Applications of proportional chambers and drift chambers in high energy physics and other fields. *Nature,* **270**, 479–482 (1977).
10. ALLSWORTH, F. L., AWCOCK, M. L., AND HOWES, J. H. *A design of rugged nuclear radiation detector for medical and biological applications. AERE R* 7878 (1975).
11. HOWES, J. H. Ion implanted p-n junctions in near intrinsic n-type silicon for nuclear particle detectors. In RUGE, I, and GRAVL, J. (eds.). *Proc. Int. Conf. on Ion Implantation in Semiconductors.* Springer-Verlag, Berlin (1971).
12. KANDIAH, K. *Radiation measurements in nuclear power*, Inst. of Physics and Phys. Soc., London (1966).
13. KANDIAH, K., STIRLING, A., TROTMAN, D. L., AND WHITE, G. *A fast high resolution spectrometer for use in nuclear radiation detectors. In* International symposium on nuclear electronics, Versailles 1968. Societé Française des Electroniciens et des Radioélectriciens. Paris (1968). Paper 69.
14. GOULDING, F. S. *Nucl. Inst. Meth.* **71**, 273 (1969).
15. GOULDING, F. S., AND LANDIS, D. A. Some electronic aspects of energy measurements with solid state detectors. *IEEE Trans. Nucl. Sci* **NS 25** (2) pp. 891–901 (1978).
16. KANDIAH, *K. Nuclear Instr. and Methods* **95**, 289–300 (1971).
17. KANDIAH, K., SMITH, A. J., WHITE, G. *A pulse processor for X-ray spectrometry with Si(Li) detectors. In Proceedings of the 2nd Ispra Nuclear Electronics symposium, Stresa, 20-23 May, 1975*, European Communities Commission, Report No EUR 53702, Luxembourg (1975) pp. 153-160.
18. DEIGHTON, M. O. *The simple theory of noise in nuclear pulse amplifiers. AERE R* 5439 (1967).
19. NICHOLSON, P. W. *Nuclear Electronics.* John Wiley & Sons, London (1974).
20. DEME, S. *Semiconductor Detectors for Nuclear Radiation Measurement.* Adam Hilges Ltd., London (1971).

Suggestions for further reading

WILKINSON, D. H. *Ionization chambers and counters.* Cambridge Press (1950).
RICE-EVANS, P. *Spark, streamer, proportional and drift chambers.* The Richelieu Press, London (1974).

SHARPE, J. *Nuclear Radiation Detectors* (2nd edn). Metheun (1964).

OUSEPH, P. J. *Introduction to nuclear radiation detectors*. Plenum Press (1975).

DEARNALEY, G. AND NORTHROP, D. C. *Semiconductor detectors for nuclear radiations* (2nd edn) Spon., London (1966).

BIRKS, J. B. *The theory and practice of scintillation counting*. Pergamon (1964).

LEAME AND HOMEWOOD. *Liquid scintillation counting*. Butterworth (1974).

BROMLEY, D. A. (ed.). Detailed reviews of separate topics on the subject of scintillation counting by several authors. *Nucl. Inst. Meth* (two special issues June 1979).

GILLESPIE, A. B. *Signal, noise and resolution in nuclear counter amplifiers*. Pergamon Press, London (1953).

21

Environmental pathways of radioactivity to man

T. F. JOHNS

In recent years a very considerable amount of effort has been devoted to the study of the pathways which can lead to the irradiation of people when radioactive materials (e.g. from the operation of the nuclear power industry) are discharged into the environment. As a consequence there is now an enormous fund of knowledge about these pathways and a very detailed and extensive literature on the subject; but because the subject is complex and extensive, it is not easy for the non-specialist to form a general impression of the relative importance of the various pathways, or indeed to form an impression of the overall importance of these environmental pathways in causing irradiation of man. An attempt has therefore been made in this chapter to discuss environmental pathways and their significance in a way which will hopefully be understood by non-specialists who have neither the time nor the knowledge to study all of the relevant literature.

After some introductory remarks, §2 explains the role of these environmental pathways in the general structure of radiological protection. The more important pathways to man from releases into the air, and to the acquatic environment, respectively, are then discussed in a general way in §§3 and 4. The various mechanisms which lead to the dispersion or reconcentration of radioactive materials are discussed at some length in these sections, and their importance is stressed.

The important pathways for particular groups of radionuclides from the nuclear power industry are then discussed in detail in §5, and the extensive information about these, resulting from many theoretical and practical studies of the situations at particular locations, is summarized. There is detailed discussion about the doses to local population groups, and about the doses which are received world-wide as a result of the release of certain long-lived radioactive species.

The discussion of these environmental pathways enables general conclusions to be drawn, such as the following. The extent to which man is irradiated is rarely known directly from actual dose measurement; normally the doses can only be estimated by measuring (for example) the concentration of radionuclides in foodstuffs, or water, etc., and then calculating or predicting the resulting doses. In that process one has to make assumptions about the magnitude of various parameters (e.g. the amount of rainfall). Since in practice these parameters often vary from place to place, or from time to time, the answer can never be very precise; nevertheless the final value of the calculated dose is often not critically dependent on the detailed nature of the assumptions made, and often the results coming from patently pessimistic assumptions differ from those involving more realistic assumptions by only an order of magnitude. Since such calculations frequently show that the resulting doses are trivially small compared with those from natural radioactivity, it is obvious that one does not need to be able to calculate the resulting doses very precisely.

The whole question of the corresponding pathways from naturally occurring radio-active materials, and the resulting doses to man, are discussed in some detail at the end of §5, in order to illustrate that the doses resulting from the operation of the nuclear power industry are very small compared with those from naturally occurring radio-activity.

Section 6 considers briefly the doses to animals and plants resulting from the nuclear power industry, and concludes that there is no reason to expect that these doses will lead to significant harm.

Finally, §7 reiterates some of the points made in this summary and notes that it has been possible to obtain the very extensive knowledge of the behaviour of radionuclides in the environment only because of the extreme sensitivity of the techniques available for their detection, identification and assay. As a result a fund of knowledge has been built up about the behaviour of radioactive materials in the environment which is far more extensive than our knowledge of the behaviour of the many highly toxic chemicals which are also discharged into the environment.

Contents

1   Introduction

The generation of electricity by nuclear reactors involves the use and production of large amounts of radioactive materials, and a small fraction of these will inevitably be discharged into the environment during the various stages of the nuclear fuel cycle. A great deal is known about the various pathways which can lead to the irradiation of people when such materials are discharged into the environment. The purpose of this article is to draw attention to the most important of these pathways.

The main stages in the nuclear fuel cycle are the mining of uranium, the fabrication of fuel elements, their use in nuclear reactors, and the storage or reprocessing of spent fuel. Discharges of radioactive materials into the environment can occur at all stages of the normal operation of the fuel cycle, although in practice the most significant discharges occur from storage or reprocessing operations, with some smaller discharges during reactor operations. Radiologically significant discharges may also occur in accident conditions.

The original material may be discharged into the environment either in gaseous, liquid or solid forms. If it is discharged into the air, exposure of man can occur from a variety of causes, such as:

1 inhalation of the discharged material (or, in the case of tritiated water vapour, absorption through the skin);
2 external irradiation from a cloud of radioactive material or from material deposited from the air on the ground; and
3 contamination of plants and animals used to provide foodstuffs, and subsequent ingestion by man.

In the case of materials which are discharged in liquid or solid forms, almost all of the pathways to man are via the aquatic environment (seas, rivers, reservoirs); the materials may enter the aquatic environment directly, or by mixing or leaching processes.

There are many environmental pathways from fresh or sea water to man, such as:

1 exposure of local populations resulting from consumption of contaminated fish caught recreationally or commercially, or of edible seaweed used for human consumption;
2 ingestion of contaminated water, or of foodstuffs contaminated by uptake via the roots, e.g. from land irrigated with contaminated water;

3 external radiation from radionuclides re-concentrated on estuarine silt or beaches, or deposited on fishing gear; and

4 inhalation of airborne material arising from resuspension of any material which has been contaminated with radioactivity.

The relative importance of these pathways can vary enormously, depending on the nature of the discharged material and the characteristics of the local environment.

One of the ways by which radioactive materials from the nuclear industry will get into the environment is as a result of the controlled disposal at various stages of the nuclear fuel cycle of various sorts of waste material (which may be in either gaseous, liquid, or solid form), and particular attention has been paid in this article to the study of the associated pathways.

In the case of relatively low-activity waste, where either the amount or the concentration (or both) of the activity is small, the objective in waste disposal operations will normally be to ensure that the radioactive material becomes dispersed into a large volume of air or water before it reaches man, so that the concentrations to which people may be exposed are minimal. On the other hand, in the case of high-activity waste, the objective will be to use a method of disposal such that the waste will remain contained and undispersed at the disposal site for a long time, where its radioactivity will decay without affecting people. Even in this case, as a result of an eventual loss of containment and subsequent leaching, some of the stored material may escape from the disposal site; in this case also the objective will be to ensure that any such material also becomes dispersed into a large volume of water before reaching man.

In both cases there is considerable interest in the processes which cause dispersal of radioactive materials in the environment, and in ways in which materials in the environment may be reconcentrated (e.g. by biological processes). Consequently rather detailed attention is paid in this chapter to both dispersal and reconcentration processes.

In the case of the nuclear power industry, in contrast to the situation involving world-wide fallout of radioactivity from nuclear explosions, interest generally centres on the doses to groups of people living near particular installations. As a consequence of this interest in local groups, certain pathways involving relatively short-lived isotopes (e.g. certain isotopes of xenon and krypton), and certain radionuclides whose properties may make them of particular significance to man in a particular environment (e.g. waterborne ^{106}Ru) give exposure to defined population groups following pathways which are of no great relevance when considering the effects of fallout from weapon tests. In a few cases, however, consideration has to be given to the world-wide situation, since the collective dose (see §2.2) to the world population may be greater than that to local populations, even though the individual doses, world-wide, are very small. In these cases the world-wide doses must clearly be considered, and compared with those from other causes, such as the natural radioactivity in the environment.

2 Environmental pathways in the general structure of radiological protection

Figure 21.1 shows diagrammatically that there are a very large number of routes by which radioactive materials released into the environment might (theoretically) cause irradiation of man; but while some of these pathways are actually or potentially important in causing the irradiation of man, others are of little interest except perhaps to those engaged in environmental research. One of the main objectives of this chapter is to provide sufficient quantitative information to enable the reader to draw his own conclusions about the relative significance of various pathways. Much detailed information will be provided about radiation doses from a variety of practices. In order that the significance of such statements may be clearly understood, and that the whole matter may be seen in proper perspective, we shall discuss briefly in this section the principles which are used internationally as a basis for controlling radiation doses resulting from the operation of facilities such as those in the nuclear power industry, and the ways in which these principles are used to determine the importance of particular environmental pathways, and to control the disposal of waste materials.

2.1 The harmful effects of radiation

It is, of course, not a new phenomenon for members of the general public to be exposed to radiation and radioactive materials. Man has always been exposed to ionizing radiation from various natural sources. Distinguishing characteristics of this natural irradiation are that it involves the entire population of the world and that it has been experienced at a relatively constant rate over a very long period of time. On the other hand, even the natural exposure varies substantially from place to place, as well as locally (e.g. even within one building). Although man has developed in this naturally radioactive environment, there is little doubt that natural radiation causes the induction of some of the apparently spontaneously occurring deleterious genetic effects and malignancies which occur in all populations. It is also generally believed that any increase in radiation doses due, for example, to the operation of the nuclear power industry, will lead to some increase in the number of such effects.

There is absolutely no reason to suppose that any effects due to radiation or radioactivity from the nuclear power industry will be different in nature from the effects due to natural radiation; only the number of such effects may be increased.

Although it is important to recognize at the outset that the increase due to the nuclear power industry will almost certainly represent only a very small fraction of the natural incidence of such effects, a great deal of attention has been devoted internationally to the question of how large an increase can be considered acceptable. For many years the International Commission on

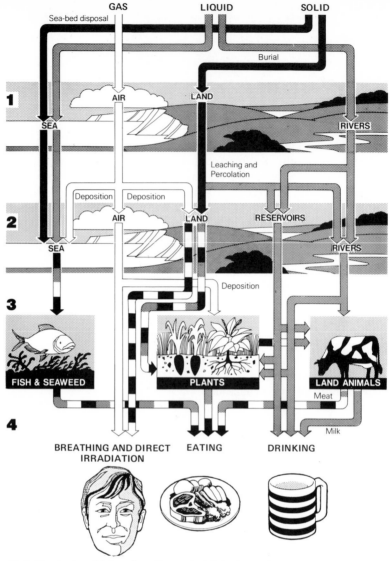

Fig. 21.1 Routes by which radioactive materials in the environment could theoretically lead to irradiation of man.

Key to Figs 1-4

The form of the released material is indicated at the top of the figure

1 indicates the medium (air, rivers, land, etc.) into which the material is originally released.

2 indicates the medium in which it remains or to which it is subsequently transferred.

3 indicates the way in which such material may be taken up by plants and animals.

4 indicates the ways in which man can eventually be irradiated or contaminated.

	Gaseous route
	Liquid route
	Solid route
	Transfer route
	Direct (external) irradiation of man

Radiological Protection (ICRP) has continuously studied in depth all of the available information about the biological effects of radiation, and has made recommendations regarding the levels of radiation exposure which are considered permissible not only for individuals exposed to radiation during their work, but for individual members of the general public, and for populations. The recommendations of ICRP are used world-wide as a basis for legislation in the field of radiation protection, and are used by government departments in all countries as a basis for judging the acceptability of various operating procedures in the nuclear industry.

2.2 The quantification of radiation doses

Before discussing the ICRP's recommendations in more detail, it is desirable to discuss briefly some of the terms used later in this chapter, and to specify the units used for their measurement. Throughout the chapter, doses to individuals are given in rads, i.e. the numbers quoted give a measure of the amount of energy deposited by ionizing radiation in body tissues; this has been done because the rad is the unit generally quoted in the relevant literature. It should be noted that $1 \text{ rad} = 10^{-2} \text{ J/kg} = 10^{-2} \text{ gray}$, the gray (Gy) being the 'strict' SI unit of absorbed dose; where doses are quoted in rads in this chapter, the equivalent value in grays is generally quoted in parenthesis. For similar reasons, quantities of radioactive materials are quoted in curies (Ci), or millicuries, picocuries, etc., with equivalent values in becquerels (Bq) quoted in parenthesis.

In assessing the significance of doses quoted in rads, it should be borne in mind that a given dose in rads due to alpha particles (or neutrons) may be expected to have a greater biological impact than the same dose in rads due to gamma or beta rays. In this respect it is fortunate that most of the doses referred to in the article are due to gamma or beta rays, so that straight-forward comparison is possible. In those cases where the dose is due to alpha particles (e.g. the greater part of doses due to daughters of radon) the dose should be multiplied by the appropriate quality factor (20) to get a measure of the dose-equivalent and hence of the relative biological significance.

Discussion of collective dose is given in man-rads or man-grays. Collective dose is the summation of the doses to individual members of the population considered.

If the dose or the collective dose arises for example from the passage overhead of a cloud of radioactive gas, the exposure stops as soon as the cloud has passed. However, in some cases exposure may continue for a very long time after the release; this applies particularly in the case of certain long-lived materials which remain in the air or the sea for very long periods and become distributed world-wide.

In this case one is interested in the dose commitment or collective dose commitment, i.e. the total dose which will eventually be received as a result of a given practice, either by an individual or by a group of people. If a long-lived material such as ^{14}C is released as a result of the operation of a nuclear reactor or a reprocessing plant, that will add a little more ^{14}C to the existing global pool of that material, and as a consequence every member of the world community will receive a slightly enhanced dose from ^{14}C, not only at the present time, but for thousands of years to come. The individual doses will be very low, but because the number of people affected will be very large, the collective dose commitment may be as large or larger than it is in those cases where small local communities are receiving much larger individual doses.

In the case of materials such as tritium or ^{85}Kr, with half-lives of about 10 years, the amount of them present in the global pool as a result of a given installed capacity of nuclear power stations will increase for a few years, but will soon reach an equilibrium value due to radioactive decay. But if nuclear power production were to continue indefinitely, then for a material such as ^{129}I with a half-life of 17 million years, this equilibrium state would not be reached for millions of years, during which time the value of the collective dose commitment would steadily increase. However, it has been pointed out by the United Nations Scientific Committee on the Effects of Atomic Radiation (UNSCEAR) that it is not reasonable to assume that current practices will continue unchanged for such a long period. They have proposed that the assessments of collective doses should be made on the assumption that these practices might continue for 500 years. In this case the annual collective dose would increase steadily during this period, reach a maximum after 500 years, and then slowly decrease. All the figures for the maximum annual collective doses quoted in this article have been calculated on this basis, and hence refer to the doses which would be received after 500 years.

2.3 ICRP recommendations on dose limitation

The ICRP has adopted the following principles:

1 no practice which involves radiation exposure shall be adopted unless its introduction produces a positive net benefit;
2 all exposure shall be kept as low as reasonably achievable, economic and social factors being taken into account; and
3 the doses to individuals shall not exceed the limits recommended by the Commission.

The assumption is made that the risk of deleterious effects is directly proportional to dose down to the lowest levels (though it is generally recognized that this probably overestimates the risk at low doses). As far as individuals are concerned, ICRP now recommends that when the human body is exposed to radiation non-uniformly (e.g. when a radioactive material concentrates primarily in a few organs) the risk of deleterious effects is obtained by a summation of the risks of such effects in different organs of the body, each component of the risk being obtained by multiplying the dose in a given organ by an appropriate weighting factor. When one is concerned with populations, the assumption of a linear relationship between risk and dose implies that the total risk of harm to the population is proportional to the collective dose in the population.

The dose limits recommended for individual radiation workers and members of the general public respectively are set by ICRP at levels intended to ensure that the risk for radiation workers is no greater than that in other occupations recognized as having high standards of safety, while the highest level of risk for members of the general public is an order of magnitude lower and corresponds roughly to the level of many everyday risks such as the use of public transport; average risk to the general public from radiation will be much lower than this. Although the Commission previously also recommended limits for whole populations, it no longer considers it necessary to do so.

Using these criteria as a basis, the ICRP recommends that, when there is relatively uniform irradiation of the whole body, the dose for an individual radiation worker should not exceed 5 rad (or 0.05 Gy) per year. The corresponding figure for an individual member of the general public is 500 mrad (5 mGy) per year. (For comparison, the average member of the population receives a dose of nearly 100 mrad (1 mGy) each year from natural radioactivity—see § 5.4.) Permissible doses to individual organs or parts of the body are higher than the permissible dose when the whole body is irradiated.

2.4 Derived working limits

In practice it is often necessary to set limits on quantities other than dose; these are called derived working limits (DWL). For example, it is easy to calculate a DWL for the concentration of a particular radionuclide in drinking-water. This is such that a person deriving all his drinking-water over a very long period from a source having this concentration would ultimately get exposed at the limiting dose-rate recommended by ICRP. It is similarly possible to derive a DWL for the amount of a particular radionuclide in fish (flesh), though in this case it is a little more difficult since the amount of fish eaten by different individuals varies enormously.

2.5 Critical pathways and discharge limitation

By the use of appropriate models it is possible to calculate the concentrations which would occur in a variety of materials such as drinking-water or fish, if a certain amount of a particular radionuclide were to be discharged at a particular location. Normally it would be found that one such material reaches the DWL when the levels in the others are well below their DWLs. That material is referred to as a *critical material*. The level of discharge at which the DWL is reached in the critical material enables one to set a DWL for the discharge itself. Normally these limits are derived using a conservative model, in such a way that limitation to the DWL will certainly imply compliance with the basic dose limits; on the other hand, exceeding the DWL during a short period does not generally or necessarily imply that the basic dose limits will be exceeded. The pathway by which the radioactivity reaches the critical material is callled a *critical pathway*. Frequently the highest doses are received only by a small group of people living near the discharge point. They are called the *critical population group*. The situation is more complicated when a mixture of radionuclides is discharged, but the principles are the same.

When discharges have actually taken place, the situation can be assessed on a more realistic basis. Actual discharges can be related directly to concentrations, and the relationship between discharge rate and probable dose can be verified in a satisfactory way. It should be noted that the identification of potential critical pathways permits the most sensible deployment of resources on monitoring. Such monitoring rarely permits the direct measurement of radiation exposure; instead, estimates of radiation exposure are made using data from the monitoring of materials related to the critical pathway in conjunction with data relating to local habits, e.g. the amount of fish eaten by the most voracious eaters.

It is important to realize that critical path analysis needs to be a continuing operation in the context of each discharge situation in order to take account of possible changes in the composition of the discharged material, or even of the habits of the local population. Later in the chapter, examples will be noted where the critical path has changed completely, as a result of such changes. It should also be noted that even when a critical pathway has been identified, other pathways cannot be ignored, because they may contribute very significantly to the total collective exposure of the population.

The type of consideration described above is used by government organisations, such as the Ministry of Agriculture, Fisheries, and Food in England, to determine the numerical values of discharge limits within which operators of plant are required by law to operate—e.g. to determine how much liquid radioactive effluent may legally be discharged from a particular locality. The authorization will certainly not exceed the corresponding DWL, and may be much smaller than the DWL if it is considered reasonably practicable to work to a lower limit (economic considerations being taken into account).

3. Pathways to man from releases into the air

The various pathways involving airborne releases are summarized in Fig. 21.2. Radionuclides may be discharged into the air by the nuclear power industry in gaseous, vapour, or particulate form. Because of the availability and use of *absolute* particulate filters, very little particulate matter is released during normal reactor operations; the only materials which are released during such operations are the more volatile fission or activation products, particularly the noble gases and (to lesser extent) the radioisotopes of iodine.

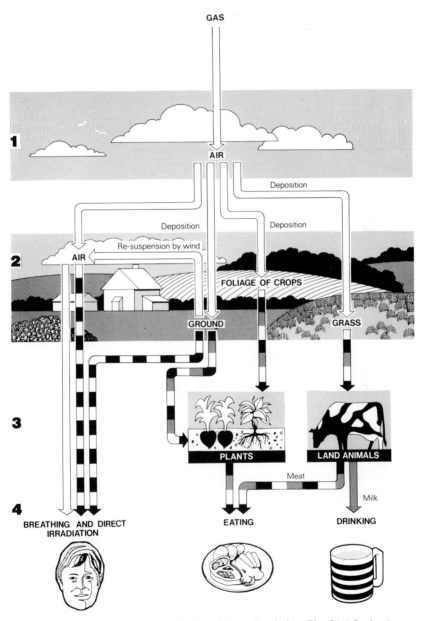

Fig. 21.2 Pathways to man from discharges into the air (see Fig. 21.1 for key).

If an operating reactor were to be involved in an accident, it is again the noble gases and radioisotopes of iodine which would be most likely to escape. In addition, one might anticipate smaller but possibly significant releases of other less volatile substances, such as caesium, strontium, tellurium, and ruthenium, and possibly plutonium. The characteristics of the radioactive materials which might escape in such an accident, their behaviour in food-chains and their metabolism by man, indicate that isotopes of iodine, strontium, and caesium should receive the most detailed consideration.

Generally speaking, the most significant releases of radioactive materials to atmosphere occur at reprocessing plants rather than at reactor sites. Prior to reprocessing, the radioactive materials in the fuel are retained within the high-integrity cladding of the fuel elements. Reactor fuels are deliberately stored for several months, or even years, before reprocessing, and consequently a very large proportion of the more volatile fission products originally present in the fuel have decayed to insignificant levels before reprocessing takes place; for example nearly all of the isotopes of krypton, xenon, and iodine come in this category. However, certain volatile radionuclides remain in the fuel at the time of reprocessing, and a significant fraction of these may be released to atmosphere unless and until special steps are taken to avoid such discharges. The most important radioisotopes in this category are the long-lived but volatile radionuclides ^{85}Kr, tritium, ^{14}C, ^{129}I. Some other less-volatile radionuclides may be discharged in smaller quantities from reprocessing plants, and if reprocessing is carried out after only a relatively short cooling period, a small but significant amount of short-lived but volatile ^{131}I may also be discharged.

3.1 Physical factors involved in the dispersion of radioactive materials released into the air

Dispersion is usually calculated using techniques devised by Pasquill,[1] and more recently refined by Smith;[2] these methods were in turn based on treatments of atmospheric diffusion originally developed by Sutton.[3] The rapidity of dispersion depends on various factors, e.g. wind speed and the state of the weather. Pasquill's method makes it easy to allow for the effects of these variables, and of the height above ground at which the release occurs. Extensions of the method enable allowance to be made for the effects of releases over built-up areas, the effects of dispersion from stacks only a little taller than the surrounding buildings, etc. Satisfactory allowances can also be made for the effects of deposition on the ground of material from the plume as a result of dry deposition or washout by rain.

The rate of deposition varies with the physical and chemical form of the released material. Dispersion data for particular situations have been provided [4,5] in graphical form. Given such dispersion data, the calculation of doses resulting from given releases of particular radioactive materials, due either to exposure from material external to the body (either in the air or deposited on the ground), or to inhaled material, is a relatively straight-forward problem.

In the special case of tritiated water, account must also be taken of intake via the skin.

A number of computer programs have been written for the purpose of calculating the radiation exposures to people downwind which would result from the release of radioactive materials following postulated accidents. In writing such programs, it is necessary to make assumptions both about the proportions of various materials released in the accident, and about their subsequent dispersion. There is generally greater uncertainty about the fraction released than there is about its dispersion. Both in the WEERIE code and the TIRION code,[6] the dispersion calculations are based on the methods referred to above, but allowance is also made for a variety of factors such as plume rise, etc. It is widely accepted that programmes such as WEERIE or TIRION provide estimates of exposure which are already sufficiently accurate for determining how airborne material will be dispersed. Nevertheless, further refinements of the techniques are still taking place.

In the USA, a computer-based system known as the Atmospheric Release Advisory Capability (ARAC), which has been developed at the Lawrence Livermore Laboratory during the last few years,[7] can be used to provide predictions in real time of the dispersion of radioactive material on a regional scale in the event of a nuclear accident; that is, a prediction of the dispersion can be made as the material drifts downwind. Data about the local weather situation is fed directly and continually to the computer from installed instruments on certain sites, and the computer is also provided with frequently updated information about the regional weather situation.

3.2 Processes which lead to the concentration of radioactive materials deposited on the ground

The computer programs mentioned in the previous subsection enable the external radiation doses resulting directly from the deposition of radioactive material on the ground to be taken into account. However, they generally do not take into consideration other less direct methods by which some materials (notably radio-iodines) may be rather efficiently transmitted to man, e.g. via milk after deposition on pasture grazed by dairy cows. This route is important for the following reasons. If grass is contaminated with radionuclides of iodine, strontium, or caesium, a substantial fraction of the contamination deposited from the air on the large area of grass grazed by the cow will be eaten by the cow and concentrated into a small volume of milk. In turn this milk may be drunk by small children, for whom the radiation dose resulting from a given intake is highest. This particular pathway is one of the most important routes of exposure to man as a result of releases of the isotopes of

Table 21.1 Routes to man of radioactivity deposited on the ground

Pathway	Radionuclides for which pathway may be important	Notes
Grass–cow–milk	Iodine isotopes (especially ^{131}I) ^{89}Sr and ^{90}Sr, ^{137}Cs	Generally the dominant route
Grass–cow–cheese	^{89}Sr and ^{90}Sr, ^{137}Cs	Unlikely to be important for ^{131}I
Lettuce, cabbages, etc.	All volatile fission products except noble gases	Likely to be important only for ^{131}I, ^{137}Cs
Grass–animals–meat	^{137}Cs, ^{89}Sr, ^{90}Sr	
Cereals	^{137}Cs, ^{89}Sr, ^{90}Sr	

iodine, strontium, and caesium, and has been studied in some detail. It is discussed further in § 5.1.2. The grass–cow–milk pathway is not of great importance for radionuclides of other elements, mainly because they are not absorbed significantly from the gut of the cow to its bloodstream or milk. In addition to the grass–cow–milk pathway, there are a number of other routes involving animals and foodstuffs. The most likely routes are summarized in Table 21.1. Any or all of these could provide significant pathways to man following a serious reactor accident, but the grass–cow–milk pathway is likely to be far more important than the others.

4 Pathways to man via the aquatic environment

A substantial fraction of the radioactive material from the operation of the nuclear power industry which reaches man does so via the aquatic environment. Radioactivity can get into rivers, lakes, or the sea directly, e.g. as a result of controlled discharges of low-level liquid wastes; or indirectly, e.g. as a result of leaching of radioactive materials from sites where solid material has been deposited. At the present time the direct routes are far more important than indirect methods in causing irradiation of people. Nevertheless there is considerable interest in the indirect routes for two reasons:

(1) because low-level solid waste encapsulated in concrete and arising in several European countries is periodically placed in the deep waters of the Atlantic ocean; and

(2) because many discussions and investigations are currently taking place relating to the controlled ultimate disposal of the high-activity waste from reprocessing plants (which is currently concentrated and stored in water-cooled steel tanks of high integrity).

With regard to item (2), there is a wide international consensus that although storage in tanks is a satisfactory interim practice, it will be more satisfactory in the longer term to convert the wastes into a solid (glassified) form, which requires less supervision and which is clearly even less likely to leak into the environment. The solid material would probably be stored for at least some tens of years in a store where it could be kept under surveillance, but could then in due course be disposed of in a repository which would require no human surveillance or attention. Present proposals are that the containers of glassified wastes should ultimately be deposited on the ocean floor or in sediments on the bed of the ocean, or be buried underground in stable geological formations. The effectiveness of the disposal methods being considered depends primarily on containing the material for long periods at the disposal site, where its radioactivity will decay without affecting people. Discussions of these aspects are not dealt with in this chapter, since they have been recently and adequately reviewed elsewhere.[8] Only the pathways by which radioactive materials might ultimately reach man from sites used for the disposal of such wastes, as a result of ultimate loss of containment and slow leaching of the glassified material, are considered in the following sections of this chapter.

4.1 Pathways to man via fresh water

The various routes by which radioactive materials may get into fresh water, and the routes by which such materials can then cause irradiation of man, are shown in Fig. 21.3.

If material is discharged in liquid form, directly into rivers or lakes, it may contaminate drinking water. Some large towns derive a high proportion of their drinking-water from rivers, and as a consequence very small concentrations of radioactive materials in those rivers can lead to significant collective population exposures. There is also the possibility of contamination of crops and vegetables, via the roots, as a result of radioactive materials getting into ground water or into water used for irrigation.

As discussed above, radioactive materials could also get into fresh water supplies indirectly, e.g. as a result of eventual leaching and seepage from sites used for the burial of solid waste. Before reaching water supplies used by man, however, the water would have to percolate for a considerable distance through the ground. This is an extremely slow process, because of various sorption processes such as adsorption, ion exchange mechanisms, precipitation, colloid filtration, etc. As a result of such processes, it is likely to be many years (see below) before such materials reach drinking-water supplies, during which time a very large fraction of the radioactive material will have decayed. Convincing evidence for this slow transport of radioactive materials through the ground has been obtained from studies of situations where there have been accidental spillages of radioactivity into the ground, for example following an incident at Hanford in 1973, when about 500 m³ of high-activity liquid waste leaked from an underground storage tank.[9] Studies by Hill and Grimwood[10] have suggested that the first radionuclides (^{99}Tc and ^{129}I) to reach potable water supplies, after ingress of water to an underground area used for storage of high-activity waste, would reach their peak concentration after about 200 years. Other nuclides such as ^{237}Np would not reach their peak concentration for about 10^4 or 10^5 years.

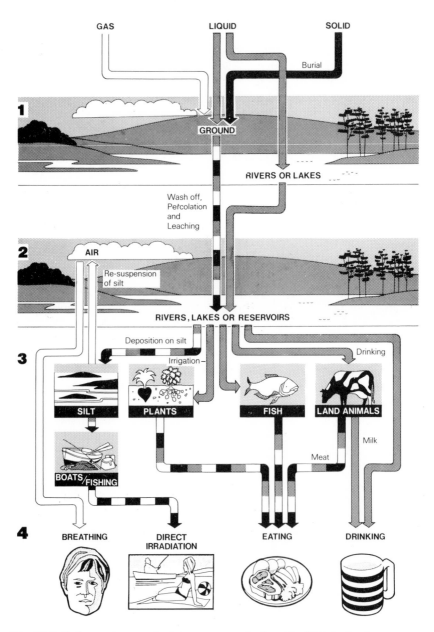

Fig. 21.3 Pathways to man via rivers or reservoirs (see Fig. 21.1 for key).

Irradiation of man can also arise as a consequence of the uptake by fish or shellfish or radioactive materials in lakes, rivers or estuaries; fish and shellfish have the capacity to concentrate a number of elements which are normally present in river or estuary water at very low concentration, either directly from the water or by intake from mud or other organisms living on the bed of the river or estuary (see further discussion in §4.3.3).

There are a large number of other pathways by which radioactive materials in fresh water can cause irradiation of man, but most of them are of small significance.

4.2 Pathways to man via the sea

The various ways in which radioactive materials can get into estuaries or into the sea are shown in Fig. 21.4. Also shown in Fig. 21.4 are the important pathways to man; almost all of these involve the uptake of radioactive materials by living organisms.

The most important route is that in which liquid wastes containing radioactive materials are discharged directly into the sea. Less direct is the route by which liquids discharged into rivers or lakes or into the ground later find their way into the sea via streams and rivers.

Material originally discharged into the air in gaseous forms can also get into the sea, and for certain long-lived radionuclides, that is where most of it will later reside. The material may be deposited in the sea directly from the air, or indirectly via deposition on land and subsequent washout by rain into rivers which then flow into the sea.

If solid waste containing radioactive material is deposited on the ocean floor, or buried underneath it, certain radionuclides may be removed from the solid by leaching processes, and become available for all of the processes described in the following paragraphs.

Once radioactive materials have got into the sea, their subsequent fate, and the extent to which they cause irradiation of man, depends on many factors such as:

(1) whether the material is discharged into nearshore areas, into the waters overlying a continental shelf, or into the deep ocean;

(2) the chemical behaviour of the material when released into the sea—i.e. whether it dissolves (or remains in soluble form), remains suspended in colloidal or particulate form, or deposits on silt etc; and

(3) the extent to which the material concentrates in particular species when it is taken up into the complex of organisms living in the sea.

Radioactive materials in the sea may be taken up by seaweeds and by phytoplankton (microscopic plants growing in the sea). These organisms are producers of organic material in the sea, using solar energy and taking nutrient salts from the sea. Both seaweed and the phytoplankton grow in surface layers in the sea, where it is light, rather than in deeper darker water.

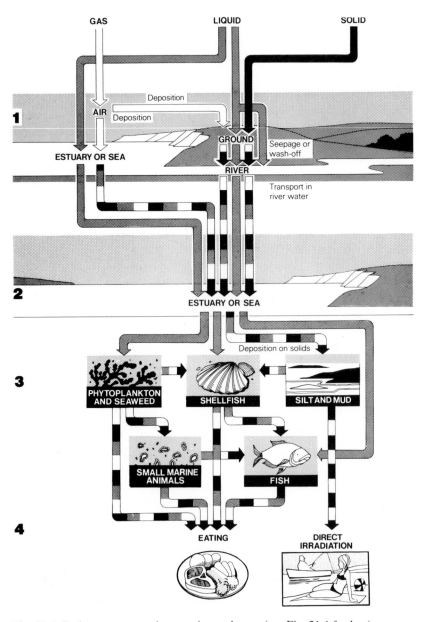

Fig. 21.4 Pathways to man via estuaries or the sea (see Fig. 21.1 for key).

In some places seaweed is incorporated into foodstuffs; for example the seaweed *Porphyra* used in the manufacture of laverbread, which is eaten by some people in Wales (see §5.1.4). Seaweed can also be used in the production of alginates (food additives), or in making animal foodstuffs or fertilizers.

Associated with the phytoplankton and other particulate matter in the sea are the marine bacteria, whose main ecological function is the decomposition of organic matter. Besides taking up substances from the decomposable organic matter, they can also take up dissolved elements directly from sea-water. The bacterial populations increase or decrease rapidly at certain times of year, and this can lead to certain changes in the content of specific elements in the sea. For example, marine bacteria are the main producers of vitamin B_{12}, and consequently accumulate ^{60}Co. They may take up much of this radionuclide at certain seasons and release it again to the sea later in the year following the decay of the phytoplankton.

Phytoplankton is hardly ever used directly as human food; but it is consumed by zooplankton and other small animals living on the phytoplankton, and this provides the most important route of entry into such organisms—though radioactive materials can also be absorbed directly from sea-water. Some small marine organisms such as squids are used directly as human foods. More importantly small pelagic (surface-dwelling) fish feed on plankton, and larger pelagic fish usually feed on small pelagic fish. Thus a likely pathway of radioactivity to man is via phytoplankton, zooplankton and surface-dwelling fish, the latter being eaten by man.

Another route is via shellfish, which spend most of their life on the bottom of the sea. Some of them, e.g. oysters, lobsters, crabs, are of commercial importance as human foodstuffs. They may be divided into:

(1) filter feeders, filtering sea-water and suspension;
(2) detritus feeders, collecting organic particles actively or passing mud through the digestive tract; and
(3) hunters, which eat other animals living on the sea-bed.

The feeding processes in each case provide routes by which these animals may absorb radioactive materials, thus in turn providing another possible way in which man may be irradiated.

Demersal fish, such as plaice and cod, spend part of their time on the sea bottom and feed partly on smaller animals living on the sea-bed. They can also absorb radioactivity directly from the sea-mass.

Studies have been and are being made of pathways to man for radioactive materials deposited on silt, other than those just discussed which involve the food chain. There is the possibility of external irradiation of fishermen and others if such material gets deposited in estuaries or beaches. There is also the possibility that such material deposited in estuaries or on beaches might be resuspended in the air and travel downwind, causing irradiation of people who inhale it. Finally, radioactive material in the sea may become wind-borne in the form of sea-spray, and hence get deposited on the land.

4.3 **Factors involved in the dispersion of radioactive materials in rivers or the sea**

4.3.1 *Physical factors*

1. *Rivers and estuaries.* When soluble radioactive materials are discharged into rivers, the material usually becomes rapidly and uniformly distributed in the stream of flowing water, and (except at very short distances from the discharge point) it may be assumed that the concentration is equal to the ratio of the quantity of radioactive material discharged per unit time, divided by the volume of water flowing per unit time in the river. This can of course be modified for a variety of reasons, e.g. if the material deposits on silt, etc.—see §4.3.2.

When the material is discharged into an estuary, the situation is more complex. In some cases the discharged material may remain for a long time in an estuary, becoming gradually dispersed as the to and fro movement of the tides takes the discharged material out to the sea. The amount of dilution occurring in a particular case can often be predicted fairly well without making local studies, but in some cases it is necessary to study the local situation.

2. *Coastal waters.* In terms of physical (as distinct from chemical or biological) factors, the most important factor controlling the dispersion of material discharged into the sea is whether it is discharged into shallow coastal waters or into the deep ocean. In the former case (inshore discharge) the dispersion depends on the local geographical and tidal situation. Several extensive studies have been made by the Ministry of Agriculture, Fisheries, and Food[11] [12] [13] of radionuclides, especially the caesium isotopes, in the sea near Windscale, where liquid radioactive waste is discharged by pipeline into the Irish Sea. These studies have shown that, during the first few days, much of the effluent simply moves to and fro with the tide, but it is then gradually dispersed by diffusion and by a general residual southerly tidal drift along the coast. Thereafter it joins the circulation of water in Liverpool Bay, where most of it remains for some months, eventually to be flushed from the area by the general movement of Atlantic water which enters the area in the south and leaves it in the north between Mull of Kintyre and Ireland, and is then carried into the deeper waters of the Atlantic.

The rate at which radioactive materials are removed from coastal waters in this way obviously varies considerably from place to place. In the Irish Sea the water is turned over with a half period of about one year. During that time, the greater part of some radionuclides will already have been removed from the sea by other processes. For example, a large proportion of the plutonium and americium will be removed by deposition on sediments in the vicinity of the discharge point. For such materials, the rate at which the inshore seas are scoured by general tidal movement is only of secondary importance. The tidal movement of water in the immediate vicinity of the discharge point is important however, even in these cases. For other radionuclides, such as ^{137}Cs, which are not substantially removed from sea-water by such means as sedimentation, the tidal movement of water determines the equilibrium concentration which will build up in the area if there is a continuing discharge. In the case mentioned above, the total amount of ^{137}Cs present at any one time in the Irish Sea is likely to be about equal to the quantity discharged from Windscale in the past year. However, at equilibrium it will not, of course, be uniformly distributed. A typical distribution profile is shown in Fig. 21.5. Even for those materials where substantial deposition occurs on sediments, the part remaining in the sea is somewhat similarly distributed—see Fig. 21.6.

Jefferies, Preston, and Steele[13] have shown that even when the material (^{137}Cs) gets outside of the Irish Sea, it does not become distributed uniformly. Instead, localized regions of high concentration (especially in surface water) can be identified along the west and north coasts of Scotland and even into the northern part of the North Sea, as shown in Fig. 21.7.

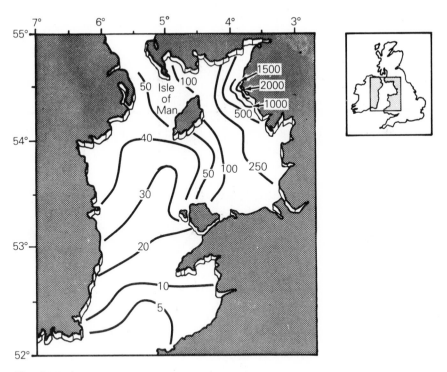

Fig. 21.5 Caesium-137 distributed in the Irish Sea (July 1975). (concentrations in pCi/kg)

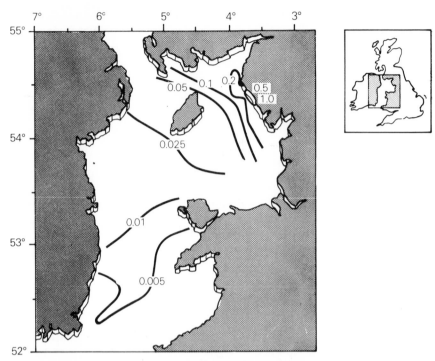

Fig. 21.6 Plutonium distributed in the Irish Sea (July 1974). (concentrations in pCi/kg).

3. *Surface waters*. Radioactive material which in various ways gets into the surface waters of the oceans becomes fairly rapidly mixed in those surface waters as the result of the action of waves and tidal movement, though as already noted quite large concentration gradients can still exist near land as a result of discharges into coastal waters. Mixing between the surface layer of the ocean and deeper layers, however, is extremely slow. The mixing which occurs in the surface layer extends down to depths which may vary from 50–200 m. Below that is the thermocline which acts as a barrier to the vertical transport of materials; the water below this is generally colder and more saline than the surface layer.

One consequence of the slow mixing between the surface layer and the deeper waters is that only a small fraction of any relatively short-lived radionuclides which get into surface waters will ever reach the deeper waters. This applies even to materials (such as tritium) with half lives of the order of 10 years. Very little of the tritium produced during the nuclear tests in the early part of the decade 1960–1970 has penetrated into the deeper waters of the oceans. As a result, the concentration of such materials in surface waters is markedly higher than it would have been if there had been rapid mixing with deeper waters; even so, concentrations of man-made radionuclides in surface waters are low, since the volume of even the surface layer is very large.

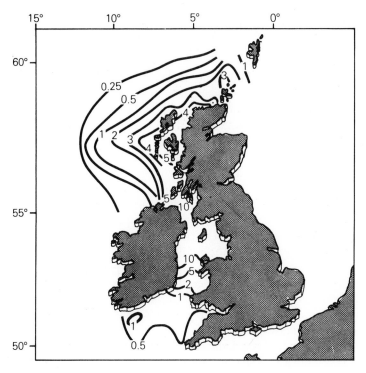

Fig. 21.7 ^{137}Cs distribution in Scottish coastal waters (July 1974)

4. *Deeper ocean waters*. There has for a long time been interest in the behaviour of radioactive materials in deep ocean waters, since low-level solid waste encapsulated in concrete has regularly been dumped in deep Atlantic waters under the auspices of the Nuclear Energy Agency, within the terms agreed in 1972 at the London Convention on the dumping of waste at sea. Although various authors have calculated that the amounts of radio-active material which one could safely deposit in the deep ocean is many orders of magnitude greater than the quantities being dumped at the present time, the Convention prohibits the disposal in this way of high-activity waste, or major amounts of alpha-active waste, presumably in part because not enough is yet known about the dispersion of radioactive materials in deep oceans. Disposal of high-activity waste on the ocean floor, as described earlier in this section, has a number of technical attractions. This has encouraged careful calculations of the radiation doses from a given waste-disposal practice. Both the National Radiological Protection Board (NRPB) and the Ministry of Agriculture, Fisheries, and Food (MAFF) have published preliminary assessments of the possible radiological consequences of the disposal of some or all of the world's nuclear waste on the ocean bed.[14][15] In the NRPB study, Webb and Grimwood[14] employed two different models of

mixing in the ocean waters. In determining the concentrations in the deeper waters in the vicinity of the disposal site they assumed that the major transport process in the deeper ocean waters was diffusion. While they recognised that other processes could be important, they stated that other processes such as vertical currents do not significantly affect the overall conclusions. In considering the situation in the longer term and at places more remote from the original disposal site, Grimwood and Webb used the compartment model shown in Fig. 21.8. This is a crude model for the circulation of waters between the different compartments in the Atlantic Ocean, viz. north and south, surface and deep waters, and between the Atlantic and the Arctic and Antarctic. All of their proposed transfer co-efficients are small, the largest being of the order 10^2 per year; thus residence times in each compartment are of the order of hundreds of years.

Shepherd of MAFF has also proposed a simple model[15] to be used for calculating the slow dispersion of radioactive materials in a deep ocean, and has used the model to estimate the equilibrium concentrations of radioactive materials which would arise from a continuous release of such material on the ocean bed, as a result of an earlier dumping of solid waste in deep oceanic waters. Using parameters appropriate to the North Atlantic ocean, he found that (except in extreme conditions) the surface concentrations do not exceed the long-term average value which would be established in a perfectly mixed ocean. He has suggested that safety assessments of deep-sea dumping of solid waste could be based on this premise, using a safety factor of no more than 10 to allow for possible effects of pluming and upwelling.

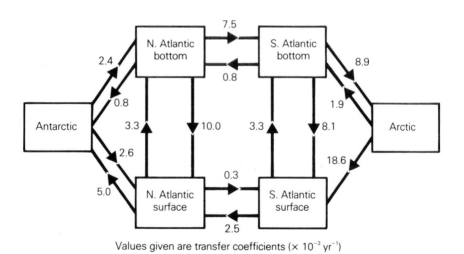

Values given are transfer coefficients ($\times 10^{-3}$ yr^{-1})

Fig. 21.8 A model of the Atlantic, Arctic and Antarctic oceans

4.3.2 *Chemical and physico-chemical factors*
The chemical form of a radionuclide is of vital importance in determining its fate when discharged into a river or into the sea. A large fraction of certain materials have been shown to deposit on sediments in the immediate vicinity of the discharge points; whereas in contrast, for some other radionuclides there is relatively little deposition of this kind.

The uptake of fission products and actinides by sediment (at least in parts of the Irish Sea) has been shown to be primarily a surface absorption phenomenon.[16] The absorptive capacity of sedimentary materials is a function of several factors, including organic content; but one of the most important is particle size, with the specific activity increasing steadily from (coarse) sand to (fine) clay. Having deposited on sediment, the radioactive material may be quite rapidly transported elsewhere due to movement of the sediment: at Windscale there is evidence for the movement of plutonium and other materials in this way into the Ravenglass estuary to the south.

4.3.3 *Biological re-concentration*
Many of the chemical elements which are essential to marine life are present at only very low concentrations in fresh water or in the sea. Those organisms which spend the whole of their lives in water have developed biological processes whereby they can extract adequate quantities of those elements from the water, either directly or by feeding on other organisms which have done so. Consequently the amount of those elements in the living organism per unit mass of flesh, bone, or other organ is very much greater than the amount in the water in which they live, per unit mass of sea-water. The ratio of these two quantities is known as the concentration factor.

For those elements which are homeostatically controlled in the body of an organism, it is absolutely necessary for the well-being of the organism that it should contain a specific amount of that element, irrespective of the concentration of the element in its surroundings. Since the amount of element needed is fixed, the concentration factor observed is inversely proportional to the concentration of the element in the water. If a radioactive isotope of an element is present in the water, in the same physical and chemical state as the stable isotopes, it is concentrated to roughly the same extent as the stable isotopes of the same element. Thus natural ^{40}K is concentrated to the same extent as stable potassium. The process also extends to radioactive isotopes of some elements which are not essential to life but have chemical properties similar to an element which is essential. Thus because caesium and potassium have similar chemical properties, ^{137}Cs is also concentrated, though not to the same extent as if it were an isotope of potassium.

4.3.4 *Examples of behaviour in particular localities*
The concepts which have been discussed in general terms in the preceeding sections may be illustrated in more quantitative terms by reference to concrete examples of waste disposal operations at particular locations. Several

examples of this type relating to the behaviour of certain radioactive materials such as ^{137}Cs, ^{106}Ru, and plutonium in the marine environment are given in §6. In this sub-section information is given concerning some of the rather detailed studies (which were made some years ago) of the behaviour of radioactive materials discharged into rivers at Oak Ridge and Hanford in the USA.

Studies at Oak Ridge National Laboratory (ORNL). ORNL is a large and complex establishment at Oak Ridge, Tennessee, USA; it stands on the White Oak Creek drainage basin, which drains to the Clinch River, which in turn is a tributary of the Tennessee River. Its activities included research and development studies of reactors and fuel reprocessing, radioisotope work, radioactive waste treatment, and the operation of national low-level (solid) waste burial grounds. A detailed and comprehension study of the movement of radioactive nuclides discharged into the White Oak Creek has added significantly to our knowledge of the consequences of the release of radioactive materials to an inland river environment.

A study was made of the hydrology of the Clinch River basin, including studies of the dilution capacity of the Clinch River for the inflowing White Oak Creek waters, the mixing characteristics, and the dispersion and accumulation in sediments.[17] The most important nuclides in the discharge were shown to be ^{60}Co, ^{90}Sr, ^{106}Ru, and ^{137}Cs. The following are the principal conclusions that were drawn.

1. The nuclides ^{90}Sr, ^{60}Co, and ^{106}Ru were associated mainly with 'dissolved' solids, and so was most of the ^{137}Cs which reached the Tennessee River; but the bulk of the ^{137}Cs which remained in the White Oak Creek was associated with suspended solids of large particle size.

2. Virtually all of the ^{90}Sr and ^{106}Ru, about 90 per cent of the ^{60}Co, and 80 per cent of the ^{137}Cs released to the creek passed through the river system, in the water, as far as Chattanooga, some 200 km downstream.

3. The radionuclide content of the bottom sediment in the whole river system was only about 1 or 2 per cent of the total radioactivity discharged from the creek.

4. Of the relatively small fraction which was retained in the river system, most of it was held on sediments. In the upper reaches, the sediments had concentrated along the sides of the stream channel, whereas lower down where the flow was slower, the radioactive sediment accumulations were distributed generally over the whole stream bed.

5. The amount of radioactivity accumulated at any one time in biological materials was only an insignificant fraction of the total load of radionuclides in the whole system.

6. A large part of the river system appeared to act essentially as a pipeline, with no significant accumulation of the discharged radionuclides either in sediments or in the biota.

Surveys were made of water usage from the river system for drinking, industrial usage, irrigation, and other purposes, and the important pathways of the radioactivity to man were identified. The results of this investigation showed that the critical nuclides were ^{90}Sr and ^{137}Cs, and that the critical pathways were drinking of river water and eating fish from the river system. While crop irrigation was not a critical pathway, it could become one. The critical population groups were young people living on the Clinch and Tennessee rivers; even for these, however, the estimated doses which had resulted from releases of over 10 000 Ci (3.7×10^{14} Bq) of these radio-nuclides into the creek were less than 10 per cent of the relevant ICRP dose limits.

Studies at Hanford. Hanford is located in Washington state in the USA, on the Columbia River, a large swiftly flowing river which empties into the Pacific Ocean some 550 km downstream from Hanford. Originally established as a plutonium production facility, it has undertaken work on many aspects of nuclear technology.

The principal sources of radionuclides reaching the Columbia River were the reactors used for plutonium production. Of the wastes arising from other operations, the high-level wastes from reprocessing were stored in tanks, while low- and intermediate-level wastes were discharged after suitable treatment into a highly suitable soil formation which retained the radio-activity. Evidence shows that these wastes did not reach the river.

The original reactors at Hanford had single-pass cooling systems operated on treated river water, to which sodium chromate was added as a corrosion inhibitor. As a consequence the nature and quantity of discharged material was different from that on more modern reactors which have closed-circuit primary cooling systems. Fission products contributed only a small fraction of the total radioactivity discharged. The most abundant radionuclides present were ^{24}Na, ^{31}Si, ^{51}Cr, ^{56}Mn, and ^{64}Cu, together with smaller quantities of a large number of other radionuclides, of which the most important from the viewpoint of irradiation of man were ^{32}P, ^{65}Zn, and the radioisotopes of iodine.

In studies made in 1967 and reported in 1969 it was found that a large fraction of the radioactivity released to the Columbia River rapidly became associated with the river sediments.[18] Some of the sediments settled on or near the river bed, and in the case of some radionuclides up to 90 per cent of the radioactivity was removed in this way; the remainder was carried to the Pacific Ocean. The deposited activity amounted to about 30 000 Ci (about 10^{15} Bq); a large part of this was associated with sediments trapped behind the McNary dam, (some 120 km downstream of Hanford) the first major deposition point downstream. The nuclides were tightly bound to the sediments and could not easily be removed again, e.g. by salt solutions.

Since Columbia River water is used for drinking-water supplies at several cities, e.g. Richland, Pasco, and Kennewick some 50–70 km downstream from Hanford, it was obvious that transfer of radionuclides to man via drinking-water was likely to be one of the most important exposure pathways. Other pathways likely to be important were the consumption of fish and waterfowl from the river, and the consumption of foodstuffs grown on land irrigated with river water. It was found that, in fact, for the typical resident in Richland the most important pathway was from drinking water, which led mainly to bone doses from ^{32}P, thyroid doses from iodine isotopes, and doses to the gastro-intestinal tract from various isotopes, including ^{24}Na, ^{51}Cr, and ^{64}Cu. Most of the doses were only a few per cent of the relevant ICRP dose limits; it was considered, however, that one or two individuals probably got considerable additional doses from the consumption of fish containing ^{32}P and ^{65}Zn; these individuals conceivably ingested enough material to give a bone dose equal to 12 per cent of the relevant ICRP dose limit for a member of the general public; most of this dose would come from ^{32}P.

5   Important pathways for particular groups of radionuclides

Because of their different chemical and physical properties, the many different radioactive materials in the nuclear power industry do not all behave in the same way when released into the environment, and the ways in which they cause irradiation of man are also different. The same is true of naturally occurring radioactive materials which have always been present in the environment. In this section it will be shown how the properties of a radionuclide determine which are the important pathways by which it causes irradiation of people. Fortunately for present purposes, many of the radio-nuclides which are produced in the nuclear power industry can be classified in a relatively small number of groups, within each one of which the behaviour of the materials in the group are similar. These main groupings are:

> noble gases,
> iodines,
> tritium,
> other fission products,
> metallic activation products,
> transuranic elements, and
> carbon-14.

Typical examples of each group are shown in Table 21.2.

The behaviour of these various groups of nuclides which are of particular interest in relation to the nuclear industry are discussed in the following sections of this chapter. As has been pointed out in the *Introduction*, interest generally centres on the effects of these nuclides on groups of people (often very small groups) near the point of release, and it is primarily these effects which are discussed in §5.1. However, in some cases there is also interest in the world-wide effects of releases, and these are discussed in §5.2. Doses resulting from both local and global exposures are summarized in §5.3, and

Table 21.2 Important pathways for particular groups of nuclides

Type of radionuclide	Examples	Radiotoxicity class*	Important pathways‡	Type of exposure	Part of body irradiated
Noble gases	^{133}Xe	4	Directly from airborne material	External irradiation	Whole body
Iodines	^{131}I	2	Directly from airborne material Air–ground–cow Air–ground–vegetables	Inhalation Ingestion	Thyroid
Tritium	^{3}H	4	Directly from airborne material also via water	Inhalation and direct absorption via skin; ingestion	Whole body
Other fission products	^{106}Ru	2	Various, including discharge to sea, contamination of seaweed, and hence of foodstuffs	Ingestion	GI tract (^{106}Ru)
	^{90}Sr	2	Various, including discharge to rivers or sea, contamination of fish	Ingestion	Bone (^{90}Sr) Whole body (^{137}Cs)
	^{137}Cs			Ingestion	
Metallic activation products	^{60}Co	2	Discharge into ground, rivers, sea; then to fish	Ingestion	GI tract or whole body
	^{65}Zn	3			
Trans-uranic elements	^{239}Pu ^{241}Am ^{242}Cm	1	Various, including discharge to sea, then incorporation into foodstuffs	Ingestion	Bone, liver
	^{237}Np		Resuspension of contaminated sediment	Inhalation	Lung
Carbon 14	^{14}C	3	Various	Inhalation, ingestion	Whole body

* radiotoxicity class: 1 high, 2 medium, 3 medium low, 4 low
‡ in order to avoid undue complexity in the table, only the most important routes of exposure have been included

then, to give some sense of perspective in relation to the magnitudes of the resulting radiation doses, the doses resulting from the presence of naturally occurring radionuclides in the environment are discussed in §5.4.

5.1 **Irradiation of local populations by particular groups of radionuclides**

5.1.1 *Noble gases*

Those fission products which are isotopes of krypton and xenon are gaseous, and hence are among the fission products most likely to escape from a reactor if there is a defect in the metallic cladding of a fuel element. Consequently, they are among the materials most likely to escape into the environment surrounding a nuclear reactor; but because they are not taken into the body to any extent, the noble gas radionuclides are of low radiotoxicity. (Some of the factors which determine the radiotoxicity of a nuclide are discussed in the appendix.) Consequently the radiation doses resulting from a given release are much smaller than they would be from a similar release of other more radiotoxic nuclides. In addition to the noble gas fission products, ^{41}A is released from many reactors; it is produced by neutron irradiation of argon in air which penetrates into areas where the neutron flux is high.

Once released, the noble gases tend to remain in the air; deposition on the ground is negligible, and they do not dissolve much in water. The only significant route of exposure of man is by external irradiation from the cloud of radioactive gas, which may pass overhead or may envelop him if he is immediately downwind of a release point. The dose-rate falls off rapidly with distance from the release point, and the most significant individual exposures occur within a few kilometres. Appreciable collective doses can occur at larger distances, however, if the released material passes over large towns.

Most of the noble gases emit both beta and gamma rays. The former cause primarily irradiation of the skin, whereas gamma rays cause fairly uniform irradiation of all of the body tissues. The whole-body dose resulting from a given radionuclide is proportional to the effective energy of the gamma rays

Table 21.3 Effective energies of gamma rays from noble gases

Radionuclide	Effective energy (MeV)
^{85m}Kr	0.15
^{87}Kr	0.85
^{88}Kr	2.00
^{133}Xe	0.05
^{135}Xe	0.34
^{135m}Xe	0.10
^{138}Xe	0.65
^{41}A	1.28

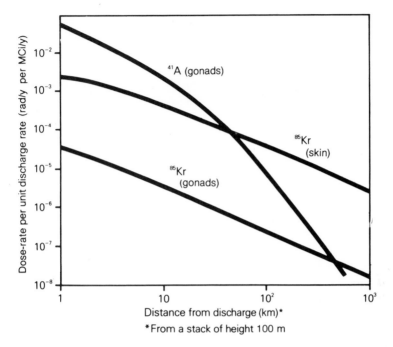

Fig. 21.9 Doses due to noble gas release

emitted by it. The effective energies of some of the more important noble gases are shown in Table 21.3.

When a mixture of such gases is released (the normal situation), the total dose-rate is not proportional to the total quantity released C, in curies (Ci), but to the summation of $C_i E_i$, where C_i is the quantity of one particular nuclide and E_i its effective energy. Consequently, discharge-rates are often expressed in Ci MeV. The dose-rates at various ranges resulting from discharges of noble gases from a stack of height 100 m are shown in Fig. 21.9.

Most of the fission noble gases have half-lives of less than a few days, and consequently when they are released from an operating reactor they decay before there has been any significant build-up globally. More significantly, their half-lives are such that they have decayed almost totally before the reactor fuel is reprocessed. Consequently, there is no significant release of them at reprocessing plants. The one important exception to this rule is ^{85}Kr, which has a half-life of about 10 years. It is still present at the time of reprocessing, when most of it is released to atmosphere (using current practice).

The released ^{85}Kr rapidly becomes widely dispersed in the atmosphere, where it remains for a long time because of its long half-life, causing small doses to all members of the world's population as a result of the accumulation of this material in the atmosphere (see §5.2) (using current practice). Because ^{85}Kr primarily emits beta rays, this leads to a small amount of exposure of the skin of people living near the release point.

5.1.2 *Radio-iodines*

Because a substantial fraction of any radio-iodine which is inhaled or ingested accumulates in the thyroid, the radio-iodines are of relatively high radio-toxicity, especially ^{131}I, which has a longer half-life than most of the others. Since they are comparatively volatile, the iodine isotopes are also among the materials most likely to be released from faulty fuel elements in operating reactors (second only to the noble gases). By the time the reactor fuels are processed, a large fraction of the ^{131}I and almost all of the shorter-lived iodine isotopes will have decayed. Nevertheless, a small fraction remains (and also the long-lived ^{129}I—see below), and some of this may be released to atmosphere during reprocessing. If radio-iodine isotopes are released from reactors or reprocessing plants, the most important pathways leading to irradiation of people are:

(1) inhalation,
(2) the grass–cow–milk pathway, and possibly
(3) via foliar contamination of vegetables.

The pathway involving milk is generally the one leading to the biggest value of dose per unit release. Numerically, the importance of the grass–cow–milk pathway compared with the inhalation pathway can be illustrated by the following comparison.

1. *Inhalation.* If the time integral of concentration of ^{131}I$=Q$ μ Ci s/m^3 (e.g. 1 μ Ci/m^3 for Q s, or Q μ Ci/m^3 for 1 s), then dose to a child's thyroid due to inhalation$=(7.5\times10^{-4})Q$ rad.

2. *Grass–cow–milk.* If time integral of concentration is Q μ Ci s/m^3,

(i) deposition on grass$=0.01Q$ μ Ci/m^2,
(ii) peak value to which concentration of ^{131}I in milk will rise after 2/3 days$=0.0014Q$ μ Ci/litre.

Thereafter the contamination of milk will fall off with a half-life of about 5 days as a result of radioactive decay and actual losses from the foliage. Thus,

(iii) if cows remain on the pasture indefinitely, the value of time integral of concentration$=0.014\times Q$ μ Ci d/litre, and
(iv) resulting thyroid dose to a child who drinks 0.7 litres of this milk each day$=0.16Q$ rad.

Hence,

$$\frac{\text{thyroid dose resulting from drinking milk}}{\text{thyroid dose from inhalation}}$$

$$= \frac{0.16Q}{(7.5 \times 10^{-4})\,Q} = 200 \text{ (approx).}$$

In practice the ratio may be smaller than that for a number of reasons, e.g.

because the cows derive part of their foodstuffs from other sources than contaminated grass, or because the milk is mixed with uncontaminated milk before consumption. It should not be inferred that inhalation can be ignored. For example, if there were to be a serious reactor accident, in which irradiation of people as a result of drinking or eating contaminated milk or vegetables was avoided by controlling the sale and consumption of such commodities, it might still be necessary to adopt other countermeasures to avoid excessive exposure of persons downwind of the reactor site resulting from inhalation, e.g. by evacuation of the local population, or by the prompt administration of stable iodine to 'block' uptake to the thyroid.

The very long-lived ^{129}I, like ^{85}Kr, produces small exposures on a world-wide scale; these are discussed in §5.2.4.

5.1.3 *Tritium*

Tritium is produced in all reactor systems, and in most, but not all cases this occurs predominantly by fission. It can be, and is, released into the environment both at reactor sites and at reprocessing plants, in either gaseous or liquid form. In the latter case it is usually present as tritiated water, whereas in the former it may be either tritium gas or tritiated water vapour.

Although the physical half-life or tritium is long (≈ 12 years), the biological half-life when it is taken into the body is short (≈ 10 days); it is rapidly excreted in urine. Because of this rapid excretion from the body, and because of the very low energy of the beta rays which it emits (5.7 keV average), the radiotoxicity of tritium is low, even when it is taken into the body (as it frequently is) in the form of tritiated water. If tritium gas is inhaled, it is even more innocuous, since only a very small fraction of the inhaled material is retained in the lung.

The discharge of tritium in airborne form leads to the irradiation of man via the following routes:

(1) inhalation and skin absorption of tritiated water vapour in air, and

(2) ingestion of foodstuffs and water contaminated during the down-wind passage of the radioactive cloud, principally from the washout of the tritium in the cloud by rain.

The dose-rates arising from discharges of tritiated water from a stack of height 100 m have been calculated by Kelly *et al*[19]; the results of their calculations are shown in Fig. 21.10, as a function of distance from the discharge point. The doses via inhalation and skin absorption have been averaged over dispersion conditions typical of the temperate latitudes, and are based on a water intake via these routes of 320 g per day, equivalent to an average water content in air of 8 g/m³ (which is typical of UK conditions). Kelly *et al* assumed that foodstuffs and drinking-water would be contaminated at the same level as rain. Approximately equal contributions to the daily water intake to the body arise from the two sources (foodstuffs and drinking water). The level of contamination in rain, and hence in these other materials, was derived on the basis of rain occurring solely in Pasquill's 'C' and 'D' weather categories, rain being assumed to fall for 17 per cent of the time

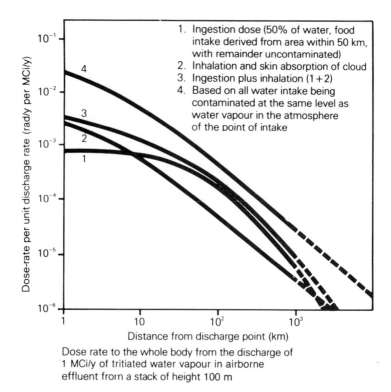

1. Ingestion dose (50% of water, food intake derived from area within 50 km, with remainder uncontaminated)
2. Inhalation and skin absorption of cloud
3. Ingestion plus inhalation (1 + 2)
4. Based on all water intake being contaminated at the same level as water vapour in the atmosphere of the point of intake

Dose rate to the whole body from the discharge of 1 MCi/y of tritiated water vapour in airborne effluent from a stack of height 100 m

Fig. 21.10 Doses due to tritium releases

during the downwind passage of the cloud. Removal of tritiated water from the cloud during rainfall was evaluated using a washout coefficient of 10^{-4} s^{-1} and the concentrations in rain were based on an average rainfall of 750 mm per year. Account was taken of evaporation and subsequent redeposition of tritium removed from the cloud by rainfall. The calculated doses do not depend critically on the detail of many of these assumptions; for example they are almost totally independent of the assumed water vapour content in the air. However, the magnitude of the ingestion doses depends rather critically on the fraction of food and water derived locally, parameters which are likely to vary widely from one region to another. Kelly *et al*[19] assumed that 50 per cent of the food and water are contaminated at the mean level in the area contained within 50 km of the release point, the remaining 50 per cent being essentially uncontaminated. On this basis the inhalation dose, is the major contributor to the total dose out to about 10 km, the ingestion route dominating beyond this distance. An extreme upper limit to the dose from airborne discharge of tritiated water vapour was also obtained (see upper graph in Fig. 21.10) by assuming all food and water to be contaminated at the same level as the water vapour in the air at the range of the exposed person.

The calculations of Kelly *et al* have been quoted at some length to illustrate the following points.

1. In calculations of this type it is necessary to make assumptions concerning the magnitude of various parameters (e.g. the rainfall). Since in practice these often vary from place to place, the final answer can never be very precise, though more precise calculations for a given locality can always be made.
2. None the less the final value of the calculated dose is often not critically dependent on the detailed nature of the assumptions made, and often the results coming from patently pessimistic assumptions differ from those involving more realistic assumptions by only an order of magnitude, which is often sufficiently precise for the intended purpose.
3. Several pathways have to be taken into account; one pathway often predominates at short range and another one at longer range.

Tritiated water may also be discharged as a liquid. Discharges into the sea in the foreseeable future will certainly be of low radiological significance as far as local population groups are concerned. Doses to the world population are discussed in §5.2.2. The importance of discharges into the fresh water environment depends rather critically on the nature of the water body into which the discharge is made, and the subsequent use of that water. An interesting case to which detailed attention has been paid is that of discharge into the river Rhine,[20] because of the use of water from the river for drinking purposes. The assessment considered the discharges likely to occur from nuclear reactors only (not reprocessing plants) expected to be built in the Rhine catchment area by about 2000 corresponding to a capacity of 100 GW(e). Assuming that all of the reactors were of the light water variety, half PWRs and half BWRs, with discharge rates of 2000 CiGW(e)$^{-1}$ y^{-1} for PWRs and a factor 100 less for BWRs, it was estimated that a whole-body dose rate of 0.14 millirad (1.4×10^{-6} Gy) per year would result (i.e. about 0.2 per cent of the dose from natural radioactivity in the environment); that figure was derived on the pessimistic assumption that the tritium concentration in all routes of water intake is equal to that in the Rhine.

5.1.4 *Other fission products*
Most fission products, other than the noble gases and radio-iodines, are likely to cause irradiation of man via pathways which are quite different from those discussed in §§5.1.1–5.1.3. Since most of them are not very volatile, they are generally not released in significant quantities on reactor sites; but many of them are long-lived and may be released during subsequent storage and reprocessing of irradiated fuel or as a result of waste disposal operations. Most of the important pathways are via the aquatic environment.

Caesium 137. Considerable amounts of ^{137}Cs have been discharged to the sea at Windscale in recent years,[28] primarily as a result of leakage from fuel elements being stored underwater prior to reprocessing, due to corrosion of Magnox fuel cladding. The ^{137}Cs is also accompanied by ^{134}Cs, which behaves somewhat similarly though it has a much shorter half-life. For reasons of simplicity, the discussion which follows will generally be limited to ^{137}Cs, though the doses resulting from the [134]Cs are not insignificant.

Although some of the caesium discharged into the sea associates with sediment, most of it stays in the water and disperses from the area of discharge off the Cumbrian coast as this water moves through the Irish Sea and mixes with further distant waters. The dispersal of such materials in the Irish and North Seas has been discussed in §4.3.1 and the variation of the concentration of ^{137}Cs in those seas is shown in Figs 21.5 and 21.7. These waters support important fisheries and the intake of ^{137}Cs through consumption of fish by the local fishing population is now the critical pathway for Windscale discharges. Previously this was the consumption of seaweed contaminated with [106]Ru—see §4.2.

The caesium content of the fleshy edible parts of fish and shellfish in the sea is about a factor of 50 times greater than the concentration in sea-water. As a consequence, the flesh of fish and shellfish caught in the Windscale area in 1975 contained between about 10 000 and 50 000 pCi/kg wet weight[21] compared with concentrations of about 200–1000 pCi/kg in the sea (Fig. 21.5). The members of the coastal fishing community local to Windscale form the critical group in this case. Surveys of this group have shown that the mean and maximum consumption rates of fish and shellfish are 57 g per day and 265 g per day, respectively. If it assumed that the 'maximum consumer' ate 265 g per day of fish, all of which was caught in the small area where the highest concentrations in fish are found, then the resulting radiation whole-body exposure to his tissues was calculated to have been 170 mrad in 1975, i.e. 34 per cent of the ICRP recommended dose limit; doses to the 'average consumer' in the same fishing community would be about five times smaller than this. Only data for one year (1975) are quoted in the text to facilitate comparison, for example, with Fig. 21.5; levels of ^{137}Cs in fish were somewhat higher in 1976, when the estimated dose to the 'maximum consumer' rose to 220 mrad.[22] [23]

The above calculations assume that the concentration of ^{137}Cs in all of the fish eaten by this fishing community is the same as that in fish caught in special fishing surveys undertaken in an area about 2 km wide and 3–4 km long, parallel to the shore, and with its northerly side at the end of the pipeline through which the ^{137}Cs is discharged into the sea. It seems unlikely that any person's all-the-year-round consumption of fish would be caught in such a small area, and hence the figures quoted for doses are probably over-estimates of the true doses. The results are summarized in Table 21.4, which also contains estimates of doses to other groups. The ^{137}Cs situation in the Windscale area is a good example of one in which consideration needs to be given, not only to the doses received by the quite small critical group of local fish eaters, but to the collective dose received by a much bigger and far less localized population. Radio-caesium of Windscale origin can be detected in a large area (not only of the Irish Sea) in which there are very large fish stocks and intensive fishing of these stocks. As a

Table 21.4 Maximum rates of radiation exposure from Windscale discharges in 1975/6 due to consumption of fish and shellfish from the Irish Sea[21, 22]

Population group and persons concerned	Assumed consumption rate and source	Radiation exposure (% of ICRP–recommended dose limit of 500 mrad per year total body)	
		1975	1976*
Coastal fishing community (maximum consumer)	265 g/d Local supplies	34‡	44‡
Coastal fishing community (average consumer)	52 g/d Local supplies	7	9
Other fish eaters: critical group average	300 g/d Commercial: Whitehaven/ Fleetwood landings	12	17
Public at large:	40 g/d Commercial: Whitehaven/ Fleetwood landings	1.6	2.4

* doses expected to reduce in future years—see text
‡ probably over-estimates; see text

consequence radio-caesium has in recent years contributed the largest component to the collective dose from radioactive releases from the Windscale reprocessing plant. During 1975 such releases are estimated [21] to have caused a collective dose of about 14 000 man-rad (140 man-Gy), of which about 8500 man-rad (85 man-Gy) was to the United Kingdom population. In comparison, note that the dose received by the UK population in 1975 from natural causes was approximately 4 000 000 man-rad (40 000 man-Gy).

It is anticipated that both the doses to the local fish eaters and the collective dose from ^{137}Cs in the Windscale discharge will be reduced by at least a factor of three within a few years as a result of the introduction of treatment facilities for removing caesium from pond water.

If ^{137}Cs is discharged into fresh water or waters of relatively low salinity, the concentration factor in the flesh of fish will be considerably higher than the factor of 50 quoted above, which applies when it is discharged into the sea. The behaviour of ^{137}Cs can best be understood by remembering that chemically it behaves rather like potassium. The lower the concentration of potassium in the water, the more the fish need to concentrate it in order to satisfy their biological needs—and hence the greater the extent to which they concentrate ^{137}Cs, which behaves similarly. Studies in Germany[24] in a bay on the Baltic Sea, in rivers, and in lakes have shown concentration factors varying from about 30–300, where the potassium concentration is 100 mg/litre, to values between 1000 and 3000, where it is 1 mg/litre. The concentration factors observed in these studies are shown in Fig. 21.11. Each set of points corresponds to a given locality; the different points in each set correspond to different species of fish living at that locality.

The concentration factor in these circumstances is found to depend not only on the potassium concentration of the water, but also to a more limited

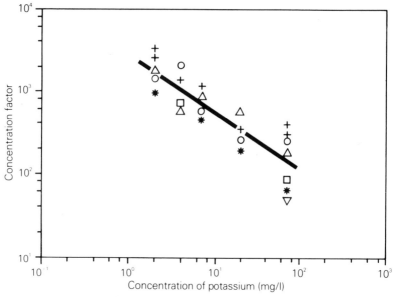

Dependence of ^{137}Cs concentration factor on potassium
concentration in water

Fig. 21.11 Concentration factors for ^{137}Cs

extent on the feeding habits of the fish. The general rule is that concentration
factors are higher for those predatory fish (such as pike and perch) which
feed on other small fish, than it is for fish feeding on all bottom sediments or
for those (such as roach and bream) which eat very small organisms.

Because the concentration factors are higher, and the dilutions which
occur are smaller, where ^{137}Cs is discharged into rivers or lakes than when it
is discharged into the sea, the amount which can safely be discharged is
correspondingly (much) smaller.

It should be noted, however, that in the freshwater regime, ^{137}Cs is more
strongly removed by suspended matter and river muds than in the sea, where
most of the ^{137}Cs remains in the water. The difference is presumably simply
related to the different relative proportions of solid and liquid available in
the two cases. However it is not so strongly absorbed on sediments as some
other nuclides, such as ^{60}Co and ^{65}Zn.

Ruthenium 106. In reprocessing plants, uranium and plutonium are extracted
by solvent extraction from the liquor obtained by acid dissolution of irradiated
fuel; the remaining aqueous–acid liquor, containing nearly all (»99 per cent)
of the fission products originally present, is concentrated by evaporation to
considerably less than 1 per cent of the original volume, and then goes to
long-term storage in water-cooled steel tanks. Following this *primary* separation the plutonium and uranium are further purified to free them from
residual fission product contamination; this produces a number of waste
streams each containing a small fraction of the original fission products
dissolved in a relatively large volume of liquor. These liquors, which are of

medium activity, are neutralized, stored, and possibly given other treatments before being discharged into the sea, together with the material from cooling ponds already discussed; they contain most of the activity discharged to the sea at the reprocessing plant. Other waste liquors from laundries, laboratories, etc., contain only small amounts of radioactivity.

The liquors arising from this *secondary* purification of plutonium and uranium contain a considerable proportion of ^{106}Ru, and about 30 000 Ci (about 10^{15}Bq) of ^{106}Ru are discharged into the sea each year at Windscale. As a consequence, seaweed grown on the Cumbrian coast is contaminated with ^{106}Ru, at a level of 200–300 pCi/g (about 10 Bq/g) wet weight. The concentration factor in the seaweed is about 2000. The seaweed *Porphyra* grown on this coast was previously gathered and sent down to South Wales to be made into laverbread, a delicacy normally fried and eaten with bacon. Some individuals with a particular liking for laverbread formed a critical group. Studies showed that the material dispatched to South Wales could generally be regarded as equivalent to an equal mixture of seaweed from the immediate area of Windscale and from Walney Island (further down the coast); the consumption rate by the critical group was about 130 g/d of laverbread.

If ^{106}Ru is ingested, the matter of greatest radiological protection significance is the irradiation of the lower large intestine (LLI) by the rather high energy beta rays which it emits. The dose to the LLI for the laverbread eaters can be calculated from the facts given above. The dose was typically about 10 per cent of the maximum permissible at a time when about 30 000 Ci (10^{15}Bq) a year of ^{106}Ru were discharged; however, because of changes in local habits, *Porphyra* from this coast is no longer used in the production of laverbread and hence this pathway, which was previously the critical pathway, has ceased to be of much significance.

The *Porphyra* (which has been shown to concentrate ^{106}Ru by a factor, *CF*, of about 2000) also concentrates ^{144}Ce (*CF*=1000), ^{95}Zr–^{95}Nb (*CF*=400), and some other nuclides, though none of these has or had the same radiological significance as ^{106}Ru.

External irradiation due to deposition in estuaries. Exposure of man can occur as a result of the uptake of radioactive materials by sediment, and the subsequent transport of that sediment to estuaries, especially those where large areas of mud banks are left bare by receding tides. The sediments composed of fine mud or silt often found in estuaries take up a number of fission products very readily: in particular ^{95}Zr–^{95}Nb, ^{106}Ru, and the rare earths (e.g. ^{144}Ce) are removed from water to a high degree (so too are ^{60}Co and ^{65}Zn—see §5.1.5). Fishermen and others may be irradiated, primarily by gamma rays from the deposited material. There may also be irradiation resulting from the handling of fishing nets contaminated with such materials; in this case the main concern is with doses to the hands from beta rays. A case to which particular attention has been paid is that at

Ravenglass, near Windscale. Some of the fission products discharged from Windscale and deposited on silt near the discharge point are transported by water currents and deposited in this estuary, causing dose-rates of about 0.15 mR/h (1.5×10^{-6} Gy/h); this only affects a small number of individuals, mainly the few who spend substantial amounts of time on the mud banks surrounding the salmon traps there.

Table 21.5 Properties of some metallic activation products

Radio-nuclide	Radioactive half-life	Mean gamma or X-ray energy/ disintegration (MeV)	Typical concentration factor in fish		
			Fresh-water fish	Salt-water fish	Salt-water shellfish
^{51}Cr	28 d	0.025	40	100	1 000
^{54}Mn	310 d	0.84	100	3000	50 000
^{58}Co	71 d	0.82	20	100	10 000
^{60}Co	5.3 y	2.50	20	100	10 000
^{65}Zn	240 d	0.50	1000	5000	50 000
^{59}Fe	45 d	1.21	100	1000	4 000
^{55}Fe	2.9 y	0.006	100	1000	4 000

5.1.5 Metallic activation products

Metallic activation products are formed in all reactor systems, but are perhaps most important in water reactors. Although great care is taken to purify the feed water in such reactors, this water always contains minute amounts of iron, cobalt, nickel, etc., as a result of corrosion or erosion of steels and other metals in the reactor circuit. Some of that material deposits on the surface of fuel elements and becomes activated by the neutrons in the core of the reactor; much of the activated 'crud' so formed (which consists mainly of iron oxide) is later transferred to other out-of-core parts of the circuit. Some of this material may later be discharged as liquid effluent at reactor sites or at reprocessing plants. Some of the properties of the more abundant metallic activation products produced in this way are shown in Table 21.5.

Because shellfish absorb metals and concentrate them beyond their biological needs, large concentration factors are observed to occur for many of these activation products. Bivalent and trivalent ions such as copper, zinc, and chromium are accumulated to a very high degree. This may be important in limiting the amount of such materials which can properly be discharged into river estuaries, on account of the existence of important shellfish populations that usually live in the same area of an estuary throughout their lives. As they are normally resident on the bed of the estuary, they may continually receive radionuclides, both from the water and from the flocculation, precipitation, and sedimentation processes which occur.

Aqueous radioactive effluent from the Bradwell nuclear power station in

Essex contains a number of activation products such as ^{51}Cr, ^{65}Zn, ^{60}Co, ^{55}Fe, ^{59}Fe, ^{54}Mn, and ^{35}S, arising from the cooling ponds in which fuel elements are stored after irradiation. They arise from neutron activation of impurities in the Magnox alloy used for cladding the fuel elements. The effluent is discharged into the estuary of the Blackwater.

Many of these radionuclides (including ^{65}Zn) are removed to a high degree on sediments in the estuary. Before the station came into operation, it was concluded that the critical nuclide in the discharge would be ^{65}Zn, because of a very large concentration factor (approaching 10^5) for this nuclide in the flesh of oysters which are grown in the estuary of the river Blackwater. This is a classic case of a minor constituent of a discharge being the critical radionuclide due to the fact that it has a very high concentration factor. A detailed study of the eating and other habits of the local population led to the conclusion that the critical group would be that fraction of the local population who each consume about 75 g per day of oyster flesh.[25] The ^{65}Zn concentration in the estuary water arising from a discharge of one curie per day of this nuclide was estimated to be about 1.5×10^{-4} Ci/1. Taking all these factors into account, it was concluded that the maximum permissible daily discharge of ^{65}Zn form Bradwell was 0.2 Ci/d. This very low figure is a direct reflection of the very large concentration factor. The value of the discharge authorization was conservatively set at 5 Ci/y (about 1.8×10^{11} Bq/y). It should be noted that values obtained in this way before operations begin can be modified if necessary in the light of actual operating experience. After a period of operation, monitoring at Bradwell in 1965/6 showed that in practice the concentration of ^{65}Zn in the flesh of oysters from the bed nearest the effluent outfall was only 3.4 pCi/g, compared with the level of 2900 pCi/g which would lead to the most highly exposed individual in the critical group being exposed at the ICRP-recommended dose limit (500 mrad/y or 5 mGy/y—see §2.3). The levels have subsequently decreased still further.

5.1.6 *Plutonium and other transuranic elements*

Most of the plutonium and other transuranic elements present in spent fuel elements are recovered for reuse in reactor fuels in the chemical separation process described in §5.1.4 (under Ruthenium-106), but a small fraction of them is discharged to sea in the large volume of low-level liquid waste. In recent years about 1000–1500 Ci (about $3–5 \times 10^{13}$ Bq) of alpha-active plutonium (mainly ^{239}Pu and ^{240}Pu), and similar but more variable quantities of ^{241}Am have been discharged in this way each year from Windscale. In addition, larger quantities (30 000 Ci/y or about 10^{15} Bq/y) of the much less radiotoxic beta-emitting ^{241}Pu have been discharged. The current certificate of authorization issued by the Ministry of Agriculture, Fisheries, and Food in March 1971 permits the annual discharge of up to 6000 Ci (about 2×10^{14} Bq) of alpha activity and up to 300 000 Ci (10^{16} Bq) of beta activity (with additional more-severe restrictions on certain radionuclides such as ^{106}Ru). The basis for such authorization was discussed in §2.

The plutonium reaching the final low-activity waste tanks is in a stream which is strongly acidic, and at this stage it is in a soluble form; but before discharge to the sea the effluent is neutralized by addition of ammonium hydroxide, and this converts the plutonium to a form more likely to precipitate out or to deposit on suspended material.

Experience has shown that at least 90 per cent of the discharged plutonium is in fact incorporated into the sea sediments quite close to the point of release. The material remaining in the sea has a distribution similar to that of the ^{137}Cs discharged at the same point (see Fig. 21.6), and it is this material in the sea which seems to be the main reservoir from which some (albeit small) uptake to biological systems is currently taking place. The equilibrium inventory in the water of the Irish Sea was found to be about 60 Ci (2×10^{12} Bq) at a time (1973/4) when 1800 Ci (6×10^{13} Bq) per year was being discharged; most of the material discharged in this and earlier years was deposited on sea-bed sediments. Because the amount in sea-water is relatively small, only a small fraction of the released plutonium is removed from the area by tidal movement.

Hetherington *et al*[26] have suggested that the loss of plutonium from the sea on to sediments is due to hydrolysis and subsequent precipitation of material (originally present in the effluent in soluble form) either as a hydroxyl complex of the element itself or in association with material already present in the sea-water. The observed value of the concentration factor between the sediment and the sea is however a function of the particle size of the sediment, suggesting that absorption plays a part in the process; concentration factors of between 2×10^4 and 2×10^5 have been observed close to the release point.

Measurements of ^{239}Pu have been made on samples of edible algae, of fish flesh, and of the soft parts of shellfish taken from the Irish Sea, and by comparing these with the measured values of sea-water concentrations, values for the concentration factor in each material have been found. These vary from about 10 for dab and plaice to 2000 or 3000 for mussels, winkles, and *Porphyra*.[26]

Preston[26] has concluded that the radiological significance of the plutonium so far discharged to the Irish Sea has been negligible, and has said that there is no evidence of long-term build-up in biological materials. Bowen and his co-workers,[27] who have mainly studied the behaviour of fall-out plutonium in aquatic environments in Buzzards Bay, Massachusetts, have concluded that the fallout plutonium in Buzzards Bay may be both more mobile and more involved with biological process than one would have supposed from the studies reported by Preston near Windscale. In particular they have argued that the amount of ^{239}Pu found at a depth of several centimetres below the surface of silty deposits below shallow water in Buzzards Bay cannot be accounted for on the basis of sedimentation, which is too slow. They suggest that the material could only have reached the observed levels as a result of chemical or biological processes. They have also suggested that the deposited plutonium can reconcentrate in fish, particularly in rarely eaten parts of fish, and that such food items as anchovies, sardines and canned salmon, which are consumed whole, could form important transfer vectors of plutonium into humans via the food chain. However, Preston[25] has concluded that there is no evidence that such processes are taking place for the plutonium which came from fuel reprocessing and is now deposited in the Irish Sea sediments; if such processes are taking place there, the fraction of plutonium involved is very small and quite insignificant compared with the plutonium entering food chains more directly.

Studies have shown there is some movement of sediment from the Windscale outfall into estuaries such as the Ravenglass estuary to the south. If such sediment is deposited in places where it can dry out, it may subsequently become airborne and produce an inhalation hazard. Studies in the Ravenglass area have shown that airborne concentrations arising from this pathway are currently extremely insignificant[28] (see Table 21.6).

Table 21.6 Doses due to resuspension of actinides at Ravenglass

Radionuclide	Concentration in air (Ci/m^3)			
	Northern site		Southern site	
	Mean	Max.	Mean	Max.
$^{239}Pu + {}^{240}Pu$	2.2×10^{-16}	7.3×10^{-16}	0.6×10^{-16}	1.5×10^{-16}
^{241}Am	2×10^{-16}	8×10^{-16}	0.4×10^{-16}	1.2×10^{-16}

Note
For a member of the general public, exposed to airborne material continuously throughout the year, the maximum permissible concentrations recommended by the International Commission on Radiological Protection are:

For soluble material	^{239}Pu or ^{240}Pu	$6 \times 10^{-14} Ci/m^3$
	^{241}Am	$2 \times 10^{-13} Ci/m^3$
For insoluble material	^{239}Pu or ^{240}Pu	$10^{-12} Ci/m^3$
	^{241}Am	$4 \times 10^{-12} Ci/m^3$

The Solway Firth has been receding throughout recorded history, with all the channels being slowly filled with marine-derived material, and sediment is undoubtedly accumulating in areas like the Ravenglass estuary. Measurements of sea-bed samples show that the amount of plutonium on the bed of the Irish Sea to the east of the Isle of Man is nearly the same as the integrated amount discharged from Windscale, and this suggests that the amount of plutonium being removed from the area as a whole on sediment is small. Consequently the total amount of plutonium deposited in places like the Ravenglass estuary can be expected to increase slowly but progressively in future years. However, airborne levels of plutonium will be related to the activity per unit mass of sediment, which will reach an equilibrium value even though the total amount of plutonium deposited in the area continues to rise. Careful monitoring of these processes is currently taking place.

Deposition on open beaches can in principle also be another source of airborne material, and plutonium can also be transported to land in wind-borne sea-spray; but concentrations resulting from either of these pathways is known to be insignificant in the Windscale area at the present time.

It will be seen from Table 21.6 that levels of ^{241}Am at Ravenglass are similar to those of ^{239}Pu+^{240}Pu. Much of this material arises from the decay of ^{241}Pu, but some of it is actually discharged as ^{241}Am. The behaviour of ^{241}Am in the sea is similar to that of plutonium, most of it being absorbed on sediments and transported with them.

5.1.7 Carbon-14

^{14}C is formed in most reactors as a result of neutron irradiation of ^{13}C, ^{14}N, and ^{17}O. Production rates are of the order $10 \, CiGW(t)^{-1} \, y^{-1}$, and most of the ^{14}C produced is released either at the reactor site or at the reprocessing plant, mostly in the form of carbon dioxide, carbon monoxide, or hydrocarbons.

^{14}C discharges to the environment are important because the ^{14}C becomes incorporated into the carbon content of the .biosphere; and once there it remains for many generations, its half-life being 5700 years. Since carbon participates in almost all biological and biochemical processes, and is a constituent of proteins and molecules such as DNA and RNA, the presence of ^{14}C in the body obviously leads to irradiation of significant tissues. Fortunately, however, it decays with emission of beta rays of low energy (mean 50 keV). It might have been anticipated that its radiological significance would be enhanced because of the decay of nuclei of atoms forming part of the genetically important DNA; the limited data available however suggests that the resulting enhancement is insignificant.

If ^{14}C is discharged as CO_2 in airborne effluents, this will lead to irradiation of man via two routes, direct inhalation of the released material and ingestion of contaminated foodstuffs. The exchange rate between atmospheric carbon dioxide and living vegetation is rapid and hence the vegetation becomes contaminated at very nearly the same specific activity as in the cloud of released material. Kelly et al[19] have calculated the doses resulting from discharges from reactors and reprocessing plants. Their results are shown in Fig. 21.12. The resulting doses prove to be small compared with those from other radionuclides such as ^{85}Kr and tritium, which invariably accompany the ^{14}C.

Apart from the local effects referred to above, ^{14}C releases also lead to world-wide effects. These are discussed in §5.2.3.

5.2 World-wide effects of certain gaseous releases

It has already been pointed out that most of the more important pathways involve small groups of people living near particular installations. However, in the case of a small number of long-lived isotopes which can relatively

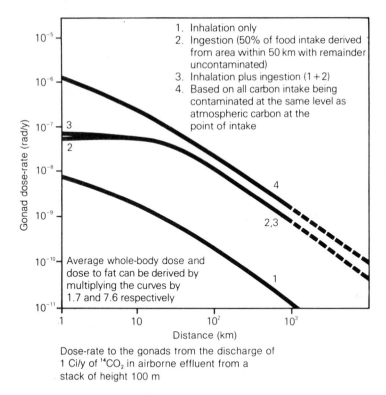

1. Inhalation only
2. Ingestion (50% of food intake derived from area within 50 km with remainder uncontaminated)
3. Inhalation plus ingestion (1 + 2)
4. Based on all carbon intake being contaminated at the same level as atmospheric carbon at the point of intake

Average whole-body dose and dose to fat can be derived by multiplying the curves by 1.7 and 7.6 respectively

Dose-rate to the gonads from the discharge of 1 Ci/y of $^{14}CO_2$ in airborne effluent from a stack of height 100 m

Fig. 21.12 Doses due to ^{14}C releases

easily become widely dispersed, the world-wide effects add substantially to the collective dose commitment. Various assessments have indicated that ^{85}Kr, tritium, ^{14}C, and ^{129}I are the radionuclides most likely to constitute long-term sources of world-wide irradiation. All of these substances are produced in nuclear reactors and can be released to some extent from operating reactors, but especially in the case of ^{85}Kr and ^{129}I they are much more likely to be released at reprocessing plants.

All of these radionuclides can also cause irradiation of populations living near reactors and reprocessing plants. Those effects have already been discussed in §5.1; only the world-wide effects will be considered here.

5.2.1 *Krypton-85*

Unlike the other shorter-lived isotopes of krypton and xenon, which have decayed to insignificant levels when the reactor fuel is reprocessed, most of the ^{85}Kr remains in the fuel at the time of reprocessing, and can be discharged to atmosphere at this time. The quantity involved is about 10^5 CiGw(t)$^{-1}$ y^{-1} (about 4×10^{15} Bq Gw(t)$^{-1}$ y^{-1}), implying a world total of about 60 MCi/y (about 2.2×10^{18} Bq/y) at the present time (1980); at present no steps are taken to limit such discharges, so nearly the whole of this material is discharged into the environment. The radiation doses resulting from the world-wide distribution of [85]Kr have been calculated by Bryant and Jones.[29] They assumed that virtually all of the [85]Kr is discharged in latitudes 35° N to 60° N, and that this rapidly becomes uniformly distributed within this latitude band up to a height of 10 km. Transfer from this band to the whole of the troposphere of the Northern hemisphere is assumed to occur with a half-time of 100 days, and mixing between Northern and Southern hemispheres about 10 times more slowly. The results of their calculations do not depend at all critically on the precise nature of these assumptions. [85]Kr deposition on land is negligible, and so is its solubility in the sea: consequently all of the [85]Kr is assumed to remain in the atmosphere until it disappears by radioactive decay. These calculations show that the dose-rate to the whole body of an individual in the latitude band 35°–60° N arising from the present accumulation of [85]Kr in the atmosphere external to his body, is about 7×10^{-7} rad/y (or 7×10^{-9} Gy/y), i.e. about a factor 10^5 smaller than the dose-rate due to natural radiation and radioactivity. Skin doses are higher than whole-body doses by a factor of about 180 ([85]Kr is primarily a beta emitter). Doses resulting from transport in the body of inhaled [85]Kr are negligible in comparison with doses due to the material external to the body.

Although the individual doses resulting from the world-wide distribution are at present very small, they will increase as more nuclear power stations are built. It is feasible to trap [85]Kr from reprocessing plants and to allow the trapped [85]Kr to decay. Appropriate processes are currently being developed, which will be available in future if it should be considered necessary to limit the magnitude of the collective doses.

5.2.2 *Tritium*

Within perhaps a year or two, most of the tritium discharged from reactors or reprocessing plants becomes widely dispersed into the circulating surface waters of the hemisphere into which the discharge is made; at present most of these plants are in the northern hemisphere.

As discussed in §4.3.1, penetration into deeper ocean waters is very slow, but the material fairly rapidly becomes dispersed in the surface waters, generally assumed to have a depth of about 75 m and volume of about 10^{16} m³. Kelly *et al*[19] have calculated the resulting global doses on the assumption that body fluids of individuals become contaminated to the same level as the surface waters of the sea; this is somewhat pessimistic because some of their drinking water is probably derived from sources having a lower tritium concentration. The global circulation was assumed to behave in the way shown in the model of Fig. 21.13; the calculated doses do not depend critically on the detail of this model. The results of their calculations are shown in Fig. 21.14. Globally, the doses due to trituim are about the same as those due to [85]Kr. As with [85]Kr, methods of trapping tritium, rather than releasing it, are being developed in case of need.

5.2.3 *Carbon-14*

The global circulation of ^{14}C discharged from all nuclear reactors has been

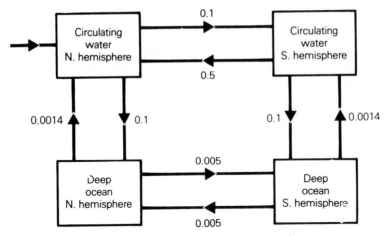

Transfer units are given in units of y^{-1}

Fig. 21.13 Model for global circulation of tritium and ^{129}I

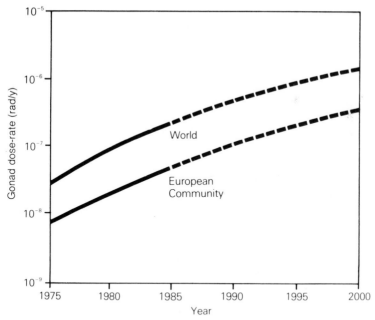

Dose-rates to the whole body from the global
circulation of tritium discharged from the European Community
and world nuclear power programmes

Fig. 21.14 Global dose rates from tritium

considered by Kelly *et al.*[19] They assumed that all the ^{14}C is discharged as carbon dioxide into the troposphere in the latitude band 35°–60° N, and that uniform dispersion up to a height of 10 km occurs very rapidly. They assumed that transfer to the remaining troposphere in the Northern hemisphere occurs with a half-time of 100 days, with slower transfer to humans, to the oceans, etc. The results of their calculations are shown in Fig. 21.15.

The world-wide collective dose commitment from ^{14}C releases from nuclear power installations has been calculated on the assumption that the world population will reach an equilibrium value of 10^{10} persons. If it is assumed that power production from nuclear fission might continue for (say) 500 years, the resulting maximum annual collective dose from ^{14}C will be 0.9 man-rad (9×10^{-3} man-Gy) per MW(e).[30] This is about a factor of 10 greater than the corresponding dose from either [85]Kr or [3]H.

5.2.4 *Iodine*

[129]I is produced in small quantities as a fission product. It is of interest because of its very long half-life of 17 million years; once released into the environment, it remains there for a very long time. Most of the [129]I

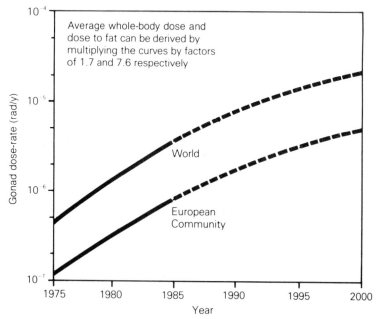

Dose rates to the gonads in the latitude band 35-60°N
from the global circulation of carbon −14
discharged from the world and European Community nuclear power programmes

Fig. 21.15 Doses from global circulation of [14]C

produced as a fission product is likely to be discharged as liquid waste at fuel-reprocessing plants, certainly for those sited on the coast. The extent to which locally released ^{129}I participates in the global iodine cycle is not known, but it seems likely that it will become widely distributed. Of the iodine available to man, most is in sea-water. Evaporation of this contributes most to the exchange between hydrosphere and atmosphere. Atmospheric water is exchanged within about 10 days, and there is an equally rapid exchange of iodine. In the case of ^{129}I, exchange with the deep ocean, which is achieved within a few hundred years, must also be considered. This leads to a reduction in the concentration to which man is exposed by a factor of about 60. It has been estimated that the maximum value of the annual collective dose, if power production from nuclear fission were to continue for 500 years, would be approximately 0.05 man-rad (5×10^{-4} man-Gy) per MW(e) (see Table 21.7).

Table 21.7 Maximum annual collective doses to the public due to nuclear power production* (man-rad per year for each MW(e))

	Gonads	Whole lung	Thyroid
Reactor operation			
Atmospheric pathways:			
Kr, Xe, ^{41}A	0.2	0.2	0.2
^{3}H	0.004	0.004	0.004
^{131}I			0.1
Water pathways:			
^{3}H	0.03	0.03	0.03
Cs, Co, Mn, I	0.01	0.01	0.02
Fuel reprocessing			
Atmospheric pathways:			
^{85}Kr	0.0007	0.002	0.0007
^{131}I, ^{129}I			0.2
Water pathways:			
^{3}H	0.04	0.04	0.04
^{129}I			0.03
Cs, Ru, Sr	0.09	0.09	0.09
Global fuel reprocessing and			
reactor operation			
^{3}H	0.1	0.1	0.1
^{85}Kr	0.09	0.25	0.09
^{14}C	0.9	0.9	0.9
^{129}I			0.05‡
Total	1.5	1.7	2.0

* assuming the generation of nuclear power continues for 500 years
‡ value quoted incorrectly as 0.5 in table 29 of annex D in the UNSCEAR Report from which these numbers were derived

5.3 Doses world-wide

Table 21.7 summarizes calculations which have been made by the United Nations Scientific Committee on the Effects of Atomic Radiation in annex

D of its 1977 report to the General Assembly[30] of the doses to the public due to various aspects of nuclear power production (see Table 29 of the annex). It will be seen that more than 50 per cent of the collective dose to the world population from nuclear power production is due to the global distribution of ^{14}C, ^{85}Kr and tritium. As already noted, in the United Kingdom and in some other countries, technologies are under development for restricting the release of these radionuclides (and also ^{129}I).

The significance of some of the figures in Table 21.7 is questionable however, especially in the case of the longer-lived materials such as ^{14}C and ^{129}I. The individual doses are very small, of the order of 10^{-7} or 10^{-6} rad/y (10^{-9}–10^{-8} Gy/y) from power stations with an installed capacity of 10^5 MW(e). The apparently large collective doses arise merely because the number of people affected is so large. The following should be noted.

1. The annual dose to an individual is, for example, about a thousand times smaller than the additional dose resulting from a single short journey in a sub-sonic aeroplane.
2. Overall detriment is only proportional to collective dose if risk is proportional to dose down to the lowest levels. Although the idea of proportionality between risk and dose is widely accepted as an acceptable basis for most radiation protection purposes, many health physicists doubt the wisdom of assuming uncritically that this relationship applies at the 1 μrad/y (10^{-8} Gy/y) level; there is a lot of evidence from the field of radiobiology which suggests that the real detriment is far smaller than a linear assumption would suggest.
3. No attempt has ever been made to calculate the world-wide detriment resulting from the global distribution of non-radioactive toxic substances.

The collective doses shown in Table 21.7 range from about 2–4 man-rad per MW(e) y. For the present installed capacity of 8×10^4 MW(e), the whole-body collective dose works out at about 1.3×10^5 man-rad (1300 man-Gy) per year. This is about the same as the global dose resulting from air travel, and about a factor 2000 lower than the dose of 3×10^8 man-rad (3×10^6 man-Gy) per year due to natural radiation sources.

5.4 Pathways to man of naturally occurring radioactive materials

Naturally occurring radioactive materials certainly reach man by each and every one of the routes discussed in this article, and the resulting exposures are far greater than those resulting from the operation of the nuclear power industry. It is not necessary or possible to discuss these pathways in detail here, but it may be appropriate to mention some of the more important pathways, and the resulting doses. Table 21.8 shows the main sources of such exposure (see reference 30, §5.2.3).

5.4.1 *External Irradiation*
On average, man is exposed to a dose of about 30 mrad/y (0.3 mGy/y) from

Table 21.8 Estimated annual tissue absorbed dose from natural sources in normal areas

Source of irradiation	Annual tissue absorbed dose (mrad)			
	Gonads	Lung	Bone lining cells	Red bone marrow
External irradiation				
Cosmic rays:				
ionizing component	28	28	28	28
neutron component	0.35	0.35	0.35	0.35
Terrestrial radiation (γ)	32	32	32	32
Internal irradiation				
Cosmogenic radionuclides:				
^{3}H(β)	0.001	0.001	0.001	0.001
^{7}Be(γ)	—	0.002	—	—
^{14}C(β)	0.5	0.6	2.0	2.2
^{22}Na($\beta + \gamma$)	0.02	0.02	0.02	0.02
Primordial radionuclides:				
^{40}K($\beta + \gamma$)	15	17	15	27
^{87}Rb(β)	0.8	0.4	0.9	0.4
^{238}U–^{234}U(α)	0.04	0.04	0.3	0.07
^{230}Th(α)	0.004	0.04	0.8	0.05
^{226}Ra–^{214}Po(α)	0.03	0.03	0.7	0.1
^{210}Pb–^{210}Po($\alpha + \beta$)	0.6	0.3	3.4	0.9
^{222}Rn–^{214}Po(α) inhalation	0.2	30	0.3	0.3
^{232}Th(α)	0.004	0.04	0.7	0.04
^{228}Ra–^{208}Tl(α)	0.06	0.06	1.1	0.2
^{220}Rn–^{208}Tl(α) inhalation	0.008	4	0.1	0.1
Total (rounded)	78	110	86	92
Fraction of absorbed doses delivered by alpha particles or neutrons (%)	1.2	31	8.5	2.1

cosmic rays, 30 mrad/y (0.3 mGy/y) from terrestrial radiation, and 30 mrad/y or 0.3 mGy/y from internal emitters. These are average values; the values vary enormously, by factors of more than 10:1, mainly due to variations in the external doses from terrestrial radiation, which are in turn mainly due to the presence of large amounts of radioactive materials on or near the ground in some inhabited parts of the world. For example in Kerala, India, 70 000 persons live in an area where the dose from external radiation is over 1 rad/y (10^{-2} Gy/y); this is due to deposits of monazite sand which contain 8–10 per cent of thorium. Similar areas exist elsewhere, e.g. in Brazil. Quite high dose-rates exist in parts of Italy and France. Within the United Kingdom, variations by a factor of two occur in the dose-rates in houses, mainly due to the variability in the amount of radioactivity in building materials.

5.4.2 *Potassium-40*
The most important source of internal radiation is ^{40}K, a primordial material with a half-life of about 10^9 years. The ^{40}K enters the body (along with

stable K) in the diet, being present in varying quantities in many items of food. Potassium is an essential constituent of nerves and muscle, and hence of living organisms. The quantity in the body is homeostatically controlled, and hence virtually independent of the concentration in diet; the body contains about 2 g of potassium per kilogram of body weight, and as a consequence the average person contains about 100 nCi of ^{40}K, giving a dose of 15–20 mrad/y to every individual in the world. The collective dose resulting from this is very large compared with doses which result from operation of the whole of the nuclear industry—see Table 21.9. This is perhaps not surprising in view of the ubiquitous nature of ^{40}K and the fact that the oceans of the world alone contain 500 000 MCi (about 1.8×10^{22} Bq) of ^{40}K.

Table 21.9 Global dose commitments from various radiation sources*

Source of exposure	Global dose commitment from that source as a percentage of total dose commitment (approximately)	
Cosmic rays	28	
Terrestrial radiation	32	78
^{40}K in nature	15	
Other natural sources	3	
Medical diagnosis	15	
Nuclear explosions	6.2	
Consumer products	0.6	
Nuclear power industry at present level‡	0.12	
Coal-fired power plants	0.04	
Commercial air travel	0.08	
Use of phosphate fertilisers	0.008	

* calculated from data in reference 30 (Tables 3 (p. 16) and 31 (p. 81)) on the assumption that present practices continue; in the case of nuclear explosions it has in effect been assumed that nuclear explosions will continue to occur at the mean level at which they occurred in the period 1951–76
‡ 80 000 MW(e)

5.4.3 *Ingestion of radium, etc*

For most individuals, doses due to ingestion of other naturally occurring radioactive materials in foodstuffs are much smaller than those from ^{40}K. It should however be noted that the amounts of radioactive materials present in various items of diet are extremely variable. Thus for example Brazil nuts contain about 20 000 times as much radioactive material as baked beans.[31] The amount of ^{226}Ra (one of the most radiotoxic materials) in Brazil nuts is surprisingly high, reaching several nCi/kg; these nuts also contain similar quantities of ^{228}Ra and even larger quantities of various isotopes of the thorium and uranium series.

The concentration of radium in Brazil nuts is of particular interest in the context of this article. Brazil nuts are the seeds of a huge tree, *Bertholletia excelsa*, which produces fruit about 15 cm in diameter, containing 12–25 nuts arranged like sections in an orange. These trees grow in the Amazon valley, on elevated ground not subject to annual floods. They have an enormous root system covering a volume of up to 10 000 m³ of earth; thus the tree is able to absorb a great amount of nutrients from the soil, even when they are present in very small concentrations. Although there are regions of Brazil which are rich in minerals containing thorium and other natural radioactive materials, the high concentration in Brazil nuts does not occur on that account; samples of soils collected near Brazil nut trees showed normal levels of radium,[32] about 1 pCi/g, compared with over 1000 pCi/g in some areas of Brazil. In contrast to most plants, which discriminate against barium, as compared with calcium, *Bertholletia* absorbs a lot of barium, which in many cases accounts for 5–10 per cent of the weight of the ash produced by burning tree samples. Because radium behaves chemically like barium, high levels of radium are found in all parts of the tree, including the nuts. A broad correlation is found between the concentrations of barium and radium in nuts.

The greatest importer of Brazil nuts is the United Kingdom. It has been estimated that people who eat Brazil nuts may ingest up to 10 times as much radium as the remainder of the population.[32] The purpose of these remarks is not, of course, to suggest that Brazil nuts are 'dangerous', but merely to point out that some ordinary items of diet contain what many people would consider to be alarmingly large amounts of one of the most highly toxic radioactive substances (radium).

5.4.4 *Long-lived daughters of ^{222}Rn*

Irradiation of people also occurs as a result of the inhalation of decay products of ^{222}Rn; the latter is a gaseous material which emanates from the ground, having arisen as a result of the decay of ^{226}Ra. The most important decay products are ^{210}Pb and its alpha-emitting daughter ^{210}Po. The amount of atmospheric ^{210}Pb produced from the decay of ^{222}Rn is about 0.6 MCi/y $(2 \times 10^{16}$ Bq), and this would lead to an equilibrium amount of about 20 MCi $(7 \times 10^{17}$ Bq) each of ^{210}Pb and ^{210}Po if radioactive decay were the only process removing them from the atmosphere. However, the tropospheric aerosols to which these radionuclides become attached are scavenged from the atmosphere by rain, so that their mean residence time in the atmosphere is only about 10 days. Hence most of the ^{210}Pb and ^{210}Po are redeposited on the ground surface on crops, etc. Some ^{210}Pb and some ^{210}Po enter the body by inhalation, particularly in the case of cigarette smokers. Rather surprisingly, although the daily intake from smoking is at least 20 times the intake from the atmospheric air, the levels of ^{210}Po found in the lungs are only about three times greater for smokers than non-smokers; presumably the ^{210}Po on cigarette smoke is more rapidly removed from the lung.

For non-smokers, consumption of food is normally the most important route by which ^{210}Pb and ^{210}Po enter the human body. The intake arises mainly from the presence of these radionuclides in cereal products, vegetables, and meat.

The concentration in milk is an order of magnitude lower, and the contribution of drinking water to the total intake is only a few per cent. High concentrations of ^{210}Po are observed in the edible portions of aquatic organisms, and hence intakes of this nuclide are enhanced in populations consuming large proportions of seafood. Vastly increased intakes also occur in the case of tens of thousands of reindeer and caribou eaters in the arctic and sub-arctic regions. Their main food is the meat of these animals, which contain unusually high concentrations of ^{210}Po because they graze on lichens which accumulate ^{210}Pb and ^{210}Po.

Table 21.10 presents information on the concentration of ^{210}Pb and ^{210}Po in the lichen–reindeer–man food-chain. Lichens, which have no root system, derive their nutrition preferentially from the air. As they present a high sorption area, live for a long time (up to 300 years), and eliminate ^{210}Pb very slowly, they concentrate ^{210}Pb and ^{210}Po to much higher levels than other plants. Reindeer consume 3–4 kg of lichen per day and consequently ingest about 10 nCi (400 Bq) per day of ^{210}Pb and ^{210}Po. The ^{210}Pb in reindeer food concentrates mainly in the bone of the reindeer, while the ^{210}Po concentrates mainly in soft tissue. Levels of several hundred pCi/kg of ^{210}Po are found in reindeer meat, and this causes doses of the order of 10 mrad (0.1 mGy) each year to the tissues of those who eat the meat of reindeer (see Table 21.10).

Table 21.10 Data relating to the lichen–reindeer–man pathway

Link in chain		Approximate concentration (pCi/kg)		Resulting doses (mrad/y)
		^{210}Pb	^{210}Po	
Lichen		8000	7000	
Reindeer or	bone	6000	7000	
caribou	meat	20	400	
	bone (ash)	250	200	10
Man				
	soft tissue	15	50	4–7

5.4.5 Short-lived daughters of ^{222}Rn

In addition to irradiation due to these long-lived decay products of ^{222}Rn, there is also some irradiation due to its short-lived daughters. These cause mainly irradiation of the lung, the dose due to outdoor exposure averaging about 1 mrad/y (10^{-5} Gy/y). Much greater exposures occur indoors, however, due to these short-lived radon daughters.

In this case the ^{222}Rn arises from radium in building materials. The radon concentration depends on many factors such as the radium concentration in the building materials, their moisture content and density, and whether or not sealants are used. It also depends critically on the ventilation rate, and consequently radon levels are often higher in modern, well-built centrally heated houses than in older draughtier houses with open fires. It has been estimated[30] that the mean lung dose from these daughters indoors is 30 mrad/y, with about five times that dose to the bronchial epithelium; the adoption of high standards of thermal insulation (via reduced ventilation) could double the natural dose-rate to the lungs.

5.4.6 *Technologically enhanced exposures*

The extra dose from radon daughters in buildings might be considered by some people to be an example of what is called a 'technologically enhanced exposure to natural radiation', although most of us would probably consider it natural to live in a house. There are other example of such exposures. For example, enhanced exposure to cosmic rays due to flying leads to a global dose commitment similar to that expected from the operation of the world-wide nuclear power industry at the present time. Additional exposures occur due to the industrial use of phosphate rocks, which contain naturally occurring radionuclides of the ^{238}U series. In the USA alone about 100 million tonnes of such rocks are mined each year, about half being used as fertilizer and the remainder for a variety of purposes including the manufacture of chemicals such as phosphoric acid. Doses resulting from the use as a fertilizer appear to be small, in spite of the fact that the rock contains about 40 pCi/g (about 1.5 Bq/g) of ^{226}Ra. Of greater radiological importance is the use of waste phosphogypsum from the phosphate industry in the manufacture of plasterboard, cement, etc. O'Riordan *et al*[33] estimated the doses received as a result of this practice. Assuming the use of a high but realistic amount of material in a building, they estimated that the use of phosphogypsum could increase the dose rate in the building by 60 mrad/y, i.e. to almost double its normal value. The radon concentration is also substantially increased.

Some radiation exposure also occurs as a result of the operation of coal-fired power stations, for example, as the result of the presence of ^{226}Ra and its daughters in coal. The doses are small, though they are comparable with doses resulting from the operation of some nuclear power plants (not reprocessing plants). The harm done by the radioactivity is however certainly negligible compared with the harmful effects of other emissions (such as SO_2) from such power stations.[34]

6 Exposure of animals and plants

In this chapter, attention has been concentrated on pathways by which radioactivity in the environment can cause irradiation of man. The irradiation of other living organisms will not be considered in detail, but a few brief comments on such matters will be made in this section.

It will be obvious that in some of the situations discussed in earlier parts of this chapter, various living organisms will be exposed to greater doses than man. The doses are likely to be greatest in the case of aquatic biota (although there are cases where one might expect high doses to some organs of animals living on dry land, e.g. the thyroids of grazing animals following a release of ^{131}I). The effects of radiation on aquatic biota have been reviewed by a number of authors.[35][36] The evidence available has been carefully evaluated; it supports the view that fish are the most radiosensitive component of aquatic ecosystems, and that damage to resources, if it occurred, would most likely stem from the direct effects of radiation on fish rather than effects produced in the less radiosensitive organisms at lower levels of the food web.[25] The elements most at risk in the life cycle of fish are the maturing and mature gametes (reproductive cells) and developing embryos. Estimates have been made of the doses to phytoplankton, zooplankton, molluscs, crustacea, and fish. These have shown that in a global context, weapon test fallout is the major source of 'artificial' exposure of aquatic organisms, with a dose-rate contribution which is in some cases of the same order as that from the natural background. Substantially higher dose-rates are occasionally produced over a relatively limited area in the immediate locality of waste disposal operations from the nuclear power industry (see Table 21.11), but in terms of collective dose to populations of organisms, the contribution is negligible.

In the past, concern was expressed mainly about the possibility of significant dose-rates from radioactive materials accumulated either on or within the egg. However, investigation of radionuclide accumulation by the eggs of plaice shows that the radiation dose experienced by eggs in a major waste disposal area (near Windscale) is much lower than that found necessary to produce significant effects in laboratory experiments. The dose to developing embryos from such material is below that due to natural background.[37]

In the context of ecosystems and their stability, it is effects at the population level rather than at the individual fish level which require attention. One

Table 21.11 Dose-rates to marine organisms from environmental radioactivity

	At 20 m depth, remote from sea bed		At 20 m depth, on the sea bed		
	Phytoplankton	Zooplankton	Molluscs	Crustacea	Fish
Natural background	2.8–8.2	3.3–16	9.5–32	10–38	4.8–21
Fallout	0.26–25	1.4–150	0.10–8.0	0.36–0.46	0.14–1.8
Waste disposal at Windscale	200–2100	530–6900	52–3400	43–3400	37–3300

Note
these values do not include the beta radiation component from the underlying sediment. For natural-activity and waste-disposal radionuclides, the beta-radiation dose-rates at the sediment–sea-water boundary are in the range 1.6–21 and 210–5400 μ rad/h respectively

should be concerned about the effects on fertility and fecundity, as well as on growth-rate, life-shortening, and damage to genetic material. At the dose-rates presently estimated, no deleterious effects would be expected at the population level. Moreover if such effects did occur they would be compensated for by density-dependent responses of the fish population. It should also be remembered that most deleterious mutations which occur in fish populations will be quickly eliminated because of the high natural mortality and compensatingly high fecundity of most aquatic animals.

7. Conclusions

Many pathways have been identified by which radioactive materials in the environment can cause irradiation of man. Those pathways which are important in relation to particular groups of radionuclides have been discussed in detail, and indications have been given of the extent of the doses resulting from particular operations. It is evident that an enormous amount is known about the processes which lead to the dispersion of radioactive materials in the environment, and about the extent to which these accumulate or recon-centrate due to physico-chemical and biological processes. Because the relationship between the dose and the magnitude of the release depends on various characteristics of the local environment, it is not feasible to produce nomograms from which one can simply calculate doses in a given situation. Nevertheless it will usually be possible for an expert to make a rough estimate of doses resulting from a given practice, and to identify clearly the studies needed to enable him to arrive at a more precise estimate of the doses.

The doses arising from operations of the various phases of the fuel cycle have been listed, and these have been compared with doses arising from naturally occuring radioactive materials which have always been present in the environment. The collective doses as a result of the operation of nuclear power plants are very small compared with those due to natural radioactivity; and the doses to the most highly exposed small groups of individuals, living near particular installations, are within the dose limits prescribed by national and international bodies, and are smaller than doses received by people living in parts of the world where there are local deposits of materials like monazite.

It should be noted that it has been possible to obtain the very extensive knowledge of the behaviour of radionuclides in the environment only because of the extreme sensitivity of the techniques available for their detection, identification, and assay. As a result a fund of knowledge has been built up about the behaviour of radioactive materials which is far more extensive than our knowledge of the behaviour of many of the highly toxic chemicals which are discharged into the environment. Indeed, in many cases information gleaned using radioisotopes has thrown considerable light on the behaviour of stable analogues, which may themselves be of high chemical toxicity.

While this chapter was being written, a report entitled *Methodology for evaluating the radiological consequences of radioactive effluents released in normal operations* was published by the Commission of the European Communities.[38] The report, prepared jointly by the UK National Radiological Protection Board and the French Commissariat a l'Energie Atomique, gives a detailed description of methods which have been developed by those two organizations for assessing the doses resulting from the discharge of radioactive effluents into the atmospheric or aquatic environments. Numerical models have been developed for many of the processes described rather qualitatively in this article. The CEC report contains a very comprehensive account of preferred methodology in the 'pathways' field, and should be studied by anyone who is interested in studying the subject at greater depth than has been possible in this chapter.

Appendix Factors determining radiotoxicity

The materials discussed in this chapter are of widely varying radiotoxicity. The main factors which determine radiotoxicity are:
(1) the extent to which the material is taken up into the body by inhalation or ingestion;
(2) the physical half-life of the isotope;
(3) the extent to which the material concentrates in particular organs and the rate at which it is subsequently excreted; †
(4) the type and energy of the radiation emitted by the isotope.

The most highly radiotoxic materials tend to be alpha-emitting substances with half-lives which are rather long, so that once in the body they may remain there for long periods. However, materials with very long half-lives (millions of years) are not of such great importance because their specific activity is low.

† When a person continuously inhales or ingests radioactive material, the quantity in his body does not generally continue to increase indefinitely; on the contrary, the quantity of radioactive material in his body usually reaches an equilibrium value after some weeks or months. For example, when tritium (which has a physical half-life of about 10 years) is taken into the body, such an equilibrium is reached within a few weeks, because the tritium is rapidly excreted from body fluids, mainly in urine, the *biological* half-life being only about 10 days.

Acknowledgements

Figs 21.5, 21.6, and 21.7 have been copied, with permission, from the following reports by staff of the Fisheries Radiological Laboratory of the Ministry of Agriculture, Fisheries, and Food: Fig. 21.5 from technical report *FRL* 12 of the Fisheries Radiological Laboratory, Lowestoft (1975); Fig. 21.6 from page 196 of reference 26; and Fig. 21.7 from technical report *FRL* 11 of the Fisheries Radiological Laboratory, Lowestoft (1976). Fig. 21.8 has been copied, with the permission of the National Radiological Protection Board, from reference 14. Figs 21.9 and 21.10, and Figs 21.12–21.15, have been copied, with the permission of the Health and Safety Directorate of the Commission of the European Communities, and with the permission of the National Radiological Protection Board, from reference 19. Fig. 21.11 is derived from *The fish/water accumulation factor*, by E. Ettenhuber and W. Röhnsch (1975) by permission of the IAEA, Vienna.

References

1. PASQUILL, F. The estimation of the dispersion of windborne materials, *Met. Mag.* **90**, 33 (1961).
2. SMITH, F. B. A scheme for estimating the vertical dispersion of a plume from a source near ground level. In: *Proc. Third Meeting of the Expert Panel on Air Pollution Monitoring*. NATO–CCMS Report 14, NATO, Brussels (1973).
3. SUTTON, O. G. *Micrometeorology*. McGraw–Hill Publishing Co., New York (1953).
4. BRYANT, P. M. *Methods of estimation of the dispersion of windborne material and data to assist in their application*. UKAEA Report *AHSB (RP)R*42 (1964).
5. BEATTIE, J. R., BRYANT, P. M. *Assessment of environmental hazards from reactor fission product releases*. UKAEA Report *AHSB(S)R*135 (1970).
6(a). CLARKE, R. H. The Weerie program for assessing the radiological consequences of airborne effluents from Nuclear Installations. *Health Phys.* **25**, 267 (1974).
6(b). KAISER, G. D. *A guide to the use of Tirion: a computer programme for the calculation of the consequences of releasing radioactive material to the atmosphere*. UKAEA Report *SRD-R*62 (1976).
7. ORPHAN, R. C. *Study of applying the atmospheric release advisory capability to nuclear power plants*. Lawrence Livermore Laboratory Report *UCRL* –52525 (1978).
8. ROBERTS, L. E. J. Radioactive waste: policy and perspective. *Nucl. Energy*, **18**, 85–100 (1979).
9. ROBINSON, R. A. The leak of tank 106-T at Hanford, *Nuclear Safety*, **15**, 460–466, (1974).
10. HILL, M. D., GRIMWOOD, P. D. *Preliminary assessment of the radiological protection aspects of disposal of high-level waste in geological formations*. National Radiological Protection Board Report *R*69 (1978).
11. (a)TEMPLETON, W. and PRESTON, A. Transport and distribution of radioactive effluents in coastal and estuarine waters of the United Kingdom. In: *Disposal of radioactive waste into seas, oceans and surface waters*, pp. 267–289. International Atomic Energy Agency, Vienna (1966).
    (b) MITCHELL, N. T. Monitoring of the aquatic environment of the United Kingdom and its application to hazard assessment. In: *Environmental contamination by radioactive materials*, pp. 449–464. IAEA, Vienna (1969).
    (c) PRESTON, A., JEFFERIES, D. F. Aquatic aspects in chronic and acute contamination situations. In: *Environmental contamination by radioactive materials*, pp. 183–211, IAEA, Vienna (1969).
12. PRESTON, A., JEFFERIES, D. F., AND MITCHELL, N. T. Experience gained from the controlled introduction of radioactive waste to coastal waters. In: *Nuclear Techniques in Environmental Pollution*, pp. 629–644. IAEA, Vienna (1971).
13. JEFFERIES, D. F. PRESTON, A., AND STEELE, A. K. Distribution of caesium-137 in British coastal waters. *Mar. Pollut. Bull.*, **4**, 118–122 (1973).
14. GRIMWOOD, P. D., AND WEBB, G. A. M. *Assessment of the radiological protection aspects of disposal of high level waste on the ocean floor*. NRPB Report *R*48, 101 (1976).
15. SHEPHERD, J. G. *A simple model for the dispersion of radioactive wastes dumped on the deep-sea bed*. Fisheries Research Technical Report, No 29, Ministry of Agriculture and Fisheries and Food, Lowestoft (1976).
16. HETHERINGTON, J. A., and JEFFERIES, D. F. The distribution of some fission product radionuclides in sea and estuarine sediment. *Netherlands J. Sea Res.* **8**, 319 (1974).

17. STRUXNESS, E. G., CARRIGAN, P. H., CHURCHILL, M. A., COWSER, K. E., MORTON, R. J., NELSON, D. J. AND PARKER, F. L. *The Clinch River study*. Report ORNL–4035 (1967). National Technical Information Service, Springfield, Virginia.

18. WOOLRIDGE, C. D. *Evaluation of the radiological conditions in the vicinity of Hanford for 1967*. Report BNWL–983 (1969). National Technical Information Service, Springfield, Virginia.

19. KELLEY, G. N., JONES, J. A., BRYANT, P. M., AND MORLEY, F. *The predicted radiation exposure of the population of the European community resulting from discharge of ^{85}Kr, tritium, ^{14}C and ^{129}I from the nuclear power industry to the year 2000*. Document V/2676/75. The Commission of the European Communities, Luxembourg (1975).

20. INTERNATIONAL KOMMISSION ZUM SCHUTZE DES RHEINS GEGEN VERUNREINIGUNG, ARBEITSGRUPPE R (RADIOACTIVITÄT). *Uber die folgen der ableitung radioactiver stoffe in den einzugsgebiet des rheins*. Reichsinstitut für Volksgesundheit (1974).

21. MITCHELL, N. T. *Radioactivity in surface and coastal waters of the British Isles, 1975*. Fisheries Radiological Laboratory Technical Report *FRL* 12. Ministry of Agriculture, Fisheries and Food, Lowestoft (1977).

22. PARKER, MR. JUSTICE. *The Windscale Inquiry*. vol. 1, p. 46. HMSO, London (1978).

23. PRESTON, A., JEFFERIES, D. F., AND MITCHELL, N. T. The Impact of ^{134}Cs and ^{132}Cs on the marine environment from Windscale. In: *Proc. Seminar on Radio-active Effluents from Nuclear Fuel Reprocessing Plants, Karlsruhe*, pp. 401–420. Commission of the European Communities, Luxembourg, (1977).

24. ETTENHUBER, E., AND ROHNSCH, W. The fish/water accumulation factor—an important parameter for determining the environmental capacity of surface waters. In: *Impacts of nuclear releases into the aquatic environment*, pp. 473–481. IAEA, Vienna (1975).

25. PRESTON, A. The radiological consequences of releases from nuclear facilities to the aquatic environment. In: *Impact of nuclear releases into the aquatic environment*, pp. 3–23. IAEA, Vienna (1975).

26. HETHERINGTON, J. A., JEFFERIES, D. F., AND LOVETT, M. B. Some investigations into the behaviour of plutonium in the marine environment. In: *Impacts of nuclear releases into the aquatic environment*, pp. 193–212, IAEA, Vienna (1975).

27. BOWEN, V. T., WONG, K. M. AND NOSHKIN, V. E. Plutonium-239 in and over the Atlantic Ocean. *J. Mar. Res.*, **29**, 1 (1971).

28. PARKER, MR. JUSTICE. *The Windscale Inquiry*, vol. 1, pp. 46–54. HMSO, London (1978).

29. BRYANT, P. M., AND JONES, J. A. The future implications of some long-lived fission product nuclides discharged to the environment in fuel reprocessing wastes. In: *Proc. NEA/IAEA Symp. on the management of radioactive wastes from fuel reprocessing*, p. 131. OECD, Paris (1973).

30. UNITED NATIONS. *Sources and effects of ionising radiation*. Report to the General Assembly by UNSCEAR (United Nations Scientific Committee on the Effects of Atomic Radiation) (1977).

31. TURNER, R. C., RADLEY, J. M., AND MAYNEORD, W. V. The naturally occurring alpha-ray activity of foods. *Health Phys.* **1**, 268 (1958).

32. PENNA-FRANCA, E., FISZMAN, M., LOBÃO, M., AND COSTA-RIBERIRO, C. Radio activity of Brazil nuts. *Health Phys.* **14**, 95 (1968).

33. O'RIORDAN, M. C., DUGGAN, M. J., AND ROSE, W. B. *The radiological implications of using by-product gypsum as a building material*. NRPB Report *R7* (1972).

34. HAMILTON, L. D. AND MANNE, A. S. *Health and economic costs of alternative energy sources*, pp. 44-58. IAEA Bulletin 20. IAEA, Vienna (1978).
35. AUERBACH, S. I., NELSON, D. J., KAYE, S. V., REICHLE, D. E., AND COUTANT, C. C. Ecological considerations in reactor power plant siting. In: *Environmental aspects of nuclear power stations*, pp. 804–820. IAEA, Vienna (1971).
36. OPHEL, I. L., HOPPENHEIT, H., AND ICHIKANA, R. Effects of ionising radiation on aquatic organisms. In: *Proc. Panel on the Effects of Ionising Radiation on Aquatic Organisms and Ecosytems*, IAEA, Vienna (1974).
37. WOODHEAD, D. S. The assessment of the radiation dose to developing fish embryos due to the accumulation of radioactivity by the egg. *Radiat. Res.* **43**, 582–597 (1970).
38. COMMISSION OF THE EUROPEAN COMMUNITIES. *Methodology for evaluating the radiological consequences of radioactive effluents released in normal operations*. Document No. *V*/3865/79—En, Fr. Luxembourg (1979).

22

Risk assessment

G. H. KINCHIN

After defining risk and introducing the concept of individual and societal risk, this chapter goes on to consider each of these risks, restricting considerations to risk of death. Some probabilities of death arising from various causes are quoted, and attention is drawn to the care necessary in making comparisons between sets of data and to the distinction between voluntary and involuntary categories and between early and delayed deaths. The presentation of information on societal risk is discussed and examples given.

The chapter next outlines the history of quantified risk assessment, particularly as related to the nuclear industry and goes on to discuss the process of assessing risk: identification of hazard causes, the development of accident chains and the use of event trees, the evaluation of probability through the collection of data and their use with fault trees, and the assessment of the consequences of hazards in terms of fatalities. Reference is made to the human element and common-mode failures, and also to studies supporting the development of reliability assessment techniques.

Finally, the chapter discusses the difficult topic of acceptance criteria for both individual and societal risk in the nuclear field and shows that proposed criteria lead to risks which are conservative by comparison with risks from day-to-day accidents and from other potentially hazardous industries.

Contents

1   Introduction

A risk may be defined as a hazard, or the chance of commercial loss.[1] This chapter is concerned with the methods available for identifying accidents which lead to losses, and for quantifying the frequency and severity of such accidents. Otway[2] regards risk assessment as 'interdisciplinary studies which provide information for use in decisions relating to the management of risks'. Given methods for the assessment of risk, it is of interest to consider criteria which might be used to decide on the acceptability of different risks. Here, although relatively little attention can be given to it in this chapter, the topic of risk perception must be kept in mind. Accident rates due to some causes appear to be accepted with equanimity by press and public, whilst similar death-rates due to other causes give rise to considerable public concern. An understanding of the reasons for these different perceptions of risk could be useful in arriving at acceptance criteria.

Two forms of risk will be considered—that to the individual and that to society as a whole. The former concerns the probability of harm (economic loss, injury or death, for example) to an individual, whilst the latter concerns the probability of harm to different numbers of people. An accident which may kill 1000 people represents a greater societal risk than an equally probable accident which may kill 10.

It was at one time thought that it might be possible to design reactors, and indeed other industrial plant, which would be absolutely safe. A variety of systems, such as surrounding the plant by an airtight containment, making the plant characteristics *fail safe*, etc. were proposed, but were in turn shown merely to reduce the probability of accidents, rather than to eliminate them. No human activity can be entirely free from risk and, as the size of industrial plant increases, it becomes ever more desirable to assess the probabilities and magnitudes of accidents before the plant goes into operation, making design changes if necessary to make the probabilities sufficiently low. It is particularly in the nuclear industry and, perhaps even earlier, in the aircraft industry that the necessary consideration of probabilities and consequences has been carried furthest. The alternative, used in other industries and more acceptable to them in the past, was to build plant and make changes retrospectively after accidents had occurred. The methodology for assessing risks will be outlined in this paper and some reference will be made to the difficult question of what is *sufficiently low* in discussing acceptance criteria.

Emphasis will be given to the important human, rather than economic consequences, and examples will reflect the growth of the methodology in the field of nuclear reactor safety, although precisely the same methods can be used in other industries.

2 Risk

2.1 **Individual risk**

Restricting considerations to the risk of death, rather than injury or economic loss, it is useful to assemble some of the existing risks from other forms of activity or from natural causes as a background against which acceptability of risks might be considered. Some (but not all) risks of death in Great Britain are shown in Table 22.1[3][4] calculated on the basis of an average risk over the individual's lifetime rather than the risk whilst the individual is, for example, driving a car. Since 140×10^{-6} is approximately equal to $1 \div 7000$, the figure of 140×10^{-6}/year against road accidents implies that there is one chance in 7000 of dying during each year, or that on average one member of a group of 7000 people will die each year as a result of a road accident.

It should be noted that the risks given in Table 22.1 refer to Great Britain and that significantly different risks of death may apply in other countries. Table 22.2[5] shows some comparative figures for Great Britain and the USA to illustrate the point. The chance of accidental death in the USA may be seen to be almost twice that in Great Britain. Since 630×10^{-6} is approximately equal to $1 \div 1600$ and 340×10^{-6} is approximately equal to $1 \div 3000$, the chance of accidental death every year in the USA is 1 in 1600, compared with the smaller annual chance of 1 in 3000 in Great Britian. Remember that a million to one chance is very unlikely, whilst an evens chance is quite likely to come off; these correspond to probabilities of 10^{-6} and 0.5.

Although the differences in Table 22.2 are quite large, even wider differences are found in the data for other countries.[6]

It is necessary to use care in making comparisons between different sets of published risk data in order to avoid drawing misleading conclusions. In the

Table 22.1 Individual risks in Great Britain (Probability of death/year)

Cause	Risk
All natural causes	$11\,000 \times 10^{-6}$
Smoking (20 cigarettes/day)[4]	$5\,000 \times 10^{-6}$
Neoplasms (excluding lung cancer)	$1\,800 \times 10^{-6}$
Lung cancer	700×10^{-6}
All accidents	340×10^{-6}
Road accidents	140×10^{-6}
Accidental falls	110×10^{-6}
Fire	16×10^{-6}
Electrocution	2.5×10^{-6}
Lightning	0.1×10^{-6}

Table 22.2 Individual risks (Probability of death/year)

Cause	Risk GB	USA
All accidents	340×10^{-6}	630×10^{-6}
Road accidents	140×10^{-6}	250×10^{-6}
Falls	110×10^{-6}	100×10^{-6}
Fire	18×10^{-6}	40×10^{-6}
Drowning	11×10^{-6}	33×10^{-6}
Electrocution	2.4×10^{-6}	6.3×10^{-6}
Lightning	0.2×10^{-6}	0.5×10^{-6}

particular case of Great Britian, it is easy to confuse statistics for Great Britain with those applicable to the United Kingdom or to the British Isles, and there is also a need to check the classification of accidents due to different causes. The point is illustrated by the small differences between the figures for Great Britain in Tables 22.1 and 22.2. The reasons for these differences are that Table 22.1 gives average values for 1971 to 1975, whilst Table 22.2 gives the figures for the single year of 1973 for Great Britain. The USA column in Table 22.2 refers to 1969 and must be compared with the 1973 British figures in the knowledge of the timing difference.

Individual risks are sometimes separated into *voluntary* and *involuntary* categories, but the distinction is not always clear. Smoking and rock-climbing represent two activities which can be accepted or rejected without significant effect on the life-style; they may be clearly defined as voluntary. Other activities, such as travelling by car, are less clearly voluntary in some locations, although in principle it may be possible, by moving house and job, to find a location where a car is no longer needed. The degree to which a risk is voluntary must be kept in mind in determining its relative acceptability.

One further point to note is that, whilst some deaths may be instantaneous, such as those due to electrocution or fire, some are delayed such as those due to smoking. The acceptability of delayed death is likely to be higher than that of instantaneous death.

It is interesting to note that the probability of accidental death is relatively independent of age for adults up to the age of 65, as shown in Fig. 22.1.[3]

2.2 Risk to society

Beattie *et al*[7] have discussed the presentation of data on probabilities of accidents $p(N)$ leading to the deaths of different numbers of people, N. A somewhat easier presentation is that which relates the frequency of causing N or more deaths to the number of deaths, N. In this latter form, data are shown in Fig. 22.2 for a variety of different causes. For small numbers of fatalities, the curves use data from the British Isles. For large accidents the statistics become very poor, and use has been made of world data[8] to extrapolate the curves. In view of the comments which have already been

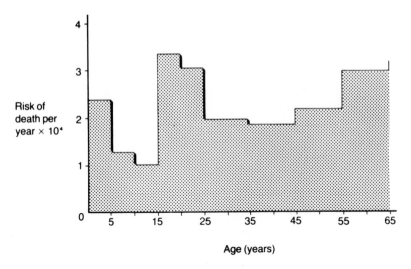

Fig. 22.1 Risk of death due to accidents

made on the differing levels of risk in different countries, the world data have been used to give only the shape of the curves at high numbers of fatalities, rather than the absolute levels.

Such indications of societal risk as these are clearly related to the size of population being considered. For comparable safety standards, the annual probability of accidents killing more than 10 people would be ten times lower in a country with a population of 5 million, than in a country with a population of 50 million. This must be kept in mind in making comparisons of societal risk between one country and another.

3 Development of quantitative risk assessment

In the early days of the nuclear industry, it was thought that absolute safety could be achieved by a variety of means—by siting, by containment, and by design.

At the first Atoms for Peace Conference in Geneva in 1955, Marley and Fry[9] evaluated some of the consequences of reactor accidents in order to make recommendations about the permissible numbers of residents within various distances from the reactor site. The exercise was essentially one of comparing different sites, and there was still a feeling that if the size of the maximum accident could be limited, it should be possible to avoid casualties altogether by remote siting.

The use of containment was pursued strongly in the USA in the 1960s and there are examples, such as the Dounreay fast reactor, of the use of steel containment vessels in the UK. For absolute safety, it must be clear that (a) all possible reactor accidents have been identified and can be held within the

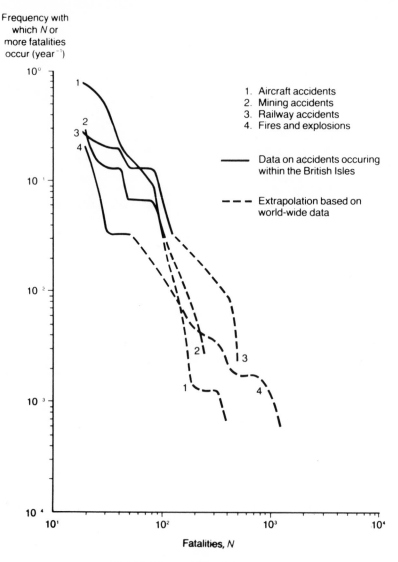

Fig. 22.2 Extrapolation of British Isles accident data

designed containment, and (b) the containment is indeed as its designer intended. With the passage of time it has become clear that it is not possible to guarantee these conditions—someone may have left a valve open, or some other valve may fail to close, for instance. Whilst the containment may be very valuable in reducing emissions, it cannot ensure absolute safety by holding all radioactivity released in a reactor accident.

The third possible line of approach was to design the system to have negative coefficients, so that if the reactor started to increase in power in an uncontrolled way, the consequent increases in fuel temperature, or the reductions of coolant or moderator density—even those caused by boiling of water—would automatically shut the reactor down. However, it was soon appreciated that accidents could be caused by the reverse of these effects, such as the sudden reduction of water temperature in a pressurized-water reactor or the collapse of voids in a boiling-water reactor. Similarly, such design moves as fixing the operating temperature of a pressure vessel above the *nil ductility temperature*, with the intention that catastrophic vessel failure would be avoided, did not prove successful. In parallel with the search for absolute safety, it was realized that steps could be taken to make accidents less likely, and codes of practice were produced with that end in view. Two examples of general criteria for UK gas-cooled reactors were:

(1) 'The possibility of failure of a circulator in the event of a single fault in any auxiliary equipment of the main circulator drive should be reduced to a minimum', and

(2) 'An adequate and reliable source of supply for the circulators is essential to ensure an adequate coolant flow under normal conditions.'

Whilst requirements such as these provide useful reminders for designers, they are open to a multitude of interpretations and act as no more than a check-list. Some sort of yardstick was needed to indicate more precisely what was *adequate* and what was *reliable*. It was necessary to be quantitative.

During the 1960s, studies of the reliability of various parts of reactor systems were being made by Siddall,[10] whilst corresponding studies of the reliability of aircraft landing gear were being made by Howard *et al.*[11] Both the nuclear and aircraft industries were feeling a way towards the quantification of risk.

Farmer[12,13] produced, towards the end of the 1960s, his criterion for the permissible probabilities of releasing various quantities of ^{131}I, the volatile fission product readily released under accident conditions. The levels shown in Fig. 22.3[14] were aimed at producing less than one death to the public for the foreseeable future of gas-cooled reactor operations. Naturally, the large releases were required to be less probable than the smaller releases.

In order to make use of the Farmer criterion, it is necessary to assess, by methods which will be described later, the probability of emission of different quantities of ^{131}I. In many cases this is difficult to achieve because of the lack of data for failure rates of different components, but the analysis can point to weak parts of design and can identify data needs, so that action can be taken to procure new data. The need for the acquisition of reliability data was appreciated in the UK and led to the setting up of the Systems Reliability Service in 1970. The Service, now part of the National Centre of Systems Reliability, has a large number of members from a variety of countries and from a variety of industries.

The first large-scale, quantitative risk assessment of this sort for a nuclear reactor was the Rasmussen report,[15] which considered the safety of pressurized- and boiling-water reactors. Although some possible improve-

Frequency (y⁻¹)

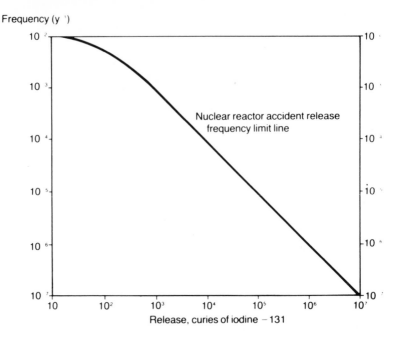

Fig. 22.3 Farmer criterion

ments were suggested in a subsequent review of the Rasmussen report by Lewis *et al*,[16] the basis of the methodology was confirmed, and Lewis recommended that fault tree/event tree analysis, which is discussed in the next section, should be amongst the principal means to deal with generic safety issues, formulation of new regulatory requirements, etc.

Subsequent studies have been carried out by the same methods for petroleum refineries, liquid natural gas and ammonia storage, and liquid petroleum gas storage on Canvey Island.[17]

4 Risk assessment methods

The process of risk analysis involves the identification of hazard causes, an assessment of the probabilities of arriving at a variety of dangerous conditions—fire, explosion, release of toxic materials, etc.—and an assessment of the consequences. This section considers first the possible range of events which can initiate an accident sequence in a plant, and then the variety of different accident chains which may result. These chains, which may branch out with various different options, are known as event trees. The ascription of probabilities to these different options, leading to an assessment of the probability of each of the various final outcomes, is then considered. Finally, the assessment of the consequences of each of the final outcomes is discussed.

4.1 **Identification of hazard causes**

In principle, each component of a plant should be ascribed a failure probability and accident chains should be followed from the initiating events.
Examples of such initiating events might be the bursting of a pressurized
coolant circuit or the failure of a component in the control system of a plant.
These events can readily be catalogued, but the difficult step is to ensure that
all of the possible events initiated by human error have been accounted for.
Additionally, external events must be considered, ranging from the failure
of external power or water supplies to the effects of earthquakes, explosions,
floods, aircraft crashes, etc.

4.2 **Accident chains**

Use is sometimes made of the event tree presentation in considering the
various possible outcomes from a given initiating event. The tree, a simple
example of which is given in Fig. 22.4, shows in diagrammatic form the
sequence of conditions governing the choice of the final outcome. Each of
the branch points of the tree relates to a particular engineered safety feature,
and at each point the question may be asked 'Does this engineered safety
feature work?' A negative answer is assigned a probability p_n, the failure
probability, leaving a probability $1 - p_n$ for the answer 'Yes'.

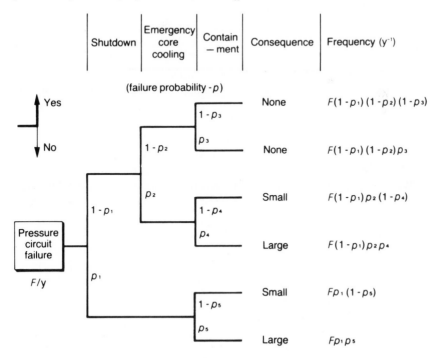

Fig. 22.4 Simplified event tree for pressure circuit failure

The first branch point of the simplified tree relates to shutting down the reactor, and includes the question of detection of the failure of the pressurized coolant circuit. There may be many alternative means of detecting the failure, such as loss of coolant pressure, excessive temperature, loss of flow, overspeeding of pumps, etc., and there may be alternative means of shutting down the reactor in addition to dropping the control rods, such as the injection of fluid neutron poisons. The nuclear industry has been concerned to ensure safety both by providing many ways of detecting pressure circuit failure and by the use of alternative methods for shutting down the reactor.

Looking at the first branch point in Fig. 22.4, the upper branch shows the outcome of detection of pressure circuit failure and reactor shutdown (the most probable outcome), whilst the lower branch represents failure to shut down, due to failure of either detection or control. At the next nodal point across, the upper branch represents operation of the emergency core cooling, whilst the lower branch represents failure of the core cooling to operate. The final branch points indicate the satisfactory operation or otherwise of the containment system.

Having established the form of the event tree, the next step is to establish the probabilities of the various different possible outcomes. The frequency of the initiating event, and the reliability of the engineered safety features must be assessed, using methods to be described later. Referring to Fig. 22.4, the frequency of pressure circuit failure (F/year) followed by reactor shutdown $(1-p_1)$, failure of emergency core cooling (p_2), with an intact containment $(1-p_4)$, will lead to an estimated frequency of small releases of radioactivity of $F(1-p_1)\,p_2(1-p_4)$/year. Since p_1 etc. are all small, this approximates to a probability of Fp_2/year, which is the probability of a small release of radioactivity through the sequence. At each of the end points it is possible to estimate a frequency and to estimate the magnitude of release of radioactivity, should there by any release.

The preceding description sounds straightforward, but in practice there are some difficulties of interpretation, partly because the answer to the question, 'Does the safety function work?' sometimes turns out to be 'Partly', rather than 'Yes' or 'No'. It may then be necessary to define some degree of partial operation which effectively separates the outcome in the two succeeding branches.

A further difficulty in real life is that the answers to each of these questions will not necessarily be independent. There are, in other words, *common-mode* failures in which a single failure of a piece of equipment causes consequent failures in one or several subsequent branches of the event tree, and this needs to be properly accounted for. An example of such a failure is the loss of an electrical supply system which is necessary both for the detection of a fault and for the operation of a number of engineered safety features. Similarly in Fig. 22.4, if pressure circuit failure inevitably leads to the containment failure, the small probabilities of containment failure, p_3, p_4 and p_5, can no longer be used, and must be replaced by unit probabilities.

There is no automatic way of identifying common-mode failures, but experience is valuable in indicating their main causes, and guidance has been produced on the best methods of defence.[18]

4.3 Assessment of probability

The frequency of failure of components and the reliability of instrumentation and mechanisms have been the subject of study for a number of years in the National Centre of Systems Reliability.[19] Failure data for different components have been collected over the last 20 years and from these data it is possible to assess the failure probability of electronic instrumentation, cooling systems, and a large variety of sub-systems in both nuclear and non-nuclear plant.

There are inevitable uncertainties in the failure data and it is by no means easy to accumulate such data. Safety assessments draw attention to important event trees and highlight data uncertainties. It may be that there is little experience of failure of a particular component in the environment of interest, or it may be that the component is new and that there are few sources of data. The Systems Reliability Service has received data from a number of sources, relating to component reliability in a wide range of industries, but it must be appreciated that the collection of data takes time and money; it is largely because of the problems of collecting and the time taken in processing data before feeding them into the Reliability Data Bank that these occupations require continuous attention from those engaged in them. Early assessments of new plant draw attention to particular areas in which data collection is needed.

Fault trees are often used for studies of the reliability of engineered safety features. A simplified version is shown in Fig. 22.5, which might relate to the detection phase of the reactor shutdown shown in Fig. 22.4. In this case the final outcome, or top event, starts the fault tree and the causes of failure are traced back through single component failures or through combinations of component failures, each of which individually will not cause the top event. If the causes are traced through to points for which failure data are available, it becomes possible to evaluate the overall failure probability by the combination of component failure probabilities through the relevant AND or OR gates. For simple systems, the fault trees can be drawn and the computations can be completed manually, but for complex systems computer programs[20] are available for automatic computation.

Fault trees and event trees basically contain the same logic and data, and to some extent it is a matter of choice or convenience which approach is used.

It is necessary to bear in mind the possibilities of human error in arriving at estimates of failure probabilities.[18] [21] Such errors can occur at any stage of the design, manufacturing or operating processes, and a variety of steps are taken to ensure that the possibility of these errors is minimized.

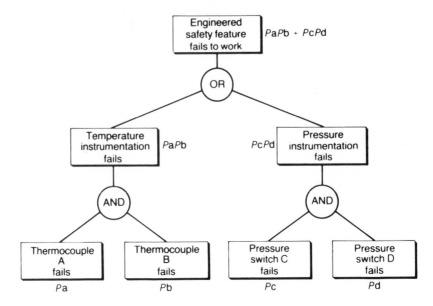

Fig. 22.5 Simplified fault tree

In the design stage, it may be that an out-dated or irrelevant design code is used, a wrong material may be specified, or the possibility may be overlooked that failure of a component necessarily leads to failure of a part of the safety system designed to protect against the component failure. The best defence against these typical human errors at the design stage is to have a design review carried out by experts not directly involved in the design.

During the manufacturing and construction of a plant, a quality assurance programme is needed to ensure that no readily detectable errors are allowed to persist through to the final plant. This involves the checking of materials, dimensions, the perfection of welds, etc. by trained inspectors throughout construction. The final check for human errors is made during the commissioning programme, which tests the plant in a variety of operating and simulated accident conditions, until it is gradually worked up to full power output.

The effects of human error in the operating phase can be minimized by ensuring that enough, but not too much, information about the state of the plant is presented to the operator, that safety actions are automatically initiated, and that plenty of time is available for thought should human intervention be necessary. In the field of maintenance, the possibility of human error is important in the context of the common-mode failures discussed earlier. For example, if a series of similar instruments such as trip amplifiers is being maintained, a common error made in setting-up each amplifier as it is returned to duty could mean that none of them would respond when required. This problem can be overcome by ensuring that at no time are all amplifiers maintained together, but it draws attention to the need to look for the effect of human error throughout plant life. Although much can be done to reduce the incidence and the effects of human errors, they cannot be completely removed.

4.4 Consequences

The consequences of accidents may range from the extremely serious, with numbers of early fatalities, through less serious accidents in which there may be a few delayed fatalities, to those accidents which produce no fatalities but which may have significant economic consequences. In arriving at the releases of radioactivity identified at the end of the reactor accident event tree in Fig. 22.4, a good deal of background information is required. Radioactivity is released from the site as a result of some of the accident chains, and it is necessary to know, for example, which fission products are released from overheated fuel and in what quantity and form, and how such fission products are retained by the coolant, absorbed on the moderator, plated out on cool surfaces, and eventually released to atmosphere. Much research and development has helped to provide the necessary methods and data which lead to estimates of fission-product release. It is then necessary to consider how the fission products are dispersed after release. Such dispersion clearly depends on weather conditions, wind velocities, etc., and computer programs such as TIRION[22] have been developed to take account of these varying conditions. Calculations are needed for a variety of weather conditions to give a properly weighted view of the hazard to the general public, and having determined the dispersion of fission products it is necessary to consider the health hazards arising from the ingestion or inhalation of radioactive materials, using the information supplied by the International Commission on Radiological Protection.[23]

Similar considerations apply, outside the nuclear field, to the dispersion of toxic and explosive gases, and some of these problems are exemplified in the contribution of the Safety and Reliability Directorate to the Canvey Island report.[17] In the case of many toxic gases and pollutants, there is less information available on the long-term effects of small concentrations than is the case for radioactive materials.[24]

5 Supporting studies

In studying the safety of any new system, uncertainties inevitably arise, partly concerning the reliability of various components, partly from incomplete knowledge of the physical and chemical processes involved in the developing accident chains, and partly beause of doubts about the assessment of consequences. Work is carried out in many countries with the objective of reducing these uncertainties, and a few examples are considered below.

Stores such as the Reliability Data Bank[25] of the Systems Reliability

Service are themselves subject to development, and the data are often collected by intensive study of records and new data over a period of about six months. The individual failure rates of links in the event tree may be quite high, although the overall probability of the completed chain of events is very low. There is more difficulty—at least to some extent because of the infrequency of the occurrences—in collecting data on events which can lead directly to major accidents (i.e. without branching of the event tree). Examples are structural failures and the failure of pressure vessels containing toxic, inflammable, or other harmful material. In such cases, much research and development work is carried out to study both modes of failure and the detection of defects which might lead to failure. The latter topic is exemplified by the international comparison of different assessments of defects in heavy-section steel plates, which contained both artificial and natural defects and which were subsequently sectioned to reveal the true state of affairs.[26]

Uncertainties in the development of accident sequences may well merit studies on such topics as the interaction of chemicals under unusual conditions of temperature or pressure, fluid flow and heat transfer in two-phase conditions, physical properties of materials, metal–water explosive interactions, rates and form of release of toxic materials, effects of missiles (produced by disintegrating machinery or pressure vessels), etc. If such studies still leave undesirable uncertainties, it may be necessary to reduce the probability of the accidents.

Finally, much work is carried out, with an increasing degree of international collaboration, on the experimental and theoretical study of the dispersion of hazardous materials.

6 Criteria for acceptability

There are virtues in quantitative assessment of risk, and in quantitative criteria for the acceptability of risk. Quantitative assessments are difficult to make, but they enable the forward programme of research work to be identified by pointing to areas in which the data are uncertain, and cannot encourage the proliferation of unsafe practices. They allow comparison between different industries and should prevent the expenditure of large sums of money on improving some plant, when the same expenditure could make far greater improvements to public safety if spent on other plant. The benefit of a quantitative set of criteria is for the designer, who can make better use of a fixed target than a diffuse one. The ALARA (as low as reasonably achievable) principle is good, but eventually requires some definition of 'reasonably'.

In the case of individual risk of early death, Webb and McLean [27] have suggested that a risk of 10^{-6}/y is one which is not taken into account by individuals making a decision and is therefore negligible. It has been suggested[28] by the present author that if an individual risk of early death of

10^{-6}/y is applied to people living close to a nuclear plant, the average risk for the population as a whole will be much lower. The figure is at the lower end of the range 10^{-6} – 10^{-5}/y suggested as acceptable by the International Commission on Radiological Protection,[23] and is much smaller than the total risk of accidental death, shown in Fig. 22.1 as several times 10^{-4}/y.

In the case of a high dose of radiation there is an increased possibility of cancer; the death-rate remains unchanged for about ten years and there is then an increased probability of cancer over the next 30 years.[29] Bearing in mind that, in the absence of radiation, there is a relatively high risk of death from cancer of about 2.5×10^{-3}/y, as indicated in Table 22.1, it has been proposed[28] that an acceptable level for delayed death due to radiation might be 3×10^{-5}/y, even though this is somewhat larger than the upper end of the range suggested by the International Commission on Radiological Protection.

For risk to society, the Farmer criterion shown in Fig. 22.3 has been in use in the United Kingdom Atomic Energy Authority.[30] The criterion gives permissible probabilities for the release of various quantities of the volatile fissile product ^{131}I, and the standards used by the Nuclear Installations Inspectorate are within a factor of three of this criterion.[31] These criteria can of course be converted to numbers of fatalities or casualities, and the Farmer criterion[12] was indeed based on a fatality rate of about 1 per 1000 reactor-years (assuming that 10 per cent of the cases of thyroid carcinoma were fatal) for relatively densely populated sties. This amounts to less than one death for a programme of 30 reactors each operating for 30 years.

Whilst the differences between one practicable site and another in the United Kingdom are not crucial, they are taken into account if the criterion is expressed in terms of the acceptable probabilities of different numbers of fatalities. The question of the inclusion of effects of other fission products, in addition to ^{131}I, is also made clear by such a criterion. For possible future use, the criteria[28] proposed by the present author and shown in Fig. 22.6 are based on the same fatality rate of 1 per 1000 reactor years as the Farmer criterion so that no fatalities are expected in a reactor programme. The probability of more than one early fatality per year is seen to be rather more than 10^{-5}/y, and this is reasonably compatible with the individual risk criterion quoted above of 10^{-6}/y. This is because, in a steady wind, any radioactive emission will spread over a sector of 30 °; if the wind is equally likely to blow from any direction, then the chance for a particular individual of being in the path of the radioactive cloud following an emission is just 30/360. If the individual risk of early death is 10^{-6}/y, it follows that the probability of an emission is $10^{-6} \times 360/30$ each year; assuming the existence of people all round the site boundary, this corresponds to a probability of rather more than 10^{-5}/year of killing one or more people.

Most of the existing and proposed criteria relate probability inversely to the possible number of fatalities. Whilst the frequencies of large familiar accidents, such as those illustrated in Fig. 22.2, are lower than would be compatible with this inverse relationship, the frequencies of large industrial

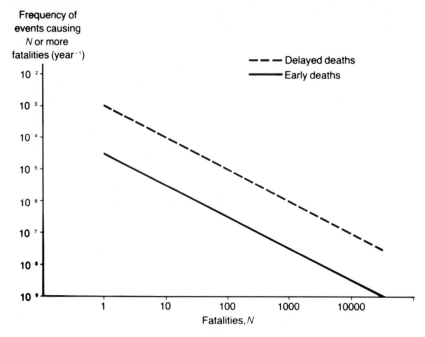

Fig. 22.6 Proposed societal risk criteria for a nuclear reactor

accidents can be relatively higher. The inverse relationship therefore seems a reasonable choice, even though it is apparent that more public attention is devoted to one accident killing ten people than to a dozen smaller accidents killing many more.

These criteria are concerned particularly with nuclear reactors. It may be seen that even with a programme of 50 reactors, the societal risk would be well below the others shown in Fig. 22.2. The suggested criteria are conservative and are unlikely to be met by other industries. Figure 22.7 shows the expected probabilities of accidents of different magnitudes for a programme of 50 reactors; these are compared with the estimated risks for the single collection of conventional industrial plants at Canvey in the mouth of the Thames.[17] Acknowledging that the estimates for this initial survey of oil refineries, gas storage, etc. were pessimistic and that recommended improvements would reduce the figures, it must also be recognized that there are other similar sites in the UK which were not included in the Canvey survey. The criteria for reactors are, therefore, stringent.

7 Conclusions

In this brief survey of the development of quantitative risk assessment in the nuclear industry it has been suggested that there is no such thing as absolute safety. There is always some risk, however small, of accidents, and by

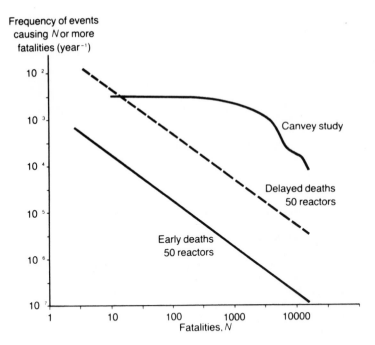

Fig. 22.7 Societal risks

quantifying such risks a proper appreciation of the importance of the accidents can be achieved. Whilst in the early stages of any industry data may be uncertain, quantitative risk analysis helps to identify important areas in which data are lacking and provides a logical framework for safety studies.

Quantitative risk assessments must be compared with quantitative criteria for acceptance and these criteria have been summarized and discussed, although it must be noted that such criteria are not sufficient to ensure the safety of any plant. Attention must also be given to the operation and maintenance of the plant to ensure that standards are satisfactorily high and that the condition of the plant remains good from the point of view of safety.

Acknowledgement

Many thanks are due to Mr. D.R. Poulter for his help in the preparation of this chapter.

References

1. *Shorter Oxford english dictionary on historical principles* (3rd edn), p. 1743 (1970).
2. OTWAY, H. J. Risk assessment and the social response to nuclear power. *J. Brit. Nucl. Energy Soc.*, **16**, 327–333 (1977).
3. GRIST, D. R. *Individual risk: a compilation of recent British data.* UKAEA Report *SRD R* 125 (1978).
4. POCHIN, E. E. *Brit. Med. Bull.* **31** (3), 184 (1975).
5. GRIFFITHS, R. F. and FRYER, L. S. *The incidence of multiple fatality accidents in the UK*, UKAEA Report *SRD R* 110 (1978).
6. FAILLA, L. *Comparison between worker-deaths in modern industries and in nuclear activities.* CNEN Report No. *RT/PRT* (77)15 Comitato Nazionale per L'Energia Nucleare, Rome (1977).
7. BEATTIE, J. R., BELL, G. D., AND EDWARDS, J. E. *Methods for the evaluation of risk*, UKAEA Report *AHSB(S)R*159 (1969).
8. FRYER, L. S., AND GRIFFITHS, R. F. *Worldwide data on the incidence of multiple fatality accidents.* UKAEA Report *SRD R* 149 (June 1979).
9. MARLEY, W. G., AND FRY, T. M. Radiological hazards from an escape of fission products and the implications in power reactor location. In *Proc. Int. Conf. on the Peaceful Uses of Atomic Energy, Geneva, 1955*, vol. 13, pp. 102–105. United Nations, New York (1956).
10. SIDDALL, E. Statistical analysis of reactor safety standards. *Nucleonics*, **17** (2), 64, (1959).
11. HOWARD, R. W., BARLTROP, R. K., BISHOP, G. S. AND BEVAN, F. Reliability in automatic landing. *Flight* (7 October 1960).
12. FARMER, F. R. Siting criteria—A new approach. In *Proc. IAEA Symp. on Containment and Siting, Vienna, April 1967*, paper SM–89/34. International Atomic Energy Agency, Vienna (1967).
13. FARMER, F. R. Progress towards the identification of safety requirements for advanced reactors. In *Proc. BNES Symp. on Safety and Siting, London, March 1969*, paper 11. British Nuclear Energy Society (1969).
14. ROYAL COMMISSION ON ENVIRONMENTAL POLLUTION. Sixth Report. Nuclear Power and the environment. CMND. 6618. fig. 15, London HMSO (1976).
15. US NUCLEAR REGULATORY COMMISSION. *Reactor safety study: An assessment of accident risks in US commercial nuclear power plants. WASH* 1400, *NUREG* 75/014 (1975).
16. LEWIS, H. W. *Risk assessment—Review Group report to the US Nuclear Regulatory Commission. NUREG/CR*–0400 (1978).
17. HEALTH AND SAFETY EXECUTIVE. *Canvey: An investigation of potential hazards from operations in the Canvey Island/Thurrock area.* HMSO, London (1978).
18. EDWARDS, G. T., AND WATSON, I. A. *A study of common mode failures.* UKAEA Report *SRD R* 146 (1979).
19. GREEN, A. E. The Systems Reliability Service and its generic techniques. *IEEE Trans. Reliability*, **R-23** (3), 140–147 (1974).
20. SHAW, P., AND WHITE, R. F. *an appraisal of the PREP-KITT and SAMPLE computer codes for the evaluation of the reliability characteristics of engineered systems.* UKAEA Report *SRD R* 57 (1975).
21. EMBREY, D. E. *Human reliability in complex systems: An overview.* UKAEA Report *NCSR R* 10 (1976).
22. KAISER, G. D. *A description of the mathematical and physical models incorporated in TIRION-2* (a computer program that calculates the consequences of a release of radioactive material to the atmosphere, and an example of its use). UKAEA Report *SRD R* 63 (1976).

23. INTERNATIONAL COMMISSION ON RADIOLOGICAL PROTECTION. *Recommendations of the International Commission on Radiological Protection.* ICRP Publication 26. Pergamon Press, Oxford (1977).
24. HEALTH AND SAFETY COMMISSION. *The hazards of conventional sources of energy.* HMSO, London (1978).
25. MOSS, T. R. *Developments in the SRS Reliability Data Bank.* UKAEA Report *SRS/GR/43* (1978).
26. ORGANISATION FOR ECONOMIC CO-OPERATION AND DEVELOPMENT. *Report from the Plate Inspection Steering Committee (PISC) on the ultrasonic examination of three test plates using the "PISC" procedures based upon the ASME XI Code.* OECD (1979).
27. WEBB., G. A. M., AND MACLEAN, A. S. *Insignificant levels of dose: a practical suggestion for decision making,* NRPB Report *R* 62. National Radiological Protection Board (1977).
28. KINCHIN, G. H. Assessment of hazards in engineering work. *Proc. Instn. Civ. Engrs.,* **64** (1), 431–438, (1978).
29. KELLY, G. N., JONES, J. P., AND HUNT, B. W. *An estimate of the radiological consequences of notional accidental releases of radioactivity from a fast breeder reactor,* NRPB Report *R* 53 (1977).
30. FARMER, F. R. and BEATTIE, J. R. Nuclear power reactors and the evaluation of population Hazards. *Advance in Nuclear Science and Technology,* **9,** 1–72, (1976).
31. DUNSTER, H. J. Private communication.

Suggestions for further reading

1. STARR, C. Social benefit versus technological risk. *Science.* **165,** 1232–1238 (1969).
2. FARMER, F. R. Quantitative safety analysis, *Nucl. Engng. Des.* **13,** 183–244, (1970).
3. GREEN, A. E. AND BOURNE, A. J. *Reliability technology.* John Wiley & Sons, New York (1972).
4. POCHIN, E. E. The acceptance of risk. *Brit. Med. Bull.,* vol. 31(3), 184–190 (1975).
5. VINCK, W. AND REIJEN, G. Van. Quantitative risk assessment, the promised but not the sacred. In *Proc. ANS/ENS Int. Conf. on World Nuclear Power, Washington DC, 14–19 November, 1976.*
6. FARMER, F. R. Nuclear reactor safety. In *Nuclear science and technology.* Academic Press, London (1977).
7. COUNCIL FOR SCIENCE AND SOCIETY. The acceptability of risks. In *The logic and social dynamics of fair Decisions and effective controls.* Barry Rose (Publishers) Ltd. (1977).
8. ROWE, W. D. *An anatomy of risk.* Wiley Interscience, New York (1977).
9. GIBSON, S. B. The quantitative measurement of process safety. In *Proc. Inst. Chem. Engrs. Symp. on Chemical Process Hazards,* 1–11 (1977).
10. KLETZ, T. A. The risk equations. What risks should we run? *New Scientist,* 320–322 (1977).
11. McGINTY, L. AND ATHERLEY, G. Acceptability versus democracy. *New Scientist,* 323–235 (1977).
12. ADVISORY COMMITTEE ON MAJOR HAZARDS. *Health and Safety Commission first report,* HMSO, London (1976).
13. —. *Second report.* HMSO, London (1979).

23

Radioactive isotopes in medicine

J. G. CUNINGHAME

Radioactive isotopes are used in medicine mainly for the diagnosis of disease, but they also have a limited application in the treatment of cancer.

In clinical medicine by far the most important diagnostic isotope is ^{99m}Tc, while for therapy it is ^{60}Co; some thirty or so other isotopes are also used to a greater or lesser extent. A far larger number (over 100) have been tried in medical research at one time or another.

This chapter starts by describing the properties required of isotopes for medical use and goes on to explain the way in which they are used and what equipment is needed. Tables giving the properties, production routes and specific uses of the more important medical isotopes are provided and, in conclusion, actual diagnosis carried out with a number of them are illustrated by a selection of examples.

Contents

1 Introduction

Although there are branches of medicine which do not directly concern themselves with sick people, medical effort is in the main devoted to the diagnosis of illness, probably followed by its treatment. The major use of radioactive isotopes[1] in medicine is for diagnosis, usually carried out by departments of nuclear medicine or medical physics in hospitals. Procedures of this kind are comparatively quick and cheap, and additionally have the advantage of generally being *non-invasive* and in consequence not very traumatic to the patient. This latter feature is important in *in vivo* diagnosis (i.e. carried out on the patient's body). (This same advantage does not of course apply in the case of *in vitro* analysis—the laboratory examination of tissue samples.) Isotopes also however play an important part in therapy, particularly of cancer; therapy of this kind is normally the province of radiotherapy departments in hospitals. Isotopes have of course a wide range of medical applications—notably in research—and this chapter will aim to cover a number of promising uses which are still under development. The primary concern will, however, be with the application of isotopes in clinical medicine, in therapy, and in diagnosis.

This chapter will examine the isotopes used in medicine, how they are made and how they are used.

2 The isotopes

2.1 Properties required for an isotope useful for diagnostic purposes

It is important to understand the very clear distinction between the purposes of diagnostic procedures on the one hand and of therapy on the other. In diagnosis it is necessary to examine the working of some part of the body in order to be able to decide what, if anything, is wrong with it; where this is carried out *in vivo*, the aim is to ensure that the minimum possible disturbance is caused to the patient and that there is a minimum of damage to bodily tissues. In therapy involving the use of radioactive isotopes the objective is usually to destroy bodily tissues that is, to destroy a tumour.

The properties required for the isotopes are very different for these two contrasting purposes. For diagnosis the objective is to obtain maximum information on the form or function of the affected organ. Radioisotopes have a valuable role to play here in allowing the behaviour of some chemical compound in the body to be followed, i.e. by acting as *tracers*. The approach is first to choose some chemical compound, drug, or pharmaceutical which, when introduced into the patient's body, has the property either of accumulating in the organ to be investigated or of passing through the body in such a way as to give information as to how some bodily system is working. The chosen compound is *labelled* with the isotope to be used, that is, the isotope is attached to it by chemical reactions. The labelled compound is then either injected into the patient or alternatively, inhaled or swallowed. After sufficient time has been given for it to pass to the organ of interest, its radiations (usually γ-radiations) are examined, normally by means of a γ-camera as discussed later. To summarize this chain of events: a compound is chosen which delivers the isotope with which it is labelled to the correct part of the body; the isotope's radiations then provide the required information Since the objective is to acquire maximum information for minimum dose to the patient the isotope should have the following properties.

1. It should emit γ-rays of just the energy required for the γ-camera (or other diagnostic instrument used). Normally γ-rays in the range 0.1 – 0.2 MeV are required.

2. It should not emit any other radiations, since these would increase the patient's radiation dose; the emission of particles, that is of pieces of matter ejected by the isotope, is particularly undesirable.

3. Its *half-life*, that is, the time taken for half its atoms to decay radioactively, must be suitable. The concept of half-life will be discussed in detail later on and it will be seen that both the physical and the biological half-lives may have to be taken into account. For the moment, however, it may simply be stated that the physical half-life must not be so short as to inhibit its use nor so long as to increase the patient's dose unnecessarily. Physical half-lives in the range 4–48 hours are suitable.

4. Its chemistry should be such that it can be readily attached to a variety of chemical compounds. It is important that it is attached firmly to the compound and is not released from it by reactions occurring within the body.

2.2 Properties of an isotope useful for therapy

The properties of a therapeutic isotope used internally are different. Ideally it should accumulate in the tumour to be destroyed (or it may be implanted in it surgically), and its radiations should affect only that tumour. Nuclear particles such as α- and β- radiations are often suitable, such radiations being by contrast highly undesirable in a diagnostic isotope. Therapy is also carried out by bombarding the tumour with γ-rays from a source outside the body exactly as in X-ray therapy. For this type of treatment the isotope must emit copious high-energy γ-rays.

2.3 Radiation characteristics of isotopes used

2.3.1 *Low-energy γ-emitters*

At the present time the great majority of nuclear medical diagnoses are carried out by using a γ-camera to examine radiation from a labelled compound which is within the patient's body. γ-cameras work best with γ-rays in the energy range 0.1–0.2 MeV, and the most commonly used diagnostic isotopes are those which emit few, if any, nuclear particles and have the majority of their γ-rays in this range. The best isotopes for this use are those decaying by one of two modes, in neither of which are any nuclear particles emitted. In *orbital electron capture* a radioactive isotope absorbs one of its own extranuclear electrons into its nucleus. In the process one proton of the nucleus is changed into a neutron, and so the *atomic number* of the isotope is reduced by one, that is, it is transmuted into an isotope of the element one place lower in the Periodic Table. This new isotope is often left with excess energy which it loses by emitting a γ-ray.

The other useful decay mode is called *isomeric transition*. Nuclei can exist in many energy states but as a rule the states of higher energy, the *excited states*, are unstable and can only exist for a short time (much less than a second) before decaying back to the lowest-energy state, the *ground state*, by emitting γ-rays. Sometimes, however, an excited state has a longer half-life than usual—a *metastable state* (indicated by the use of the affix 'm' with the mass number)—and if this half-life is suitable the metastable state of the isotope may be of use for diagnosis. It is this type of decay which is termed isomeric transition.

In addition to the ideal γ-emitters which are pure electron-capture isotopes or isomeric-transition isotopes, there are others which decay by a mixture of both particle emission (commonly positive or negative electrons) and one or the other of the above modes, or alternatively by particle emission alone. Although not so ideal, if they also emit an abundance of suitable γ-rays they may well be useful.

2.3.2 *Positron emitters*

Positrons, or β^+-particles, are positive electrons, and the emission of one transmutes the isotope into one of the element one place lower in the Periodic Table as in the case of electron capture; indeed the two modes of decay frequently occur together in the same isotope. Positron emission can be followed by γ-rays of any energy. The characteristic behaviour of positrons is however to fuse almost immediately with a *negatron* (a β^--particle or negative electron), with the resultant simultaneous emission of a pair of 0.511 MeV γ-rays moving in opposite directions. Because this form of decay is common, and because some special techniques can make use of the fact that the two γ-rays are emitted simultaneously, modified forms of γ-camera (*positron cameras*) have been developed.

2.3.3 *Negatron emitters (β⁻-emitters)*
Negatrons, or negative electrons, are β^--particles. As mentioned in §2.3.1, they may be emitted as part of the radiation from isotopes which have been selected for use in diagnosis owing to the suitability of their γ-ray emission. Such particles generally prove to be an undesirable complication since, although their penetration of tissue is not large, they cause damage to it with no corresponding gain. This property of damaging tissue is, however, turned to good effect in therapy in which a β^--emitter is attached to a compound which preferentially accumulates in a tumour, so allowing the β^--particles to destroy it.

2.3.4 *Alpha emitters*
Some isotopes, mainly the heavier ones, decay by emitting α-particles, which are nuclei of the element helium. The α-particles have only slight penetrating power and cannot normally do much harm. However, if the α-emitter becomes lodged inside the body close to sensitive tissue it may be very dangerous indeed since, during their short travel through tissue, the α-particles cause intense damage. Some therapeutic uses have been suggested for α-particles but they are, in general, shunned in nuclear medicine.

2.3.5 *High-energy γ-emitters*
Isotopes which emit mainly γ-rays of high-energy (say, ≈ 1 MeV or more) are not suitable for diagnosis, but may be used to bombard tumours in cancer therapy.

2.4 Physical forms of the isotopes

2.4.1 *Element or simple compound*
Generally speaking isotopes are supplied in the form of a simple chemical element or compound. Some, for example $^{11}CO_2$, $^{13}N_2$, and $^{15}O_2$,[2] are normally used in this form because their physical half-life is too short to make the preparation of really elaborate compounds practicable. It is one of the unfortunate quirks of Nature that she has not seen fit to provide us with isotopes of the most important organic elements, hydrogen, carbon, and oxygen, with half-lives ideal for nuclear medicine.

From a strictly medical point of view, half-lives for most diagnostic purposes should be short—say less than 10 hours. Such short lives, however, give rise to a major difficulty in that fresh supplies of the isotope are required daily. In some cases, however, Nature does act in our favour in the following way. An isotope with a reasonably long half-life (called the *parent*) decays radioactively into one with the desirable short half-life (the *daughter*). In such a case the laws of radioactive decay cause the activity of the daughter to grow to approximately 50 per cent of that of the parent during one daughter half-life, to 75 per cent in two half-lives, and so on, until the two activities are about equal. (See Chapter 24.) If the daughter is now separated in some way from the parent, it may be used in diagnoses, while, in the meantime, a fresh batch grows in with the parent.

Such a parent–daughter system is called a *generator* or *cow* and the process of removing the daughter is called *milking*. An advantage of the system lies in the fact that, while the daughter isotope used in diagnosis has a desirable short half-life, the generator as a whole has the long half-life of the parent and can produce several batches of the daughter isotope before it needs to be replaced. The milking process is designed to be very simple: normally the parent is fixed to an ion exchange column (this works like a domestic water softener) and the daughter is removed from it by pouring a small quantity of some specified liquid through it.

The most important diagnostic isotope of all. ^{99m}Tc, is produced as a daughter product in a system of this kind. ^{99m}Tc has nearly perfect physical properties for diagnosis but were it not the daughter of a generator system, its half-life of six hours would make its routine use quite impracticable. Fortunately its parent, ^{99}Mo, which is produced in nuclear reactors either directly or as a product of nuclear fission, has a half-life of 66 hours, and this is sufficiently long for a generator to be usable for a week.

2.4.2 Labelled compounds

For most diagnoses the isotope must be attached to a chemical compound which will behave in the body in the required way. Thus the eluant from the generator or the simple compound from the isotope production process will be chemically compounded with other substances so as to produce the desired drug or pharmaceutical for introduction into the patient's body.

Because the chemistry of the human body is exceedingly complex, there is a whole host of chemical compounds to which radioactive isotopes might be attached, each compound having particular potential advantage in the diagnosis of one or another of the many conditions that may need to be examined.

In the simplest cases, it is the properties of the element itself which will determine the organ by which the compound will be taken up. An example of this is the use of radioactive iodine, usually given orally as sodium iodide and used for examinations of the thyroid; this works because it is a property of the thyroid to remove iodine from the bloodstream.

Sometimes a compound which is an actual constituent of the body is labelled; when introduced into the system it will then behave in its normal way. An example of this is the labelling of red blood cells with ^{51}Cr so as to measure their survival and detect the rate of their destruction.

Some compounds merely act as a physical support for the isotope. An example of this is when ^{99m}Tc is absorbed by small particles of human serum albumin, which are then inhaled by the patient. They lodge in the lung tissue, so allowing the γ-camera pictures to be taken, but are eventually metabolized and excreted.

Finally, there is a huge number of complex organic compounds whose behaviour in the body is not substantially changed by the addition of a radioactive isotope, and which behave in some way that allows the required information about the patient's condition to be deduced from the γ-emission of the radioisotope. An example of this is the dye *Rose Bengal* which, with the addition of a radioactive isotope of iodine, accumulates in the liver and is used to study it.

3 Producing the isotopes

3.1 The specific activity problem

All isotopes are produced by reactions in which one atomic nucleus is changed into another; this is a *nuclear transmutation*. Sometimes the new isotope is of the same chemical element as the one from which it was made; this is often the case when a nuclear reactor is employed to effect the transmutation. In this case the product will be a mixture of the new isotope and the old; isotopic separation, although possible, is not a feasible proposition owing to its great expense and complexity. The *specific activity* of the product is the amount of radioactivity per unit weight of the element concerned, and it is one of the disadvantages of this type of reaction that it may not be sufficiently high for diagnostic or therapeutic purposes. This is not normally a problem when the nuclear reaction is induced by means of a particle accelerating machine, because the product is usually an isotope of a different element from the target material; this means that the target and product isotopes can be separated chemically and the product can be *carrier-free*, or else prepared with very high specific activity.

3.2 Producing the pure isotope

3.2.1 *In reactors*
In these days of frequently exaggerated concern about the possible hazards of operating nuclear reactors, it is often forgotten that without them many forms of medical diagnosis would become impossible, and people would die who might otherwise have been saved. Not only the most important diagnostic radioisotope (^{99m}Tc) but all of the radioisotopes used in therapy are reactor products, and could not possibly be effectively made in any other way.

The commonest reactor nuclear reaction for isotope production is called an $X(n,\gamma)Y$ reaction. The symbolism means that the nucleus X absorbs a neutron and is converted into the nucleus Y, emitting γ-rays in the process. The effect is that Y is an isotope of the same chemical element as X but one atomic mass unit heavier. It is a reaction which usually has a high *cross-section* (a measure of the ease with which the reaction can take place) and only requires low-energy neutrons. One of the reactions often used for production of the ^{99}Mo–^{99m}Tc generator described earlier is of this type:

$$^{98}\text{Mo(n, }\gamma)^{99}\text{Mo} \xrightarrow{\beta^- \text{-decay}} \,^{99\text{m}}\text{Tc}.$$

A second method of ^{99}Mo–$^{99\text{m}}$Tc production involves the fission of ^{235}U (or of any other reactor fuel material). ^{99}Mo is one of the medically used isotopes which arise as otherwise unwanted by-products during the operation of nuclear reactors (others, used in cancer therapy, are ^{90}Sr and ^{137}Cs). Generators produced by this route allow the elution of $^{99\text{m}}$Tc at far higher concentration than do those produced by the first method.

Two other reactions sometimes used for isotope production in reactors are $X(\text{n,2n})Y$, in which Y is of the same chemical element as X but one atomic mass unit lighter, and $X(\text{n,p})Y$, in which Y is an isotope of the same mass as X but of the element one lower in the Periodic Table. Cross-sections for these two reactions are considerably lower than for the first two.

To make an isotope, the target material is sealed up in a suitable container and inserted into an operating nuclear reactor, one with a high flux of neutrons being preferred since this flux controls both the specific activity which can be attained and the amount of the isotope which can be made in a specified time. When this time has elapsed the container is unloaded from the reactor directly on to a shielded transport container. Figure 23.1 shows

Fig. 23.1 A member of the Isotope Production Unit of Amersham International unloading isotopes from the DIDO reactor at Harwell

such an operation being carried out at the Harwell DIDO reactor by one of the staff of Amersham International's Isotope Production Unit.

3.2.2 *In cyclotrons*

In the case of reactors the isotopes are produced by bombardment with neutrons and consequently they are almost all *neutron excessive* that is, they have more neutrons than they require for stability; these they lose by β^--emission. On the other hand, bombardment by charged particles from accelerators (normally cyclotrons) gives rise to *neutron-deficient* isotopes. This is because in these reactions a compound nucleus is first formed by a fusion of the target nucleus with the bombarding particle. This compound nucleus is formed with too much energy for stability and the easiest way it can lose this is by emitting neutrons. The isotopes which are finally produced, after this complex process has finished, decay by positron emission, by electron capture, or by a mixture of the two; they are thus a completely different group from those produced in reactors and with quite different characteristics. Some examples of the sort of reactions used are:

$$X(p,2n)Y,$$
$$X(^2H,n)Y, \text{ and}$$
$$X(^4He,3n)Y.$$

In the first, Y is one mass unit lighter than X and one place higher in the Periodic Table; in the second it is one mass unit heavier and one place higher; while in the third it is one mass unit heavier but two places higher. Note that in all three cases an isotope of a different chemical element is formed, thus permitting the achievement of high specific activity.

One fundamental difference between reactors and cyclotrons is that isotope production within a reactor is normally a side activity which does not much affect the main task of the reactor; it is a *parasitic* operation. With cyclotrons, however, this is not normally the case; they are *dedicated*, that is, nothing else can go on at the same time as an isotope is being made. This means that it is normally uneconomic to irradiate for long periods in cyclotrons and this, in turn, restricts their use in practice to the shorter-lived isotopes. Another major difference is that in a reactor the target material is immersed in a sea of fairly low-energy neutrons which move in all directions and are quite easily able to penetrate to the depths of the target. In a cyclotron the particles have a high energy but fairly low penetration of matter, and are in the form of a concentrated beam aimed in one direction. The design of cyclotron targets is thus more difficult. The target material must be formed into a compact shape, must be cooled well enough to carry off the heat deposited in it, and must be readily removable from the system after the irradiation is ended—this last requirement being harder to achieve than in the reactor case.

While any cyclotron can be used to prepare isotopes, the characteristics of the machine will have a profound effect on the range and type of products that can be made. Small cyclotrons may well be cheap enough for them to be owned by a hospital. Such machines are usually designed to give high currents of the four important isotope production beams; these are protons (hydrogen nuclei; usually represented by the symbol ^{1}H or p), deuterons (heavy hydrogen nuclei; ^{2}H or d), helium-3 (light helium nuclei; ^{3}He), and alpha particles (helium nuclei; ^{4}He or α). The maximum energies to which the small machine can accelerate the particles are fairly low and this restricts the number of nuclear reactions they can use. Sometimes this restriction is a nuisance, as in the case of the important diagnostic isotope ^{123}I, which needs a much larger machine for its efficient production in pure form, but they are perfectly capable of making the majority of neutron-deficient medical isotopes. Furthermore, if they are situated in a hospital (as for example, the MRC cyclotron at Hammersmith), the doctors can then use the very short-lived isotopes, particularly ^{11}C (half-life 20 minutes), ^{13}N (10 minutes), and ^{15}O (2 minutes). Such cyclotrons can also be used for long-lived isotope production. Amersham International's machine, shown in Fig. 23.2, which is fully automated, can run overnight with no staff present, and is the source of most of the longer-lived cyclotron isotopes produced in the UK.

Large cyclotrons designed for nuclear physics and nuclear chemistry research are expensive to operate, and are only used for isotope production

Fig. 23.2 View of Amersham International's cyclotron, used for isotope production. Target heads can be attached to the target chassis shown on the turntable and the targets can be put into and taken out of the cyclotron beam, all by remote control

if there is some special reason, as in the case of ^{123}I production, where they permit the use of a very good nuclear reaction denied to the smaller machines. Figure 23.3 shows one such machine, the variable-energy cyclotron at Harwell, which is one of the small number of machines in the world producing ^{123}I of high purity and, indeed, the only such machine in the United Kingdom.

3.3 Chemical processing and labelling

Once the irradiation in reactor or cyclotron is complete, the target material must be removed from its container; in most cases, the desired isotope is then chemically separated. This work has to be carried out in cells suitably shielded to protect the operator from the radiations. Figure 23.4 is an example of one such cell with 175 mm thick lead walls; it is situated at Amersham International. Figure 23.5 shows a series of much smaller ones with 50 mm thick lead walls used at Harwell for separation of ^{123}I.

The preparation of the target material for chemical treatment may simply consist of tipping it out of its container, or may involve some operation such as the milling of a thin layer of irradiated metal off the surface of a metal target. Once the material is ready, conventional radiochemical operations are performed on it which result in the separation of the required isotope in some simple chemical form, usually a concentrated solution. Measurements and tests for radionuclidic, radiochemical, and chemical purity, pyrogenicity[3] etc. are carried out on the product, following which it will either be dispensed and sterilized for subsequent despatch to the user, or alternatively used for the labelling of a drug or pharmaceutical.

3.4 Quality control

When medical materials, including isotopes and labelled compounds, are manufactured for human use the process is controlled at all stages by the provisions of the Medicines Act. The finished product must conform to its stated specifications which, for a substance to be introduced into a patient's body, include sterility and freedom from pyrogens. The manufacturer has to have quality control staff with the power to insist on the rejection of materials not reaching specification, who check on the manufacture of the product at all stages.

Sterility is not a problem for products which can be subjected to steam at 120 °C for 20 minutes, but if time does not permit this (for example, in the case of very short-lived isotopes) or if such treatment would destroy the product (as is the case for some complex compounds), it may be sufficient to pass the product through a very fine filter (usually with a pore size of 0.22 μm). Pyrogenicity, however, is a much greater problem, and considerable effort may be needed to ensure that the standards set for pyrogenicity are not exceeded. Pyrogenic material may be present in the apparatus used for the chemical processing or may be introduced in reagents or from the atmosphere. The filtering of air and the use of pyrogen-free reagents suffice

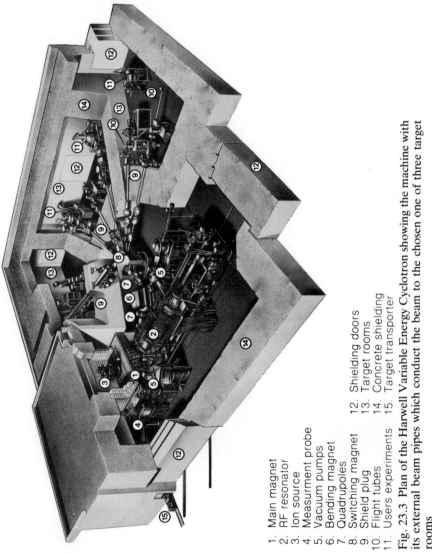

1. Main magnet
2. RF resonator
3. Ion source
4. Measurment probe
5. Vacuum pumps
6. Bending magnet
7. Quadrupoles
8. Switching magnet
9. Shield plug
10. Flight tubes
11. Users experiments
12. Shielding doors
13. Target rooms
14. Concrete shielding
15. Target transporter

Fig. 23.3 Plan of the Harwell Variable Energy Cyclotron showing the machine with its external beam pipes which conduct the beam to the chosen one of three target rooms

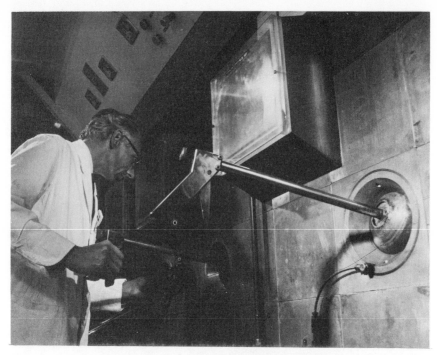

Fig. 23.4 External view of a shielded cell at Amersham International. This cell has 17.5 cm thick lead walls and is used for handling irradiated target discs

Fig. 23.5 A bank of small isotope production cells built into fume hoods at Harwell. These cells have 5 cm thick lead shields and are used for production of ^{123}I

to deal easily with the last two sources of pyrogens; the removal of pyrogens from apparatus before use involves the use of a special anti-pyrogen cleaning fluid, which can be tedious and time-consuming.

The finished product must be subjected to tests to ensure that it conforms to specification. Some of these tests, for example sterility and pyrogenicity, take several days and, for short-lived radioactive products, cannot therefore be performed before use. In such a case samples prepared using identical apparatus and procedures have to be exhaustively tested before the product is used with patients, and every batch must be sent for testing even though the results will not be available until after the product has been used. Other tests which have to be carried out on a radioactive product are:

(1) radionuclidic purity, i.e. absence of radioactive isotopes other than the required one;
(2) radiochemical purity, i.e. product in the correct chemical form; and
(3) chemical purity, i.e. absence of all ions apart from those required.

The quality control staff are responsible for checking that firstly, the apparatus and reagents used and the procedures followed conform to production specifications and secondly, that the final product meets the specification on all the criteria outlined above. The quality control manager and his staff must be independent of the production manager, and must act as a parallel organization, reporting directly to higher management.

3.5 Sources of UK-produced isotopes

Amersham International Ltd. is by far the most important UK isotope producer, supplying a high proportion of medical (and other) isotopes used in the UK and also supplying a world-wide export market. They may certainly be regarded as unique in the wide range of products and services they provide. There are other suppliers of isotopes however who, while of smaller importance, still make a significant contribution. Table 23.1 summarizes UK sources of medical isotopes.

The supply of a huge range of medical isotopes and compounds, many of them having quite short half-lives, to customers all over the world requires a highly efficient system. It must be capable of manufacturing the products to demanding specifications, processing orders for them quickly, and then despatching the materials by a wide variety of transport methods and under a set of rigid, internationally-agreed packaging and documentation regulations.

4 How radioisotopes are used in medicine

4.1 Purposes for which they are used

The uses of radioisotopes in medicine can conveniently be divided into diagnosis and therapy as has been discussed earlier. It should also be

Table 23.1 Sources of UK–produced medical isotopes

Place	Machine used	Isotopes produced	Comments
AERE Harwell	DIDO and PLUTO reactors	Most of the reactor isotopes produced in UK	All handling of the isotopes is by the Isotope Production Unit (IPU) of Amersham International Ltd., located at Harwell. Processing is at Amersham
	Variable-energy cyclotron	^{123}I	Processed by Harwell
Birmingham University	Cyclotron	Various	Small amounts for local use only
British Nuclear Fuels Ltd., Chapelcross	Power reactors	^{14}C, ^{60}Co	Sent to Amersham for processing
ICI, Billingham	Research reactor	Various	Small amounts for local use only
MRC Cyclotron Unit Hammersmith Hospital	Cyclotron	Most of the shorter-lived cyclotron isotopes produced in the UK; includes ^{11}C, ^{13}N, ^{15}O, ^{18}F used clinically in hospital	Processed by MRC cyclotron unit
Scottish Universities Reactor Centre, East Kilbride	Research reactor	Various	Small amounts for local use only
Amersham International Ltd.	2 Cyclotrons	Most of the longer-lived cyclotron isotopes produced in the UK	Processed by Amersham

remembered however that within both categories there will be a difference between clinical use and research. Many isotopes are tried out in research and may prove entirely satisfactory for some particular investigation, but this is a far cry from their becoming accepted for routine use on patients. For this reason, while over a hundred radioisotopes have been mentioned in the medical literature, extensive clinical use is made of only a dozen or so in diagnosis, while therapy is restricted to even fewer.

In diagnosis the overriding principle is to obtain the required information while subjecting the patient to the minimum possible dose of radioactivity. In this respect one advantage of isotope diagnosis *in vivo* is that this dose is fixed by the amount of isotope introduced into the body. No matter how many tests are made or pictures are taken the dose does not increase; this is in sharp contrast with X-rays where the dose increases each time a picture is taken. All kinds of investigations can be undertaken, some examples of which are:

(1) the shape and position of organs,
(2) the functioning of organs and bodily systems,
(3) estimation of body spaces,
(4) blood flow measurements, and

(5) estimation of trace elements in the body.

New compounds are constantly being tried to see whether they may have a helpful diagnostic application, and occasionally one will be found which may revolutionize some aspect of diagnosis—for example the current acceptance of ^{201}Tl as an agent for myocardial examination.

In therapy the purpose is straightforward—to destroy the tumour if possible or at least to retard its growth. The attack may be made by radiations striking the tumour from a radioactive source outside it; alternatively the source may be inserted into the body in such a way that its radiations impinge primarily on the tumour.

4.2 The most commonly used isotopes

It is worth repeating that by far the most important medical isotopes for diagnosis and for therapy are respectively ^{99m}Tc and ^{60}Co. In Table 23.2, which is a list of diagnostic isotopes, ^{99m}Tc is therefore shown at the top, the remaining isotopes being in order of their position in the Periodic Table. The order of importance of these other isotopes is largely a matter of opinion and is strongly dependent on local conditions, that is on the specialities and strengths of particular hospitals using the isotopes; it also depends very much on such extraneous factors as cost, availability, and convenience. Table 23.2 does, however, attempt to include the most important isotopes used clinically. Table 23.3 lists the few isotopes used for therapy. In this case ^{60}Co is at the top, the rest being in Periodic Table order. Note that all the isotopes in Table 23.3 are reactor produced.

4.3 Methods of use

4.3.1 The half-life

Before going into detail of actual methods of isotope use, it is important to be clear about this concept of half-life and to distinguish between the three varieties of it in medical use. Radioactive decay is a process expressed by the simple equation:

$$-\frac{dN}{dt} = \lambda N.$$

In words this simply states that the rate of break-up of radioactive atoms $(-dN/dt)$ is equal to the number present (N) multiplied by a constant (λ), whose value is a fundamental property of the isotope concerned. From this beginning, some simple mathematical manipulations lead to the conclusion that, for any radioactive isotope there is a constant quantity, the *physical* half-life, which indicates the length of time taken, on average, for the radioactivity present to be reduced by half.

The physical half-life is determined solely by the properties of the isotope concerned. The *biological* half-life is by contrast a very much less precise

Table 23.2 Diagnostic medical radioisotopes for clinical use

Isotope and name of element	Reactor(R) or cyclotron(C)	Nuclear reaction commonly used for production	Half-life	Type of radiation emitted	Principal γ-ray energies (MeV)	Medical applications† Labelled compound	How introduced into body	Organ examined	Remarks
^{99m}Tc Technetium	R	$^{98}Mo(n,\gamma)^{99}Mo \rightarrow {}^{99m}Tc$ $^{235}U(n,f)^{99}Mo \rightarrow {}^{99m}Tc$	^{99}Mo: 66 h ^{99m}Tc: 6 h		0.141	Pertechnetate Sulphur colloid DTPA; Phosphates Red blood cells Fibrinogen Human serum albumin MAA*	IV§ IV IV IV IV IV IV	Brain, thyroid Liver Kidney Bone, heart Spleen Blood clot detection Blood pool Lungs	^{99m}Tc-labelled compounds have been used for almost all nuclear medical diagnoses. Although for some there may be better agents labelled with other radioisotopes the cheapness and convenience of ^{99m}Tc will often dictate its use in spite of their existence
^3H Hydrogen	R	$^6Li(n,\gamma)^3H$	12.3 y		—	Tritiated water	IV	Exchangeable body water	Also enormous biological usage
^{11}C Carbon	C	$^{10}B(d,n)^{11}C$ $^{11}B(d,2n)^{11}C$	20.4 m		0.511	CO, CO_2 Red blood cells Many organic compounds	Inhalation IV Various	Pulmonary function Blood pool definition Many—but mainly in research	Because of short half-life a local cyclotron is required
^{14}C Carbon	R	$^{14}N(n,p)^{14}C$	5730 y			Glycine cholate Various	Oral *In vitro*	Breath tests Assay, including radio-immuno and saturation	Awkward to analyse because emits no gamma rays
^{13}N Nitrogen	C	$^{12}C(d,n)^{13}N$	9.8 m		0.511	N_2 NH_3	Inhalation IV	Pulmonary function studies Cerebral blood flow and myocardial imaging	Because of short half-life a local cyclotron is required
^{15}O Oxygen	C	$^{14}N(d,n)^{15}O$	2.1 m		0.511	O_2, CO_2, CO O-haemoglobin and CO-haemoglobin	Inhalation IV	Lung ventilation Cerebral circulation and cerebral oxygen metabolism	Because of short half-life a local cyclotron is required

(Table 23.2 *Continued*)

Isotope and name of element	Reactor(R) or cyclotron(C)	Nuclear reaction commonly used for production	Half-life	Type of radiation emitted	Principal γ-ray energies (MeV)	Medical applications† Labelled compound	How introduced into body	Organ examined	Remarks
^{18}F Fluorine	C	^{16}O(^{3}He,p)^{18}F ^{20}Ne(d,α)^{18}F	1.83 h	EC	0.511	Very many fluorinated organic compounds	IV	Most types of diagnosis, but particularly for bone imaging	Because of short half-life requires a nearby cyclotron. Its ubiquity arises because the F ion can replace H or OH in organic compounds
^{51}Cr Chromium	R	^{50}Cr(n,γ)^{51}Cr	27.8 d	EC	0.320	Red blood cell EDTA^{11} Blood proteins Heat-damaged red blood cells	IV IV IV IV	Red cell survival and mass Glomerular filtration rate Demonstrates bleeding into GI‡‡ tract Spleen imaging	Red cells labelled by chromate *in vitro* and then reinjected†
^{52}Fe Iron	C C	^{52}Cr(^{3}He,3n)^{52}Fe ^{50}Cr(d,2n)^{52}Fe	8.3 h	EC	0.511 0.169	Citrate	IV	Bone marrow	Rather short half-life has meant that this isotope is scarce
^{59}Fe Iron	R	^{58}Fe(n,γ)^{59}Fe	44.6 d		1.292 1.099	Citrate Chloride Ascorbate Damaged red blood cells	IV IV Oral IV	Iron kinetics in blood studies Iron absorption and plasma turnover Iron absorption Spleen function	Radiations are much less satisfactory than those of ^{52}Fe but ready availability dictates its use
^{57}Co Cobalt	R C	^{58}Ni(n,2n)^{57}Ni ^{57}Co ^{58}Ni(p,2p)^{57}Co ^{58}Ni(p,pn)^{57}Co	270 d	EC	0.136 0.122 0.014	Cyanocobalmin Various	Oral *In vitro*	Investigation of malabsorption of Vitamin B12 in diagnosis of pernicious anaemia. Volume marker in radio-immunoassay	^{58}Co also used for same purpose
^{67}Ga Gallium	C	^{68}Zn(p,2n)^{67}Ga	78.1 h	EC	0.394 0.300 0.185 0.093	Citrate	IV	Abscesses Localization of soft tissue tumours (lymphomas, Hodgkins disease)	One of the most important cyclotron produced isotopes

(Table 23.2 Continued)

Isotope and name of element	Reactor(R) or cyclotron(C)	Nuclear reaction commonly used for production	Half-life	Type of radiation emitted	Principal γ-ray energies (MeV)	Medical applications[†] Labelled compound	How introduced into body	Organ examined	Remarks
^{75}Se Selenium	R	^{74}Se$(n, \gamma)^{75}$Se	120 d	EC	0.400 0.279 0.264 0.135 0.121	Methionine Cholesterol	IV IV	Pancreas scanning Adrenal scanning	
^{81m}Kr Krypton	C	^{82}Kr$(p,2n)^{81}$Rb ^{81m}Kr ^{82}Kr$(d,3n)^{81}$Rb ^{81m}Kr	^{81}Rb:4.7 h ^{81m}Kr:13s		0.190	Gas	Inhalation	Lung function studies Cerebral perfusion studies	A generator system which would be more widely used if more readily available
^{111}In Indium	C	^{112}Cd$(p,2n)^{111}$In	283 d	EC	0.245 0.171	DTPA‡, EDTA[11] transferrin Oxine	Intrathecal In vitro	Cisternography and other CSF‡‡ studies, e.g. in spina bifida Blood cell labelling	
^{113m}In Indium	R	^{112}Sn$(n, \gamma)^{113}$Sn ^{113m}In	^{113}Sn:115d ^{113m}In: 1.66 h		0.391	Citrate DTPA[2]	IV IV	Liver scanning Brain and kidney scanning	This is special case. This generator is useful in places where supplies of ^{99m}Te are uncertain. In developed countries it is not so important
^{123}I Iodine	C	^{127}Te$(p,2n)^{123}$I ^{123}I$(p,5n)^{123}$Xe ^{123}I	13.3 h	EC	0.159	Hippurate Rose Bengal, BSP§§ Iodine	IV IV Oral	Kidney scanning Liver scanning Thyroid uptake and scanning	Only lack of easy availability prevents this isotope from replacing ^{131}I for most of its diagnostic uses and ^{99m}Te for some
^{125}I Iodine	R	^{124}Xe$(n, \gamma)^{125}$Xe ^{125}I	60.14 d	EC	0.035	Fibrinogen Human serum albumin Various	IV IV In vitro	Deep vein thrombosis Plasma volume estimation	Very important in vitro label

(Table 23.2 *Continued*)

Isotope and name of element	Reactor(R) or cyclotron(C)	Nuclear reaction commonly used for production	Half-life	Type of radiation emitted	Principal γ-ray energies (MeV)	Medical applications[†] Labelled compound	How introduced into body	Organ examined	Remarks
[131]I Iodine	R	$^{130}\text{Te}(n,\gamma)^{131}\text{Te} \rightarrow {}^{131}\text{I}$	8.06 d		0.637 0.364	Iodine Hippurate Human serum albumin Rose Bengal MAA*	Oral IV IV IV IV	Thyroid uptake and scanning Kidney scanning Blood pool studies Liver studies Lungs	One of the first radioisotopes to be used. Has radiations which are very much less than ideal and it is being rapidly replaced by ^{99m}Te or by ^{123}I where this is available
[133]Xe Xenon	R	$^{132}\text{Xe}(n,\gamma)^{133}\text{Xe}$	5.29 d		0.081	Gas Saline solution	Inhalation IV or intra arterial	Lung ventilation Regional peripheral blood flow	
[200]Tl Thallium	C	$^{200}\text{Tl}(p,3n)^{200}\text{Pb} \rightarrow {}^{201}\text{Tl}$	73.5 h	EX	0.167 0.135	Chloride	IV	Myocardial visualization and in examination of isochaemia in coronary heart disease	

† only a selection given under this heading
‡ DTPA = diethylenetriaminopentacetic acid
§ IV = intra-venous
* MAA = macroaggregated albumin
‖ EDTA = ethylenediaminetetracetic acid
†† GI = gastrointestinal
‡‡ CSF = cerebrospinal fluid
§§ BSP = bromsulphthalein

Table 23.3 Therapeutic medical radioisotopes for clinical use

Isotope	Nuclear reaction commonly used for production	Half-life	Type of radiation emitted	Principal γ-ray energies (MeV)	Medical applications			Remarks
					Type of therapy	How used	Organ treated	
^{60}Co Cobalt	^{59}Co(n,γ)^{60}Co	5.26 y	β^- γ	1.33 1.17	Teletherapy	Machine	General treatment of tumours	By far the most important therapeutic use of radioisotopes. Many ^{60}Co teletherapy machines are in use as a complement to X-ray machines
^{32}P Phosphorus	^{32}S(n,p)^{32}P	14.3 d	β^-	—	Systemic	As colloidal suspension given IV	To treat polycythaemia vera	
^{90}Sr Strontium ^{90}Y Yttrium	^{235}U(n,f)^{90}Sr $\rightarrow$ ^{90}Y	^{90}Sr: 28.5 y ^{90}Y: 64.1 h	β^-	—	Brachytherapy Brachytherapy Systemic	^{90}Y rods ^{90}Sr-^{90}Y applicators ^{90}Y colloids	Pituitary Opthalmic work Palliation	
^{125}I Iodine	^{124}Xe(n,γ)^{125}Xe $\rightarrow^{125}$I	60.14 d	EC γ	0.035	Brachytherapy	Seeds	Various	
^{131}I Iodine	^{130}Te(n,γ)^{131}Te $\rightarrow^{131}$I	8.06 d	β^- γ	0.637 0.364	Systemic	As sodium iodide given IV	Thyroid cancer, hyperthyroidism	One of the earliest isotopes to be used for cancer treatment
^{137}Cs Caesium	^{235}U(n,f)^{137}Cs $\rightarrow^{137m}$Ba	^{137}Cs: 30.0 y ^{137m}Ba: 2.5 m	β^- γ	0.661	Teletherapy Brachytherapy	Machine Intracavitary and as needles	General tumour treatment General treatment	Now relatively little used for teletherapy because γ-ray energy is rather low, but is replacing ^{226}Ra for brachytherapy
^{192}Ir Iridium	^{190}Ir(n,γ)^{192}Ir	74.2 d	β^- γ	0.612	Brachytherapy	Wires, rods	Various	
^{198}Au Gold	^{197}Au(n,γ)^{198}Au	2.7 d	β^- γ	0.412	Brachytherapy Systemic	Grains Colloids	Various Palliation	
^{226}Ra Radium	Natural	1600 y	α γ	2.43 -0.19	Brachytherapy	Needles and tubes	Various	While of great historical importance, now being rapidly replaced by ^{137}Cs

idea. It is the length of time taken for the radioactivity to be halved by removal from the body by biological processes such as excretion, exhalation, etc. The same isotope will behave differently in different people and even in the same person at different times, and so quoted values for this half-life may have a wide margin of error.

The *effective* half-life is the one that really matters, since this is the time over which the radioactivity in the body will actually be halved by a combination of physical and biological processes. Knowing the physical half-life $t_{1/2}$, and the biological half-life, t_B, the effective half-life, t_E, is

$$t_E = \frac{t_{1/2} \times t_B}{t_{1/2} + t_B}$$

It may easily be shown that if either $t_{1/2}$ or t_B is very much shorter than the other, then t_E is effectively equal to the shorter one. The maximum divergency of t_E from both values occurs when $t_{1/2}$ is equal to t_B; under those conditions t_E is half of their value.

4.3.2 *Diagnostic methods*

Radioisotopes are normally introduced into the body by intravenous injection. Some procedures, however, involve oral ingestion or inhalation of the material. There is also the possibility that they may be generated in the body *in situ* through *in-vivo activation analysis*. In this fairly uncommon method the patient is irradiated with a small dose of low-energy neutrons, which then interact with some inactive isotope which is a constituent of the body and turn it into an active one by the $X(n, \gamma)Y$ reaction. The radioactivity of Y is then measured, usually with a whole-body monitor. An example of this type of diagnosis is the assessment of activated calcium in the body in order to study the response to treatment of patients suffering from certain diseases that affect the skeleton. The measurement techniques are described in §4.4.

Finally, it must not be forgotten that there are a number of diagnostic techniques in which the radioactivity is never put into the patient at all: *in-vitro* analysis. A sample of one of the patient's body fluids is taken and examined by using the radioactive isotopes in the laboratory. One example of this is the *T-4 test* for the thyroid hormone, thyroxine. Thyroxine is transported through the body bound to serum proteins. A sample of these is taken from the patient; the thyroxine is separated from the proteins and is then added to a test-tube containing an aqueous solution of ^{125}I-labelled thyroxine bound to a protein. Some of this labelled thyroxine is replaced by the thyroxine from the sample, and so is released into the solution, where it is trapped by absorbent granules in the test tube and removed. The radioactivity in the solution is thus reduced and this gives us a measure of the amount of thyroxine in the sample. This may be assessed quantitatively by means of a calibration prepared using a known amount of thyroxine.

^{125}I is also commonly used in the technique known as *radioimmuno assay* used for the *in-vitro* assessment of hormone concentrations in blood. An antibody of the hormone to be assayed is prepared, together with a quantity of the hormone itself, which is labelled with ^{125}I. This labelled hormone, the unknown blood sample containing the (same) hormone, and the antibody are mixed. The antibody reacts with both labelled and unknown hormone to form a complex which is filtered off and counted. There will thus be competition between the labelled and unlabelled hormone for the available binding sites on the antibody, and where the blood sample contains a high concentration of hormones a relatively low amount of ^{125}I radioactivity will pass into the complex. Conversely, where the hormone concentration in blood is low, the radioactivity of the complex will be correspondingly high.

4.3.3 *Therapeutic methods*

There are, broadly speaking, three different methods of radiation therapy with isotopes. In the first, called *teletherapy*, the isotope is placed in a shielded enclosure with collimators arranged so that the γ-radiation can be formed into a beam of the desired shape. This beam of radiation is allowed to fall on the particular area of the patient's body behind which is the tumour to be treated and will, it is hoped, destroy it. Of course, the rays also pass through healthy tissue both in front of and behind the tumour and it is normal practice to irradiate it from a number of different angles in turn, so arranged that all the beams converage on the tumour. The healthy tissue receives much less radiation than the tumour by the use of this technique. For this to be possible, the machine must be able to move round the patient. Figure 23.6 shows a ^{60}Co machine which can be used in this way.

Treatment by γ-rays as just described is similar to the treatment by X-ray machines. For the sake of completness it should be noted that considerable effort is going into an alternative non-isotopic, non-X-ray method for the irradiation of tumours. This uses fast neutrons. The method was pioneered by the MRC Cyclotron Unit at Hammersmith Hospital, but is now being tried in many countries. The neutrons are produced by a large accelerating machine, usually by the reaction

$$^9Be(d, n)^{10}B$$

In the UK the MRC has a second cyclotron for this purpose at Edinburgh, shown in Fig. 23.7, while some preliminary experiments are also being conducted by an MRC/NHS collaboration on the Harwell variable-energy cyclotron.

The second treatment method is known as *brachytherapy*. Here the isotope is administered in a form which will be insoluble in the body fluids, either by forming it into, say, metallic seeds, wires, or rods, or else by encapsulating it in a suitable container. The isotope is inserted into the body near to, or in, the tumour or else applied to it externally. Energetic particles, as well as γ-rays, can play a part in this kind of irradiation.

Finally, in some forms of treatment the isotope is transported to the site of the tumour by normal processes as in the case of the diagnostic methods

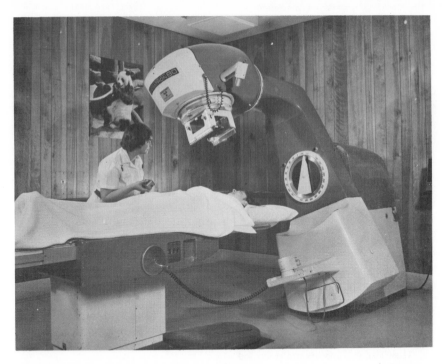

Fig. 23.6 A ^{60}C teletherapy machine. (Courtesy of the Churchill Hospital, Oxford)

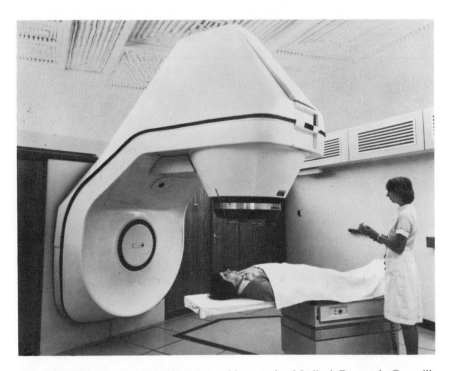

Fig. 23.7 The neutron teletherapy machine at the Medical Research Council's Edinburgh cyclotron. (Courtesy of the Controller, HMSO.)

earlier discussed. An example of this *systemic therapy* is in the treatment of thyroid cancer by ^{131}I administered orally.

4.3.4 *Heart pacemakers*

One minor use of radioisotopes in medicine, which is totally different from any of the others, should be mentioned in passing. The hearts of some people develop an irregular rhythm because the natural pacemaker fails to control them properly. Such people can have a surgically implanted artificial pacemaker powered by a small battery, which gives the heart regular small jolts of electricity. Normal chemical batteries last for a year or two only, and a further operation then has to be carried out in order to replace them. However, it is possible to build a battery which works on the Seebeck effect, i.e. the production of electricity by heating the junction of two dissimilar metals; the heat is here supplied by the radioactive decay of a small amount (0.15 g) of ^{238}Pu.[4] Such batteries last for about 10 years before they need to be replaced and thus offer an advantage over chemical batteries of the conventional type. Recent advances in chemical batteries have however made it possible to bring their life up to several years, and the future of isotope-fuelled batteries is thus uncertain.

4.4 How the radiations are detected

4.4.1 *Detection of radioactivity*

While occasionally clinical diagnoses or research experiments may involve the counting of α- or β-particles, the vast majority of requirements in medicine are for the detection of electromagnetic radiations, that is, X- or γ-rays. The reasons are not hard to find: firstly such rays readily penetrate matter whereas particles, do not, and secondly they cause far less damage to tissue.

All γ-ray detection methods depend on the interaction of the ray with the detector material producing *ionization*, that is the removal of electrons from the detector atoms. Sometimes the electrons are collected at the detector anode as an electric pulse. Most medical detection systems however use scintillators (typically crystals of sodium iodide), in which the ionization produces photons of light; these are then converted back to electricity by a *photomultiplier*. The electrical pulse produced by this process will be proportional to the energy of the γ-ray striking the scintillator and thus provides a measure of the strength of radiation. Some of the more important detection systems will now be discussed.

4.4.2 *Gamma cameras*

By far the most important detection apparatus today is the γ-camera, invented by H.O. Anger in 1958, which produces pictures showing the distribution of the radioactivity. There are several different kinds, but most of them consist of a single crystal of sodium iodide in the form of a disc 12.5 mm thick and with a diameter up to 500 mm or more. Behind this are photomultiplier tubes—up to 91 in some cases; each tube views a circular area slightly larger than itself. Every time a γ-ray strikes the crystal, a shower of photons is produced. Each tube generates electrical pulses indicating its position relative to the centre of the crystal, the intensity of the pulses being determined by how near the tube is to the point of impact of the γ-ray upon the crystal. The information from all the tubes is combined and gives X and Y co-ordinates for each γ-ray to hit the crystal. This allows a picture to be eventually built up on an oscilloscope screen which may either be photographed or sent to a computer for storage or numerical processing.

The picture would be hopelessly fuzzy if γ-rays were allowed to strike the crystal at any angle, and an essential part of the camera is a heavy metal collimator designed to ensure that γ-rays always enter the crystal more or less at right angles; there are different types of collimators for various purposes. There are also γ-cameras made up of a large number of small crystals and an array of photomultipliers. A typical γ-camera is shown in Fig. 23.8.

4.4.3 *Positon cameras*
For various reasons the crystals of γ-cameras are limited to about 12.5 mm thickness and this restricts the γ-ray energies which can be used to a maximum of around 0.4 MeV, with the best energy being in the range 0.1–0.2 MeV. If

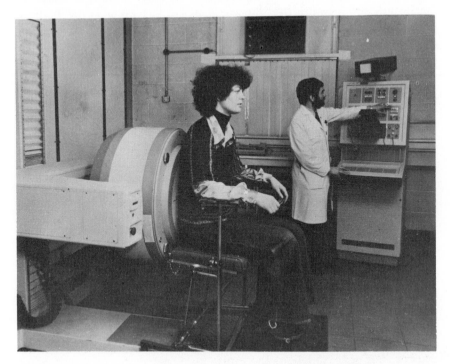

Fig. 23.8 A gamma camera in operation. (Courtesy of Manchester Royal Infirmary)

it is recalled however that many neutron-deficient isotopes, including the important short-lived ^{11}C, ^{13}N and ^{15}O, decay by positron emission (with the resultant production of two simultaneous γ-rays) it is clear that there may be advantages in constructing a *positron camera* which can make use of these γ-ray pairs.

Several kinds of positron camera exist, all of these showing the essential feature of being able to detect both of the two 0.511 MeV γ-rays *in coincidence*. Often one is detected by a single sodium iodide crystal and the other by a γ-camera. Alternatively the single crystal can be replaced by a whole crystal array or even by a second γ-camera.

Since these cameras make use of pairs of γ-rays which are moving at 180 ° to one another, collimators are not required. Positron cameras are a valuable tool for the detection of lesions deep in the body: they have low backgrounds, and can supply *tomographic* data, that is, pictures at different depths in the body which can be built up to give three-dimensional information.

4.4.4 *Scanners and fixed detectors*
Until a few years ago, most diagnostic tests aimed at producing a map of the activity levels over a particular area of the patient's body were performed by scanners. These comprise sodium iodide crystal detectors which are collimated so that they view only a small area of the subject; the detectors move backwards and forwards over the whole area of interest in a *raster* pattern. The number of counts at each point on the raster is recorded, usually by a chart recorder, which prints spots of different colours depending on the level of radioactivity at that point. Suitably modified versions also exist for positron scanning.

Although scanners are still in use for some purposes, most of the procedures for which they were employed now use γ-cameras instead.

4.4.5 *Fixed detectors*
Sometimes what is wanted is a measure of the activity moving past a certain point in the body, for example in blood moving along a vein, and it may be convenient to place fixed detectors over the spot in question. Sodium iodide crystal detectors supported in heavy metal shielding are used and positioned appropriately in relation to the patient. (See Fig. 23.9).

4.4.6 *Whole-body monitors*
If it is required to look at radioactivity distributed throughout the body, a *whole-body monitor* is necessary. If the activity levels are reasonably high, a γ-camera can be used in what is effectively a scanning mode, moving the length of the body. Often, however, the activity level to be detected is extremely low; this is so in the case of *in-vivo* activation analysis, or again in an examination aimed at detecting a possible small ingestion of ^{239}Pu by the patient. For such situations there may be advantage in using a monitor consisting of a number of large sodium iodide crystals 125 mm or more in

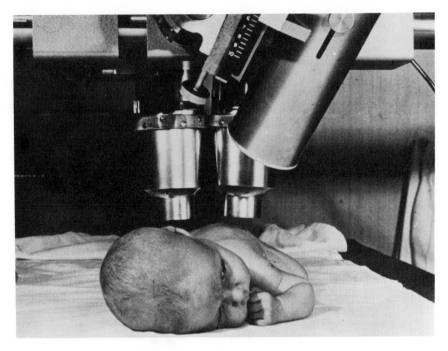

Fig. 23.9 Fixed detectors being used to investigate kidney function in a baby. (Courtesy of the Royal Hospital for Sick Children, Glasgow)

diameter, positioned both above and below the patient. The whole system is located inside a small cell having metal shielding walls specially selected for their low radioactivity levels (for example, pre-war battleship armour up to 250 mm thick); this shield is necessary to reduce the background activity from cosmic rays and other natural sources to a minimum, and it may be supplemented by electronic devices which further reduce the background. Figure 23.10 shows one of the whole-body monitors at Harwell.

4.4.7 *Other in-vivo detectors*
Occasionally it may be necessary to detect β-particles in organs or at the body surface. Various shapes of detectors are available for this; they are normally either Geiger–Müller tubes or semiconductor detectors.

4.4.8 *Detectors for in-vitro analysis*
Medical *in-vitro* analysis is no different from any other laboratory analysis of radioactive material and exactly the same sorts of detectors may be used. Counting of particles *in-vitro* is much easier than *in vivo*, and so it is possible to make use of particle emitters. As in other radioactive laboratories, however, X- and γ-ray analysis remains the preferred analytical methods.

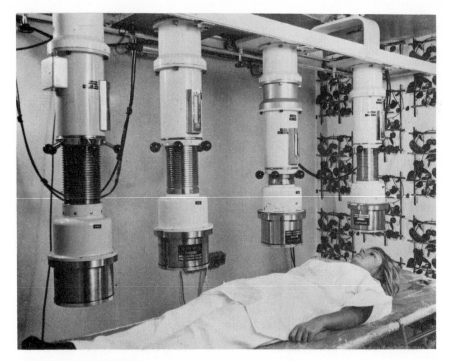

Fig. 23.10 One of the whole body monitors at Harwell

4.5 Health physics and waste disposal in hospitals

The dose of radiation to critical organs within the patient's body is carefully calculated before the isotope is introduced into it. As with normal X-ray diagnois, the annual dose to the patient will inevitably be increased to some extent by the use of these techniques, and this is a factor which will need to be taken into consideration in evaluating the risks and benefits of a particular diagnostic or therapeutic procedure.

Risks to be evaluated in nuclear medicine include not only those to the patient but also those to hospital staff. It may be that the patient's condition is serious enough to justify, say, the risk of injection of even a large amount of a radioactive isotope, but this activity has to be handled and measured by hospital staff, who have nothing to gain from the radiations and who must be protected from them, all the more so since they have to handle many patients. Furthermore, after the diagnostic procedure is finished, some part of the radioactivity will almost certainly be excreted by the patient and this could also present a hazard to others.

Hospitals are well aware of these problems. Prior to their use on patients, isotopes are handled in shielded fume hoods and with equipment similar to that used in all radioactive laboratories. Shielded syringes are used for injecting the isotopes into the patients, and the diagnostic equipment is designed so that the operators do not have to remain close to the patients while the measurements are being made. If the patient is excreting radio-activity, it is treated in exactly the same way as is radioactive waste in all laboratories and comes under the same regulations. Fortunately, most such activity is short-lived and so the problem is not really serious.

5 Examples of the use of radioisotopes

Table 23.2 shows that the range of investigations which can be carried out using radioisotopes is very wide. In this section we shall not attempt to do more than give a few examples, making use of γ-camera pictures to illustrate them.

Figures 23.11 and 23.12 show two aspects of kidney examination. Hippuric acid can be readily labelled with iodine isotopes, the preferred isotope, where available, being ^{123}I. Normal kidneys readily remove this compound from the blood stream and pass it into the bladder. The use of labelled hippuric acid thus allows both the shape of the kidneys and their functioning to be investigated. Figure 23.11 shows the result of such an examination; the

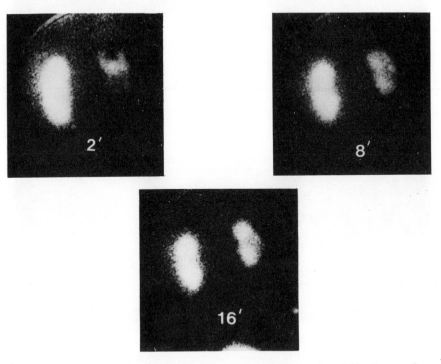

Fig. 23.11 Three renograms taken using ^{123}I-hippurate at 2, 8 and 16 minutes after injection. The poor uptake in the right kidney indicates incorrect functioning. (Courtesy of the Liverpool Clinic.)

right kidney is clearly not taking up the activity effectively. Figure 23.12 shows a transplanted kidney, ^{99m}Tc in the form of sodium pertechnetate being used as the source of the γ-rays. The aorta, branching into the two iliac arteries, is clearly visible during this period immediately after intravenous injection. The kidney image is well defined over the right iliac artery. If immunological rejection of the kidney had been developing, this would have been evidenced by a reduction, possibly to zero, of the visible activity. This kind of investigation is evidently of great value after kidney transplant surgery.

Figure 23.13 is an adrenal scan using the labelled compound ^{75}Se–methylcholesterol which accumulates in the adrenal glands. Interest in developing in adrenal scanning owing to the connection between these organs and hypertension. ^{123}I–iodocholesterol is another compound which has been suggested for clinical use; it has the advantage over ^{75}Se of giving a smaller dose of radioactivity to the patient for the same resolution.

There are a number of liver scanning agents in use. Figure 23.14 shows how effectively the liver can be viewed using, in this case, ^{123}I–

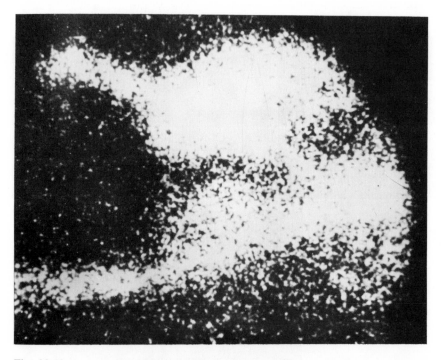

Fig. 23.12 A transplanted kidney visualized using ^{99m}Tc as sodium pertechnetate administered intravenously as a bolus. The image shows the aorta at the top, bifurcating into left and right iliac arteries and that the kidney is well perfused, radioactivity in the vascular bed appearing on the left of the picture, over the right iliac artery. (Courtesy of Western Infirmary, Glasgow.)

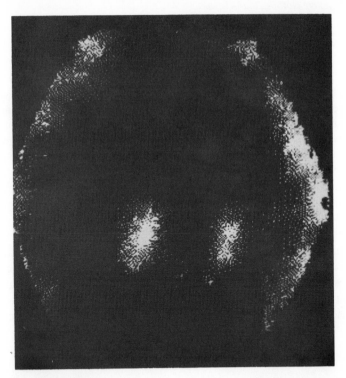

Fig. 23.13 Normal adrenal scan using ^{75}Se-methylcholesterol. (Courtesy of St. Bartholomew's Hospital, London.)

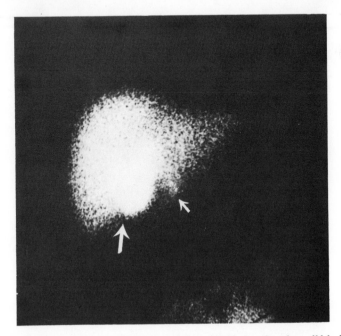

Fig. 23.14 Liver scan using ^{123}I bromsulphalein (BSP) showing the gall bladder (large arrow), bile duct (small arrow) and activity in the gut (below). (Courtesy of the Liverpool Clinic.)

bromsulphthalein. The gall bladder and bile duct are clearly seen in this picture.

Figure 23.15 shows, in three separate pictures, how the skeleton can be examined by means of isotopes as an alternative to using X-rays; several metastases are shown as regions of increased uptake. ^{99m}Tc compounds are now nearly always employed in such investigations, methylene diphosphonate being the one used in this case. Before the advent of the Tc bone-scanning agents some hospitals which could obtain ^{18}F used it for this purpose. The half-life of ^{18}F (1.83 hours) and the fact that it is a positron emitter means that it is not a convenient isotope, and it was rapidly dropped by the majority of hospitals once the Tc agents appeared. However, some nuclear medical experts believe the results obtained with it to be superior to those from Tc and, now that positron cameras are becoming more widely used, hospitals having ready access to a medical cyclotron are beginning to use it again.

Heart disease is now such an important problem that considerable effort continues to be put into finding more effective diagnostic methods for detecting it. It seems probable that ^{201}Tl will soon become a major diagnostic isotope, not only for visualization of the myocardium of victims of

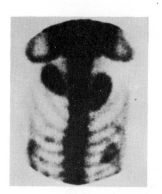
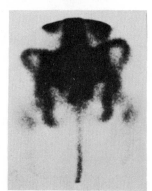

Fig. 23.15 Skeletal images following intravenous administration of ^{99m}Tc-methylnediphosphonate (MDP) showing metastases (Courtesy of Manchester Royal Infirmary.)

heart infarcts, but also for examination of ischaemia (a pre-infarct state) in coronary heart disease. So important is this cyclotron-produced isotope that it may, in the view of some American drug companies, be necessary to build a new cyclotron every two years simple to make this one isotope. Figure 23.16 shows a normal heart after exercise; both ventricles can be clearly seen. This test used ^{201}Tl. It is worth noting that ^{123}I–hexa- and hepta-decanoic acid are also being tried out with some success as myocardial scanning agents; however, the longer half-life of ^{201}Tl gives it an obvious advantage.

^{99m}Tc in the form of pertechnetate can be used for brain scanning as shown in Fig. 23.17, in which two tumours can be observed.

Finally, Fig. 23.18 shows pictures of yet another organ in operation—the stomach. In these it can be seen that the ^{99m}Tc, in this case attached to a meal of cornflakes, has passed from the fundus (top part) of the stomach to the antrum (bottom part) in the 40 minutes between the taking of the right-hand picture and the left. It is worth emphasizing once again that series of pictures like those shown in this article can give valuable information about how an

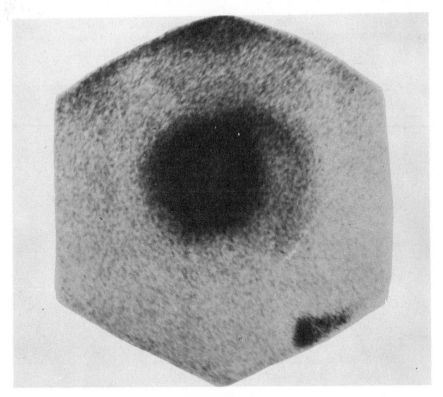

Fig. 23.16 Heart scan with ^{201}Tl, taken after exercise. Picture shows the left ventricle (the circular structure) and the right ventricle (the semi-circle joining it on the left.) (Courtesy of St. Bartholomew's Hospital, London.)

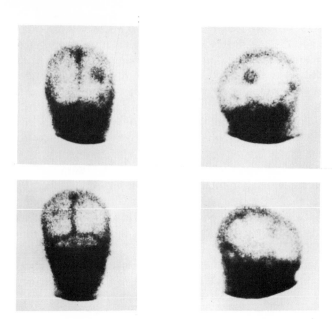

Fig. 23.17 Brain scans with $^{99m}TcO_4$—showing two tumours. (Courtesy of Manchester Royal Infirmary.)

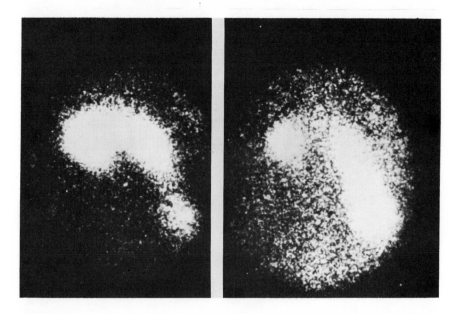

Fig. 23.18 Gastric emptying after a meal of ^{99m}Tc-cornflakes. The right hand image (10 minutes after consumption) shows most of the activity in the upper part of the stomach while the other (at 50 minutes) shows most of it in the lower part. (Courtesy of Western Infirmary, Glasgow.)

organ is behaving dynamically and that, in contrast to X-rays, the dose to the patient remains the same however many pictures are taken.

6 Conclusions

In concluding this survey of medical isotopes, three main points will be reiterated.
1. The use of radioactive isotopes in medicine is developing rapidly, because they provide better or alternative methods for the detection and diagnosis of disease. They also have very important applications in cancer therapy.
2. These methods are non-invasive and non-traumatic for the patient.
3. Of the main isotopes in clinical use, many of the diagnostic ones, including the most important (^{99m}Tc), and all the therapeutic ones are produced in nuclear reactors. The rest are made by irradiation in cyclotrons or other accelerating machines whose development has been closely associated with nuclear power.

Acknowledgements

It is a pleasure to acknowledge the help given to me by my medical colleagues in various hospitals in supplying information, pictures, and advice on the writing of this chapter. In particular I wish to thank Dr. K.E. Britton, Dr. A.T. Elliott, Mr. P.W. Horton, Mr. W.A. Little, Dr. H.J. Testa, Mr. R.A. Shields, Dr. N.G. Trott, Dr. G. Wiernik, and Dr. E.P. Wraight.

Notes to the text

1. To be strictly correct the term 'radionuclide' should be used instead of 'radioactive isotope' or 'isotope'. We employ the latter, however because it is in common use.
2. The nomenclature $^{11}CO_2$ indicates that the carbon isotope concerned is the radioactive one of mass 11. If no prefixed number is given, as in the case of O_2, then natural oxygen is implied. Similarly, ^{99m}Tc is an isotope of the element technetium with mass 99, the affix 'm', as earlier indicated, being used to show that this is a metastable state of the isotope.
3. Pyrogens, so-called because they may cause a rise in temperature in the patient, are protein material which cannot be removed by sterilization. In extreme cases they can cause death.
4. This is a rare isotope of plutonium; the common isotope, copiously produced in nuclear reactors is ^{239}Pu.

Suggestions for further reading

A. Wide coverage publication

1. HINE, G. J. (ed.) *Instrumentaion in nuclear medicine*, vols 1 and 2. Academic Press, New York (1974).
2. HORNSEY, D. J. *Radioactivity and the life sciences*. Methuen Educational, London (1974).
3. WAGNER, H. M. (ed.) *Nuclear medicine*. H. P. Publishing Co., New York (1974).
4. SUBRAMANIAN, G. (ed.). *Radiopharmaceuticals*. Society of Nuclear Medicine, New York (1975).
5. TUBIS, M., AND WOLF, W. (eds). *Radiopharmacy*. John Wiley & Sons, New York (1976).
6. INTERNATIONAL ATOMIC ENERGY AGENCY (ed.). *Medical Radionuclide Imaging (Report of the 1976 Los Angeles Conference)*. IAEA, Vienna (1977).
7. HEINDEL, N. D., BURNS, H. D., AND HONDA, T. (eds.). *Chemistry of Radiopharmaceuticals*. Masson, New York (1978).
8. SCHMIDT, H. A. E., AND WOLDRING, M. (eds.). *Nuclear Medicine. State of the art and future*. Schattauer, Stuttgart (1978).
9. PARKER, R. P., SMITH, P. H. S., AND TAYLOR, D. M. *Basic science of nuclear medicine*. Churchill Livingstone, Edinburgh (1978).
10. MCALISTER, J. M. *Radionuclide techniques in medicine*. C.U.P., Cambridge (1979).
11. O'REILLY, P. H., SHIELDS, R. A., AND TESTA, H. J. (eds.). *Nuclear medicine in urology and nephrology*. Butterworth, London (1979).

B Medical cyclotrons in isotope production

1. HOOP, B., LAUGLIN, J. S., AND TILBURY, R. S. Cyclotrons in nuclear medicine. In HINE, G. J. (ed.). *Instrumentation in nuclear medicine*, vol. 2, p. 407–457. Academic Press, New York (1974).
2. SILVESTER, D. J. Recent developments with cyclotron-produced radionuclides. In GOMEZ-LOPEZ, J., BONMATI, J., BERRY, R. J., AND HOPEWELL, J. W. (eds.). *Radiology*, p. 350–354. Exerkpta Medica, Amsterdam (1974).
3. SILVESTER, D. J. Biomedical cyclotron in a medical centre: capabilities and problems. In SUBRAMANIAN, G. (ed.). *Radiopharmaceuticals*, p. 157–164. Society of Nuclear Medicine, New York (1975).

C In-vivo activation analysis

1. SORENSON, J. A. Quantitative measurement of radioactivity *in vivo* by whole body counting. In HINE, G. J. (ed.). *Instrumentation in nuclear medicine*, vol. 2, p. 311–348. Academic Press, New York (1974).
2. SPINKS, T. J., AND BEWLEY, D. K. Activation analysis *in vivo* of the human body using cyclotron-produced neutrons. *Proc. Anal. Div. Chem. Soc.*, **13**(7), 204 (1976).
3. BOND, C. D., THEUS, R. B., AUGUST, L. S., SHAPIRO, P., AND ROGERS, C. C. *In vivo* activation analysis. *Phys. Med. Biol.*, **3**(4), 248 (1976).
4. EILBERT, R. F., KOEHLER, A. M., SISTERSON, J. M., WILSON, R., AND ADELSTEIN, S. J. Partial body calcium determination in bone by proton activation analysis. *Phys. Med. Biol.*, **22**(5), 817 (1977).
5. ELLIS, K. J., COHN, S. H., VASWANIZ, A., ZANZI, I., ROGINSKY, M., AND ALOIA,

J. Total body sodium and chlorine in normal adults as determined by neutron activation analysis. *J. Radioannl. Chem.*, **37**(1), 333 (1977).

6. SPINKS, T. J. Measurement of body nitrogen by activation analysis. *Int. J. Appl. Radiat. Isot.*, **29**(6), 409 (1978).

7 .WILLIAMS, E. D., BODDY, K., HARVEY, I., AND HAYWOOD, J. K. Calibration and evaluation of a system for total body *in vivo* activation analysis using 14 MeV neutrons. *Phys. Med. Biol.*, **23**(3), 405 (1978).

D Production of isotopes and compounds

1. HELUS, F., AND MAIER-BORST, W. A comparative investigation of methods used to produce ^{67}Ga with a cyclotron. In *IAEA* (ed.). *Radiopharmaceuticals and labelled compounds*, p. 317–324. IAEA, Vienna, (1973).

2. HELUS, F., KRAUSS, O., AND MAIER-BORST, W. An effective, routine reactor production method of ^{18}F for medical use. *Radiochem. Radioanal. Lett.*, **15**(3), 225 (1973).

3. COMAR, D., AND CROUZEL, C. Preparation of carrier-free radioactive thallium for medical use. *Radiochem. Radioanal. Lett.*, **23**(3), 131 (1975).

4. GUILLAIMEZ, M., LAMOTTE, D., MERCHIE, G., AND WINAND, L. Possible short-lived medical radioisotope production and labelled compounds applications with an isochronous cyclotron. *Ned. Tijdschr. Ganeeskd.*, **120**(35), 1511 (1976).

5. PARKS, N. J., AND KROHN, K. A. Cyclotron production of ^{13}N compounds for environmental and biological research. *Trans. Am. Nucl. Soc.*, **27**, 215 (1977).

6. PEEK, N. F., HEGEDUS, F., LAGANAS-SOLAR, M., deNARDO, G. L., AND BERMAN, D. S. Production and characteristics of ^{81}Rb for myocardial studies. *Int. J. Nucl. Med. Biol.*, **5**(6), 273 (1978).

7. CUNINGHAME, J. G., HILL, J. I. S., NICHOLS, A. L., AND TAYLOR, N. K. The production of iodine-123 on the Harwell variable energy cyclotron. AERE Report *R* 9087 (1978).

8. FARES, Y., D³MICHAELE, D. W., GOESCHL, J. D., AND BALTUSKONIS, D. A. Continuously produced, high specific activity ^{11}C for studies of photosynthesis, transport and metabolism. *Int. J. Appl. Radiat. Isot.*, **29**(7), 431 (1978).

9. BETT, R., CUNNINGHAME, J. G., HILL, J. I. S., JONES, I. G., TAYLOR, N. K., WINTER, J. A., AND NICHOLS, A. L. Development of a process for routine production of ^{123}I using the ^{127}I (p, 5n) ^{123}Xe $\longrightarrow$ ^{123}I reaction. *J. Radioanal. Chem.*, **56**, 237 (1980).

E Use of isotopes

Popular articles

1. LASSEN, N. A., INGVAN, D. H., AND SKINJ, E. Brain function, blood flow. *Sci. Am.*. **239**(4), 50 (1978).

2. WALKER, W. H. C. Radioimmunoassay: specific, sensitive and so popular, *Chemtech*, **8**, 622–625 (1978).

3 .YALOW, R. S. Radioimmunoassay: a probe for the fine structure of biologic systems. *Science*, **200**, 1236, (1978).

4. ENCYCLOPAEDIA BRITANNICA, vol. 6, p. 805 (1978).

5. ——. vol. 15, p. 454 (1978).

More technical articles

1. MITTEN, A. E. A. Present and future of radiopharmaceuticals resulting from generators. *J. Radioanal. Chem.*, **27**(1), 129 (1975).

2. COMAR, D. Tumour localisation using compounds labelled with cyclotron-produced short-lived radionuclides. In IAEA (ed.). *Tumour localisation with radioactive agents*. IAEA, Vienna (1976).
3. BULTON, K. E. Renal radionuclide techniques in their clinical context. In IAEA (ed.). *Medical radionuclide imaging*. IAEA, Vienna (1977).
4. CLARK, J. C. Radioactive gases of short half-life for brain, heart and lung studies. *Proc. Anal. Div. Chem. Soc.*, **15**(10), 287 (1978).

F. Therapy

'Popular' articles
1. BARSCHALL, H. H. The production and use of neutrons for cancer treatment. *Amer. Scient.*, **64**, 668 (1976).
2. HERMAN, R. Tumours take a hard knock from neutrons. *New Scient.*, **77**, 154–5 (1978).
3. ENCYCLOPAEDIA BRITANNICA vol. 11, p. 836 (1978).
4. ——, vol. 15, p. 464/5 (1978).

More technical articles
1. ATKINS, H. L. *Diagnostic and therapeutic medical applications for isotopes*. Brookhaven Report *BNL* 18052 (1973).
2. GOPAL, N. G. S. Radioisotopes and radiation in biomedicine. In *Proc. Chemistry Symposium, Aligarh, 1972*, pp. 1–24. Dept. of Atomic Energy, India (1974).

24

Radioactive dating

G. V. EVANS, R. L. OTLET

The natural processes of radioactive decay provide convenient means of measuring time spans between past events. This chapter explains the principles of the various dating methods that rely on the decay of radioactivity, or the growth of decay products and describes the measurement methods and equipment employed for dating activities within a number of specified disciplines.

The history of radioactive dating methods and their impact on such scientific fields as archaeology, geology, hydrology, climatology, and environmental protection are described. Significant advances in understanding have resulted from their application, and current and future developments promise exciting advances in the areas of application and the available age ranges. New techniques, capable of determining the ages of extremely small (milligram) samples, are described allowing reliable dates to be determined for, amongst other things, art or religous treasures, previously forbidden because of the size of sample required. Enrichment techniques, e.g. using lasers, allow extension of the range of radiocarbon dating, and equipment developments allow more accurate measurements to be made.

The chapter concludes that radioisotope dating has played a considerable part in understanding the origins, history, and current behaviour of our environment and has provided us with a true sense of past time-scales that can be used as a sound basis for decisions affecting future generations.

Contents

1   Introduction

Radioactivity was discovered by Becquerel in 1896 and, although its importance was not fully realized at the time, the discovery heralded the dawn of a new scientific era. Within a matter of a few decades it was realized not only that invisible radiation emanated from the earth, but also that we are subjected to an incessant bombardment of extra-terrestrial radiations, which react with our atmosphere to produce more radioactivity. It is now understood that this natural radioactivity is an integral part of our environment, food and atmosphere and, literally, 'part of our bones'.

Radioactive decay is purely time-dependent, and this fact has provided us with a means of measuring time over extremely long periods extending beyond the age of the earth itself, and has allowed accurate time-scales to be laid against past events of a geological or man-made nature. Changes in the radioactive contents of rocks have provided estimates of the age of the earth and of major geological events. Among other things, measurements of the radioactive contents of rocks have provided us with clear indications of the presence of naturally occurring nuclear reactors that have generated power over periods of hundreds of thousands of years. Natural radioactivity in the atmosphere means that all living things contain radioactive elements, and this provides the possibility of dating ancient organic materials. Archaeology has benefited greatly from this, and radioisotope dating, in particular carbon-14 dating, is employed in investigations world-wide.

Other areas of study which have also benefited by radioisotope dating include hydrology, climatology, and environmental protection.

In addition to naturally occurring radioactivity it has been possible, in certain cases, since the 1950s, to use the increased atmospheric levels originating from nuclear weapons testing as an aid to dating. The sharp reduction of these tests in 1964 marked out a concentration pulse which can now be found in plants and rainfall and provides a useful identifier of modern materials, helping to identify such things as the presence of modern groundwaters or the age of a wine or cider.

This chapter describes the principles of radioisotope dating, its valuable contribution in several areas of study, and looks forward to future developments.

2 Principles of dating methods

The basic idea behind any absolute dating method is that of exploiting some natural scientific process to act as a 'clock'. The essential requirements of the selected process are,

(a) that there are known laws and constants governing the process throughout the whole period being dated,

(b) that the clock can be started at some well-defined, known value at time zero, the day when the event to be dated occurred, and

(c) that the change in the value can be determined at a later date by a suitable scientific measurement.

The fundamental and immutable process of radioactive decay (Appendix A) fulfils these requirements ideally. The process of gradual transmutation of one isotope (the parent) to another (the daughter) in material containing a naturally occurring radioactive substance leads to several ways in which the mechanism for the clock can be realized. Three of these are shown graphically in Fig. 24.1.

In method 1 (Fig. 24.1 top), the example is given of a clock formed simply by the observed decay of the parent isotope. At time zero this isotope has a given known value. In the case shown, carbon-14, this value is the equilibrium level, related to the carbon dioxide of the atmosphere, which is maintained in all biogenic material while it is alive. At death such material ceases to be maintained at the equilibrium level, and the clock begins to tick as the total quantity of the parent isotope gradually decays. The time lapse since this moment is determined by measuring the quantity of carbon-14 remaining and calculating how long it will have taken to reach that point.

In method 2 (Fig. 24.1 middle), the basic decay process is the same but in this case it is the build-up of the daughter isotope which is observed, and which forms the clock. It is implicit in this method that at time zero no daughter atoms are present. Some chemical or physical event is relied upon to guarantee this start or clock-set condition. In the example given, the potassium–argon method used in the dating of rocks, the event may be a volcanic eruption. During the accompanying high temperature, the rocks melt and, in this state, all gases, including argon from earlier decay, are driven off. On cooling, argon is produced by potassium decay and begins to accumulate in the now solidified rock. In dating the rocks, the time lapse since solidification is determined from analysis of the potassium content, to find the average rate of production of argon, and of the argon, which gives the total accumulation to the present date.

The third method (Fig. 24.1 bottom) is an example of a hypothetical system which is a combination of the first two. The case is that of a parent isotope decaying to a daughter isotope which is also radioactive. This, on its

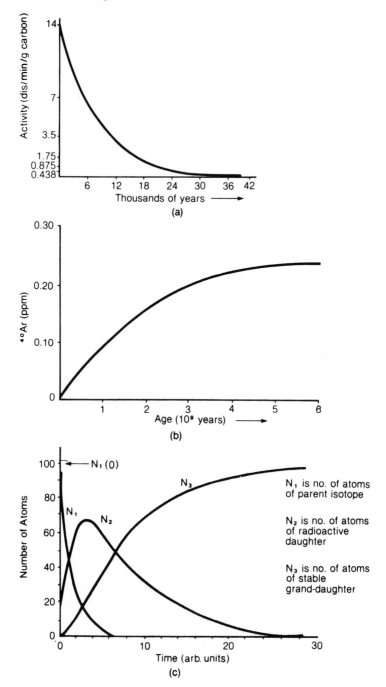

Fig. 24.1 (a) Decay of natural carbon–14
(b) Theoretical build-up of ^{40}Ar from ^{40}K in rock dating (rock initially 2%
potassium)
(c) Radioactive decay and growth in a three-component system

decay introduces a third component (the second-generation daughter isotope). Time lapse from some 'start' condition can be calculated from this system (see Appendix A) by considering the relative quantities of all three components in relation to the decay rates (characteristic decay constants) of the two radioactive species. The situation shown is a simplified one, and in real examples, such as those involving the uranium series isotopes (Fig. 24.2), not only the second but many subsequent generations of daughter isotopes may also be radioactive. The decay build-up graphs increase in complexity but, after a long decay period, a condition is reached where the decay of the whole chain is limited by the slowest rate of decay from one isotope at the head. Isotopes further down the chain are then in a condition known as secular equilibrium, which simply means that the relative specific amounts of each are controlled only by their respective decay constants. If, by some chemical or physical event, isotopes in the chain are preferentially separated, the system will be left in a state of disequilibrium; that is, the normal ratios of amounts of given isotope pairs within the chain will then be disturbed. The time-determined reattainment of the equilibrium values for these ratios provides another possibility for a clock. Disequilibrium dating between the pairs $^{234}U/^{238}U$ and $^{230}Th/^{234}U$ has been considered for certain hydrological/speleological applications. In these cases the disturbing (clock-setting) event occurs in the dissolution of rock salts into the groundwater. Uranium is dissolved and thorium is not. The dissolved uranium salts are co-precipitated with calcite in the form of a stalagmite, from which moment

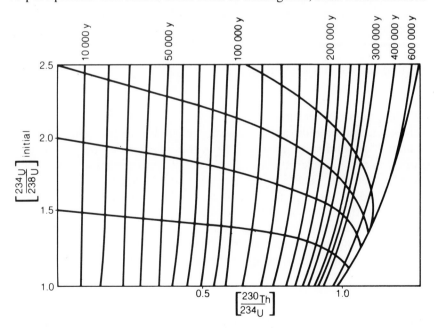

Fig. 24.2 Graphical representation of the growth of ^{230}Th towards secular equilibrium with ^{234}U

regrowth of thorium begins. A graphical representation of the regrowth of ^{230}Th towards secular equilibrium with ^{234}U in a closed system for various initial ^{234}U/^{238}U ratios is shown in Fig. 24.2.

A list of some commonly used radioisotopes for dating is given in Table 24.1 with details of their half-lives, typical age ranges they can cover, and general fields of application.

3 Measurement techniques

The relevant abundances of the parent and daughter isotopes or decay particles must be measured very accurately to achieve precision in age determinations. Furthermore, as the isotope of interest may be of very low abundance (e.g. in modern carbon ^{14}C/^{12}C is 1.5×10^{-12}), very sensitive methods of measurement are often required. However, this is not always the case. In the ^{40}K/^{40}Ar method, used for dating rocks, although the ^{40}K is only 0.012 per cent of naturally occurring potassium, the ratio is well known and the total potassium content of the rock may be several per cent. In this case potassium concentrations may be measured by one of several methods including atomic absorption spectrometry and flame photometry. These methods of measurement are, however, less specific to radioisotope dating and no detailed descriptions will be given here. Instead, attention is given to outlining the special techniques of extremely high sensitivity which are particularly used in radioisotope dating practice. A more detailed description of the methods of measuring radioactivity generally is given in Appendix B.

3.1 Radioactivity measurement

3.1.1 α-particle detection
The detection of α-particles and the accurate measurement of α-emitting isotopes such as uranium and thorium are generally effected by the use of ion chambers or solid-state detectors. Both these systems utilize the ionizing properties of α-particles, that is, the effect of liberating electrons from atoms within a detector. The free electrons produced by the passage of each particle through the detector are collected and form an electrical signal that can be recorded. The size of this signal is proportional to the energy of the particle, so that it is possible not only to measure the gross number of particles passing through the detector per unit time, but also to make specific measurements in selected energy regions. As the energies of α-particle emissions are specific to the isotope concerned, such measurements can also identify the isotopes being measured.

A typical α-particle spectrometer used for dating from uranium series isotopes is shown in Fig. 24.3. This facility is capable of simultaneous measurement of eight prepared samples. All the spectral data are recorded on magnetic tape and can be displayed visually.

Table 24.1 Radioisotopes commonly used for dating

Radioisotope decay	Principal emissions	Emission energy (MeV)	Half-life (years)	Useful age range (years)	Application*	Measurement‡
³H–³He	β	0.018	12.4	0–25	H, E, O	decay counting
¹⁴C–¹⁴N	β	0.155	5730	0–4 × 10⁴	H, A, G S, E, O	decay counting accelerators
³²Si–³²P	β	0.1	280	0–1.5 × 10³	H	decay counting accelerators
³⁶Cl–³⁶Ar	β	0.7	3.08 × 10⁵	10⁵–2 × 10⁶	H, E	decay counting accelerators
³⁹Ar–³⁹K	β	0.6	270	0–1.5 × 10³	H	decay counting
⁴⁰K–⁴⁰Ar	EC, γ	1.46	1.28 × 10⁹	10⁶–4.5 × 10⁹	G	MS
⁴⁰K–⁴⁰Ca	β	1.32				
⁸⁷Rb–⁸⁷Sr	β	0.3	4.9 × 10¹⁰	10⁶–4.5 × 10⁹	G	XRF, MS
²³⁵U–²⁰⁷Pb (series)	α β γ	(α) 4.39 to 7.37	various up to 7.13 × 10⁸	10³–10⁶	G, C, S, O	decay counting MS
²³⁸U–²⁰⁶Pb (series)	α β γ	(α) 4.19 to 7.69	various up to 4.51 × 10⁹	various within 10⁶–4.5 × 10⁹	G, H, S, O, C	decay counting Ms

* H, hydrology; S, sedimentology; G, geology A, archaeology; E, environmental;
  C, climatology; O, oceanography;
‡ MS, mass spectrometry; XRF, X-ray fluorescence spectrometry

Fig. 24.3 Typical spectrometer for α-particle measurement

3.1.2 β-particle detection

Radioisotopes which decay by β-particle emission eject an electron from the nucleus in the process of a neutron changing to a proton. Compared with α-particles, the energy of the emitted electrons is very low. This tends to be the case particularly with those isotopes which are used in dating, e.g. tritium (maximum energy 0.018 MeV) and carbon-14 (maximum energy 0.155 MeV). Specialized techniques are required to deal with the detection and measurement of β-particles of such low energies. As if this were not enough, however, two further constraints add to the problem of measurement and these can be highlighted by the example of carbon-14.

Firstly, the quantities occurring naturally are low. Even in modern (live) biogenic sources, the abundance of carbon-14 is only enough to produce approximately 13.6 disintegrations of carbon-14 per minute (≈ 0.23 Bq) for every gram of natural carbon (13.6 dis min^{-1} g^{-1} carbon) as shown in Figure 24.1(a). The counting rate produced by even several grams of carbon is thus low compared with the natural background rate (i.e. the usual counting rate from cosmic radiation and surrounding radioactive impurities observed by any detector even with no source/sample applied). Special low-level shielding is thus necessary to exclude as much as possible this extraneous background. Large *passive* shields of dense material are necessary to reduce the gamma component of background radiation. Many laboratories use pre-1940 steel armour plating, salvaged from old battleships, for this, because of its low level of radioactivity. Other components of background radiation, principally of cosmic ray origin, are reduced either by electronic methods or, if they are neutrons, by hydrogenous shield material containing boron (Appendix B).

Secondly, in some dating work, particularly archaeology where errors of even a hundred years may have a profound effect on interpretation, high precision and accuracy of measurement are required. For carbon–14 (half-life 5730 y), an activity measurement even of such a high accuracy as ± 1 per cent produces an equivalent uncertainty in the date of ± 83 years, and the usual requirement is for something better than that.

The original counting system, developed by W.F. Libby[1] for carbon-14 in the late 1940s, was to prepare pure carbon from the sample and to introduce this as a thin coating inside a screen-wall geiger counter. From further development two practical counting systems have emerged (Fig. 24.4), gas counting and liquid scintillation counting.

In the gas counting system the carbon is introduced as a gaseous compound (e.g. CH_4, CO_2). The emitted β-particles are detected (and measured) from the ionization produced by the loss of their initial kinetic energy as they track through the counter filling gas. The gas counter used is called a proportional counter because it works on the principle of proportional gas amplification to convert the minute initial ionization, produced by the β-particle, to a measurable electrical signal (Appendix B). Proportional gas counting techniques have been in common use for low-energy β-particle measurements

Gas counting
Sample prepared as an acceptable gas for counter filling (CO_2,CH_4,C_2H_2 etc.).
0.3 g Carbon → 0.2 ℓ } CO_2 at 3 atm.
6 g Carbon → 4.5 ℓ } pressure.
Gives high sensitivity but volumes are large and shielding becomes massive. Requires custom made instrumentation.

Liquid scintillation counting
Sample prepared as C_6H_6 and made up with a solvent/scintillant mixture.
1 g Carbon → 1.2 ml } C_6H_6
14 g Carbon → 18 ml }
(5 g Carbon → 6 ml / typical).
Small physical size of product sample enables multiplication of count rate when large initial samples are available.
Instrumentation obtainable commercially and relatively inexpensive.

Fig. 24.4 Practical techniques for ^{14}C (β-particle) measurement

for many years although, in the early days, it was difficult even with gas amplification to obtain output signals which could be unequivocally separated from background electrical *noise* at the lower end of the energy spectrum. Improvements in electronic amplifiers have now largely overcome this problem.

Another early problem was that of the stability of the gas amplification itself. Even minute amounts of electron-capture (electronegative) impurities such as chlorine, oxygen, water, etc. drastically reduce the overall gas gain. Elimination of this effect has been achieved by progress in gas purification techniques and in choice of construction materials for the counters, i.e. materials which will not exude impurities during the counting periods. Counters have recently been reported that allow stable counting with even carbon dioxide (a gas which is particularly sensitive to electronegative impurities) over periods of several months. This feature has enabled counters of just a few millilitres gas volume to be designed which, in the case of carbon-14, permit measurements on samples down to approximately 10 mg of carbon, utilizing long counting times to attain the required precision.

The other main method of measuring β-emitting radioisotopes is liquid scintillation counting. In this method, the sample to be measured is made into a liquid which is mixed with a liquid scintillator, usually a 'cocktail' of an organic solvent such as toluene or benzene and a fluorescent organic solute. The passage of an ionizing particle through the solution causes the solute to fluoresce. The small flashes of light produced are detected as a single electrical pulse by the photomultipliers placed adjacent to the sample vial (Fig. 24.5).

In all dating work the counting time of whatever system is to be used is a prime consideration. As stated, the abundances of the long-lived naturally occurring radioisotopes are invariably low, and the need for precision is generally severe. This results in long counting times to achieve acceptable counting statistics. Since the variation in the number of radioactive disintegrations occurring in a measurement period is described by the Poisson distribution, the standard deviation on the result of counting N events is $\sqrt{N}$. For a relative standard deviation of 1 per cent, it is therefore necessary to count long enough to collect 10 000 events. Often 24 hours of continuous counting is necessary to do this, but with the very small gas proportional counters mentioned earlier (volumes down to 5 ml) counting times of more than three months may be required (Fig. 24.6).

3.2 Spectrometric methods

An extremely sensitive method of measuring the concentration of a particular isotopic ratio, which can be used for some elements, is by means of a mass spectrometer. This instrument separates atoms and molecules according to their mass by utilizing the behaviour of charged particles moving in a magnetic field. Basically it consists of three components: (1) a beam of

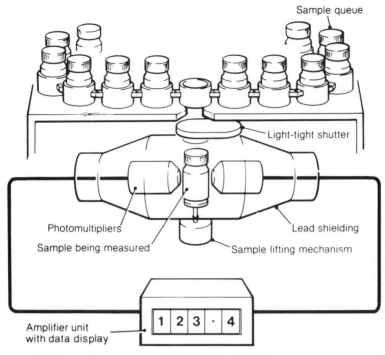

Fig. 24.5 Schematic diagram of liquid scintillation counter

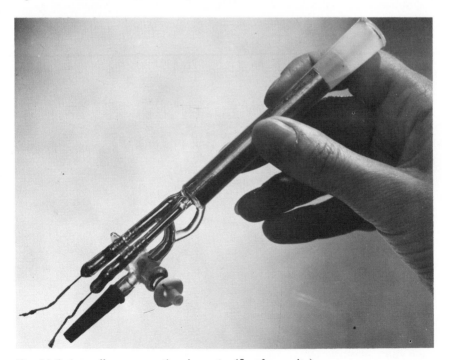

Fig. 24.6 A small gas proportional counter (5 cm³ capacity)

positively charged ions of constant energy; (2) a magnet producing a magnetic field through which the ion beam is passed, which causes a deflection of the ions depending on their mass; and (3) a device for measuring the number of ions received at the exit of the magnetic field. All these sections are operated under vacuum conditions of approximately 1 μ Pa absolute pressure.

For the analysis of gases, the positive ions are produced by electron bombardment from a heated filament. Solids are ionized by deposition of a salt of the element on to the filament or from a spark source. The ions once formed are accelerated towards the exit slit by the action of an electric field and then passed through a magnetic field at right angles to the direction of motion. This causes the beam to deflect in a circular arc of radius r according to the relationship:

$$r = \frac{1}{B}\sqrt{\frac{2\,mV}{e}},$$

where B is the magnetic flux, m is the mass of the ion, V is the accelerating voltage, and e is the charge on the ion.

Thus, when an ion detector is placed at the exit of the magnetic field at some defined radius, beams of ions of different masses can be detected by adjustment of the accelerating voltage V or the magnetic field B to align the beam of interest with the detector. In this manner the ratio of isotopes of an element can be measured by the ratio of the detector signals. A schematic diagram of a mass spectrometer is shown in Fig. 24.7.

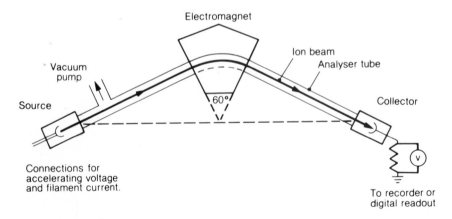

Fig. 24.7 Schematic diagram of a 60° sector mass spectrometer showing arrangement of ion source, electromagnet and collector

3.3 **Other measurement methods**

Other methods of measurement include those which can be used either in conjunction with, or independently of, the ones already described and are generally based on associated effects of radioactive decay or radiation damage. These include the accumulation of stored energy, as in thermo-luminescent dating, or observable crystal damage, as in fission-track dating, or simply the accumulation of ^{4}He from absorbed α-particles. These methods have applications in generally distinct fields such as archaeology (in particular the dating of kiln-fired clays or synthetic glass) or geology (mica, obsidian, and natural glass). Although these methods are less known to the authors a brief description of them is included for completeness.

3.3.1 *Thermoluminescence method*
The basis for this method of dating is that certain non-conducting materials when subjected to ionizing radiation (α-particles, β-particles, γ-rays etc.) absorb and store some of the deposited energy in the formation of free electron–hole pairs, which become trapped in deformations of the crystal lattice. The energy states of the particular atoms involved are thereby raised. When the temperature of the material is increased, as in the firing of a clay pot, the trapped electrons are released and the atom returns to its base energy level, the excess energy being emitted as light. In the period following firing, the material begins again to accumulate energy (the main source being from natural radioactive constituents, external terrestial and cosmic radiation). This accumulation is time-dependent and provides a measure of the time that has elapsed since firing, i.e. of the age of the pot. In practice, a sample of this material is heated, and the accumulated energy is released in the form of light, the amount of which is measured with sensitive light detectors. The calibration of light output, in terms of the energy accumulation, is obtained by artificial irradiation of the samples using a radioactive source of known radiation intensity. The relationship of the accumulated energy to age is then calculated by considering the dose-rate, from all sources, to which the sample has been subjected since firing.

3.3.2 *Fission track method*
When charged particles travel through a crystalline solid, they leave a trail of damage resulting from the transfer of energy from the particles to the atoms of the solid. With high-energy particles, the resulting tracks can be viewed and counted with high magnification microscopes, and their density can be used as a measure of the time elapsed since some original annealing event (such as glass melting). Suitable tracks are formed from fragments caused by fission in minerals containing uranium. Such tracks can again also be formed in natural glass (obsidian) or in certain man-made glasses. In practice the tracks are usually observed by grinding and polishing the surface of a selected fragment, and then enlarging the tracks by etching so that they can be seen under a microscope. The average number of tracks per unit area is

determined by counting them over a sufficient area to accumulate a statistically significant number, usually several hundreds or more. The age is calculated either from a knowledge of the radioactive constituents of the material or by irradiating a previously annealed sample with thermal neutrons and measuring the number of tracks produced.

4 Fields of application

4.1 Archaeology

Radioisotope dating, and in particular radiocarbon (carbon-14) dating, is now so much an accepted tool in archaeology that it is perhaps sometimes forgotten how little would be known of real time-scales without it. The earlier confusions over dating, even little more than thirty years ago, are rarely referred to in present day archaeological journals. But it was, in fact, only in 1949 that it all began. The story is told by Sir Mortimer Wheeler of how he and O.G.S. Crawford, editor of *Antiquity*, first heard the news and how Crawford's eyes lit up as he responded, 'It's a scoop'.[2] It was published in the editorial of the next edition of *Antiquity* in the following memorable report.[3]

A discovery has been made in America which may be of the greatest use to archaeologists. It consists of a method of dating dead pieces of formerly living substances (such as wood and bones) by means of their radiocarbon. The details are highly technical and beyond the comprehension of those who are not specialists.

The discovery referred to was W.F. Libby's Nobel-Prize-winning work on formulating the principles and making the first practical demonstrations of the radiocarbon-dating technique. The first dates were for samples of wood beams from the tombs of the Egyptian Kings Zoser and Sneferu. Within the limits of the measurement procedure of those days, Libby obtained good agreement with the 'known age' of these samples, thus proving the method. A new era had begun for archaeologists: the 'radiocarbon revolution' was here.

The impact of this new technique was enormous. Here for the first time, was a means of dating which was totally independent of archaeological assumptions and personal assessment. The archaeologist simply provided the scientists with a few ounces of a suitable organic sample removed from the site or artefact to be dated and received back, in due course, a seemingly incontrovertible date result. Little wonder that radiocarbon was hailed as 'a godsend'.

But how were estimated dates and chronologies arrived at before the advent of radiocarbon? From some areas, Egypt in particular, historical records had fortunately been preserved. These, once deciphered (c. AD 1820) provided the initial basis for *cross-dating* and hence the construction of chronologies elsewhere. Cross-dating from the culture with records to neighbouring ones without was possible because of trading links between the countries. For example, imports from Egypt were recognized in Crete and Greece and this provided time calibration markers for the chronology of the Minoan and Mycenean civilisations, respectively. Of course this type of calibration only applied to a limited geographical area, the eastern Mediterranean and the Aegean, and in age range it could not extend beyond the starting point, the known Egyptian chronology ($\approx$3000 BC).

In more distant areas, cross-dating could only be attempted by assuming diffusion from one culture to another, and through associations based on an assumed rate of typological development. Thus it was believed that the passage graves of Brittany were later than their supposed prototypes in the Aegean. The applicability of this argument was clearly limited and its validity not without question. The lack of clear explanation of how it was done in some cases was commented upon by J.G.D. Clark:[4] 'By and large I think we can say that the more eminent the prehistorian the less willing he was to commit himself on the matter.'

Other than the direct comparison of cultural development, the only tools available to the early archaeologists were means of ordering chronologies, but without any knowledge of the timespans involved. Because of the relevance to present-day archaeology, two systems should perhaps be mentioned. The first has as its basis the idea of stratigraphical succession, and it is, of course, still an essential concept in excavation technique. It logically assumed that deposits build up in order one above the other, in sequence, lower levels being the oldest and upper ones the most recent. Thus it could be said that one layer was earlier than another but, without absolute dating evidence in each, there was no way of measuring the timespan between them, or the precise age of either.

The second system used as its basis the idea of the 'three Ages' for the classification of the prehistoric past, Stone Age, Bronze Age, and Iron Age. Sub-divisions within these Ages could be ordered from typological developments, but again information regarding timespans was largely absent. In both these methods a net compression of the estimated time-scales occurred, and 'guess dates', if attempted, inevitably tended to be conservative.

It was against this background that radiocarbon dating entered the scene. However, some surprisingly early dates began to appear, and controversies soon began to rage regarding the validity of results from the new technique. In particular, the archaeology of the Near East was immediately upset, and the results of two samples from Tell es-Sultan (the site of ancient Jericho) were hotly debated.[5] Both samples were charcoal taken from upper layers of a pre-pottery Neolithic complex. The results, 6250 ± 200 BC and 5850 ± 160 BC, were consistent with each other but their mean, 6050 BC, was at least 1000 years earlier than any previous estimate for the site. Further, as the samples were from the upper occupational levels of this complex, an even earlier assignment for the original settlement was inevitable, making the discrepancy with the original archaeological 'guess date' even greater. As much as 3000 years was suggested. The initial opposition was largely crushed by the emergence of an increasing number of apparently good correlations with 'known-age' material. For example, one of the earliest ever dates to emerge from radiocarbon, 13 600 ± 900 BC, came from charcoal, from the occupational level in the splendidly painted cave at Lascaux, France. Here, however, there was a different surprise, the paintings were younger than expected!

Not all archaeologists were convinced, and criticism continued to build up from some quarters. Later, the doubters appeared to be proved correct when further research began to show that some of the basic assumptions made by Libby in the application of the technique were not as incontrovertible as first hoped. In the confusion that followed, an eminent professor is reported to have said: 'If a carbon-14 date supports our theories we put it in the main text; if it does not entirely contradict them we put it in a footnote; and if it is completely out of range we just drop it.'[6]

The principal assumption called into question was the value of the initial carbon-14 specific activity assigned to the once-living material for the age calculation. It was known that carbon-14 is produced by the interaction of neutrons with atmospheric nitrogen according to the nuclear reaction:

$$^{14}N + neutron \longrightarrow {^{14}C} + proton.$$

The neutrons are products of the extra-terrestrial cosmic radiation which continuously bombards our planet. The maximum cosmic radiation intensity occurs at high altitude and it is here that most of the carbon-14 is produced. Individual carbon atoms are chemically very reactive and quickly form carbon dioxide. Thus, $^{14}CO_2$ exists as a small component of the general carbon dioxide of the atmosphere. In the lower levels of the atmosphere, carbon dioxide is at the head of the food chain for all living substances. On land it is incorporated in plants, by photosynthesis, and in animals through the plants or other animals which they eat. In the sea it is absorbed in the water by equilibrium exchange and is therefore present in the food chain of all life depending on dissolved carbon dioxide and carbonates.

The first major worry was that there could be variations in carbon-14 across the globe caused by preferential time-dependent dispersion of the atmospheric carbon-14. However, concern over this was shown to be unnecessary by observation of the behaviour of carbon-14 introduced into the atmosphere during the weapons trials from 1954 to 1963. Atmospheric mixing, world-wide, proved to be rapid (in relation to the carbon-14 half-life) and uniform. The first assumption, therefore, which is sometimes referred to as the concept of 'simultaneity', was fully supported.

The second worry was concerned with the long term constancy of carbon-14 production. Libby had not ignored the possibility that carbon-14 production might not have been constant over all time, but had believed his checks on known-age material[1] to be sufficient evidence that any variations were small in comparison with the measurement precision. (At this time, and in the age range over which he was working, measurement uncertainties were equivalent to ±100-200 years.) As precision improved, the position was seen to be rather different. The first alarm was raised by De Vries[7] who, on taking carbon-14 measurements at intervals through a section of a long-lived tree, demonstrated that variations as large as 1 per cent had certainly occurred since 1500 AD. The importance of these variations was immediately realized and also the key role of long-lived trees in providing the chronological record of them. A tree puts on one ring of wood each year as it grows and locked within that ring is the radiocarbon content specific to the year. If, therefore, long-lived trees are found, measurements of radiocarbon content can be made ring by ring through them and variations of atmospheric input with time precisely recorded. Following the work of De Vries, a curve was produced of the radiocarbon content going back over the last 1300 years.[8] Variations as large as 3 per cent were predicted from measurements of an American giant redwood tree, which would cause errors in radiocarbon ages of up to 240 years if allowance were not made.

Clearly a major extension to the time-scale was required, and a break-through came as the result of work begun some years previously by A.E. Douglas and E. Schulman of the Tree-Ring Laboratory, Arizona, on the bristlecone pine found in the White Mountains of California. With ages greater than 4000 years for some specimens, they had identified the bristle-cone pine as the oldest living inhabitant of the world. Their work was continued by W. Ferguson and, eventually, by the matching of tree-ring widths from overlapping sections of living and extinct trees, a chronology stretching back to 5400 BC was made. Essentially this meant that known-age material covering a continuous span of over 7000 years was available and, if measurements of radiocarbon were made on this, a 'calibration curve' could be produced which would correct ages calculated from radiocarbon to true calendar ages. Samples of bristlecone pine were offered to a number of laboratories and the first results were produced by Suess[9] and were followed by those of Ralph and Damon.[10] Figure 24.8 gives a possible mean curve which is a combination of all results. The characteristic trend line is clear, and a particular feature is that the correction is small up to approximately 100 BC. Beyond this point, however, the deviation increases to a maximum of approximately 800 years at around 5000 BC. This means that, in the worst case, the conventional radiocarbon date (i.e. the date calculated on the simple assumption of a constant atmospheric input and on agreed half-life) would be 800 years too recent if no calibration were applied. Although there is much discussion about the validity of the original calibration curves, there is little doubt that results are more correct by using them and, as further work continues, more precise versions will enable more accurate corrections in the future.

With this calibration of radiocarbon dating, the early criticism of the method has now been overcome, and it is nowadays very difficult to imagine archaeology without radiocarbon. In fact, world-wide, radiocarbon dating is

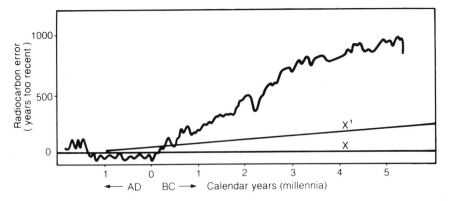

Fig. 24.8 Possible mean curve of the bristlecone pine calibration corrections. Readings about the X axis refer to dates calculated on the original Libby half-life of 5568 years; readings about the X^1 axis correspond to dates calculated on a 5730 years half-life

accepted and extensively used as a service tool. Other dating methods have emerged since radiocarbon, and they may be used in parallel, but the undeniable strength of radiocarbon is probably best illustrated by the fact that almost all other techniques evidence their reliability by comparison with radiocarbon, and many rely on it entirely for their calibration.

There are approximately 130 active laboratories measuring radiocarbon, most having a fair amount of archaeological work as well as their own research areas. The Radiocarbon Laboratory at Harwell devotes 50 per cent of its capacity of 450 samples per annum to archaeology. In the years of operation since 1973, dates have been produced for many archaeological sites. Some have been measured as part of major on-going studies involving many disciplines, for example dendrochronology, palaeobotany, etc., others have been single measurements. Whatever the type of sample or its context, the magic that was felt by the first workers in this field still remains—the excitement of seeing the actual date result appear as an unknown sample is examined.

One of the larger, more interesting, and certainly most publicized exercises of the Harwell laboratory was the dating of 'King Arthur's Round Table', at Winchester. This table, a magnificent, painted, circular (5.5 m diameter, 1.25 tonnes) object hangs in the Great Hall at Winchester. When the Winchester Research Unit was set up, it had, as part of its brief, the study of this artefact. In 1976, therefore, as the excavations in the ecclesiastical areas (Cathedral Green) and within the town (Brook Street) were drawing to a close, the Research Unit gathered together a team of experts to look at this 'table' from all aspects, in an attempt to find out more of its history than was given in the written records.

Although it was by tradition a table, and in particular the Round Table of King Arthur (the writing round the Tudor rose painted on the centre of the table reads, 'This is the round table of King Arthur with XXIV of his named knights.'), no historical records provide any clues as to when or why it was made, nor the occasion of its first use. The earliest reference is found in Harding's *Chronicle* of 1450 AD, where he states that it is the table of Arthur and 'hangeth yet' in the hall at Winchester, implying that it had been there for some considerable length of time (as measured by man's memory alone). After this we know that Henry VIII displayed it to the Holy Roman Emperor, Charles V in 1522, but little else.

As part of the investigations in 1976, the table was, therefore, removed from the wall for renovations and study. The construction and painting were scrutinized, a dendrochronologist examined every one of the radial planks making up the top to see, amongst other things, whether a single tree or a number had been used, and samples were taken for radiocarbon dating. The first secure date, however, did not come from radiocarbon dating. When some reinforcing planks were removed from the rear, it was found that the Victorian carpenter involved in this work, at the time the table was last removed from the wall, had signed and dated his name beneath one of them!

A total of 29 samples were taken from the timbers for radiocarbon dating, providing the laboratory with a marvellous opportunity to test multiple sampling from a single artefact. The age of the table and its history were assessed from radiocarbon dating, dendrochronology, technology of its carpentery, and other scientific investigations. The results of the comprehensive study, in which the radiocarbon dating made a major contribution, showed that the table belonged to the medieval period, as the historians had always believed, and in fact to the mid-thirteenth century. It was certainly built as a table and, as it is known that festivities called *Round Tables* were held at this time in imitation of Arthur and his Knights, it may be conjectured that this table was made for such an occasion. After its use at some feast or gala, it was adapted to hang on the wall, and the popular myths began to be woven around it. These have now been exploded by the scientific study and, alas, the table has no connection with the real Arthur, who is believed to have lived in about the fifth century AD. However, the 'detective' investigation which has uncovered more of this object's story, is, in many ways, just as exciting as the legends and has added a further chapter to its history.

4.2 Geology

The realization by Rutherford, Holmes, and Boltwood[12-14] early this century that rocks could be dated by radioactive decay radically altered current estimates of the age of the earth. As late as the seventeenth century, geological interpretations were based on biblical events. It was thought that the earth was created around 4000 BC and that the sedimentary rocks were formed following the Flood. At the turn of the last century, William Thompson (Lord Kelvin) estimated the age of the earth from calculations of its cooling from its molten state. This eminent physicist calculated a value of less than 40 million years but some geologists were doubtful. They considered that this 'physical' time-scale was too short to account for the complex geological history of the earth. Kelvin's calculations had not allowed for the then unknown heating effect of the decay of radioactive elements in the earth. When Rutherford presented a lecture in 1904, at the Royal Institution, on the heat production of radium and its effect on the rate of cooling of the earth, he was embarrassed to see Lord Kelvin, then in his eightieth year, in the audience. Rutherford avoided a difficult situation by praising Lord Kelvin for actually anticipating the discovery of radioactivity because he had calculated the age of the earth from its thermal history and had expressly stated 'provided no new source of heat was found'. This seemed to please Lord Kelvin as much as the later revised dates pleased the geologists!

In 1907, Boltwood estimated ages of approximately 500 million years for three uraninite specimens based on the decay of uranium to lead, although, at this stage, it was not known that lead is also produced by the decay of thorium. Similar ages had been determined by Rutherford from measurements of the amount of helium accumulated in the samples from the decay of uranium. Later measurements, based on the decay of uranium and thorium isotopes to lead isotopes, increased the estimated age of the earth to 2250 million years. Although this estimation did not include any contributions of lead from the ^{235}U decay series, which had not then been recognized, it was at least the first of many to show that the age of the earth was of the order of a few thousand million years. Since this early work, the application of radio-isotope dating has provided irrefutable evidence that even this age was a gross underestimate, and scientists are now universally agreed that the true age is about 4600 million years.

The dating of the earth is based on the principle of the decay of uranium and thorium to different isotopes of lead, ^{238}U decaying to ^{206}Pb, ^{235}U to ^{207}Pb, and ^{232}Th to ^{208}Pb. The remaining naturally occurring lead isotope, ^{204}Pb, is essentially stable (it is actually radioactive but has a half-life of approximately 10^{17} years). The isotopic composition of all lead-bearing minerals is made up of the sum of the original lead composition plus that produced by the decay over the period since formation. If there has been no external loss or gain of materials since its formation (i.e. it has remained a *closed* system), the growth of each radiogenic lead isotope should correspond to the same age. Lead-bearing minerals carrying different initial uranium/lead ratios will yield different values of the ratio ^{206}Pb to ^{204}Pb and ^{207}Pb to ^{204}Pb which, when plotted on a graph, will give a straight line. The slope of this line is related to the age since formation. The same result may be obtained from values of the ratio of uranium to lead when normalized for the presence of primordial lead to the isotope ^{204}Pb.

When the closed-system condition does not apply, different dates will result from dating different minerals in the same rock. This can provide extremely useful geological data on subsequent thermodynamic events such as metamorphic heating. Such heating would, by allowing some of the elements of the decay chain of one of the minerals to escape from the mineral, destroy the previously established closed-system conditions and effectively reset one of the radioactive clocks. This type of discordant age dating is shown in Fig. 24.9. The age of formation, T (4580 million years), is given by the upper intersection of the straight-line relationship of lead/uranium measurement with the curve corresponding to the isotope relationships expected from samples of different ages. The lower intersection t corresponds to the age of a thermodynamic event (90 million years).

It is an interesting fact that since the formation of the earth, 4.6 billion years ago, approximately 50 per cent of the original ^{238}U has decayed to ^{206}Pb, 99 per cent of the original ^{235}U to ^{207}Pb, and 20 per cent of the original ^{232}Th to ^{208}Pb.

Other radioisotopes have been used for the dating of rocks[15] most notably $^{40}K/^{40}Ar$ and $^{87}Rb/^{87}Sr$ (Table 24.1). Apart from the obvious application of dating the formation of metamorphic and sedimentary rocks, it has been possible with these methods to identify and date events such as volcanic eruptions and reversals of the earth's magnetic field. The developments have led to refinements in understanding such phenomena as sea-floor *spreading*—the continuous creation of oceanic crust from the earth's mantle, and have provided some of the best evidence supporting continental drift.

In another branch of geology, sedimentology—the study of deposition and movements of sediments—radioisotope dating is increasingly important. Two examples will be mentioned.

In studying sediment deposition, rates of formation of deep-sea sediments can be obtained from measurement of their ^{230}Th content. Approximately

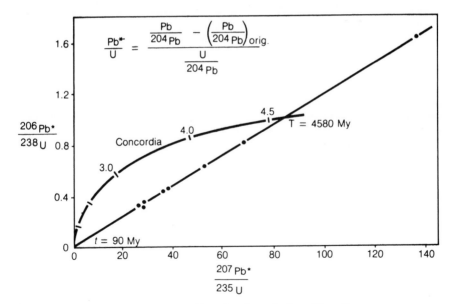

Fig. 24.9 Isotope evolution of lead in volcanic rocks from Hawaii

75 per cent of the ^{230}Th in sea-water is derived from the decay of ^{234}U in the sea. The rest is from surface streams, where it is found in company with ^{232}Th. Because of its chemical characteristics, thorium is rapidly removed from the sea-water by adsorption on to the surface of solids. This preferential removal of thorium gives rise to levels of ^{230}Th in the sediments in excess of that supported by their ^{234}U contents. The excess decreases with time according to the half-life of ^{230}Th of 7.5×10^4 years.

The second example concerns more recent rates of sedimentation. In environmental or ecological studies, sedimentation of inland lakes may be determined by measuring the variation of ^{210}Pb with depth of extracted cores. This isotope is in equilibrium with radon gas (^{222}Rn), which is constantly present in the atmosphere, derived as a decay product of radium (^{226}Ra, 1600 year half-life). The lead is precipitated and is incorporated in the sediments where it is isolated from its source of radon. A dating system is thus established, the residual ^{210}Pb being measured to determine the age of the sediment from precipitation. As the half-life of ^{210}Pb is 22.3 years, dating can be achieved over a period of approximately 200 years. The sedimentation rates are determined from the variation of age with depth of sediment. This method of dating has also been used to study deposition rates of snow in Antarctica, Greenland, and Alpine glaciers.

The most exciting recent geological contribution from radioisotope dating has been associated with the investigations of a naturally occurring nuclear reactor found in North East Gabon in West Africa.[16] The first clue to the existence of such a reactor was found in 1972 by H. Bouziques during a routine analysis of a standard sample of uranium hexafluoride. Bouziques was on the staff of a uranium enrichment plant at Pierrelatte in France, and his job was to check the grade of samples of uranium prior to enrichment. By mass spectrometer measurements he found that the ratio of ^{235}U/^{238}U was lower than the normal ratio of 0.7202 per cent by 0.003 per cent, a small but significant difference. There seemed to be no plausible explanation why the isotopic ratio should be so different. Further investigations identified the ore as coming from the Oklo mine, which from then on became the subject of a great deal of scientific investigation. Various fission products were identified in the area in quantities and ratios to one another which clearly indicated that substantial nuclear reactions had occurred. Measurements of uranium/ lead ratios identified that the reactors—a total of six separate sites had been found—started around 2000 million years ago.[17] Estimates of fuel burn-up indicated that 15 000 megawatt years of heat were produced and measurement of ^{239}Pu showed that the reactor operated for longer than 500 000 years.

4.3 Hydrology

The science of hydrology is a conglomerate of physical geography, geophysics, hydraulics, and water resource engineering. It may be defined as the science dealing with the various phases of the hydrological cycle. This is the term given to the passage of water from the oceans through evaporation, subsequent precipitation, surface water run-off, evapotranspiration, movement through unsaturated soil zones to water tables, with consequent delays, and movement back to the seas. The times involved in large parts of this cycle have, until recently, been unknown and have limited an understanding of water resource evaluation and the planning of its utilization. This area represents one of the most recent to which radioisotope dating has been applied, and the significance of the application and extensions of the methods are still growing.

One man-made event has had a significant effect on the understanding of hydrology. This was the development and testing in the atmosphere of nuclear bombs which released measurable quantities of the radioactive hydrogen isotope, tritium. Increasing numbers of tests from 1954 raised the level of tritium in the stratosphere until this kind of testing was limited by international agreement. Tritium thus found its way into modern waters—that is waters in exchange with atmospheric tritium—and now acts as an effective marker to distinguish between these and waters which were isolated from precipitation before 1954. A diagram of tritium concentration in rainfall in the UK between 1952 and 1979 is given in Fig. 24.10. Apart from providing a means of identifying the presence of mix of recent waters in groundwaters, so assisting in developing groundwater recharge models, the

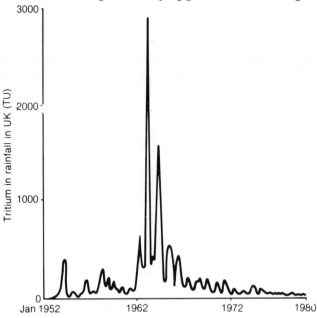

Fig. 24.10 Distribution of tritium concentration in rainfall in the UK, 1952–80

high peak concentration of tritium present in rainfall in 1963 has also provided a valuable tracer pulse. The measurement of the movement of this pulse through the ground has important implications for environmental pollution studies and is dealt with more fully in §4.5.

Measurements of tritium in groundwaters may also be used in studies of groundwater seepage from dams[18] or again in helping identify whether water discharging from around the base of spoil tips is of modern origin or from confined waters. This may be of relevance in considerations of the stability of such tips, the failure of which may have tragic consequences, as at Aberfan in 1966.

The use of tritium in groundwater studies and its decreased level in waters sampled downstream of outcrop areas led to the use of carbon-14 for dating older water. As well as deriving the 'age' from precipitation, differences in groundwater ages may be used to infer the general groundwater movement patterns and give indications of the water transport parameters such as permeability of the host rock. The importance of groundwater studies can be gauged from the fact that in the UK as much as 35 per cent of water used for public supply is derived from the ground,[19] and in arid countries the contribution is much higher. Such water is stored in the pores of rocks such as limestone or sandstone, generally termed aquifers, and may emerge as surface water streams or else may be extracted, either by pumping or, in the case of artesian wells, by hydraulic pressure forcing it out of the ground.

Carbon-14 (half-life 5730 years) is incorporated into the groundwaters from dissolved carbon dioxide occurring from respiration at the root zone of plants and from buried decaying biogenic material. This carbon reacts with the carbonate in the strata to produce soluble bicarbonate, which then contains a mixture of biogenic and geologically derived carbon according to the simplified chemical equation:

$$CO_2 + H_2O + CaCO_3 \rightleftharpoons Ca(HCO_3)_2.$$

Further dissolution and precipitation of carbonate can occur, thus affecting the amount of biogenic carbon remaining in solution. The carbon-14 in the biogenic carbon component provides a method of measuring the time the groundwater has been in closed-system conditions isolated from the atmosphere.

In order to obtain a sample suited to carbon-14 measurement, the carbonate from approximately 100 litre samples of water is precipitated in the field in the form of barium carbonate by the addition of barium chloride and a flocculating agent. In the laboratory, the carbonate is reduced to CO_2 and is then treated in the same way as that from archaeological samples. Unlike archaeological dating, hydrological interpretation of carbon-14 measurements to obtain an age depends on correcting for the geochemical carbonate exchange processes occurring during its passage through the ground and the mixing of waters of different carbonate concentrations. These corrections may be inferred from examining the amounts of the isotope carbon-13 exchanged between the groundwaters and rock in areal studies. Although there is still no universal correction procedure that can be applied for ^{14}C dating of groundwater, surprising facts have been revealed about the storage times of certain groundwaters.

Studies have been carried out by Harwell in collaboration with other organizations on the dating of groundwaters in a number of major aquifers in the UK and overseas.[20] It was indeed a surprise to find that the ages of some of the groundwaters in the Lower Greensand, London Basin, and Lincolnshire Limestone aquifers actually exceed 20 000 years. Water abstraction in these areas is effectively 'water-mining' with only low rates of recharge, so that the reserves are essentially finite and are diminishing as extraction continues. This information has had important implications for water resource planning and utilization.

In addition to the tritium and carbon-14 methods, groundwater ages can be determined also by measurement of dissolved gases derived from radioactive decay. The α-particle decay of uranium and thorium in the rocks accumulates helium (^{4}He) in the groundwater, and it is possible to use this fact to determine groundwater age from measurement of the rock composition and the helium content of the groundwater. The method is particularly attractive to dating old groundwaters (more than 10 000 years old) because the helium content increases with age. It is also attractive where overestimation of the age must be avoided (e.g. in studies involving the disposal of wastes), because any loss of the helium from the groundwaters by diffusion would give underestimation. Helium concentrations up to five orders of magnitude (i.e. 100 000 times) above atmospheric saturation level have been found in groundwaters.[21]

4.4 Climatology

A great deal of attention has been paid to determining the climatic variations which have occurred during man's existence. The Glacial Epoch, Ice Age, or Pleistocene are all synonyms for the latest geological episode lasting some 1.5 to 2 million years. In this period considerable climatic changes have occurred which have had strong influences on our present landscape.[22] Interest in this period has been mainly due to the geographical evidence of glacial erosion and the consequences of movements of vast ice sheets. Climatic investigations have indicated relatively large variations in temperature which would have greatly influenced the prehistory of man. Further, questions have been raised concerning the speed at which these temperature changes occurred and, as we have no reason to suppose that the conditions which might lead to repeat glaciation have ceased, the question of how soon we plunge into the next is posed.

Prior to the development of radioisotope dating, the relative time-scales of this study of climate were determined from stratigraphy, the deposition in sequence of various climatic indicators such as river terraces. Limited chronometric dating was available from tree-rings, varve clays, or laminated sediments. Radioisotope dating has allowed quantification of these time-scales over a wide range (Table 24.2). Radiocarbon dating, in particular, has

Table 24.2 Outline chronology of the pleistocene[22]

Time-scale 10³ y (not linear)	¹⁴C N–W Europe	Europe	K/Ar — Africa	K/Ar — N. America	²³⁰Pa/²³⁰Th related to ¹⁸O/¹⁶O episodes in Caribbean marine deposits	²³⁰Th/²³⁴U (coral, oolite shell near or above present sea level—i–g) Mediterranean, Morocco	elsewhere
10	*Flandrian*						
20	10 250 BP*						
30	⎫						
40	⎪ Weichselian						
50	⎬ Brrup i–s						
60	⎭				colder (g)		
70							
80	Eemian i–g				warmer (i–g)	Ouljian (5–8 m) sl	Bahamas sl
90							
100					colder (g)		
125		Holstein i–g			warmer (i–g)		
150					colder (g)	Tyrrhenian? sl	Eniwetok, Florida Keys sl
200		Mindel g (Rhine middle and old Middle Terrace)				Anfatian sl (25–34 m)	
250							
300							
350		Cromer i–g					
400		Günz g					
450		(Rhine High Terrace)					
500							
600							
1000		Villafranchian f (S. France)		Irvingtonian f			
2000			Olduvai (Villafranchian f)				
3000				Blancan f			

features dated: f fauna; g glacial; i–g interglacial; i–s interstadial; sl sea level
* BP = before present

been used extensively to date within the latest interglacial period, the Flandrian, extending back some 10 000 years, and in some cases, to the Early Weichselian period of 60 000 years ago. One of the first geologists to advocate the systematic use of the radiocarbon method in the study of Pleistocene drifts was Richard F. Flint at Yale University. He sent a large number of datable materials from the Wisconsin drift of·the eastern and central United States to Meyer Rubin of the United States Geological Survey for radiocarbon analysis. These results showed that the previous supposition of a single glaciation was incorrect, and that the Wisconsin drift was due to two glaciations, one beyond the age range of radiocarbon method and the other reaching its maximum extent 18 000 years ago, with its rapid disappearance some 8000 years later.

The radiocarbon method has also been used to establish vegetational history, by calibration of pollen zones, and identification of sea-level changes, from peat layers. An example of such measurements is shown in Fig. 24.11.[23] Several older glacial advances have been identified from developments of uranium series dating methods, which extended the existing age range of dating methods.

The relative abundances of oxygen isotopes, ^{18}O and ^{16}O, in biogenic

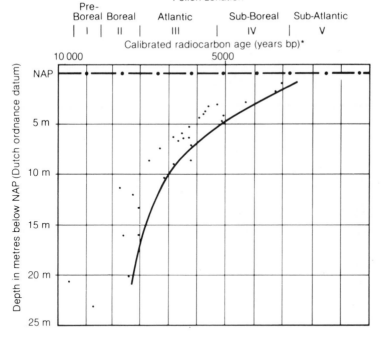

Fig. 24.11 Time-depth graph showing radiocarbon ages of peats at depth in the Netherlands. (The curve is drawn through the lowest points at any given age on the assumption that peat growth may have started at different heights above high tide level) *Before present.

carbonates (shells) secreted by aquatic creatures depends upon the temperature of the water. A decrease in temperature of 1 °C causes an enrichment in
^{18}O of approximately 0.02 per cent. This fact has been used with radioisotope
dating methods to determine changes in past climate from isotope variations
in Caribbean marine deposits.[24] Ages of deposits of up to 175 000 years have
been determined from measurements of the isotopic ratio $^{231}Pa/^{230}Th$, which
is derived from the decay of the uranium isotopes ^{235}U and ^{238}U and their
temperature variations determined from $^{18}0/^{16}0$ measurements. The climatic
variations so derived are very similar to those determined from stable-
isotopes analyses of deep ice cores from Greeland and Antarctica (Fig.
24.12).[25,26]

Temperatures of formation of cave deposits have been determined from
stable isotope composition with dating by carbon-14 or uranium disequilibrium methods. Carbon-14 and stable isotope analysis of groundwaters in
the Sahara show that very old water deposits exist and indicate that the
precipitation derived from westerly air movements, a situation which is
similar to that of today for North Africa and Europe.[27]

Thus, it is clear that the combination of modern analytical techniques with
radioisotope dating has provided considerable, information on historical

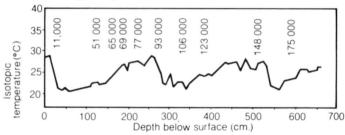

(a) Measured temperature variations from Caribbean marine shells
using $^{231}Pa/^{230}Th$ methods of dating

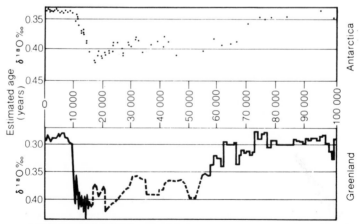

(b) Measured $\delta^{18}O$ ‰ variations in ice cores with dates calculated
from ice flow considerations. [25, 26]

Fig. 24.12 Temperature records derived from tropical marine shells and ice cores

climatic changes. Further developments will no doubt improve the base of understanding in this field and perhaps allow better means of predicting future climatic change.

4.5 Protection of the environment

The scientific, technical, and industrial progress in the developed countries of the world has accelerated in this century at a phenomenal rate when compared with all previous endeavours. This progress has not only increased the impact of man's activities on his environment, but has also increased his awareness of the fact. Greater emphasis is now being placed on studying the environmental consequences of present day practices, thereby planning to reduce pollution and control the disposal of the waste by-products of industrial activity.

Radioisotope dating methods are being used in environmental studies to investigate rates of sedimentation in lakes and coastal waters, and the movement of groundwater which may carry a pollutant far from the site of deposition. In some cases, it may not have been realized that the material being deposited would act as a pollutant. This was the situation when increased use of artificial fertilizers raised the levels of nitrate in groundwaters in the main aquifers of the United Kingdom, which supply over 30 per cent of all potable water. It is now known that increased nitrate levels exist within the unsaturated zones of these aquifers and considerable attention has been paid to the movement of nitrates in these zones.[28] Thermonuclear tritium has played an important part in these investigations as a dating marker for the movement of water through the strata.

As described in §4.3, a large increase of tritium in precipitation was observed around 1963 (Fig. 24.10), and this has been used to identify this water in the unsaturated zone. Water is extracted from samples of drilled cores, by vacuum distillation, and measured for tritium content. Many measurements of tritium have been made for the water industry in the UK, and these have shown that 1963 rainfall is present at various depths in the unsaturated zones of the Chalk and Permo-Triassic Sandstone aquifers, giving estimated penetration rates of less than 1 metre/year. This information combined with laboratory data on relative movements of tritium and nitrate ions in soil columns provides valuable information on expected future degrees of pollution of groundwater supplies from nitrate contamination and assists in developing suitable abstraction strategies.

Groundwater dating methods employing tritium and carbon-14 are also used to investigate the hydrology beneath existing and potential buried waste (land-fill) sites. This information is of importance in evaluations of the likely extent and degree of leached pollutants carried by the water flow.

Currently, considerable international attention is being paid to identifying potential sites for the safe disposal of radioactive waste produced by nuclear reactor operation. The local environment is intended to be one component of what is termed a *multi-barrier* containment. Waste is incorporated in a solid, contained in a metal container, sealed in a surrounding low-permeability medium within a geological formation, or buried in deep sea sediments. Various geological formations such as crystalline rocks, salts, and clays are under investigation. In all these formations, the presence of water and its behaviour is important in evaluating the remoteness of the site to the hydrosphere and assessing possible routes of pollution to man. Radio-isotope dating of groundwaters is one positive means of assessing the historical degree of 'remoteness', and there has been considerable interest in the development of these methods for the dating of old groundwaters (>50 000 years).

Carbon-14 dating methods are generally suitable for dating up to 30 000 years and with enrichment techniques (§5) to 75 000 years. However, for older groundwaters, uranium disequilibrium methods (§2) have been developed for dating up to approximately 1 million years, and are being extensively applied in this area of environmental protection studies. The method relies on the fact that in most natural grondwaters ^{234}U is in disequilibrium with ^{238}U (i.e. the decay rates of $^{234}U/^{238}U \neq 1$). Generally, the waters are enriched in ^{234}U due to its preferential leaching from rock or that of its *grandparent* isotope ^{234}Th. Preferential leaching is possible because of crystal lattice damage, caused by recoil of the nucleus when an α-particle is emitted during the decay of ^{238}U to ^{234}Th. Enrichment is also enhanced by direct recoil from the lattice into the surrounding waters. The relative excess of ^{234}U over ^{238}U in groundwater therefore depends on the ratio of uranium in the rock to that in the water, the relative surface area of the rock, and the time of co-existence of the rock and water. If precipitation of uranium has occurred in part of the aquifer, preferential uptake of ^{234}U will be greater, because the shallow surface deposition of the uranium will increase the number of atoms likely to escape from the surface by recoil. Subsequent movement of these waters into a closed system allows equilibrium to be re-established. These uranium dating methods are the subject of research and their full potential has yet to be realized.

5 Current and future developments

Apart from the further development of existing methods, exciting advances in radioisotope dating are promised. Research aims fall into four main categories:

(1) to obtain better accuracy of measurement within the range of isotopes currently in use and the time-scales they provide.

(2) to extend the time-scale range currently achieved.

(3) to be able to operate with small quantities of sample material, and

(4) to prove dating methods with lesser-known isotopes such as, for example, ^{36}Cl, ^{10}Be, and ^{53}Mn.

The solution of each problem is not independent. They are separate needs, but one particular development, the use of accelerators for dating measurements, may satisfy at least three of them simultaneously. This development will therefore be described first.

An outline diagram of one scheme which uses a tandem accelerator for the measurement of carbon-14 is given in Fig. 24.13. The basic principle is that of an ultra-sensitive mass spectrometer capable of directly measuring the abundance ratio of the radioactive to stable nuclei. Simple though the idea appears, the ratios involved are so large (^{14}C: ^{12}C $\approx$ $1:10^{12}$, ^{36}Cl: ^{35}Cl $\approx$ $1:10^{13}$) that even up to 1977 such a measurement was thought completely impracticable. A burst of enthusiasm in 1977 led to a number of independent workers[29] reporting successful exploratory measurements both with cyclotrons and tandem accelerators. Features of the new machines which made possible these unexpectedly low measurements included:

(1) large initial negative ion beams obtained from solid *sputter* ion sources (which in itself is a discriminatory process—nitrogen, which has also mass 14 and is a major atmospheric contaminant, does not easily form a negative ion whereas carbon does so readily);

(2) separation of extraneous molecular ions, by passing the beam through a *stripping* foil;

(3) further selection using a crossed-field mass filter; and

(4) energy and energy loss discrimination of residual ions at the detection stage, which enables the separation (electronically) from any residual ions of the same mass.

The accelerator and cyclotron methods open up a new range of possibilities for radioisotope dating techniques. An important feature is that only a small

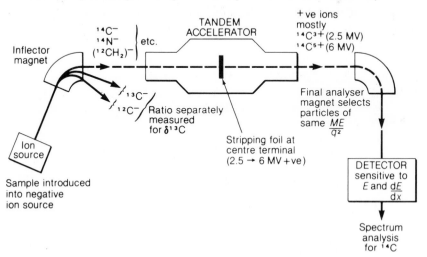

Fig. 24.13 Schematic diagram of tandem accelerator measurement principle for carbon-14

sample is required to produce a perfectly adequate ion beam for the measurement, a clear advantage when either only a small quantity is available (as in some hydrological or environmental investigations) or only a small amount of sample can be spared for the measurement (as in the case of a valuable work of art or precious relic such as the Shroud of Turin). Measurement times, too, are likely to be very much shorter in comparison with conventional counting techniques, since the number of atoms (accessible in the ion beam) which are waiting to decay is enormous compared with those which will decay naturally during the measurement period. Thus, it is a bonus that the method lends itself to measurements of certain radioisotopes which, with conventional β-counting methods, have never been a practical possibility. These include ^{10}Be (half-life 1.6×10^6 y) and ^{26}Al (half-life 7.2×10^5 y) for use in sedimentation studies, and ^{36}Cl (half-life 3.1×10^5 y), ^{81}Kr (half-life 2.1×10^5 y), and ^{39}Ar (half-life 270 y) for use in hydrology, to mention only a few of the most likely candidates in this category.

The possibility of extending the time-scales obtainable by β-counting techniques also exists for specially constructed machines dedicated to the measurement of particular isotopes. This has not been realized up to now in general-purpose machines and could not be reasonably expected because of the residues of similar ions left behind from other experiments. For a 'clean' machine, the limiting factor should be only the time of the count in relation to the time all the other factors, e.g. ion beam control, can be held stable.

An alternative method of ^{14}C dating extremely small quantities of carbon is by use of the small gas proportional counters mentioned previously (Fig. 24.6). A current development of this method at Harwell is the establishment of a ^{14}C detector system in which the detectors are housed within a large NaI crystal acting as an anticoincidence shield. The whole assembly is operated within a 28 tonne steel shield to minimize background radiation. Data is collected on a dedicated microprocessor linked to a small general-purpose computer where immediate displays of the spectra of measured cosmic radiation and ^{14}C are available. By using two sizes of counters, up to 250 samples containing less than 60 mg of carbon can be measured each year.

As far as sample preparation (not to mention sample selection) is concerned, there may be major problems in making such minute uncontaminated source samples. For example, it is easy to show that for a carbon-14 sample which is truly 100 000 years old, contamination of only 0.1 per cent of modern carbon would result in an overall measured age of 57 000 years.

Progress in the dating of very old samples by carbon-14 has come from the combination of large, low-background, gas proportional counters, and a filling gas which has been enriched by known amount in the initial $^{14}C/^{12}C$ ratio. The most practical method used so far for this is the process of thermal diffusion.[30] Gas (CO_2) prepared from the sample is introduced at the top of a column containing a hot central wire and water-cooled walls. Under the influence of the temperature gradient prevailing between the hot wire and the cold wall, a net downward convective transport of heavier molecules occurs. Large quantities of the initial sample material are needed (kilograms) and, even with a battery of such columns, processing time may be of the order of weeks to obtain an enrichment of even a factor of 12. However, extension of the measurement capability to about 75 000 years is obtainable.

In the future, development of enrichment techniques based on selective gas dissociation using tuned laser beams may be expected.[31] In principle, (again for carbon-14) formaldehyde (H.CHO) prepared from the sample to be enriched may be exposed to a tuned beam of a suitable power laser. Molecules contianing ^{14}C atoms are selectively dissociated to form carbon monoxide which, because of the higher dissociation probability of ^{14}CO than that of ^{12}CO or ^{13}CO, is then enriched in carbon-14. The processing of large quantities of sample this way is not expected, but a residual product of say 100 mg after three hours' laser irradiation seems a reasonably practicable proposition. This quantity is clearly more than ample for either conventional counting in the recently developed 'micro' gas proportional counter, mentioned earlier (Fig. 24.6), or, with further chemical processing to graphite, by an accelerator technique.

Other developments to be pursued for future applications are concerned with attaining higher accuracy. This will be of increasing importance in archaeology when, as more is known of the general structure of cultural and historical growth, more will be asked of the time detail within the broader timebands. Increased precision will also enable better discrimination of the measured levels in other fields, such as hydrology, when operating with low-abundance isotopes generally at close to background levels (e.g. uranium series isotopes). Until now, improvements have come simply by taking more care to follow the well defined principles of low-level measurements. For example, modern electronic equipment continues to provide better stability and better signal-to-noise ratios. Improved purification procedures for counting gases enable better long-term stability of the in-counter pulse amplification and hence longer counting times are practicable. Much attention has also been paid to achieving lower and more stable backgrounds than hitherto. One method has been to construct deep underground counting rooms to escape residual counts from cosmic radiation. The residual is then largely γ-radiation and this too has been reduced by revising ideas of guard counter (anticoincidence) design and using a more efficient γ-ray guard counter (e.g. a large sodium-iodide crystal) acting to detect (and then subtract) the scattered components of the primary γ-ray interactions in the sample counter.

6 Conclusions

It can be judged from the foregoing that radioisotope dating has played a considerable part in understanding the origins, history, and current behaviour of our environment. The impact has been so great and the results of application so embedded in our current scientific thinking that it is difficult to appreciate what state development would have reached without it. Many areas of study have benefited, a few of which have been described in this paper, and there is great potential for extensions to other areas. Developments are in progress to extend the range, accuracy, and application of these methods in many fields. The more refined techniques have applications in protection of the environment from industrial activities, in the planning of use of precious resources, such as water, and in understanding the history of our climate. Above all, because of the unambiguous nature of radioactive decay, radioisotope dating has reduced the areas of contention in many fields of study and has, hence, provided us with a true sense of past time-scales, that can be used as a sound basis for scientifically based decisions affecting future generations.

Appendix A

Principles of dating by radioisotope decay

Nuclei of radioactive atoms are unstable because of an excess or deficit of neutrons. Stability is achieved either by emitting a particle (a- or β-particle or positron (β^+)), or by capturing an orbital electron. Emission of electromagnetic radiation, in the form of γ-rays or characteristic X-rays, often accompanies the event. In the process of radioactive decay, the initial, unstable nucleus (the parent) changes to another (the daughter), which then belongs to an atom of a different isotope and element, which may or may not be stable.

Precisely when any particular radioactive nucleus will undergo this transformation cannot be predicted, but, when considering radioactive isotopes on a macro scale (i.e. involving very large numbers of individual atoms), the usual statistical concepts of probability apply. Each individual radioactive atom has a small but equal probability (p) of undergoing the decay process within a specified period. The product of their total numbers (N) and probability (p) is finite, so that the number of atoms decaying in a given period follows the Poisson distribution. The rate of decay is proportional to the number of radioactive atoms present at that moment, i.e.,

$$\frac{dN}{dt} = -\lambda N,$$

where λ is the constant of proportionality known as the decay constant.

Solution of this equation shows that the radioisotope decays exponentially according to the form,

$$N_1(t) = N_1(0)e^{-\lambda t}, \tag{1}$$

where $N_1(0)$ is the number of atoms at $t = 0$ of the parent isotope 1 and, $N_1(t)$ is the number at time t.

Rewriting this expression enables the introduction of the notion of *half-life* ($t_{1/2}$), which is more generally used than decay constant, to characterize the decay of particular isotopes. Thus, in the period ($t_{1/2}$) when the number of atoms present falls to just half the number originally present,

$$\frac{N_1(0)}{N_1(t'_{\frac{1}{2}})} = 2,$$

i.e.

$$e^{-\lambda t_{\frac{1}{2}}} = \tfrac{1}{2}, \qquad \lambda t_{\frac{1}{2}} = \ln 2, \quad \text{and} \quad \lambda = \frac{0.6931}{t_{\frac{1}{2}}}.$$

Thus, equation (1) becomes,

$$N_1(t) = N_1(0) \exp \frac{-0.6931t}{t_{\frac{1}{2}}}.$$

In terms of elapsed time (t), the expression is,

$$t = \frac{t_{\frac{1}{2}}}{0.6931} \cdot \ln\left(\frac{N_1(0)}{N_1(t)}\right). \tag{2}$$

This is the basic equation for 'age' calculations in the case of a radioactive *clock* formed by the simple decay of a radioactive isotope from a known initial level ($N_1(0)$) to some lower level ($N_1(t)$) at some time t later on (see Fig. 1(a)).

Alternatively, where the radioactive isotope (the parent) is decaying to form a stable (daughter) isotope, the growth from zero of this second isotope ($N_2(t)$) can be considered. Thus,

$$N_2(t) = N_1(0)(1 - e^{-\lambda t}).$$

This gives rise to the second example for a radioactive clock, illustrated in Fig. 1(b) for ${}^{40}K/{}^{40}Ar$ dating.

In many applications, it is more convenient to work in terms of the number of parent atoms remaining ($N_1(t)$) rather than the number at time zero. In this case, eqn (3) becomes,

$$N_2(t) = N_1(t)(e^{\lambda t} - 1) \tag{4}$$

or

$$t = \frac{1}{\lambda} \ln\left(\frac{N_2(t)}{N_1(t)} + 1\right).$$

In the case of the potassium–argon method of dating, ${}^{40}K$ decaying to ${}^{40}Ar$, a complication arises because the decay of ${}^{40}K$ branches. This means that not all decays result in ${}^{40}Ar$ production. In fact, the predominant branch, taking 89 per cent of total ${}^{40}K$ decays, is from ${}^{40}K$ to ${}^{40}Ca$, which has an entirely different decay constant.

Eqn (4) for this case becomes,

$$N_2(t) = \frac{\lambda_{Ar}}{\lambda} N_1(t)(e^{\lambda t} - 1) \tag{5}$$

or

$$t = \frac{1}{\lambda} \ln\left(\frac{N_2(t)}{N_1(t)} \cdot \frac{\lambda}{\lambda_{Ar}} + 1\right),$$

where $N_2(t)$ is the number of daughter, ${}^{40}Ar$, atoms which have been produced in the elapsed time t, $N_1(t)$ is the number of parent, ^{40}K, atoms also present at time t, λ_{Ar} is the decay constant of the decay branch ^{40}K to ^{40}Ar, and λ is the total decay constant for ^{40}K.

When the daughter isotope (N_2) is also radioactive and its presence is only due to the decay of the parent isotope (N_1), the relationships of decay and production are given by expressions,

$$N_1(t) = N_1(0)e^{-\lambda_1 t}$$

and

$$N_2(t) = \frac{\lambda_1}{\lambda_2 - \lambda_1} N_1(0)(e^{-\lambda_1 t} - e^{-\lambda_2 t}).$$

Further, if the radioactive daughter isotope is stable, the number of atoms (N_3) of this isotope can be shown to be,

$$N_3(t) = N_1(0)\left[1 + \frac{\lambda_1 e^{-\lambda_2 t}}{\lambda_2 - \lambda_1} - \frac{\lambda_2 e^{-\lambda_1 t}}{\lambda_2 - \lambda_1} \right],$$

where, λ_1 and λ_2 are the decay constants of the parent and daughter isotope, respectively.

These expressions are shown graphically in Fig. 24.1(c) and represent the decay and growth curves of the parent and daughter radioactive isotopes and the stable daughter product.

In the special case when the half-life of the parent is considerably longer than that of the daughter (i.e. $\lambda_1 \ll \lambda_2$), $e^{-\lambda_2 t}$ will approach zero considerably faster than $e^{-\lambda_1 t}$ for increasing values of t. Then,

$$\lambda_1 N_1 \approx \lambda_2 N_2.$$

This condition is termed secular equilibrium, in which the rates of decay of the daughter is equal to that of its parent. In a radioactive decay series, such as the uranium-238 series, which consists of a very long-lived parent (^{238}U, $t_{1/2} = 4.5 \times 10^9$ years) and a series of relatively short-lived daughters (^{234}Th, 24 days; ^{234}Pa, 1.18 minutes; ^{234}U, 2.48×10^5 years ... ^{206}Pb, stable) secular equilibrium is such that:

$$\lambda_1 N_1 = \lambda_2 N_2 = \lambda_3 N_3 = \lambda_n N_n, \quad \text{etc.,}$$

and the number of atoms present of the unstable daughters would be:

$$N_n = \frac{\lambda_1 N_1}{\lambda_n}$$

where the suffix n, denotes the daughter under consideration.

In disequilibrium dating, the change observed is the reattainment of secular equilibrium after some separating event (time zero) which disturbed it. An example, for the pairs $^{234}U/^{238}U$ plotted against $^{230}Th/^{234}U$, is given in Fig. 24.2. The mathematical representation of these graphs becomes considerably more complicated than the previous examples and will not be described here.

Appendix B

Measurement techniques used in radioisotope dating

The techniques of measuring the decay rates of the particular radioisotopes used in dating are not basically different from any other radioactivity detection and measurement. The main differences are generally to be found in the practicalities of the systems, which often need special adaptation because the radioactivity levels being measured are very much lower than usually encountered in nuclear experiments. Some of the constraints concerning the need for low backgrounds and high stability over long counting times are mentioned in the main text and will not be repeated here. The purpose of this appendix is to complement what is given there with some further description on the principles and details of the practical application.

Radioisotopes used in dating work are exclusively α-particle or β-particle emitters and their measurement is discussed under these two main headings.

B.1 α-particle measurements

An α-particle is made up of two protons and two neutrons. Because of its relatively high mass and charge, it is able to *strip* electrons from atoms in its path, forming one electron-ion pair for each 34 eV of its energy until all its energy is absorbed. This property, termed ionization, is used to detect the particle and also measure the characteristic energy of its emission, enabling identification of the radioactive isotope from which it was emitted. Detection systems capable of high energy resolution are commonly based on gas ion chambers or solid-state *surface barrier* detectors.

Samples of the chemical element to be measured (e.g. uranium or thorium) are prepared by chemical separation methods and electrodeposited as thin films on stainless steel planchets. In the case of measurement by an ion chamber, one of which is shown in Fig. 24.14, a planchet is placed inside the chamber which is filled with an argon–methane (90/10 per cent) mixture to an absolute pressure of approximately two bar. The α-particles ionize the gas in their paths, and the liberated electrons are accelerated by a driving voltage to the collector plate positioned above the planchet. Effects of the slower moving positive ions are shielded from the collector by a grid and guard ring held at intermediate voltages.

As the size of the electrical charge at the collector due to the arrival of the electrons is proportional to the number of electrons produced by the ionization, it is also proportional to the energy of the emitted α-particles. The

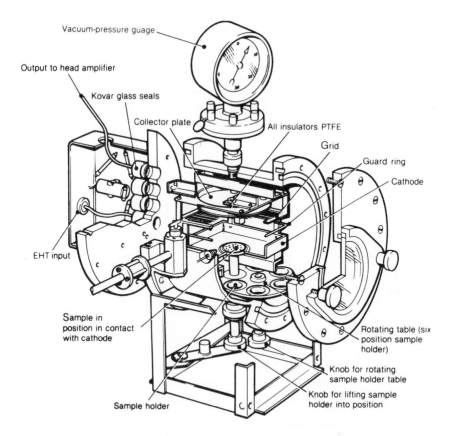

Fig. 24.14 Diagram of ion chamber for α-particle measurement

corresponding voltage pulses from the ion chamber are pre-amplified and sorted in a pulse-height or multi-channel analyser so that the energy spectrum of the α-particles is obtained, as well as the number of particles detected per unit time. As each particular radioisotope displays a characteristic spectrum of energy of its emitted radiation, it is possible with a calibrated ion chamber to determine both the identity and the amount of a particular radioisotope in the sample.

Semiconductor surface barrier detectors are also used for α-particle spectroscopy and have certain advantages over gridded ion chambers. These include better energy resolution, lower background electrical noise, higher permissible count rates, lower cost, and superior stability. These detectors operate in an analogous way to ion chambers, in that the incident α-particle produces electron–hole pairs in the depletion layer of a semiconductor in a similar manner to the electron–ion pairs in the gas detector. The energy required to produce one electron–hole pair is only about 3.5 eV compared with 34 eV for an electron–ion pair. A high electric field sweeps the electrons and holes to their respective enriched surfaces to produce a charge pulse which can be processed in an identical manner to that described previously. The overall resolution of a semiconductor detector is approximately 15 keV compared with about 50 keV for the best gridded ion chamber.

A typical α-particle spectrometer used for dating from uranium series isotopes is shown in Fig. 24.3. This facility is capable of simultaneous measurement of eight prepared samples. All the spectral data are recorded on magnetic tape and can be displayed visually.

B.2 β-particle detection

Radioisotopes which decay by β-particle emission eject an electron from the nucleus in the process of a neutron changing to a proton. Unlike α-particles, β-particles are not emitted at discrete energies but rather as a continuous spectrum up to characteristic maximum energy. Accurate measurement of a β-emitter demands integration of the spectrum produced, and integration of background over an identical energy range. Compared with the energies of α-particles emitted by actinides, the energy of the emitted electrons is lower, but it is still ample to produce significant ionization in passing through a detector gas or liquid.

In measuring low-energy β-emitters used in radioisotope dating, only two practical systems are currently employed, gas counting and liquid scintillation counting. Examples of each are demonstrated for carbon-14 in Fig. 24.4.

In the gas counting system, the emitted β-particles are detected (and measured) from the ionization produced in the loss of their initial kinetic energy as they track through the counter filling gas. In comparison with α-particles, βs are less effective in producing ionization and tend to have much greater ranges, i.e. the ionizing events in their wake are more widely spaced. For high sensitivity and precision of measurement, it is necessary to obtain a larger signal output per emitted particle than that which would be given by simple collection of the ion pairs produced in the β-particle track. Multiplication of this initial ionization is achieved as follows. A high electrical field gradient is obtained in a counter which uses a fine anode (collector) wire and an applied voltage which is greatly in excess of that required for simple primary ionization collection. In this field, the initial electrons are sharply accelerated towards the anode and quickly gain enough energy to cause secondary ionization when colliding with the containing gas molecules. Thus, more electrons are produced, which also accelerate and collide, multiplying the initial event over and over again. Over a particular range of applied voltage, this multiplication (gas amplification) for a given voltage is constant and hence, as in the case of α-particles, the output signal of the counter is proportional to the initial number of ionizing events and hence to the energy of the β-particle. Operating in this mode the counter is called a proportional gas counter.

It is important, for it to work satisfactorily, that all electrons produced by collision should go on to multiply again. The presence of even small amounts of electronegative impurities such as chlorine and oxygen, which capture electrons, greatly reduces the overall gas amplification. Reduction of this effect has been achieved by progress in gas purification techniques and in choice of suitable materials with which to construct the counters.

In the case of liquid scintillation counting, the sample to be measured is made into a liquid and mixed with a liquid scintillator, which usually consists of a fluorescent organic solute in an organic solvent such as toluene or benzene. The main effect of the passage of an ionizing particle through the solution is to cause ionization and excitation of the molecules of the solvent. Due to thermal diffusion and migration of these molecules, they soon come in close proximity to solute molecules, where the excited state is transferred from the solvent to the solute, which fluoresces. The small flashes of light produced are detected as a single electrical pulse by the adjacent photomultipliers (Fig. 24.5). The amplitude of the output pulse from the combined photomultiplier tubes is proportional to the energy of the β-particle, and so the energy spectrum can be recorded as described in §B.1.

Sample preparation techniques depend upon the radioisotope being measured. In carbon-14 dating, the carbon from the sample is reduced first to CO_2 by oxidation. For gas counting, CO_2 can be used directly as a counter filling gas, following processing for the removal of impurities. Alternatively, it may be further processed to CH_4 (by catalytic reaction with hydrogen), which is less susceptible to electronegative residuals. For liquid scintillation counting, the CO_2 is reacted with lithium to form lithium carbide, and acetylene is formed by the addition of water. The acetylene is synthesized with a vanadium catalyst to form benzene (C_6H_6), which contains most of the carbon from the sample in a liquid form suitable for counting by liquid scintillation.

For tritium measurements, the starting point is generally water. When it is, a valuable aid to the measurement step is obtained by first enriching the tritium-to-protium ($^3H/^1H$) ratio in the water. This is achieved by electrolysis.[32] The enriched water can then be counted by gas proportional or liquid scintillation techniques. For gas counting, the water is reduced to hydrogen over magnesium (600 °C) and, after catalytic hydrogenation using ^{14}C or ^3H free ethylene, forms ethane for the counter filling. Two-litre volume counters are frequently used, which, operating at a filling pressure of two bars, means the hydrogen (with its tritium) from approximately 4 ml of enriched water (80 ml of original water) is actually counted.[33] Alternatively, for liquid scintillation counting, the enriched water can be mixed with an emulsifier-type scintillant and directly counted. Generally this method is not regarded as reliable, and it is certainly not as sensitive as gas counting for very low-level tritium measurements.

As mentioned earlier, the amount of activity available in dating work is usually extremely small, and considerable effort must therefore be made to shield the detector from extraneous cosmic and terrestrial radiation. Figure 24.4 demonstrates the scale of such shielding for a typical gas proportional counter and liquid scintillation sample vial. In a practical set-up, the gas counter is shielded from the following three main sources of background.

1. *γ-radiation*. Using a 20–30 cm steel shield, an attenuation of about 10:1 is usual.
2. *Cosmic particles*. These high-energy charged particles occurring in showers, mainly muons, pass relatively unattenuated through the steel shield, but produce an ion pair track in the gas counter. To remove their effect, the sample counter is surrounded by a set of guard counters arranged in an electronic anticoincidence circuit. Since a cosmic particle will produce ion pair tracks in both the guard and sample counter simultaneously, all pulses occurring in coincidence are rejected (at very low counting rates the probability of accidental coincidences is negligible). Anticoincidence gives an attenuation ratio of, say, a further 50:1.
3. *Neutrons*. Background neutrons originate mainly from cosmic particle showers, but can migrate quite large distances (metres) before being absorbed. Any neutrons which are unrelated to a close cosmic particle shower might thus produce an event in the sample counter which would not be rejected as background. Some will be absorbed in the steel shield, but at high energies it is first necessary to thermalize them (slow them down). Neutron shields are generally placed between the steel shield and the guard counters. They are made of a suitable hydrocarbon, e.g. paraffin wax (to slow neutrons down by collison) into which is mixed a compound of boron. Boron has a very high capture cross-section (absorption probability) for slow neutrons. The background reduction obtained by neutron absorption depends upon the counter gas filling (methane is more susceptible than CO_2) but can be as large as 2:1.

As demonstrated (Fig. 24.4), the liquid scintillation vial is considerably smaller and, therefore, intercepts a much smaller fraction of the background radiation flux than a gas counter holding the same quantity of sample. The shields can accordingly be much simpler, generally no more than a simple γ-ray shield, 25 to 50 mm of lead. Lower backgrounds can be obtained by additional shielding but most commercial instruments—one feature of the liquid scintillation method is that the instrumentation is available commercially—do not easily lend themselves to greater elaboration.

Initially, liquid scintillation counting was seen as a major advance for β-emitter counting in radioisotope (particularly radiocarbon) dating. In that it has enabled the rapid expansion of counting facilities to many more laboratories than might otherwise have contributed to dating investigations, the early promise has been realized. Experience has shown, however, that unless great care is taken, certain important drawbacks arise. With standard commercial instruments special attention has to be paid to achieving the required calibration and background stability throughout long counting sequences.[34] Certainly the chemistry of sample preparation, sample vial make-up, and counting efficiency determination are considerably more difficult than the equivalent procedures in present-day gas counting. In the authors' opinion, the net result is that good sample-to-sample reproducibility is more difficult to achieve in liquid scintillation counting. There is, then perhaps good reason not to quote counting statistics alone as the overall error of a measurement result, unless very special care is taken to test that the assumption is valid.[35]

Acknowledgements

Figures 24.1 (c), 24.7, and 24.9 are reprinted from *Principles of isotope geology* by G. Faure (1977) by permission of John Wiley & Sons Ltd., New York. Figure 24.8 is reprinted from *Physics and archaeology* by M. J. Aitken (1974) published by the Oxford University Press. Figure 24.11 is reprinted from *The Ice Age in Britain* by B. W. Sparks and R. G. West (1972) by permission of Methuen & Co. Figure 24.12 is reprinted from *Absolute dating of deep-sea cores by the* $^{231}Pa/^{230}Th$ *method* by J. N. Rosholt, C. Emiliani, J. Geiss, F. F. Koczy, and J. Wangersky (1961) by permission of the University of Chicago Press.

References

1. LIBBY, W. F., *Radiocarbon dating*, University of Chicago Press (1952).
2. WHEELER, M. *Antiquity*, **32**, 4 (1958).
3. CRAWFORD, O. G. S. Editorial. *Antiquity*, **23**, 91 (1949).
4. CLARK, J. G. D. Radiocarbon dating and the expansion of farming culture from the Near East over Europe. *Proc. Prehistoric Soc.*, **31**, 58–73 (1965).
5. BRAIDWOOD, R. J. Jericho and its setting in Near-Eastern history. *Antiquity*, **31**, 73 (1957).
6. JOHNSTON, J. O. D. The problems of radiocarbon dating. *Palestine Explor. Rev.*, 13–26 (1973).
7. VRIES, H. De. Variation in concentration of radiocarbon with time and location on earth. *K.Nederlandse Akadmie van Wetneschappen, Amsterdam* B, **61**, 1–9 (1958).
8. WILLIS, E. H., TAUBER, H. AND MUNNICH, K. O. Variations in the atmospheric radiocarbon concentration over the past 1300 years. *Amer. J. Sci. (Radiocarbon Supplement)*, **2**, 1–4 (1960).
9. SUESS, H. E. Bristlecone pine calibration of the radiocarbon time-scale 5200 BC to the present. In OLSSON, I., (ed.). *Radiocarbon variations and absolute chronology*, pp. 303–312. Wiley, New York (1970).
10. RALPH, E. K., MICHAEL, H. N. and HAN, M. C. Radiocarbon dates and reality. *Masca Newsl.*, **9** (1), 1–20 (1973).
11. DAMON, P. E., LONG, A., AND WALLICK, E. I. Dendrochronologic calibration of the carbon-14 timescale. In *proc. 8th Int. Conf. on Radiocarbon Dating, Wellington, New Zealand, 1972*, vol. 1 pp. 429–457. Royal Society of New Zealand, Wellington (1973).
12. RUTHERFORD, E. *Radioactive transformations*. Charles Scribner's Sons, New York (1906).
13. HOLMES, A. *The age of the earth*. Harper Brothers, London (1913).
14. BOLTWOOD, B. B. On the ultimate disintegration products of the radioactive elements. *Amer. J. Sci.*, **4**(23), 77–88 (1907).
15. FAURE, G. *Principles of isotope geology*. Wiley, New York (1977).
16. INTERNATIONAL ATOMIC ENERGY AGENCY. *The Oklo Phenomenon, Proc. IAEA Symp. Libreville, Gabon, 1975*. IAEA, Vienna (1975).
17. GANCARZ, A. J. 2.05×10^{9} year U/Pb age of the Oklo uranium deposit. In *Proc. IAEA Technical Committee on Natural Fission Reactors, Paris, 1977*. IAEA, Vienna (1978).
18. RHODDA, J. C (ed.). *Facets of hydrology*. Wiley, London, (1976).
19. RHODDA, J. C., DOWNING, R. A., AND LAW, F. M., *Systematic hydrology*. Newnes-Butterworths, London (1976).
20. EVANS, G. V., OTLET, R. L., DOWNING, R. A., MONKHOUSE, R. A., AND RAE, G. Some problems in the interpretation of isotope measurements in United Kingdom aquifers. In *Proc. IAEA Symp. on Isotope Hydrology, Neuherberg, 1978*, vol. II. IAEA, Vienna (1979).
21. FRITZ, P. Comments on isotope dating of groundwater in crystalline rocks. In *Proc. Advisory Group Meeting on the Application of Isotope Techniques in Mining and Waste Disposal Hydrology*, IAEA, Vienna (1979).
22. SPARKS, B. W., AND WEST, R. G. *The Ice Age in Britain*, Methuen & Co. Ltd., London (1972).
23. JELGERSMA, S. Holocene sea level changes in the Netherlands. *Med. Geol. Stichting*, C-**VI**, no. 7 (1961).
24. ROSHOLT, J. N., EMILIANI, C., GEISS, J., KOCZY, F. F., AND WANGERSLEY, P. J. Absolute dating of deep sea cores by $^{231}Pa/^{230}Th$ method. *J. Geol.*, **69**, 162–185 (1961).

25. DANSGAARD, W., JOHNSEN, S. J., MOLLER, J., AND LANGWAY, C. C. One thousand centuries of climatic record from Camp Century on the Greenland Ice Sheet. *Science*, **166**, 377–381 (1969).

26. EPSTEIN, S., SHARP, R. P., AND GOW, A. J. Antarctic ice sheet. Stable isotope analyses of Byrd Station cores and interhemispheric climatic implications. *Science*, **168**, 1570–2 (1970).

27. SONNTAG, C., KLITZSCH, E., LÖHNERT, E. P., EL-SHAZLI, E. M., MÜNNICH, K. O., JUNGHANS, C. L., THORWEIHE, U., WEISTROFFER, K., SWAILEM, F. M. Palaeo-climatic information from deuterium and oxygen-18 in carbon-14 dated North Saharian Groundwaters: groundwater formation in the past. In *Proc. IAEA Symp. on Isotope Hydrology, Neuherberg, 1978*, vol. II. IAEA, Vienna (1979).

28. YOUNG, C. P., GRAY, E. M. *Nitrate in groundwater*. Water Research Centre Technical Report No. *TR*69 (1978).

29. BENNETT, C. L. Radiocarbon Dating with accelerators. *Amer. Scient.* **67**, 450–456 (1979).

30. GROOTES, P. M., MOOK, W. G., VOGEL, J. C., VRIES, A. E. de, HANING, A., AND KISTEMAKER, J. Enrichment of radiocarbon for dating samples up to 75 000 years. *Z. Naturforsch.*, **30a**, 1–14 (1975).

31. GRIBBEN, J. Extending the radiocarbon calender. *New Scient.*, **83**, 98–100 (1979).

32. ALLEN, R. A., SMITH, D. B., OTLET, R. L., AND RAWSON, D. S. Low-level tritium measurements in water. *Nucl. Instrum. Meth.*, **45**, 61–71 (1966).

33. OTLET, R. L. Low-level tritium measurements for hydrological applications. In *Proc. Conf. on Nucleonic Instrumentation*. Institute of Electrical Engineers, Reading (1968).

34. OTLET, R. L. AND WARCHAL, R. M. Liquid scintillation counting of low-level ^{14}C. In COOK, M. A., AND JOHNSON, P. (eds.). *Liquid scintillation counting 5*. Heyden & Sons Ltd., London (1978).

35. OTLET, R. L. An assessment of laboratory errors in liquid scintillation methods of ^{14}C. In BERGER R., AND SUESS, H. (eds.) *Proceedings of the Ninth International Radiocarbon Dating Conference*, pp. 256–267. University of California Press (1979).

Glossary

Absolute filter: an efficient filter for removing particulate matter from gases.

Absorbed dose: the energy deposited by ionizing radiation per unit mass of material (such as tissue).

Absorber: material which reduces radiation by removing energy from it; the magnitude of the reduction depends on the type of radiation, the type of material, its density, and its thickness. A sheet or body of such material.

Absorption process: a process where a component in a gaseous or liquid mixture is removed by contacting the gaseous or liquid mixture with a liquid or solid absorber. Silica gel is a common solid absorber.

Accelerator: a machine for producing high-energy charged particles by electrically accelerating them to very high speeds. Types include betatron, cyclotron, synchrotron, Cockcroft-Walton, Van de Graaff, tandem generator, and linac (linear accelerator).

Accident transient: the variation with time of the neutron population, the power, and the temperature of a reactor following some postulated accident.

Actinides: actinium and the elements following it in the Periodic Table; the most important are actinium, thorium, uranium, neptunium, plutonium, americium, and curium. Many of them are long-lived alpha-emitters.

Activation: the process of inducing radioactivity by irradiation, usually with neutrons, charged particles, or photons.

Activation cross-section: effective cross-sectional area of target nucleus undergoing bombardment by neutrons, etc. Measured in barns.

Active: often used to mean radioactive.

Active area: part of a laboratory where radioactivity may be present, and where exposure to individuals is constantly controlled.

Activity: the number of nuclear disintegrations occurring per unit of time in a quantity of a radioactive substance. Activity is measured in curies. Often used loosely to mean radioactivity.

Activity, specific: the activity per gram of material.

Additive compounds: compounds formed by additive reactions, in which a double bond is converted into a single bond by the addition of two more atoms or radicals.

Adiabatic: without loss or gain of heat.

Adsorption: the retention of dissolved substances on the surface of a substance (adsorbent).

Advanced gas-cooled reactor (AGR): the successor to the Magnox reactors in the UK nuclear power programmes. It uses slightly enriched oxide fuel canned in stainless steel with graphite moderator and carbon dioxide coolant.

Aerosol: a colloidal system such as a mist or fog, in which the dispersion medium is a gas.

Aggressive salts: these are chemicals like sodium and magnesium hydroxides or chlorides which are very corrosive if they exist in high concentrations at high temperature (200–300 °C).

Alara: as low as reasonably achievable.

Alpha particle: a charged particle having a charge of 2 and a mass of 4 atomic mass units. It is emitted in the decay of many heavy nuclei and is identical with the nucleus of a helium atom, consisting of two protons and two neutrons.

Alpha (radiation): helium nucleus emitted by some radioactive substances, e.g. plutonium-239.

Americium: artificially made transuranic element.

Anharmonic: said of any oscillation system in which the restoring force is non-linear with displacement, so that the motion is not simple harmonic.

Anhydrous: a term applied to oxides, salts, etc. to emphasize that they do not contain water of crystallization or water of combination.

Anisotropic: said of crystalline material for which physical properties depend upon direction relative to crystal axes. These properties normally include elasticity, conductivity, permittivity, permeability, etc.

Annihilation: spontaneous conversion of a particle and corresponding antiparticle into radiation, e.g. positron and electron, which yield two gamma-ray photons each of 0.511 MeV.

Annihilation radiation: the radiation produced by the annihilation of a particle with its corresponding antiparticle.

Antibody: a body or substance invoked by the stimulus provided by the introduction of an antigen, which reacts specifically with the antigen in some demonstrable way.

Antigen: material which sensitizes tissues in an animal body by contact with them and then reacts in some way with tissues of the sensitized subject *in vivo*, or with his serum *in vitro*.

Aqueous phase: the 'watery' solution in a solvent-extraction process.

Argillaceous rocks: sedimentary rocks having a very small mineral grain size, as in clay.

Aspect ratio (torus): the ratio R/r of the major to minor radii.

Atom: the smallest particle of an element, which has the chemical properties of that element. An atom consists of a comparatively massive central nucleus of protons and neutrons carrying a positive electric charge, around which electrons move in orbits at relatively great distances away.

Atomic: strictly, relating to the behaviour and properties of entire atoms—nuclei and orbital electrons; it is more usually a synonym for *nuclear*, it is as in 'atomic energy'.

Atomic absorption spectrometry: a method of physical analysis. A small aliquot of the sample to be analysed is introduced into a flame, the heat from which excites the outer electrons of the atoms causing the emission of light characteristics of the constituent elements. This light preferentially absorbs light of identical wavelengths when this, emitted from a standard comparison lamp, is passed through the flame. This provides a means of identifying elements of a given material as well as an estimate of the amount of each present from the extent of absorption.

Atomic displacement cross-section: a measure of the probability of a neutron displacing an atom from its normal position in the crystal lattice structure of a material. The probability is expressed as a target area or cross-section.

Atomic mass unit (amu): one-twelfth of the mass of an atom of carbon-12. Approximately the mass of an isolated proton or neutron.

Atomic weight: the average mass of the atoms of an element at its natural isotopic abundance, relative to that of other atoms, taking carbon-12 as the basis. Roughly equal to the number of protons and neutrons in its nucleus.

Atomic number (Z): the number of protons in an atomic nucleus. Nuclei with the same atomic number but different mass numbers are isotopes of the same chemical element.

Attenuation: reduction in intensity of radiation in passing through matter.

Autoclave: a vessel, constructed of thick-walled steel for carrying out chemical reactions under pressure and at high temperatures.

Average effective dose-equivalent: the measure of the risk from exposure to radiation, which takes account of the different sensitivity of various organs of the body and allows for the effects of different types of radiation.

Azimuthal power instability: eccentric neutron behaviour which results in uneven nuclear conditions in the reactor.

Backfitting: making changes to plants already designed or built.

Background: (1) in discussing radiation levels and effects, it refers to the general level of natural and man-made radiations against which a particular added radiation component has to be considered; (2) in discussing radiation measurement techniques, it may also include spurious readings due to the *noise* characteristics of the instrument and its power supplies, and to the presence of local radioactive contamination, etc.

Bare sphere critical mass: the mass of pure fissile material which if formed into spherical shape, with no outer layer of neutron reflecting material, will just sustain a chain fission reaction.

Barn: a unit of area (10^{-24} cm^2) used for expressing nuclear cross-sections.

Barytes: barium sulphate, a common mineral in association with lead ores, occurring also as nodules in limestone and locally as a cement of sandstones.

Base load: in electricity generation, the minimum steady power demand on the system over a period.

Batch (process): a process not operated continuously.

Bearing pads: pads attached to the outer faces of fuel rod wrappers which contact with similar pads on neighbouring elements either initially (restrained core) or as a result of distortion (free-standing core).

Bearing resonances: low-speed synchronous whirling frequencies, which are determined by the inertia of the rotor and the support stiffness of the bearings.

Bearing systems: the supports to hold a rotating shaft in its correct position.

Becquerel (Bq): the new unit of activity in the SI System; it is equivalent to 1 disintegration per second or roughly 2.7×10^{-11} Ci.

Belt grinding: an abrasive belt process for removal of a thin surface layer from a tube outer surface.

Benchmark: a name of American origin to describe a well-defined problem or experiment which then provides a reference standard for inter-comparison of various methods of solution or prediction.

Beta particle: an electron or positron emitted from a nucleus in certain types of radioactive disintegration (beta-decay).

Beta quenching: rapid cooling of uranium from the β-phase region.

Beta radiation: nuclear radiation consisting of β-particles.

Bifurcate: twice forked, forked.

Binder/binderless routes: pelleting methods employing or not employing a binder to assist the powder compaction.

Binding energy: the energy theoretically needed to separate a nucleus into its constituent protons and neutrons; it gives a measure of the stability of the nucleus.

Biological shielding: heavy concrete shielding erected around certain sections of plant containing radioactive materials in order to protect the operators from nuclear radiations.

Biosphere: that part of the earth and the atmosphere surrounding it, which is able to support life.

Blanket: *fertile* material (usually depleted uranium) arranged round a fast reactor core to capture neutrons and create more fissile material (usually plutonium); in a fusion reactor the blanket may be of lithium to capture neutrons and create more tritium.

Bled-steam feed-heating train: a series of heat exchangers in which steam is *bled* or extracted from the main expansion path through a steam turbine and is used to raise the temperature of feed water being returned to a steam generator from the condenser at the exhaust of the turbine.

Blowdown: rejection of liquid from a vessel under pressure to reduce dissolved solids.

BNFL: British Nuclear Fuels Limited.

Boiling-water reactor (BWR): a light water reactor in which the water is allowed to boil into steam which drives the turbines directly.

Boltzmann equation: the fundamental particle conservation diffusion equation based on the description of individual collisions, and expressing the fact that the time rate of change of the density of particles in the medium is equal to the rate of production less the rate of leakage and the rate of absorption.

Boral sheeting: a composite formed of boron carbide crystals in aluminium with a cladding of commercially pure aluminium.

Bore grinding: a grid abrasion process to remove a thin surface layer from a tube bore.

Boron: element important in reactors, because of large cross-section (absorption) for neutrons; thus, boron steel is used for control rods. The isotope ^{10}B on absorbing neutrons breaks into two charged particles ^{7}Li and ^{4}He, which are easily detected, and is therefore most useful for detecting and measuring neutrons.

Boron counter: an ionization chamber or proportional counter for detecting thermal neutrons by their interaction with boron-10 nuclei.

Brachy-therapy: treatment of tumours by radiation from sources placed in or near to the tumour.

Branching: alternative modes of radioactive decay which may be followed by a particular nuclide.

Brazing: the process of joining two pieces of metal by fusing a layer of brass or spelter between the adjoining surfaces.

Breeder: short for fast breeder reactor.

Breeding: the process of converting a fertile isotope, e.g. ^{238}U into a fissile isotope, e.g. ^{239}Pu. Fast reactors can be designed to produce more fissile atoms by breeding that are lost by fission. The process is also referred to as conversion.

Bremsstrahlung: X-rays produced when rapidly moving charged particles, e.g. electrons, interact with matter (from German 'braking radiation').

Broad-group library: a set of nuclear cross-sections tabulated as average values over a few (about 40) relatively broad energy groups.

Buffer tank: a vessel usually charged with a gas connected to a system containing a liquid, allowing the liquid to be expelled from the system and the out-flow brought to rest in a controlled manner by the cushioning effect of the gas in the tank as it is compressed above the liquid.

Bundle: see *fuel assembly*.

Burn-up: (1) in nuclear fuel, the amount of fissile material burned up as a percentage of the total fissile material originally present in the fuel; (2) of fuel element performance, the amount of heat released from a given amount of fuel, expressed in megawatt-days per tonne.

Burst: a fuel cladding defect which allows fission products to escape into the coolant; it need not be more than a very small crack or pin-hole.

Busbar: an electric conductor of large current capacity connecting a number of circuits.

Butex: name given to dibutyl ether of diethylene glycol, an organic liquid used in solvent-extraction processes.

Calandria: a closed tank penetrated by pipes so that liquids in each do not mix.

Calorimetry: the measurement of thermal constants, such as specific heat, latent heat, or calorific value; such measurements usually necessitate the determination of a quantity of heat, by observing the rise of temperature it produces in a known quantity of water or other liquid.

Campaign: the period from plant start-up to plant shutdown in a nuclear fuel reprocessing operation—usually a few months long.

Can: the container (usually of metal) in which nuclear fuel is sealed to prevent contact with the coolant or escape of radioactive fission products etc., sometimes also to add structural strength and to improve heat transfer. It may be made of Magnox, Zircaloy or stainless steel and may carry fins to increase the rate of heat tranfer.

CANDU: a type of thermal nuclear power reactor developed in Canada and widely used there; it uses natural (unenriched) uranium oxide fuel canned in Zircaloy, and heavy water as moderator and coolant.

Canyon concept: a reprocessing plant layout favoured in the USA, where the plant is constructed partly below ground in concrete-lined vaults or canyons.

Capture: the process in which a particle (e.g. a neutron) collides with a nucleus and is absorbed in it.

Carbon-dating: a means of dating by measuring the proportion of radioactive carbon. Atmospheric carbon dioxide contains a constant proportion of radioactive ^{14}C, formed by cosmic radiation. Living organisms absorb this isotope in the same proportion. After death it decays with a half-life 5.57×10^3 years. The proportion of ^{12}C to the residual ^{14}C indicates the period elapsed since death.

Carbon-14: see *carbon-dating*.

Carcinogenesis: the production and development of cancer.

Carcinoma: a disorderly growth of epithelial cells which invade adjacent tissue and spread via lymphatics and blood vessles to other parts of the body.

Carrier-free: a carrier-free preparation of an isotope consists of atoms of that isotope alone.

Cartridge: a unit of nuclear fuel in a single can.

Cascade: (1) in nuclear fuel processing etc., a progressive sequence of operations in which the process material flows from one stage of the plant to the next, for example, in solvent-extraction processes (in gaseous diffusion or gas centrifuge separation processes there may be several hundred almost identical stages—flow may be in both directions); (2) the emission of gamma rays by a radioactive nucleus in sequence separated by a very short time interval.

Cascade (ideal): a cascade in which the flow is graded along it to avoid mixing losses, yielding maximum separative power.

Cascade (jumped): a cascade in which the product or waste from a stage is not necessarily connected to the stage above or stage below, respectively. If the cut is small, the waste may be connected to a point several stages below in the cascade.

Cascade (squared off): a cascade built in sections whose outlines follow those of an ideal cascade—each section of a squared-off cascade is a square cascade.

Catalytic hydrogenation: chemical reactions in which molecular hydrogen is added to the organic compound in the presence of a secondary element or compound, the catalyst. The catalyst effectively takes no part in the reaction but is essential for its completion. Typical hydrogenation reactions are the hydrogenation of olefins to paraffins, aromatics to napthenes, and the reduction of aldehydes and ketones to alcohols. Typical catalysts are Ni, Pd, V_2O_5, etc.

Cation exchange: the process by which suitable solid agents such as zeolites, artificial resins or clays can remove cations (i.e. positively charged atoms or molecules) from solution by exchanging them with another cation. Commonly used in water softening whereby calcium and magnesium ions are replaced by sodium ions; the removed ions are held by solid cation exchanger. In the context of radioactive waste disposal the process would be typically the removal of strontium and plutonium ions by replacement by sodium or potassium ions from a mineral.

Cave: a heavily shielded compartment in which highly radioctive materials can be safely kept, handled or examined by remote manipulation; sometimes called a *hot cell*.

Centrifuge: apparatus rotating at very high speed, designed to separate solids from liquids, or liquids from other liquids dispersed therein.

Ceramic: hard pottery-like materials having high resistance to heat, e.g. oxides and carbides of metal; it is used for nuclear fuels operating at high temperatures.

Cermet: an intimate mixture of metallic and ceramic particles which combine some of the desirable qualities of both, e.g. for reactor fuels.

Chain reaction: a process which, once started, provides the conditions for its own continuance. In the chain reaction of nuclear fission, neutrons cause nuclear fission in uranium or plutonium, producing more neutrons, which cause further fissions, and so on.

Channelling: the escape of radiation through flaws in the moderator or shielding of a reactor, etc. leading to high levels of radiation in the regions affected.

Charcoal delay bed: beds of charcoal to which gases can be admitted providing hold-up or delay by absorption and desorption. In a nuclear plant such delays are used to allow the decay of activity.

Charge-face: of a nuclear reactor, that face of the biological shield through which the fuel is inserted.

Charge/discharge machine: a mechanical device for inserting or removing fuel in a nuclear reactor without allowing the escape of radiation and, in some reactors, without shutting the reactor down.

Charged particles: nuclear or atomic particles which have a net positive or negative electric charge; they include electrons (and beta particles), positrons, protons, deuterons, alpha particles, and positive or negative ions of any of the chemical elements, but not neutrons.

Chemisorption: irreversible adsorption in which the adsorbed substance is held on the surface by chemical forces.

Chopping: process of cutting nuclear fuel into small lengths.

Cisternography: visualisation of body spaces.

Cladding: the protective layer, usually of metal, covering the fuel in a nuclear fuel element.

Clean critical assembly: a reactor in its initial stage before irradiation has caused changes in the fuel composition; the material composition is usually very well known.

Closed cycle, closed-cycle cooling: a completely enclosed path, e.g. a Magnox coolant circuit.

Cluster: see *fuel assembly*.

Coastdown: the process of slowing down of a pump or turbine once the drive mechanism has stopped or been disengaged.

Coated fuel particle: a compact of nuclear fuel coated with a refractory material which restricts release of fission products.

Codecontamination: the decontamination of U and Pu together from fission products.

Cold criticality: the establishment of a low-power, nuclear fission chain reaction under conditions of essentially zero heat generation.

Cold drawing: a continuous cold metal working process in which a tube is pulled through a die, reducing its wall thickness and/or diameter.

Cold pilgering-type operation: an intermittent metal-working process to reduce tube wall thickness and/or diameter.

Cold work: the plastic deformation of a material at temperatures far below the melting-point, carried out usually in order to increase its strength.

Collimator: a device to confine radiation to a narrow beam by preferentially shielding against radiation in other directions.

Column: vertical, cylindrical apparatus for carrying out a chemical operation, e.g. solvent extraction, absorption, etc.

Commissioning: running a machine etc. (e.g. a nuclear reactor) up to power and checking that it complies with the specifications before the supplier hands it over to the customer.

Committed dose-equivalent: the total integrated dose-equivalent over 50 years to a given organ or tissue from a single intake of radioactive material into the body.

Common-mode failure: the failure of two or more supposedly independent parts of a system, e.g. a reactor, from a common external cause or from interaction between the two parts.

Compound nucleus: a highly excited nucleus, of short lifetime, formed as an intermediate stage in a nuclear reaction, e.g. ^{236}U prior to fission.

Concentration limits: a technique of criticality control using concentration limits as the control.

Concentration pulse: a term coined to describe an enhancement, which exists for a particular period only, in the concentration of one of the constituents of a general medium. In the case of a radioactivity concentration pulse, a graphical plot of specific activity against time demonstrates a profile rising to a maximum and, thereafter, falling towards the usual background level.

Condenser off-gas: incondensable gases isolated in the steam condenser at the exhaust of a turbine that have to be drawn off if the condensing process is to continue efficiently.

Conditioning: the addition of chemicals to a solution in order to adjust the chemical composition; it is usually carried out in a 'conditioner'.

Confinement time: in nuclear fusion research, the average life-time of a particle in a plasma containment system.

Constant-volume feeder: see *CVF*.

Contactor: (reprocessing) generic term for solvent-extraction apparatus.

Containment: physical boundaries constructed to confine radioactive material from a reactor or plant used in reprocessing.

Contamination: the presence of unwanted radioactive matter, deposited on solid surfaces, or introduced into solids, liquids or gases.

Continuous operation: a method of operation of a process or plant in an unbroken sequence (see *batch*).

Continuous refuelling: replacing fuel channels one at a time at the required interval rather than in a batch at longer intervals. Refuelling with the reactor on-load is a particular case.

Control rod: a rod of neutron-absorbing material (e.g. cadmium, boron, hafnium) moved in or out of the reactor core to control the reactivity of the reactor.

Control rod worth: the reactivity change resulting from the complete insertion of a fully withdrawn control rod into a critical reactor under specified conditions.

Conversion: a term used for breeding (see separate entry) when the main fissile element consumed is different from the main fissile element bred. Thus the term applies to reactors fuelled with ^{235}U/^{238}U as opposed to ^{239}Pu/^{238}U.

Conversion factor: the ratio of the number of fissile nuclei produced by conversion to the number of fissile nuclei used up as fuel.

Converter reactor: a reactor in which the conversion process takes place, but in which breeding, with a net gain of fissile material, does not.

Coolant: the gas, water or liquid metal circulated through a reactor core to carry the heat generated in it by fission (and radioactive decay) to boilers or heat exchangers.

Cooling, radioactive: progressive diminution of radioactivity, especially of nuclear fuel after removal from a reactor. This is accompanied by a diminution of heat output, so the word may be used in either sense.

Cooling pond: a water-filled tank in which used fuel elements are placed while cooling (in the radioactive and the thermal senses) is allowed to proceed; the water provides both radiation shielding (conveniently transparent) and means of removing the heat of radioactive decay.

Core-catcher: commonly used to describe the device designed to retain the products of the melted reactor core after a postulated accident. It may be within the reactor vessel (internal) or below the vessel (external).

Core follow: a mathematical technique for constraining the theoretical prediction of the behaviour of a reactor to follow the measured behaviour during operation.

Core, homogenous: core materials so distributed that the neutron characteristics of the reactor are homogenous.

Core power: the rate of production or use of energy in the core.

Core, reactor: the central region of a nuclear reactor containing the fuel elements, where the chain reaction of nuclear fission proceeds.

Coriolis coupling: the coupling between vibrations and rotations in a molecule.

Coulomb barrier: the potential barrier between charged particles due to mutual electrostatic repulsion.

Counter: an instrument for counting pulses of radiation, or the electric pulses that these cause, and displaying or recording them in digital form; also used loosely for any form of radiation detection or measuring instrument.

Counter-current: opposing flows, as for example, where the organic phase carrying U + Pu flows in one direction, while the aqueous phase containaing fission products flows in the other direction.

Counting rate: the rate at which radioactive events, for example, the emission of beta particles, are registered by the measuring device; it is usually expressed in counts per minute, counts per second etc. The counting rate is less than the total radioactive disintegration rate by a factor which expresses the overall counting efficiency of the particular measuring device for the radiation in question.

Coupled control system: a form of power station control which is inherently load following; in the nuclear application, the system is sometimes referred to as 'core follows turbine'.

Coupled hydrodynamic–neutronic instability: in a BWR thermohydraulic instability is complicated by a feedback through the link between the amount of steam in the core (voidage) and the power generated in the fuel. This feedback effect can be dominant when the time constant of a hydraulic oscillation is close to the same magnitude as the time constant of the fuel element. Strong nuclear-coupled thermohydrodynamic instabilities occured in early experiments at Idaho where a metallic fuel with a low time constant was operated in a low-pressure boiling-water flow.

Creep (radiation): the time-dependent, non-reversible dimensional change in a material subject to both a mechanical load and a neutron flux. Radiation creep is caused by the stress-induced preferential segregation of the atoms displaced by irradiation damage. It is observed at temperatures too low for thermomechanical creep to occur. At higher temperatures, e.g. in a reactor core, both types of creep may occur simultaneously.

Creep (thermal or thermomechanical): the low, time-dependent, non-reversible dimensional change in a material when subject to a mechanical load less than that required to produce plastic deformation. Creep is very temperature-dependent, significant only at temperatures above about 0.4 of the melting-point on the absolute scale.

Critical, criticality: a nuclear reactor or other assembly of fissile material is said to have 'gone critical' when its chain reaction has just become self-sustaining.

Critical mass: the amount of fissile material needed to maintain a nuclear chain reaction.

Critical material: the material in which the concentration of radioactivity resulting from a given discharge is highest, when expressed as a fraction of the appropriate derived working limit.

Critical pathway: the pathway by which most radioactivity reaches the critical material.

Critical population group: the group of persons whose radiation doses, resulting from a given practice, are highest.

Criticality incident or excursion: inadvertent accumulation of fissile material into a critical assembly, leading to criticality and the sudden and dangerous emission of neutrons, gamma rays and heat.

cross-section, nuclear: the target area presented by a nucleus to an approaching particle relating to a specified nuclear interaction, e.g. capture, elastic scattering, fission. The cross-section varies with the type of nucleus, the type of energy of the incident particle and the specified interaction. Cross-sections are measured in barns, and give a measure of the probability of the particular reaction.

Cryostat: low-temperature thermostat.

Curie (Ci): the unit of radioactivity, being the quantity of radioactive material in which 3.7×10^{10} nuclei disintegrate every second. Originally it was the activity of 1 gram of radium-226. The curie has now been superseded in the SI system by the becquerel (Bq), equal to 1 disintegration per second.

Curium: artificially made transuranic element.

Cut: the fraction of the feed to a separation stage which emerges in the product stream.

CVF (constant-volume feeder): a rotating device with 'buckets' on the ends of radial arms, which scoops up liquid and delivers it at a rate proportional to the rotational speed.

Cycle: in solvent extraction, used to denote one complete sequence of extraction, scrubbing and stripping.

Cyclotron: an accelerator in which charged particles follow a spiral path in a magnetic field and are accelerated by an oscillating electric field.

Dating, radioisotope: determination of the age of an archaeological or geological specimen by measuring its content of a radioactive isotope in relation to that of its precursor or decay product, or of its stable isotope; applied particularly to radio-carbon dating of archaeological specimens. (See *carbon dating*).

Daughter product: the nuclide immediately resulting from the radioactive decay of a parent or precursor nuclide. If it is radioactive, it will in due course become a parent itself.

D–D: symbol for reaction between two nuclei of deuterium atoms.

Decade: any ratio of 10:1

Decay chain: a series of radionuclides each of which disintegrates into the next, until a stable nuclide is reached.

Decay constant (decay, law of radioactive): the probability per unit time that a nucleus will decay spontaneously. If the number of nuclei is N, the rate of decay dN/dt and the decay constant λ, then the law of radioactive decay is: $dN/dt = -\lambda N$.

Decay heat: the heat produced by radioactive decay, especially of the fission products in irradiated fuel elements. This continues to be produced even after the reactor is shut down.

Decay product: synonym for *daughter product*.

Decay, radioactive: the disintegration of a nucleus through emission of radioactivity. The decrease of activity due to such disintegration.

Decommissioning: the permanent retirement from service of a nuclear facility and the subsequent work required to bring it to a safe and stable condition.

Decommissioning, stage of: the sequence of stable stages of partial or total decommissioning.

Decontamination: the process of removing radioactivity or any other unwanted impurity.

Decontamination factor: the ratio of the proportion of contaminent to product before treatment to the proportion after treatment.

Delayed neutrons: neutrons resulting from fission but emitted a measurable time after fission has taken place. They play an essential part in nuclear reactor control.

Depleted uranium: uranium with less than the natural content (0.71 per cent) of ^{235}U, e.g. the residue from an isotope enrichment plant or from a nuclear fuel reprocessing plant.

Derived working limit (DWL): a limiting value for the amount of radioactive material which may be present continuously in a given situation without risk that the basic international dose limitations will be exceeded.

Detector, radiation: a device for detecting and counting individual radiation pulses or for measuring radiation intensity. The variety of radiations and the kinds of measurements that need to be made require many forms of detector, which include: Geiger-Müller counters, proportional counters, solid and liquid scintillation counters, fission and ionization chambers, and semi-conductor detectors.

Deuterium: the hydrogen isotope of mass 2, 'heavy hydrogen'. (See *heavy water*.)

Deuteron: the nucleus of a deuterium atom, comprising one neutron and one proton.

DFR: the Dounreay fast reactor.

DFR fuel: fuel used in DFR, an alloy of enriched uranium and molybdenum.

Diagrid: the structure supporting the core, blanket and radial shield rods, which also distributes the coolant flow amongst these items.

DIDO: nuclear reactor situated at Harwell.

Die-filling: filling of a die (container) with powder prior to compressing into a pellet.

Diffractometer: an instrument used in the examination of the atomic structure of matter by the diffraction of X-rays, electrons, or neutrons.

Diffusion: in general, the random movements of particles through matter. Specifically used for: (1) diffusion of a gas through a porous membrane, notably in the enrichment of uranium by the diffusion of uranium hexafluoride gas; (2) the movement of fission neutrons through a moderator.

Diffusion plant: a plant for the enrichment of uranium in the ^{235}U isotope by gaseous diffusion of uranium hexafluoride through a porous membrane.

Direct cycle: where the turbine is driven by coolant directly received from the reactor, i.e. one primary circuit.

Disequilibrium: the converse of the stable condition described under *secular equilibrium* in the particular case where a transient preferential separation of one or more of the members in the isotopic decay chain upsets a previously established equilibrium state which then takes a time, dependent upon the longest half-life members disturbed in the chain, to re-establish.

Dishing: a shallow spherical or truncated conical depression in one or both end faces of a UO_2 fuel pellet.

Disintegration: any transformation of a nucleus, either spontaneous or by interaction with radiation, in which particles or photons are emitted. It is used in particular to mean radioactive decay.

Disposal: the removal from man's environment of unwanted or dangerous material, notably nuclear waste, to a place of safety, without the intention of retrieving it later.

Distillation: purification of a liquid by boiling it and condensing and collecting the vapours.

Distribution coefficient: the ratio of the total concentration of a substance in the organic phase (regardless of its chemical form) to its total analytical concentration in the aqueous phase.

Divergence: a nuclear chain reaction is said to be divergent when the rate of production of neutrons exceeds the rate at which they are lost, so that the fission reaction increases in intensity or spreads through a larger volume of material.

DNA: deoxyribonucleic acid (see *nucleic acid*).

Doppler broadening; Doppler coefficient; Doppler constant; Doppler effect: when the velocity of an atom (derived from its thermal energy) is comparable to that of interacting neutrons, the proportion of neutrons affected by resonances in the neutron cross-sections changes with temperature. This is because the resonances are effectively broadened as the velocity of the atom increases with temperature (Doppler broadening). The effect is important for a few isotopes present in quantity in a typical LMFBR, for example ^{238}U. As temperature increases, capture in ^{238}U increases and reactivity decreases; this is called the Doppler effect and is a very useful safety feature. The Doppler temperature coefficient is dR/dT where R is reactivity and T temperature. Because this coefficient is found to be approximately inversely proportional to the absolute temperature T, a Doppler constant D is also defined, where $D = T\,dR/dT$.

Dose commitment: future radiation doses inevitably to be received by a person or group, e.g. from a radioactive material already incorporated in the body.

Dose-equivalent: the absorbed dose multiplied by a quality factor to measure the biological effectiveness of radiation irrespective of its type in rems or sieverts.

Dose-equivalent (effective): the *dose-equivalent* to the whole body having the same risk of causing biological harm as an exposure of part of the body.

Dose-radiation: generally, the quantity of radiation energy absorbed by a body.

Dose-rate: the dose absorbed in unit time, e.g. rems per year.

Dosemeter, Dosimeter, Dose-rate meter: an instrument which measures radiation doses or dose-rates

Doubling time: (1) in a divergent reactor, the time taken for the neutron flux density, and therefore the power, to double; (2) in a breeder reactor, the time taken to produce new fuel equivalent to a full replacement charge in addition to the fuel consumed during this time.

Down time: the period during which a reactor is shut down for routine maintenance.

Dragon: a high-temperature gas-cooled reactor experiment operated at Winfrith, UK, by an OECD project team from 1964 to 1975.

Dry cooling tower: a cooling system which uses the atmosphere as a heat sink by a combination of a jet condenser, closed water circuit, heat exchangers cooled by air, and a cooling tower.

Dry well: the region around the reactor vessel which is kept 'dry' during normal operation, but through which steam and water would discharge in the event of a loss of coolant accident.

Dryout margin: the factor relating a heat flux employed in a boiling system with the critical heat flux which would cause the heating surface to be blanketed by the vapour phase thereby raising the temperature of this surface.

D–T: symbol for reaction between nuclei of deuterium and tritium.

Ductility: the maximum dimensional change per unit length of a mechanically loaded material, as measured just before the point of failure, excluding any region of gross deformation.

EBR: experimental breeder reactor.

Eddy diffusion: the mixing of isotopes due to turbulent motion.

Effective dose-equivalent: the dose-equivalent to individual organs multiplied to give the 'effective whole-body dose-equivalent'.

Effluent: a waste stream from a chemical process, usually gaseous or liquid.

Egg boxes: a constructional feature of fast reactor fuel sub-assemblies.

Eigenfunction: the solution of an equation compatible with the boundary conditions associated with possible values of a parameter of the equation (the eigenvalue).

Elastic scattering: the outcome of collisions between particles, in which the total kinetic energy of the system is unchanged, but the directions of motion of the particles are altered (i.e. the particles simply bounce off one another with no net energy loss).

Electromagnetic radiation: radiation having the nature of electromagnetic waves. In the nuclear context it includes gamma rays and X-rays.

Electromagnetic separation: the separation of ions of different masses by deflection in a magnetic field.

Electron: one of the stable elementary particles of which all matter consists. It carries a single unit of negative electric charge equal to 1.6×10^{-19} coulombs and has a mass of 9×10^{-31} kilograms.

Electronegative residuals: a term that refers to the particular impurities that might form electronegative ions left in the gas after attempts have been made to remove them. Successful operation of a proportional counter depends upon the gas it contains being as pure as possible especially in regard to certain molecular species (e.g. Cl_2, O_2, NH_3, H_2O, etc.) which readily form electronegative ions. Formation of electronegative ions limits, or may even completely prevent, the operation of the counter in its intended mode.

Electronvolt: a unit in which energy is measured in the study of nuclear particles and their interactions. It is equal to the change in energy of an electron crossing a potential difference of 1 volt. Abbreviation eV and multiples keV (10^3 eV) and MeV (10^6 eV).

Electrophoresis: motion of colloidal particles under an electric field in a fluid, positive groups to the cathode and negative groups to the anode.

Element, chemical: a simple substance which cannot (by normal chemical means) be broken down into simpler components. All its atoms have the same number of protons in their nuclei and therefore occupy the same place in the Periodic Table.

Eluant: liquid which is added to an ion-exchange column and passes through it carrying the desired product which it has removed from the column.

Emanometer: radon monitor.

Energy, atomic: popular, though not strictly accurate, synonym for nuclear energy.

Energy containment time: the total energy of a confined plasma divided by the rate of energy loss from it.

Energy fluence: the energy intensity integrated over time of a short pulse of radiation.

Energy loss discrimination: a technique by which charged particles that may be identical in certain respects, e.g. in mass and momentum-to-charge ratio, are separately distinguished by means of the different rates at which they lose energy in passing through a thin detector (thin meaning the path length within the counter, over which the energy loss is measured, is small compared with the total range of the particle).

Energy, nuclear: the energy released when the particles constituting the nuclei of atoms undergo rearrangement, especially through neutron-induced fission in uranium or plutonium.

Engineered storage: storage of spent fuel or high-activity wastes in facilities specially constructed to ensure safe keeping until such time as processing or disposal is undertaken.

Enrichment: the process of increasing the abundance of fissionable atoms in natural uranium (which contains 0.7 per cent of fissile isotope ^{235}U). This is usually done in either the *centrifuge* process (where isotopes are separated by centrifugal force) or the *diffusion* process (where a series of screens retards the heavier isotopes).

Environmental pathway: the route by which a radionuclide in the environment can reach man, e.g. by progressive biological concentration in foodstuffs.

EURATOM: European Atomic Energy Community.

Event tree: a diagram which, starting from some initiating event, identifies the possible courses of an accident by a series of branches expressing the respone 'YES' or 'NO' to the question 'does this engineered safety feature work?'

Eversafe: a description given to plant whose dimensions are limited so that a critical quantity of plutonium (or highly enriched uranium) cannot be accommodated.

Excitation: the addition of energy to a system, e.g. a nucleus, transferring it from its 'ground' state to an 'excited' state.

Excursion: a rapid increase of reactor power above the set levels of operation. This increase may be deliberately caused for experimental purposes or it may be accidental.

Exothermic: accompanied by the evolution of heat.

Expansion coefficient: the fractional expansion (i.e. the expansion of unit length, area, or volume) per degree rise of temperature.

Exponential assembly: an experimental sub-critical assembly into which thermal neutrons are introduced at one face. The neutron flux density in the assembly decreases exponentially with distance from this face. Used in studies of reactor physics, etc.

Extraction (in solvent extraction): the transfer of a dissolved substance from an aqueous phase to an organic phase.

Extraction column: solvent-extraction apparatus where the contacting is done in a vertical column with aqueous inlet at top and organic inlet at bottom.

Fall-out: deposition of radioactive dust etc. from the atmosphere, resulting from the explosion of nuclear weapons or from accidental release.

Fast neutrons: neutons travelling with a speed close to that with which they were ejected from the fissioning nucleus, typically about 20 000 km s^{-1}.

Fast reactor: a nuclear reactor in which most of the fissions in the chain reaction are caused by fast neutrons, travelling with a speed close to which they were ejected from the fissioning nucleus. It contains no moderator, and is capable of generating more fissile material than it consumes.

Fault conditions: any condition in the reactor or plant which is a departure from the designed normal operating condition and which could lead directly or indirectly to an automatic shutdown, to damage or to an accident.

Fault tree: a diagram representing possible initiating events and sequences of successive failures that could lead to an accident.

Fecundity: capacity of a species to undergo multiplication.

Feed: a solution introduced into an extraction system.

Feed train: the series of components which exist between the power station condenser and the steam generator through which the feedwater must pass. Typically these components will be condensate booster pumps, de-aerators, feed pumps, and feed heaters.

Feedwater: the water, previously treated to remove air and impurities, which is supplied to a boiler for evaporation.

Fertile: material such as uranium-238 and thorium-232 which can be transformed by neutron absorption into fissile ^{239}Pu or ^{233}U, respectively.

Fine-group library: a set of nuclear cross-sections tabulated as average values over many energy groups, usually about 2000.

Fine-structure experiment: one in which the detailed variation of the neutron reaction rates from the moderating material, through the coolant, the structural materials, and into the fuel is measured.

FINGAL: fixation in glass of active liquid.

Fissile: a material readily capable of undergoing fission when struck by a neutron, notably ^{235}U, ^{233}U, ^{239}Pu, and ^{241}Pu.

Fission-counter: a detector consisting of a tube lined with fissile material or filled with a fissile gas which detects neutrons by the ionization produced in it by the fission products.

Fission, fast: fission induced by fast neutrons.

Fission gas bubble swelling: a swelling of UO_2 resulting from the accumulation of fission gases into bubbles, mainly on grain boundaries.

Fission neutrons: neutrons produced at the time of fission.

Fission, nuclear: the splitting of a heavy nucleus usually into two nearly equal fast-moving fragments, accompanied by fast neutrons and gamma rays. Fission may be either spontaneous or induced by the absorption of a particle or a high-energy photon.

Fission product(s): the nuclide(s) formed when a fissile material undergoes nuclear fission.

Fission spectrum: (1) the energy distribution of prompt neutrons in fission of a specified nuclide (2) the energy distribution of prompt gamma radiation arising from the fission; (3) the range and abundance of nuclides formed from the fission.

Fission, spontaneous: a mode of radioactive decay in which a heavy nucleus undergoes fission without being excited by any external cause. It occurs in ^{238}U as a mode of decay having a very long half-life.

Fission, thermal: fission induced by thermal neutrons.

Fission track dating: a physical method of dating applicable to glassy materials such as obsidian. Such materials frequently contain the isotope ^{238}U, which in undergoing spontaneous fission, forms two, energetic, heavy nuclei, which lose energy in travelling through the crystal lattice and cause visible damage along their paths (fission tracks). On formation, at high temperatures, the material is fully annealed, meaning all previous crystal lattice damage is reformed and no tracks are present. Thus, from a physical count of the number per unit area in a section of a sample and knowledge of the specific U concentration producing tracks, it is possible to estimate the elapsed time since the material's formation.

Fission yield: the number of nuclei of a particular mass resulting from 100 fissions (strictly the chain fission yield).

Fissium: collective term to describe all the fission products formed by nuclear fission of a fissile material.

Flask: a heavily shielded container used to store or transport radioactive material, especially used nuclear fuel.

Flame photometry: as for *atomic absorption* a method of physical analysis, but in this case the light emitted from the samples introduced into a flame is directly examined. The presence of a particular element is demonstrated by the identification of that element's characteristic light output seen as discrete lines when viewed through a suitable spectroscope, and the intensity depending upon the quantity present.

Flashing-off: the process whereby steam is formed from hot water by a reduction in the pressure of the system.

Flocculation: separation of radioactive waste products from water by coagulation of an insoluble precipitate.

Floc process: a process where material is precipitated as a mass of fine particles.

Flow path redundancy: a way of providing a series of alternative parallel routes for a water flow, so that if one route becomes blocked or fails, other parallel routes are still available.

Flowsheet: a schematic plan giving details of all the steps in the process including quantities of chemicals required.

Fluidized bed: if a fluid is passed upward through a bed of solids with a velocity high enough for the particles to separate from one another and become freely supported in the fluid, the bed is said to be fluidized.

Fluoroscopy: examination of objects by observing their X-ray shadow shown on a fluorescent screen.

Flux density: for a given point (especially in the core of a nuclear reactor), the number of neutrons or other particles incident per second on an imaginary sphere centred at that point, divided by the cross-sectional area (1 cm²) of that sphere. It is identical with the product of the population density of the particles and their average speed.

Forced-draught cooling towers: a system used for cooling fluids, where the coolant—generally atmospheric air—is drawn or forced through a 'rain' of the fluid to be cooled under the action of motor-driven fans.

Form factor: the ratio of the effective value of an alternating quantity to its average value over a half-period.

Fossil fuel: fuel derived from fossilized organic matter; includes coal, crude oil, and natural gas.

Fractional electrolysis: concentration or separation of isotopes by application of electrolysis.

Fracture machanics: a method of analysis which can establish the response of a loaded structure to flaws or cracks postulated to be present at various locations in the material of the structure.

Free electron–hole pairs: the particle pairs formed in solid crystalline material when neutral impurity atoms contained in the material are dissociated by radiation or an electric field, and an electron is physically separated from the remaining positively charged atom (the whole).

Free energy: the capacity of a system to perform work, a change in free energy being measured by the maximum work obtainable from a given process.

Freon: a halogenated hydrocarbon. Used in refrigeration and as aerosol propellants.

Frequency following: the adjustment of the load of an electricity generator by attempting to restore the instantaneous frequency of the supply to a nominal value.

Fretting: a uniform, sometimes very rapid, removal of metal from one or both of two contacting surfaces between which there is relative movement or periodic impacting; sometimes called fretting corrosion.

Froth flotation: a method of separating particles of different densities by the use of frothing agents to vary the density of the liquid in which they are suspended.

Fuel assembly: a group of nuclear fuel elements forming a single unit for purposes of charging and discharging a reactor. The term includes bundles, clusters, stringers, etc.

Fuel channel: a channel in a reactor core designed to contain one or more fuel assemblies.

Fuel cycle: the sequence of steps involved in supplying and using fuel for nuclear power generation. The main steps are mining and milling, extraction, purification, enrichment (where required), fuel fabrication, irradiation (burning) in the reactor, cooling, reprocessing, recycling, and waste management and disposal.

Fuel cycle equilibrium: when the isotopic compositions of feed fuel, output level, and wastes become constant in a system where fuel is returned to the reactors.

Fuel element: a unit of nuclear fuel which may consist of a single cartridge, or a cluster of thinner cartridges (pins).

Fuel inventory: the total amount of nuclear fuel invested in a reactor, a group of reactors, or an entire fuel cycle.

Fuel pin threaded end plug: a modified fuel pin in which the end plug which seals the hollow Zircaloy-2 tube is extended somewhat, and the external surface is threaded to allow it to screw into the lower and upper tie plates and thus act as a structural member.

Fusion, nuclear: a reaction between two light nuclei resulting in the production of a nucleus heavier than either, usually with release of excess energy.

Gamma ray: very short wavelength electromagnetic radiation, emitted during many types of nuclear reaction.

Gamma-ray spectrometry: an analytical technique whereby radionuclides are identified and measured by determining the energies and intensities of the gamma rays they emit during radioactive decay.

Gangue: the portion of an ore which contains no metal.

Gas counter: Geiger counter into which radioactive gases can be introduced.

Gas counting: counting of radioactive materials in gaseous form. The natural radioactive gases (radon isotopes) and carbon dioxide (^{14}C) are common examples.

Gaseous diffusion: name given to the practical separation process based on the principle of molecular diffusion.

Gaseous wastes: generic term to denote gaseous fission products (e.g. iodine, krypton, etc.) or gaseous chemical wastes (e.g. steam, oxides of nitrogen, etc.).

Gas–graphite reactors: gas-cooled, graphite-moderated reactors such as Magnox, AGR, and high-temperature gas-cooled reactors.

Gas lift: technique of lifting liquor from one level to a higher level by entraining liquor in gas bubbles under pressure in a narrow tube.

Geiger-Müller counter: a simple and well-established form of radiation detector which produces electrical pulses at a rate related to the intensity of the radiation. Commonly called a 'Geiger counter'.

Gel precipitation (of fuel): a process for converting liquid metal nitrate into solid mixed-oxide spheres using a gelling agent. The plutonium is co-precipitated with uranium from the nitrate to produce the required enrichment or composition for fast reactor fuel. The process involves fairly simple fluid-handling procedures and can produce fuel with a very low dust content.

Geometric limitation: a method of criticality control which prevents neutron multiplication by appropriate design of the container of fissile material.

Germanium: a metalloid element; it occurs in a few minerals, including coal, and has exceptional properties as a semiconductor.

Glassification: see *vitrification*.

Glove box: a form of protection often used when working with alpha-emitting radioactive materials. Gloves fixed to ports in the walls of a transparent box allow manipulation of work within the box without the risk of inhalation or contact.

Granulocytes: a group of blood cells of the leucocyte division.

Graphite: a black crystalline form of carbon used as a moderator and/or reflector of neutrons in many nuclear reactors.

Gray (Gy): the unit of absorbed radiation dose (replacing the rad under the SI system).

Guide thimbles: another name for support tubes in PWR fuel elements.

Half-life: the characteristic time taken for the activity of a particular radioactive substance to decay to half of its original value—that is, for half the atoms present to disintegrate. Half-lives vary from less than a millionth of a second to thousands of millions of years, depending on the stability of the nuclide concerned.

Half-life, biological: the time required for the amount of a particular substance in the body to be halved by biological processes.

Halides: fluorides, chlorides, bromides, iodides, and astatides.

Handed: arranged as a mirror image of an adjacent section.

Hanger bar: the portion of a suspension section (q.v.) of a fuel assembly by which the fuel and scatter plug are hung from the seal plug.

Hard: of radiation, having a relatively high penetrating power, i.e. energy.

HARVEST: highly active residues vitrification engineering study.

Head end: that part of the reprocessing scheme before solvent extraction, i.e. fuel receipt, fuel breakdown, fuel dissolution, liquor clarification, and conditioning.

Health physics: the study of persons exposed to radiation from radioactive materials.

Heat exchanger: device for transferring heat from one body of fluid to another.

Heavy water (deuterium oxide, D₂O): water in which the hydrogen is replaced by 'heavy hydrogen' or deuterium. Because of the very low neutron absorption cross-section of deuterium, heavy water makes an excellent moderator and is used in, e.g. CANDU and SGHWR nuclear reactor. It is present in ordinary water at one part in about 5000.

Helical multipole coils: helical coils in which adjacent conductors carry opposing currents to produce a multipole magnetic field.

Heterogeneous core: one in which fertile or blanket sub-assemblies are loaded within the boundaries of the highly enriched core zone.

Hex: a colloquialism for uranium hexafluoride (UF₆), the gas used in isotope enrichment plants.

High-level: of radioactive wastes, those that require continuous cooling to dissipate the heat of radioactive decay.

Homogeneous diffusion reactor model: a mathematical description of a reactor in which the reactor is represented as a homogeneous medium of average material composition and the diffusion approximation of neutron transport is assumed to apply.

Honeycomb grid: description of a constructional feature of fast reactor fuel sub-assemblies

Hopping mechanism: molecules adsorbed on a surface can move by hopping from one adsorption site to another.

Hot: jargon for highly radioactive.

Hot cell: see *cave*.

Hot spot: (1) the point of highest temperature in a reactor fuel or its cladding; (2) a restricted area of comparatively intense radiation or radioactive contamination.

Hulls: small lengths of fuel pin cladding left after dissolution of the fuel.

Hydrocarbon: a compound of hydrogen and carbon.

IAEA: International Atomic Energy Agency

Immiscible: that cannot be mixed.

Immunology: the science dealing with the various phenomena of immunity, induced sensitivity, and allergy.

Imploding linear systems: fusion devices in which cylindrical plasmas are created by the implosion of material lining the reactor vessel.

In coincidence: two nuclear events occurring within a fixed (normally extremely short) space of time are said to be in coincidence. The fixed time is called the resolving time.

Indirect cycle: where the turbine is driven by steam produced from the heat of the reactor coolant, i.e. a primary and a secondary circuit.

Inertial confinement: short-term plasma confinement arising from inertial resistance to outward forces.

Individual risk: the probability of harm to an individual.

Induced activity: activity of the radionuclides produced within materials by neutron irradiation.

Inelastic collision: a collision in which kinetic energy is not conserved. With neutrons, a collision with a nucleus in which part of the initial energy is released as a gamma ray. A neutron is emitted from the nucleus which is of lower energy than the incident neutron.

Inelastic scattering: the outcome of collisions between particles, in which some energy is absorbed or emitted, i.e. they do not simply bounce off one another.

Inert gas: helium, neon, krypton, xenon, and radon are the so-called inert gases.

Infarct: death of tissue resulting from the arrest or sudden insufficiency of circulation in the artery supplying the part.

INFCE: International Nuclear Fuel Cycle Evaluation.

Infra-red radiation: invisible electromagnetic radiation with wave-lengths between those of visible light and those of radio waves, i.e. from approximately 0.8 m to 1 mm.

Integro-differential equation: a mathematical equation involving terms in which quantities are required to be integrated, and terms in which quantities require differentiation.

Intermediate-level waste: all those wastes not included in the categories 'high level' and 'low level'.

Invariant magnetic moment: the magnetic moment associated with a gyrating charged particle is an invariant of motion.

In vitro: literally 'in glass', term used to describe the experimental reproduction of biological processes in isolation from the living organism.

In vivo: term used to describe biological processes occurring within the living organism.

Ion: an electrically charged atom or group of atoms.

Ion exchange: interchange between ions of charge. The process is used to remove species from aqueous solution by exchange with other species held on an insoluble solid compound.

Ion pair: a positively charged ion together with the electron removed from it by ionizing radiation.

Ionization: the process of creating ions by dislodging or adding orbital electrons.

Ionization chamber: a device for measuring the intensity of ionizing radiation. The radiation ionizes the gas in the chamber and the rate at which ions are collected (on oppositely-charged electrodes) is measured as an electric current.

Ionization continuum: the energy region above the threshold for ionization of an atom.

Ionization radiation: radiation which removes orbital electrons from atoms, thus creating ion pairs. Alpha and beta particles are more densely ionizing than gamma rays or X-rays of equivalent energy. Neutrons do not cause ionization directly.

Irradiate: to expose to irradiation, particularly to penetrating forms such as gamma rays and neutrons. Often used to mean the 'burning' of fuel in a nuclear reactor. Also used as a measure of the extent of this burning, expressed in megawatt-days per tonne.

Irradiation swelling: changes in the density and volume of materials due to neutron irradiation.

Isomers (nuclear): nuclides having the same number of neutrons and of protons, but having different internal energy levels.

Isomorphism: the name given to the phenomenon whereby two or more minerals crystallize in the same class of the same system of symmetry and develop very similar forms.

Isothermal temperature coefficient: the rate of change in reactivity with temperature from one uniform temperature over the whole reactor to another uniform temperature.

Isotopes: forms of the same element having different atomic weights.

Isotopic abundance: in a specimen of an element, the percentage of atoms having a particular mass number (i.e. of a specified isotope).

Isotropic: said of a medium, the physical properties of which, e.g. magnetic susceptibility or elastic constants, do not vary with direction.

Jet nozzle process: process whereby isotope separation is obtained by the fast flow of uranium hexafluoride in a curved duct.

Joule: a unit of energy; 1 kW h = 3.6 million joules.

K-capture: a radioactive transformation whereby a nucleus captures one of its orbital electrons. Usually accompanied by emission of electromagnetic radiation.

Laminar flow: flow in which adjacent layers do not mix, except at molecular scale.

Laser compression: compression of matter induced by impinging laser beams

Laser fusion: fusion achieved by spherically symmetrical laser compression (q.v.)

Lattice: (1) the regular pattern of fuel arrangement within a reactor core; (2) the arrangement of atoms in the structure of a crystal.

Lattice constants: the simple factors, which characterize the neutron physics of the lattice, such as the fast fission factor, the resonance escape probability, the fuel absorption probability, and the number of neutrons produced per absorption in the fuel.

Leaching: the dissolution of a substance from a solid containing it, e.g. uranium from ore or fission products from vitrified radioactive waste.

Lead-time: the expected time required from the placing of an order for a plant to the commercial operation of the plant.

Leakage: the net loss of particles (e.g. neutrons, gamma rays) from a region or across a boundary of a region.

Leaning post: a structural item in the fast reactor core against which a group of six adjacent sub-assemblies are located or are sprung to provide radial restraint. Control rods are usually located and moved inside leaning posts. Leaning posts may be used also to contain instruments, experiments, and non-standard sub-assemblies.

Levitron: in fusion research, a toroidal magnetic trap formed by levitating a current-carrying ring in the plasma chamber.

Licensee: the holder of a licence issued by the regulatory body to perform specific activities related to the siting, construction, commissioning, operation, and decommissioning of a nuclear plant.

Light water: ordinary water, as distinct from heavy water.

Light water reactor (LWR): a reactor using ordinary water as both moderator and coolant. The term embraces boiling-water reactors and pressurized-water reactors.

Limiter: an aperture defining the boundary of a plasma.

Liquid scintillation counting: a method for measuring the rate of decay of a radioactive isotope, frequently a β-emitter, in which the material containing the isotope is converted to a liquid, which is then mixed with another liquid called a scintillant. The scintillant contains molecules of a solute (fluors), which fluoresce when excited by a transfer of energy, from, for example, an emitted β-particle. The resultant emission of light quanta (flashes of light), the number of which is proportional to the total energy of the initiating β-particle, are registered as a simple pulse by a closely placed photomultiplier tube (or tubes). The number of pulses counted in unit time (the counting rate) is thus related to the disintegration rate (activity) of the sample being measured.

LMFBR: liquid-metal-(cooled) fast breeder reactor.

load factor: the ratio of the average load during a year (or any other selected period) to the maximum load occurring in the same period. It is also used for the ratio of total output of a generating unit in a period to its designed or reference capacity.

Load throw-off: the rapid rejection of the load on an electric generator.

LOCA: loss of coolant accident. The conditions which might arise when the coolant level in the primary vessel, or in the secondary circuit, falls.

Loop-type reactor: one in which the primary coolant is piped outside the main vessel to external heat exchangers (c.f. *pool-type* reactors).

Loss-cone: in a *magnetic trap* (q.v.) the region of velocity space occupied by escaping particles.

Low-level waste: generally, those wastes which because of their low radioactive content do not require shielding during normal handling and transport. In the UK, it is usually interpreted as those solid, liquid or gaseous wastes that can be disposed of safely by dispersal into the environment.

LWR (light water reactor) box: the term used to describe the square-cross-section

sheath which encloses the fuel pins comprising the fuel element of an LWR.
LWR fuel: fuel used in LWRs, usually slightly enriched UO_2.

Magnetic confinement: in fusion research, the use of shaped magnetic fields to confine a plasma.

Magnetic field: effect produced in the region around a conductor carrying an electric current. It exerts a force on any moving electric charge, causing charged particles to travel in helical paths about magnetic field lines.

Magnetic field line: often called 'line of force', an imaginary line showing the direction of the magnetic field. The density of these lines is often used to denote field strength.

Magnetic mirror: when a particle gyrating round a line of force moves from weaker to a much stronger field, it can be reflected back. This arrangement is called a magnetic mirror.

Mangetohydrodynamics (MHD): the study of the motion of an electrically conducting fluid in the presence of a magnetic field.

Magnox: (1) an alloy of magnesium containing small amounts of aluminium and beryllium developed for cladding natural uranium metal fuel used in the Calder Hall reactors and the power stations of the first British nuclear power programme (the Magnox reactors): it absorbs few neutrons and does not react with the carbon dioxide gas used as reactor coolant (hence the name—'*magnesium, no oxidation*'); (2) the generic name given to the type of gas-cooled graphite-moderated reactor using Magnox-clad fuel, on which Britain's first nuclear power programme was based.

Mandrel: a rod inserted into a pellet die prior to filling with powder to form a central hole in the pressed pellet.

Mass balance area (MBA): section of plant or process area that can be isolated in order to determine the quantity of fissile material present.

Mass defect: the difference between the mass of a nucleus and the sum of the masses of its constituent nucleons.

Mass–energy equivalence: confirmed deduction from relativity theory, such that $E = mc^2$, where E = energy, m = mass, and c = velocity of light.

Mass limitation: technique for criticality control where the total mass of fissile material present is limited.

Mass number: the total number of neutrons and protons in an atomic nucleus.

Mass spectrometer: an analytical instrument in which accelerated positive ions of a material are separated electromagnetically according to their charge-to-mass ratios. Different species can be identified and accurate measurements made of their relative concentrations.

Mathematical modelling: the representation of a real physical process by a series of mathematical equations, whose solution thus aids the understanding of the process.

Maximum permissible level/body burden/concentration: the maximum permitted value for such quantities as radiation dose-rate, quantity or concentration of a radionuclide, as determined by health physics considerations. Usually based on the recommendations of the International Commission on Radiological Protection.

Meson: one of a series of unstable particles with masses intermediate between those of electrons and nucleons, and with positive, negative or zero charge.

Metastasis: a secondary tumour.

MeV: million electronvolts—a measure of energy.

Micrometre: one millionth of a metre.

Milling capacity: the quantity of uranium ore which can be handled by the fabricating plant. The throughput of uranium ore in a uranium processing mill will be restricted by the milling capacity.

Missile shield: a steel or concrete structure placed over the upper head of the reactor vessel to protect the containment building from missiles such as ejected control rods.

Mixed mean temperature, mixed outlet temperature: the most useful mean value of the temperature which, when multiplied by the mass flow of fluid and its specific heat, gives the transport of heat along a passage.

Mixed oxide fuel: fast reactor fuel consisting of intimately mixed dioxides of plutonium and uranium (which may be depleted). In a fast reactor the plutonium undergoes fission, while the uranium acts as a fertile material for breeding.

Mixer–breeder: the upper axial breeder zone of the fast reactor, which forms part of the core sub-assemblies and is a separate assembly of large-diameter wire-wrapped pins.

Mixer–settler: a solvent-extraction plant unit comprising two inter-connected tanks, in one of which two immiscible fluids of different densities are stirred together, then allowed to separate out in the other. The plant will comprise several such units arranged in a cascade with the two liquids flowing in opposite directions, one carrying the product and the other the impurities.

Moderating ratio: a figure of merit which accounts for both a moderator's ability to slow down neutrons and its propensity to capture them by absorption.

Moderator: the material in a reactor used to reduce the energy, and hence the speed, of fast neutrons to thermal levels, so far as possible without capturing them. They are then much more likely to cause fission in ^{235}U nuclei. The most important moderators are graphite, water, and heavy water.

Moderator coefficient: the rate at which the reactivity of the system increases with temperature.

Mole: the amount of substance that contains as many entities (atoms, molecules, ions, electrons, etc.) as there are atoms in 12 g of ^{12}C. It replaces in SI the older terms gram-atom, gram-molecule, etc. and for any chemical compound will correspond to a mass equal to the relative molecular mass in gram.

Molecular diffusion: the process by which molecules pass through very fine pores. The lighter molecules move faster and travel more easily down the holes.

Monazite sands: deposit from which thorium is mainly extracted.

Monte Carlo method: statistical procedure when mathematical operations are performed on random numbers.

MOX: mixed oxide fuel.

MTR: materials testing reactor (e.g. DIDO, PLUTO).

MTR fuel: enriched uranium–aluminium alloy clad in aluminium metal.

Multipass steam superheater: an arrangement for raising the temperature of steam above the boiling temperature associated with its pressure, wherein the steam flows successively through separate paths arranged through the heat source—for example—the core of a nuclear reactor.

Multiphoton dissociation: the process in which a molecule is dissociated by the absorption of many photons of the same energy.

Multiplication factor: the ratio of the rate of production of neutrons by fission in a nuclear reactor or assembly to the rate of their loss, symbolized by the letter k 1. When the reactor is operating at a steady level, $k = 1$, when divergent, $k > 1$, when shut down, $k < 1$.

Multi-start helical finning: a series of separate helical fins formed on the outer surface of a tube.

Muon: subatomic particle with rest mass equivalent to 106 MeV. It has unit negative charge, a half-life of about 2μs, and decays into electron, neutrino, and anti-neutrino. It participates only in weak interactions without conservation of parity.

Myocardium: the middle layer of the heart, consisting of cardiac muscle.

Neutrino: a particle having no mass or charge which is emitted in radioactive beta decay along with an electron. Although of great interest as an elementary particle, it is of little concern in nuclear technology.

Neutron: an elementary particle with mass of 1 atomic mass unit (approximately 1.67×10^{-27} kg), approximately the same as that of the proton. Together with protons, neutrons form the nuclei of all atoms. Being neutral, a neutron can approach a nucleus without being deflected by the positive electric field, so it can take part in many types of nuclear interaction. In isolation neutrons are radioactive, decaying with a half-life of about 12 minutes by beta emission into a proton.

Neutron absorber: substance with the property of absorbing neutrons, e.g. boron, gadolinium, etc.

Neutron absorption: a nuclear interaction in which the incident neutron joins up with the target nucleus.

Neutron economy: for good neutron economy losses of neutrons must be kept to a minimum. In a reactor, some neutrons are unable to take part in the chain reaction because they are captured in the nuclei of the reactor material or they leak out of the system.

Neutron-induced voidage: the presence in a material of voids, which are small aggregates of vacancies stabilized by gas atoms; these give macroscopic increases in the volume of non-fissile components subjected to irradiation by neutrons.

Neutron poisons: see *neutron absorber*: absorbers dissolved in solutions of fissile materials or incorporated into plant equipment which holds or processes fissile materials are soluble or fixed poisons, respectively.

Neutron scatter plug: an arrangement in a fuel assembly which prevents neutrons streaming out from a reactor core along the coolant pipework by causing such neutrons to be deflected back into the core.

Neutron spectrum: the energy distribution of a neutron population.

Neutron yield: the average number of fission neutrons emitted per fission.

NII: Nuclear Installations Inspectorate.

Noble gases: another name for the inert gases, comprising the elements helium, neon, argon, krypton, xenon, and radon-222. Their outer (valence) electron orbits are complete, thus rendering them inert to most chemical reactions.

Nomogram: chart or diagram of scaled lines or curves for the facilitation of calculations.

Non-invasive: not interfering directly with bodily tissues.

Nuclear (energy etc.): resident in, derived from or relating to atomic nuclei (rather than to entire atoms—see *atomic*).

Nucleic acids: the non-protein constituents of nucleoproteins. Nucleic acids play a central role in protein synthesis and in the transmission of hereditary characteristics.

Octahedral symmetric anharmonicity: a term in the potential energy of a polyatomic molecule which is octahedrally symmetric.

Off-gas: gaseous effluents from a process vessel, a chemical process, or a nuclear reactor.

OK: odourless kerosene, a hydrocarbon mixture used as a diluent for the extractant in a solvent-extraction process.

Oklo: the uranium mine in Gabon, West Africa, where the first evidence of a natural nuclear reactor was discovered. Thousands of millions of years ago the isotopic abundance of ^{235}U was much higher than it is today. Local concentrations at Oklo were high enough, when moderated by incoming water, to form critical assemblies in which fission took place over periods of millions of years.

Once-through fuel cycle: where the fuel is used only once, and is not reprocessed for reuse.

Once-through type boiler: high-pressure boiler using superheated (dry) steam.

One-group cross-section: a single, average cross-section value for the whole range of neutron energies of interest.

Orbital: of electrons, revolving around the atomic nucleus at considerable distances (on the atomic scale) from it. The number of possible orbits is limited, and when an electron changes orbit, energy is given off (as light or X-rays), or absorbed.

Osteosarcoma: a malignant tumour derived from osteoblasts, composed of bone and sarcoma cells.

Oxide fuel: nuclear fuel manufactured from the oxide of the fissile material. Oxides will withstand much higher temperatures and are much less chemically reactive than metals.

Parameter: one of the measurable characteristics or limits of a given design, system or operation. For example, in a nuclear reactor the pressure vessel dimensions, coolant temperature limits, neutron doubling time, radiation levels, power output, etc.

Parent: the immediate precursor of a *daughter product* in radioactive decay processes.

Particles, elementary: particles which are held to be simple; in nuclear energy these are neutrons, protons, electrons, positrons, photons. In the study of high-energy physics there are a great many other 'elementary' particles such as mesons, pions, quarks, neutrinos, etc.

Partition coefficient: the ratio of the total concentration of a substance in the organic phase to its total concentration in the aqueous phase.

Passage grave: one of the main categories of megalithic or chamber tomb.

Pebble bed (core): a loose bulk of pebble-shaped fuel compacts made from graphite and uranium dioxide powder.

Perfusion: use of radioisotopes to measure the blood flow per unit volume of the organ under investigation.

Periodic Table, chart: a chart of the chemical elements laid out in order of their atomic number so as to bring out the relationship between atomic structure and chemical etc. properties.

PFR: prototype fast reactor, at Dounreay, Scotland.

PFR fuel: a mixture of uranium and plutonium dioxide used as fuel in the PFR.

Photochemical: the chemical effects of radiation, chiefly that due to visible and ultraviolet light.

Photodissociation: dissociation produced by the absorption of radiant energy.

Photomultiplier: a device in which electrons striking its first stage, owing to absorbtion of a photon of light, are multiplied in number so as to produce an easily detectable electrical pulse at the last stage.

Phytoplankton: planktonic plants.

Pickling: a chemical process for cleaning metallic surfaces by the dissolving of a thin layer of metal.

Pile: the former name for a nuclear reactor, particularly of the graphite-moderated type.

Pilot plant: small-scale plant used by chemical engineers to study behaviour of larger plants which they are designing.

Pin, fuel: a very slender fuel can, as used, for instance, in fast reactors.

Pinch effect: the constriction of an electric discharge due to the action of its own magnetic field.

Pitchblende: a particularly rich ore of uranium, historically important in the discoveries of radioactivity by Becquerel and the Curies. Radium was first discovered in this mineral.

Planchet: plain disc of metal.

Plankton: small plants and animals living in the surface waters of the sea.

Plasma: an electrically neutral gas of free ions and electrons (i.e. electrons that have been stripped from the original atoms).

Plasma temperature: temperature expressed in degrees K (the thermodynamic-temperature) or in electronvolts (the kinetic temperature); 1 keV = 10 000 K.

Plate crevice (tube to tube): the very narrow gap which is formed when a tube is located in the drilled hole in the thick tube plate.

Plateout: a general term used to encompass all processes by which material is removed from suspension to form a coating (or plating) on exposed surfaces.

Plenum (fuel pin): a space provided at one or both ends of a fuel pin for the fission gases released by the fuel during operation.

PLUTO: materials testing reactor at Harwell.

Plutonium (Pu): the important fissile isotope ^{239}Pu produced by neutron capture in all reactors containing ^{238}U. Higher isotopes, plutonium 240, 241, 242, and 243, are produced in lesser quantities by further captures.

Poison: see *neutron poison*.

Poison, burnable: a neutron absorber deliberately introduced into a reactor system to reduce initial reactivity, but becoming progressively less effective as burn-up progresses. It thus helps to counteract the fall in reactivity as the fuel is burned up.

Poisson distribution: statistical distribution characterized by a small probability of a specific event occurring during observations over a continuous interval (e.g. of time or distance).

Poloidal field: the magnetic field generated by an electric current flowing in a ring.

Polonium: radioactive element, symbol Po. Important as an alpha-ray source relatively free from gamma emission.

Polyatomic: a molecule containing many atoms.

Polymerization: the combination of several molecules to form a more complex molecule having the same empirical formula as the simpler ones. It is often a reversible process.

Pool-type reactor: one in which the primary coolant circuits (i.e. including the intermediate heat exchangers and primary pumps) are within the primary vessel (cf. loop-type reactor).

Positron: the anti-particle of the electron, having a positive charge instead of the more usual negative charge. It is the only anti-particle of significance in the context of nuclear power.

Positron annihilation: a positron, or positive electron, can annihilate with a negative electron to produce electromagnetic radiation consisting of two gamma rays of 0.511 MeV energy emitted (if the positron and electron are at rest) in exactly opposite directions (180 ° to each other). If the electron is in a solid, the distribution of angle between the gamma rays provides information on the distribution of electron velocities in the solid, and hence about the physical structure of the material.

Posting: the name given to the transfer of radioactive or dangerous materials such as plutonium from store to sealed glove box or plant or from plant to plant etc. in such a manner that the materials are never exposed to personnel.

Power density: rate of production of energy per unit volume (of a reactor core).

Power ramping: an increase in reactor power from a pre-existing level to a higher level. The term is generally applied to a fairly rapid increase after a prolonged period at the lower level.

Precursor: in a radioactive decay chain any nuclide which has preceded another.

Pre-equlibration conditioning: preliminary treatment of an aqueous phase in order to convert the material to be solvent extracted into the most suitable chemical form.

Pressure-suppression containment: a form of reactor primary containment employing *pressure-suppression ponds* to reduce the pressure inside the containment, following an accident in which there was an escape of a condensable reactor coolant.

Pressure-suppression ponds: a large volume of water used to reduce the pressure in, say, the primary containment of a reactor cooled by boiling or pressurized water after a release of coolant, by condensing the steam fraction and the vapour flashed-off from the escaping liquid.

Pressure-tube reactor: a class of reactor in which the fuel elements are contained in a large number of separate tubes, through which the coolant water flows, rather than in a single pressure vessel. Examples include Britain's SGHWR, and Canada's CANDU.

Pressure-vessel: a reactor containment vessel, usually made from thick steel or prestressed concrete, capable of withstanding high internal pressures. It is used in gas-cooled reactors and light water reactors.

Pressurized-water reactor (PWR): a light water reactor in which ordinary water is used as moderator and coolant. The water is prevented from boiling by being kept under pressure and is circulated through a boiler in which steam is raised in a separate circuit for the turbo-alternators.

Primary circuit: the coolant circuit which removes heat directly from the core.

Primary separation plant: that part of a nuclear fuel reprocessing plant where the bulk of the fission product decontamination occurs, and plutonium and uranium are separated from each other.

Prismatic core: vertical columns of graphite prisms.

Proliferation: in the nuclear policy context, an increase in the size of nuclear weapons arsenals worldwide; this may involve the escalation of nuclear weapons capability to countries which currently are not nuclear weapons states.

Prompt: of neutrons or gamma rays, emitted immediately upon fission, or other interaction.

Prompt critical: the state of achieving criticality in a reactor by means of the prompt neutrons alone and therefore without the control effected through the delayed neutrons.

Proportional counter: a detector for ionizing radiation which uses the proportional region in a discharge tube characteristic, where the gas amplification in the tube exceeds unity but the output pulse remains proportional to initial ionization.

Protium: lightest isotope of hydrogen of mass unity (^{1}H) most prevalent naturally. The other isotopes are deuterium (^{2}H) and tritium (^{3}H).

Proton: the nucleus of hydrogen atoms of mass number 1 and a part of all other nuclides. The number of protons in a nucleus of any element is the atomic number, Z, of that element.

Pulsed inertial devices: fusion systems relying on *inertial confinement* (q.v.)

Purex: generic name for solvent-extraction processes using TBP as the extractant.

Pyrite: sulphide of iron crystallizing in the cubic system. It is also known as iron pyrite.

Pyrometallurgical process: process using heat to refine or purify metals.

Quality assurance (QA): a systematic plan of inspection necessary to provide adequate confidence that a product will perform satisfactorily in service.

Quality control: a statistically based procedure of operational checks and tests for the production of a uniform product within specified limits in accordance with design requirements.

Quality factor: of radiation, a factor used to express the biological effectiveness of different kinds of radiation.

Quartz fibre electrometer: an instrument which measures radiation exposures via the force between two charged quartz fibres; this charge is reduced as ionization occurs. It can be conveniently sized for monitoring personal doses, with an immediate visual display.

Rad: a unit of absorbed radiation dose, equivalent to 10^{-2} J/kg. The unit is being replaced by the SI unit, the gray (Gy), equal to 100 rads.

Radiation: electromagnetic waves, especially (in the context of nuclear energy) X-rays and gamma rays, or streams of fast-moving particles (electrons, alpha particles, neutrons, protons), i.e. all the ways in which an atom gives off energy.

Radiation area: an area to which access is controlled because of a local radiation hazard.

Radiation damage: undesired effects in a material arising from disturbance of the atomic lattice or from ionization caused by radiation. It is often deliberately incurred in the course of experimental work, especially on reactor materials.

Radiation dose: the quantity of radiation received by a substance.

Radiation risk: the risk to health from exposure to radiation.

Radiation source: a device which emits radiation, such as a quantity of radioactive material encapsulated as a sealed source, or a machine, e.g. for generating X-rays for medical purposes.

Radioactive source: any quantity of radioactive material intended for use as a source of radiation.

Radioactive waste: all materials arising from reactor operations which are deemed to be of no further value, but which, due to induced activity or contamination, or a combination of both, have a radionuclide content which exceeds a prescribed level.

Radioactivity: the property possessed by some atomic nuclei of disintegrating spontaneously, with loss of energy through emission of a charged particle and/or gamma radiation.

Radioactivity, induced: radioactivity that has been induced in an otherwise inactive material, usually by irradiation with neutrons.

Radioactivity, natural: the radioactivity of naturally occurring materials (e.g. uranium, thorium, radium, potassium-40).

Radiobiology: branch of science involving study of effect of radiation and radioactive materials on living matter.

Radiocarbon dating: (see *carbon dating*).

Radiochemistry: that part of chemistry which deals with radioactive materials, including the production of radionuclides etc. by processing irradiated or naturally occurring radioactive materials. The use of radioactivity in the investigation of chemical problems.

Radiography: a method of visually examining the interior of a specimen for defects etc. by passing a beam of penetrating radiation through it so that 'shadows' are cast by the denser or thicker parts. These can be examined on a fluorescent screen or a cathode ray tube, at the time, or recorded on photographic film. Medical diagnostic X-rays and industrial gamma-ray tests are the best known examples. A more recent development uses neutrons.

Radioiodines: radioactive isotopes of the element iodine.

Radioisotope: short for radioactive isotope.

Radiolysis: the chemical decomposition of material by radiation.

Radionuclide: radioactive nuclide.

Radiotherapy: treatment of disease by the use of ionizing radiation.

Radiotoxicity: a measure of the harmfulness of a radioactive substance to the body or to a specified organ following its uptake by a given process.

Radon: a zero-valent, radioactive element, the heaviest of the noble gases.

Raffinate: the waste stream remaining after the extraction of valuable materials from solution particularly in the reprocessing of fuel.

Rare-earth elements: a group of metallic elements possessing closely similar chemical properties. These are extracted from monazite, and separated by repeated fractional crystallization, liquid extraction, or ion exchange.

Rare-earth fission products: fission products which are rare earths.

Raster: a pattern of scanning lines arranged to provide complete coverage of an area.

Rating (linear, mass, of fuel): the rate at which heat is generated in fuel. Mass rating is expressed in watts per gram of fuel; linear rating of a fuel pin is usually expressed in watts per unit length of pin.

Reactant: a substance taking part in a chemical reaction.

Reactivity: a measure of the ability of an assembly of fuel to maintain a neutron chain reaction. It is equal to the proportional change in neutron population between one generation and the next. In terms of k_{eff} reactivity $= 1 - (1/k_{eff})$.

Reactivity worths: the reactivity change caused by a particular addition or removal of a material or sub-assembly to or from a reactor. The worth of an individual isotope is often expressed as the ratio of its reactivity at the core centre to that of a ^{239}Pu atom.

Reactor chemical: a vessel, or part of a plant, in which a chemical reaction is maintained and controlled, usually as part of a production process.

Reactor vessel: the container of a reactor in which the fuel, moderator (if any) coolant and control rods are situated.

Recuperator: an arrangement whereby hot fluid leaving a circuit, heats the incoming fluid.

Recycling: the reuse of the fissionable material in irradiated nuclear fuel after it has been recovered by reprocessing.

Reducing agent: a substance that will remove oxygen from or add hydrogen or electrons to a second substance, itself being oxidized in the process. Reducing agents are often used in the separation of Pu from U.

Reflector: an extra layer of moderator or other material outside the reactor core designed to scatter back ('reflect') into the reactor some of the neutrons which would otherwise escape.

Refractory elements: metals with a high melting point such as vanadium, niobium, tantalum, molybdenum, titanium, and zirconium.

Regulatory body: a national authority or a system of authorities designated by national government, assisted by technical and other advisory bodies, and having the legal authority for issuing of licenses.

Rem (roentgen-equivalent man): the unit of effective radiation dose absorbed by tissue, being the product of the dose in rads and the quality factor. The rem is being replaced by the SI unit, the sievert (Sv), equal to 100 rem.

Reprocessing: the processing of nuclear fuel after its use in a reactor to remove fission products etc. and to recover fissile and fertile materials for further use.

Reserves: of uranium, resources which can, with reasonable certainty, be recovered at a cost below a specified limit using currently proven technology.

Residence time: dwell time in a given section of a process.

Resin, useful lifetime: the period during which the resins arranged in a water purification plant of the ion-exchange type continue to be effective in service.

Resolved resonance region: region where the peaks in cross-section can be separately recognized.

Resonance integral: the integral cross-section value over all the energies within the resonance region, weighted by the reciprocal of the energy.

Resonance (reaction rate): the high, often narrow, peak in a reaction rate curve as a function of energy which is observed when the incident particle excites a specific energy level in a compound nucleus.

Resources: of uranium, 'reasonably assured resources' refer to ore known to exist and to be recoverable within a given production cost. 'Estimated additional resources' refer to ore surmised to occur around known deposits or in known uranium-bearing districts.

Reversed field pinch: a toroidal magnetic trap in which the toroidal field changes sign at an intermediate minor radius.

Reverse osmosis: a process essentially akin to filtration, involving the use of extremely high-quality membranes for the removal of dissolved salts from solution.

Rig: an experimental device, especially one designed to enable work to be carried out in, or in close association with, a nuclear reactor or chemical plant.

Roentgen: a unit of exposure to radiation based on the capacity to cause ionization. It is equal to 2.58×10^{-4} coulombs per kilogram in air. Generally an exposure of 1 roentgen will result in an absorbed dose in tissue of about 1 rad.

Roll and shock: motion imparted to a ship as a result of interaction with waves.

Rose Bengal: a red dye which has the property of accumulating in the liver.

Rotameter: instrument for measuring the flow of liquids or gases.

Rotating nut and translating screw device: a mechanical device consisting of a vertical threaded shaft together with a series of freely rotating roller nuts canted to match the lead angle of the threads on the shaft. As the shaft rotates the nuts turn within the threads of the shaft translating vertical motion to it, much as a turning nut would cause a bolt to raise or lower in a slot which prevents the bolt from turning.

Rotor precession: this is low-frequency orbiting motion superimposed on the high rotation frequency.

Safety rod: One of a set of additional reactor control rods used specifically for emergency shutdown and for keeping the reactor in a safe condition during maintenance etc.

Salting out: improving the extraction of a substance (in solvent extraction) by the addition of particular substances to the aqueous phase.

Saturated fluid: a liquid at its boiling-point corresponding to the imposed pressure.

Saturated steam: steam at the same temperature as the water from which it was formed, as distinct from steam subsequently heated.

Saturation temperature: the temperature at which the liquid and vapour phases are in equilibrium (at some given pressure). When the pressure is 1 atmosphere, the saturation temperature is called the boiling-point. Above the saturation temperature, the liquid phase cannot exist stably.

Scattering: general term for irregular reflection or dispersal of waves or particles. Particle scattering is termed elastic when no energy is surrendered during the scattering process—otherwise it is inelastic.

Scintillation counter: a radiation detector in which the radiations cause individual flashes of light in a solid (or liquid) 'scintillator' material.Their intensity is related to the energy of the radiation. The flashes are amplified and measured electrically and displayed or recorded digitally as individual 'counts'. (see *gamma-ray spectrometry*).

Scoop: a pipe which is used for extracting the product or waste from a centrifuge. It can also act as a braking mechanism and to stimulate friction flow in a machine.

Scram: the evacuation of a building or area in which it would be dangerous for the operators to remain; in US usage, emergency shutdown of a nuclear reactor or other potentially dangerous plant.

Scrub: the process of removing impurities from the separated organic phase containing the main extractable substances by treatment with fresh aqueous phase.

Sealed-face production lines: a design of production line for active fabrication in which all equipment is sited behind a single operating face, as distinct from the use of free-standing glove boxes.

Sealed source: a radiation source totally enclosed in a protective capsule or other container so that no radioactive material can leak from it.

Seal plug: specifically the pressure closure at the end of the channel of a tube reactor through which access may be gained for refuelling.

Secular equilibrium: the term given to the particular stable situation which exists in respect of the relative abundances of the isotopic members of a radioactive decay chain, e.g. A decays to B decays to C ... D etc., after a long decay period (long in terms of the decay constant of the longest half-life isotope at the head of the chain). Secular equilibrium is established when the quantity present of any given isotope within the chain is exactly balanced by, on the one hand, the rate of its production caused by the decay of the isotope one up in the chain, and, on the other hand, its own rate of decay to the isotope next down in the chain. At this point, the disintegration rates of all the members of the chain are equal.

Semi-conductor detector: detector for nuclear particles which makes use of a semi-conductor; this is a material whose resistivity is between that of insulators and conductors and can be changed by the application of an electric field.

Separation factor: this factor measures the difference in mole fraction of the desired isotope after passage through a separating element.

Separation nozzle process: in this process isotope separation is achieved by expanding gas through a nozzle.

Separative work: a measure, for costing purposes, of the work done in enriching a material such as uranium from the initial concentrations to the final desired enrichment.

Serum protein: protein in the blood serum; this is the fluid portion of the blood obtained after removal of the fibrin and blood cells.

SGHWR: steam-generating heavy water reactor.

Shear: a property of a twisted magnetic field whereby the amount of twist varies with depth; it is used in some plasma confinement experiments to reduce instabilities.

Shearing: cutting nuclear fuel into small lengths.

Shield, biological: a mass of absorbing material which reduces the level of ionizing radiation, e.g. from a reactor core, to an acceptably low level. It is usually made from high-density concrete, lead, or water.

Shield, thermal: in a reactor, a shield of thick metal plates placed inside the biological shield to protect it from damage by overheating.

Shim: a term used to describe a device which permits a small adjustment to be made. It may be used in relation to the small adjustment in reactivity control permitted by the use of soluble poison boric acid.

Shock heating: a method of heating plasma by a sudden increase in magnetic field.

Shroud tube: a vertical tube within the above-core structure, in which a control rod moves and is supported. Shroud tubes align with the control rod guide tubes; so that during operation a control rod may be partly within a shroud tube, partly within a guide tube, and partly within a leaning post.

Shutdown, emergency: the rapid shutdown of a reactor to remedy or forestall a dangerous condition.

Shutdown power: in a shutdown reactor, the continuing power output due to heat produced by fission product decay.

Shutdown, reactor: stopping the chain reaction of fission by inserting all control rods, making the reactor sub-critical (i.e. k less than 1).

Silanes: a term given to the silicon hydrides.

Single reheat: passing steam back to a superheater after it has been partially expanded in a turbine.

Sintering: a process of densifying and binding granules or particles. It is based on the increase in the contact area between granules resulting from the enhanced diffusion of molecules across the surfaces of granules when a material (such as mixed fuel oxide) is heated.

Site licence: a licence issued by the Nuclear Installations Inspectorate for the operation of a nuclear site. In the UK, under the 1965 Nuclear Installations Act, all nuclear sites (except those operated by government departments or the UKAEA—for which, however, similar conditions apply) must be so licensed.

Skimmer: this is used in the jet nozzle process to divide the flow into product and waste streams.

Slab geometry: a model of a reactor in which the fuel and moderating materials are represented as adjacent slabs. The slabs may be finite or of infinite extent.

Slumping (fuel): the movement of molten fuel under gravity.

Smear test: a method of estimating the loose, i.e. easily removed, radioactive contamination upon a surface. It is made by wiping the surface and monitoring the swab.

Societal risk: the probabiity of harm to numbers of people.

Sodium void coefficient: the reactivity change resulting from the loss of all coolant, or from the loss of coolant in a specified region of the reactor.

Sodium voiding: the removal of sodium from a specific location in the reactor core, or from the whole core, or from a section of the core.

Soft radiation: radiation having little penetrating power.

Sol: a colloidal solution, i.e. a suspension of solid particles of dimensions in the approximate range 10^{-4}–10^{-6} mm.

Solenoid: a cylindrical coil of wire in which an electric current through the wire sets up a magnetic field along the axis of the coil.

Sol-gel: a process in which the aqueous sol (colloidal dispersion) is converted into gel spheres by partial dehydration.

Solid waste: radioactively contaminated waste in solid form.

Solvent: the organic phase which may consist of a mixture of extractants and/or diluent and/or modifier.

Solvent degradation: deterioration of the solvent brought about by high irradiation levels.

Solvent recycle: the return of the (organic) solvent to the solvent-extraction process for reuse, usually after purification.

Somatic effects: the effects of radiation on the body of the person or animal exposed (as opposed to genetic effects).

Source term: the mathematical expression describing the source of neutrons of a particular energy at a point in space.

Spacer grids: skeletal structures which hold the fuel pins in the required spatial positions at intervals along the length of a fuel element.

Spatial modes: the components of the neutron flux distribution that can occur in a reactor analogous to the fundamental and higher harmonic standing waves in a vibrating string, or on a vibrating surface.

Spatial transient experiments: measurements on the variation of properties, such as the neutron population or the reactor temperature with time and position, following some initiating disturbance.

Sparger (sparge tube): a device consisting of a tube with holes in it through which water can be sprayed.

Specific energy loss: energy loss per unit path length.

Specific heat capacity: the quantity of heat which unit mass of a substance requires to raise its temperature by one degree.

Spectrometer: instrument used for measurements of wavelength or energy distribution in a heterogeneous beam of radiation.

Spent fuel: nuclear fuel which has reached the end of its useful life in a reactor.

Spider connecter: the device which links the control rod drive shaft to each individual absorber rod in the fuel assembly (see Fig. 4.8).

Spiked seating: fuel support allowing space for gases to circulate.

Spike (sub-assembly): the lowest part of a sub-assembly; it fits tightly into the coolant supply plenum (diagrid), and so maintains both the geometry of the coolant flow and the positional rigidity of the sub-assembly.

Spoil: waste.

Spot prices, spot market: although the majority of uranium procurement is carried out under long-term contracts, some small quantities of uranium are bought for immediate delivery on the 'spot market' at prices which tend to be considerably higher.

Sputter: the term 'sputtering' is used to denote the process whereby atoms, or clusters of atoms, charged or uncharged, are released from an electrode (generally a metal), held at a negative potential, under the impact of bombarding ions.

Square coupons: a term to describe thin square slabs of reactor material. When assembled in appropriate numbers, a desired average reactor composition is obtained.

Stage: a concept in solvent extraction where complete equilibrium between phases is attained. In mixer–settlers the concept of a stage is often synonymous with the physical unit of one mixer and one settler.

Standpipe: an open vertical pipe connected to a pipeline, to ensure that the pressure head at that point cannot exceed the length of the standpipe.

Steam driers: devices used to remove the last traces of water from steam. They usually consist of a series of passages in which the steam is made to change direction abruptly. Water droplets having inertia tend to travel straight on, impinge on the sides of the passage and the water is collected in vertical gullies or drains.

Steam-end pedestal: the structure containing the bearing and shaft-sealing glands of a turbine, specifically at the end of the cylinder.

Steam quality at TSV: the measure of the temperature and pressure of steam at the turbine stop valve. From a knowledge of the temperature and pressure of the steam, the amount of superheat can be calculated.

Stellarator: in fusion research, a toroidal magnetic trap with the magnetic fields generated entirely by conductors placed around the torus.

Step function: one which makes an instantaneous change in value from one constant value to another.

Stochastic, non-stochastic effects (of radiation): an effect is said to be stochastic if its probability is a function of the irradiation dose without threshold. If the severity of the effect is a function of the irradiation dose, with or without a threshold, then the effect is non-stochastic. Somatic effects can be stochastic or non-stochastic, while hereditary effects are usually regarded as stochastic.

Stoichiometry: exact proportion of elements to make pure chemical compounds.

Storage: emplacement in a facility, either engineered or natural, with the intention of taking further action at a later time, and in such a way and location that such action is expected to be feasible. The action may involve retrieval, treatment *in situ* or a declaration that further action is no longer needed, and that storage has thus become disposal.

Stratosphere: the earth's atmosphere above the troposphere.

Stress corrosion: crack propogation which depends on the combined action of chemical corrosion and tensile stress.

Stringer: see *fuel assembly*.

Stripping foil: a stripper, which is an essential feature of a tandem accelerator, in the form of a thin foil. Ions are accelerated towards the stripper which is maintained at the potential of the high-voltage terminal. In passing through it, molecular ions are totally disintegrated and atomic ions are stripped of the charge by which they were first accelerated and, in changing sign, are then freshly accelerated away from it. Sign changes can be either from +ve to −ve or, as in the case of carbon ion produced from a caesium *sputter* ion source (q.v.), from −ve to +ve.

Strip solution: the aqueous phase used for removing a particular solute from a loaded solvent or extract.

Sub-assembly, fuel, blanket: the basic, removable, unit of the fast reactor core. Each fuel sub-assembly has a steel, usually hexagonal, wrapper enclosing a bundle of fuel pins, usually with an inlet filter and a gag to regulate the coolant flow which removes heat from the fuel pin bundle. A blanket sub-assembly similarly contains blanket pins. The sub-assembly represents the least mass of fuel handled by the operator for movements to and from the core.

Superconductor: a material which exhibits zero resistance (at low temperature) to electric current flow.

Supercritical: exceeding the necessary conditions for the attainment of criticality.

Superheat: (1) the condition in which the temperature of a liquid is above the saturation temperature corresponding to the pressure in the liquid, where the degree of supherheat, *T*, is the difference between the superheated liquid temperature and the saturation temperature; (2) the temperature rise given to steam passing through a superheater.

Superheat channel liner: a thin metal shield arranged inside the pressure tube (of a reactor) in which the coolant is being superheated, allowing secondary coolant to be introduced so that the pressure tube can be maintained at a temperature associated with the boiling process.

Surge tank: an appropriately elevated or pressurized tank connected to, say, the suction or inlet main of a group of feedwater pumps. It is able either to accept surplus condensate or to supply extra condensate when there is demand for a change in the system flow-rate following a change in load before an equilibrium condition is re-established. In such an arrangement, the surge tank is said to be 'riding' on the feed pump suction.

Suspension section: an arrangement for 'hanging' a fuel assembly inside a reactor core.

Swirler: a device for mixing the coolant to enable fully representative recordings of outlet temperatures and possible fission product release to be obtained. In the case of PFR fuel this duty is performed by the mixer–breeder.

Swirl vane separators: devices to separate steam from water which involve imparting a centrifugal motion to the mixture, so that the water is flung out to the walls of the separator to be collected, whilst the steam passes up the centre of the device.

Synchrotron: an accelerator in which charged particles follow a circular path in a magnetic field and are accelerated by synchronized electric impulses.

Tailings: mine or mill wastes consisting of crushed uranium ore from which the uranium has been extracted chemically.

Tails: the depleted uranium produced at an enrichment plant, typically containing only 0.25 per cent of ^{235}U.

TBP: tri-*n*-butyl phosphate—the solvent used as the extractant in the Purex process.

Teletherapy: treatment of tumours by radiations from outside the body.

Theoretical or ideal stage: a stage where equilibrium is not affected by chemical or physical influences.

Thermal diffusion: process in which a temperature gradient in a mixture of fluids tends to establish a concentration gradient. It has been used for isotope separation.

Thermal neutrons: neutrons in thermodynamic equilibrium (i.e. moving with the same mean kinetic energy) with their surroundings. At room temperature their mean energy is about 0.025 eV and their speed about 2.2 km/s.

Thermal reactor: a nuclear reactor in which the fission chain reaction is propogated mainly by thermal neutrons, and which therefore contains a moderator.

Thermite-type reaction: a strongly exothermic reaction between a metal and a metal oxide in which the oxide is reduced to the metal.

Thermocouple: a device for measuring temperature using the electrical potential produced by the thermoelectric effect between two different conductors.

Thermoluminescent dating: a further physical method of dating associated with the accumulated effect of radiation (α-particles, β-particles and γ-rays) emitted in the decay of the radioactive constituents in the material concerned (e.g. pottery). In crystalline material (e.g. quartz) a fraction of the energy associated with this radiation is permanently stored in the crystal lattice of the minerals in the material (as electrons trapped at regions of imperfection). Subsequent heating of the material allows this energy to be released in the form of light (thermoluminescence), the quantity being related to the product of the time since the last heating (firing in the case of pottery) and the quantity of radioactivity present. Thus, from an assessment of the total radioactive content an estimate of the elapsed time can be determined.

Thermonuclear reaction: a nuclear fusion reaction brought about by very high temperatures.

Thermosetting resins: solid (plastic) compositions in which a chemical reaction takes place while they are being moulded under heat and pressure. The product is resistant to further applications of heat (up to charring point), e.g. phenol formaldehyde, urea formaldehyde resins.

Theta pinches: cylindrical plasmas constricted by external currents flowing in the θ-direction to produce solenoid magnetic fields.

Thorium: a naturally radioactive metal, the mineral sources of which are widely spread over the earth's surface. The main deposit from which thorium is industrially extracted is monazite sands.

Thorium cycle: a nuclear fuel cycle in which fertile thorium-232 is converted to fissile uranium-233.

THORP: the Windscale thermal oxide reprocessing plant.

Threshold energy characteristic: in the context of a nuclear reaction, the dependence upon incident neutron energy of an event, such as the probability of nuclear fission in some nuclei, which only takes place above a certain energy—the threshold energy of the incident neutron.

Time-of-flight technique: a way of measuring the neutron spectrum in which the energy or speed of neutrons is determined by the time taken by the neutrons to traverse a known distance.

Tokamak: in fusion research, a toroidal magnetic trap whose poloidal field is generated by the current in the plasma. Tokamak is an acronym of the Russian words meaning toroidal magnetic chamber.

Toroidal: having the shape of a torus.

Toroidal magnetic field: magnetic field generated by current flowing in a toroidal solenoid.

Torus: a tube bent round in a ring with the ends joined up together to give the shape of a motor-tyre tube or an American doughnut.

Toxic: of poison.

Tracer: a small amount of easily-detectable material fixed to some substance whose movement one wishes to follow. If this material is radioactive it can easily be detected by devices such as γ-cameras or other nuclear radiation detectors.

Transient over-power: an accident in which the reactor power exceeds the normal safe upper limit, but full coolant flow continues throughout.

Transient, reactor: a change in power level and/or a temperature which may be accidental or deliberate, causing other reactor or plant parameters to change from their steady-state values.

Transition, nuclear: a change in the configuration of a nucleus, usually either a disintegration or a change in internal energy level, accompanied by emission of radiation.

Tri-normal: a solution of reagent containing three gram-equivalents per litre.

Transuranic elements: the elements of atomic number 93 and higher which have heavier and more complex nuclei than uranium. They can be made by a number of nuclear reactions, including prolonged neutron bombardment of uranium.

Trip: rapid automatic shutdown of a reactor caused when one of the operational characteristics of the system deviates beyond a present limit. Often applied to spurious shutdowns caused, for example, by an instrument malfunction.

Tritium: the isotope of hydrogen having an atomic mass number of 3.

Tritium unit: a proportion of tritium in hydrogen of one part in 10^{18}.

Troposphere: atmosphere up to region where temperature ceases to decrease with height.

Tube-and-shell units: a form of heat exchanger construction comprising a tube 'nest' supported within a casing referred to as the 'shell'. One fluid flows through the tubes, while the other passes over their outer surfaces, during which it is contained within the shell.

Tube-sheet: the thick cylindrical plate which is drilled to take the very large number, typically 5000, of tubes which go to make up a nuclear steam generator.

Tunable dye laser: a dye laser, consisting of an organic dye dissolved in a solvent, which fluoresces over a broad band of frequencies, enabling the output to be tuned.

Turnings: swarf produced by machining a piece of metal.

Two-phase coolant: a coolant which can exist in significant quantities in both the liquid phase and the gaseous phase.

Two-start, helical 'rip': a helical, longitudinal fin (here, specifically, there would be two such fins at any section) produced in the outer surface of a fuel clad. Used in conjunction with fuel elements having 'plain' cladding to space one element from another along their whole length within a fuel bundle assembly.

Unsealed source: radioactive material that is not encapsulated or otherwise sealed, and which forms a source of radiation. For example, radioactive material in use as a *tracer*.

Uranium: the heaviest element found in appreciable quantities in the earth's crust. Natural uranium contains 0.0055 per cent ^{234}U, 0.71 per cent ^{235}U, (by weight) the remainder being ^{238}U. Other isotopes of uranium are produced by irradiation in reactors.

Vacuum chamber: in fusion experiments, the vessel inside which the plasma is confined, so-called because it is first highly evacuated to remove impurities before the plasma is introduced. In actual confinement, the plasma is compressed by the magnetic field into a much smaller volume than the vacuum chamber, thus isolating it from the walls.

Valence: chemical unit of combining power.

Value function: a function representing the value of a quantity of separated material which depends on the number of separating elements required to produce it.

Venturi tube: a wasp-waisted tube used to measure the flow of fluids.

Vibro-compaction: mechanical vibration and compaction.

Vicor glass tube: a proprietory glass tubing (available in the USA).

Vipak: a vibratory compaction process.

Vitrification: the incorporation of radioactive waste oxides into glass (also known as glassification).

Void coefficient: the partial derivative of reactivity with respect to a void (i.e. the removal of the material) at a specified location within a reactor. It is equal to the reactivity coefficient of the material removed.

WAGR: Windscale advanced gas-cooled reactor.

Warm twisting operation: twisting at temperature of typially, 350–450 K.

Waste disposal: the consignment of radioactive wastes to areas or facilities from which there is no intent to retrieve them.

Waste storage: the consignment of radioactive wastes to areas or facilities from which there is an intent and capability to retrieve the waste for further treatment or disposal.

Waste transport: the movement of radioactive waste from one location to another.

Water reactors: nuclear reactors in which water (including heavy water) is the moderator and/or the coolant.

Weldment: a welded assembly.

Wet (saturated) steam: steam containing particles of unevaporated water.

Whole-body monitors: an assembly of large scintillation detectors, heavily shielded against background radiation, used to identify and measure the total gamma radiation emitted by the human body.

WIMS: the name of a family of computer codes used widely to predict the properties of thermal reactors. It is an acronym of Winfrith Improved Multigroup Scheme.

Xenon effect: the rapid but temporary *poisoning* of a reactor by the build-up of xenon-135 from the radioactive decay of the fission product iodine-135. Xenon-135 is a strong absorber of neutrons and until it (and its parent) has largely decayed away reactor start-up can be difficult.

X-rays: electromagnetic radiations having wavelengths much shorter (i.e. energy much higher) than those of visible light. X-rays with clearly defined energies are produced by atomic orbital electron transitions. X-rays produced by the interaction of high-energy electrons with matter have a continuous energy spectrum, and it is these that are generally used in medical X-ray machines (see *Bremsstrahlung*).

Yellow-cake: concentrated crude uranium oxide, the form in which most uranium is shipped from the mining areas to the fuel manufacturers.

Zeolites: one of a number of minerals consisting mainly of hydrous silicates of calcium, sodium, and aluminium, able to act as cation exchangers.

Zero-power reactors: reactors not requiring high power or large coolant flow, used to study reactor physics of various designs without the build-up of significant quantities of fission products.

Zircaloy: an alloy of zirconium and aluminium used for fuel cladding in water reactors.

Zooplankton: planktonic animals.

INDEX